Notes
from the
Second Dimension

Books by Christine Kromm Henrie and David Henrie

Published by Access Soul Knowledge

The Spiritual Design, Channeled Teachings, Wave 1

The Spiritual Design, Channeled Teachings, Wave 2

Notes from the Second Dimension, Volume 1

Helig Design; Kanaliserade Budskap, Första Vågen
(*Svenska Derivat*)

Helig Design; Kanaliserade Budskap, Andra Vågen
(*Svenska Derivat*)

Notes from the Second Dimension, Volume 2

Books Scheduled for Publication in 2022

The Spiritual Design, Channeled Teachings, Wave 3

Notes from the Second Dimension, Volume 3

Notes
From the
Second Dimension

Volume 2

Christine Kromm Henrie

&

David Henrie, Sp.D.

Access Soul Knowledge
Stockholm, Sweden

Copyright © 2021 by Christine Kromm Henrie, David Henrie.

All rights reserved. No part of this book may be reproduced, stored in or introduced into an information storage or retrieval system, or transmitted in any form, or in any manner, including electronic, photographic, mechanical, recording, or otherwise, without prior written permission of the copyright owner. For information, please contact the author.

Library of Congress Cataloging-in-Publication

Names: Henrie, Christine Kromm | Henrie, David

Title: Notes from the second dimension, volume 2 /
   By Christine Kromm Henrie and David Henrie

Description: Access Soul Knowledge, 2021 |

Identifiers: LCCN 2021xxxxxx | ISBN 9781951879020 (Paperback Edition)

Subjects BISAC: 1. BODY, MIND & SPIRIT—Afterlife & Reincarnation. |
   2. BODY, MIND & SPIRIT—Angels & Spirit Guides. |
   3. BODY, MIND & SPIRIT—Channeling & Mediumship

Classification: BL515 .H74 2021 | DDC 133.9'01'35—dc22

LC record available at https://lccn.loc.gov/2021xxxxxx

ISBN 9781951879037 (E-book Edition)

Editors: Kari Pelletier | Susanne Kromm

Cover Photo Art: ID 58653311 © Dwnld777 | Dreamstime.com and Book Design by David Henrie

Printed in the United States of America
First Edition
First Printing, November 2021
   Access Soul Knowledge
   Stockholm, Sweden & Williamstown, WV, US

Publisher information at www.AccesSoulKnowledge.com

Contents

Page	Section and Date
1	**Introduction**
7	**Bob's Projects**
8	Becoming a Council Secretary (Oct 14, 2018)
12	Updates on Bob's Planet (Oct 14, 2018)
18	The Velvet Purse of Notes (April 6 and 14, 2019)
25	Bob Plans a Life for Me (July 25, 2019)
39	Presenting the Life Plan to the Council (Sept 26, 2019)
45	Refining the Life Plan (April 5, 2020)
49	All Life Plans Involve Astrology (April 18, 2020)
57	**Notes on the Human**
57	Reluctance to Accept Change (Dec 4, 2018)
66	Self–Healing (April 30, 2019)
68	Mother's Return Home (July 25, 2019)
72	The Inner Calling (Oct 13, 2019)
76	Inner and Outer Hobbies (Nov 17, 2019)
82	A Holiday Message (Dec 12, 2019)
85	Fatness is not only Physical (Dec 15, 2019)
90	**Teachings from Etena and Tiddle**
91	Bob Reads the Soil at Etena (April 21, 2019)
98	Beekeeper Bob (April 28, 2019)
107	Other Worlds for Advanced Spirits (April 30, 2019)
111	The Pyramid of Life Forms (June 2, 2019)
121	Ia brings Siah to our Session (July 13, 2019)
125	The Song of the Creator (Oct 6, 2019)
133	Twelfth Dimension of Healing (Oct 6, 2019)
142	The Washer (Nov 9, 2019)
149	Bob Recreates a Companion for Siah (Nov 13, 2019)
155	The Pyramid of Light Bulbs (Nov 21, 2019)
159	Watching over Tess (Nov 28, 2019)
167	Update on Tess (Dec 8, 2019)
168	A Little Rocket Ride (Dec 12, 2019)
171	The Big Sleep for Tess (Dec 12, 2019)
175	Previous Occupants of Earth (Dec 8, 2019
185	The Tiddle–Taffles Color the Worlds (Dec 22, 2019)

197	Siah and Tess are Reunited (Dec 25, 2019)
209	Preparing to Travel to Tiddle (Jan 13, 2020)
215	Bob Travels to Tiddle (Jan 26, 2020)
229	The Spiritual and the Manifested Blueprints (Feb 9, 2020)
238	Sneaking into the Pyramid of Knowledge (April 15, 2020)
250	**Teaching the Students**
251	The Walkie-Talkie is Off
253	The Museum of Previous Costumes (May 5, 2019)
263	So Many Questions about the Coat (May 26, 2019)
271	The Tailors and the Coat of Karma (June 15, 2019)
279	The Cells of Enslavement (June 15, 2019)
287	The Runway Show of Bodies and Personalities (June 23, 2019)
293	Mixing and Matching Personalities to the Body (June 30, 2019)
298	Role Playing to Mirror Earth Life (July 4, 2019)
313	A Field Trip to Study Earth (July 7, 2019)
328	Sending Souls to Earth (July 13, 2019)
337	Bob finds Remains of Atlantis (July 20, 2019)
345	Transitioning through the Fourth after Death (July 29, 2019)
355	Picking Guides (Sept 25, 2019)
357	The Preacher-Man and the Recipe Book (Sept 29, 2019)
365	The Traveling Magician (Oct 17, 2019)
370	Coloring the Mind (Oct 20, 2019)
379	Bob brings his Students to a Session (Nov 13, 2019)
386	The Spirit Guide's Oath (Nov 21, 2019)
389	Final Exams for the Spirit Guides (Dec 8, 2019)
392	Becoming Human is NOT the Goal (Jan 5, 2020)
401	What Happens on Earth, Stays on Earth (Jan 23, 2020)
416	Becoming a Wheel Star (Feb 23, 2020)
421	Everyone gets a Roller (April 5, 2020)
423	Travels with Old Sniffer (April 8, 2020)
433	Bake with Both Hands! (May 25, 2020)
437	Acknowledgements
438	About the Authors

Introduction

For those who are aware that life is a spiritual quest, a divine encounter is perhaps the pinnacle of experiences one can have. Receiving this type of gift frequently, as we do, is something few humans will ever experience. During the trance sessions, words pour like a waterfall out of Christine, making it hard to fully process what is being said. Later, after transcribing the audio recordings, the complexity and beauty of their teachings are inescapable to the reader. While no spirit ever claims to speak on behalf of the Creator, bit-by-bit we are being given a majestic view of the spirit world and the processes of creation and evolution within the many universes. Their goals are to educate the human mind, uplift our hearts, and compel us to seek our own spiritual identity. If we realign our thoughts and ideals to mirror the intent of our soul, we will begin to heal ourselves, humanity, and, ultimately, the planet. It is very humbling to be educated by guides and council members who must, with great patience, explain rudimentary ideas in a way we can comprehend. This is a joint project between us and the spirit world, which, they said, was our primary mission for this lifetime. They also said their teachings will continue for many years to come. The ideas shared herein build upon the previous teachings found in *Notes from the Second Dimension, Volume 1* and *the Spiritual Design, Wave 1* and *Wave 2* books. Instead of repeating the basic information in each book, we are trusting the reader to be familiar with the prior publications.

Christine and I have been receiving these lectures since 2015 and have accumulated over a million words from the various spirits who speak during our trance sessions. Christine, the trance channel and co-author, is able to place herself in a deep altered state and allow the consciousness of another spiritual being to take control of her vocal cords and upper body. The spiritual entities can then communicate directly and eloquently with me (David), the co-author who conducts all the trance sessions. From my perspective, sitting in front of her, it is undeniable that I am conversing with someone other than Christine. Each of them has a unique personality and way of speaking. The spiritual beings from the sixth, seventh, eighth, ninth and tenth dimensions sit quite still while lecturing in a precise but relatively impersonal way. Bob, the main author of this book, is the opposite. He is very animated and gives us a finely detailed narrative of his personal life as a spirit from the second dimension. This book is essentially Bob's journal or autobiography, although several other spirits from the second, such as Ia and Gergen, also contribute their wisdom. Each week he reveals, in a more-or-less chronological sequence, a little more about his life, activities, thoughts and concerns. Many of the stories that unfold in *Volume 2* are continuations of relationships and travel destinations that were presented in earlier writings. We have added clarifying comments where some jostling of the reader's memory may be helpful. His story began in *Volume 1* with his creation and covered his adventures as a sparkle and his early travels. He always comes with a specific agenda each session, but several weeks can pass before he resumes one of his many storylines. During our sessions, the Elahim Council, the Council of Nine, Ari, Eli, Ophelia, or another entity will speak first. Most of their messages can be found in the *Spiritual Design* series. We created the *Notes from the Second Dimension* series as a platform for Bob and the other spirits from the second dimension to articulate on issues they find important, which often involve human activity in relation to plants, animals, water and atmosphere. I would estimate 35 to 40 percent of our transcripts come from Bob. I asked Eli, who is an older brother to both Seth (Christine) and Lasaray (me) on the sixth dimension, how we should present his copious dialogues. He offered the following advice, which we took to heart while preparing *Volume 1*, and will continue within this *Volume 2*:

D. This book I'm working on about the second dimension; how do you think the information should be presented?

Eli. It should be presented like a journal, like he is telling you his journal. He is giving you his experience; write it from him, write it from his perspective, like he is giving out the book, not you. If you think of it as his personal journal that you simply manifest here, it will be easier for you.

Volume 2 is arranged into four main sections, although there are a lot of overlapping ideas throughout the book. We added the session date to help organize and maintain the continuity of the messages. The first chapter is an update on the solar system Bob created and a collection of his talks on creating a future life for

Lasaray. We went back and forth on whether to include those commentaries, because it may be only speculation on his part. But we also know that Ophelia and the Council of Nine wouldn't allow meaningless topics to detract from our precious channeling time. Bob describes the intricacies of planning a mission, selecting companions, evaluating the timeline, and consulting with the various councils who oversee life on Earth. Those processes are all part of the rigorous preparations that occur before any soul incarnates.

In the second chapter, Bob gives practical guidance about human behavior. Bob has been traveling to Earth in spirit form for millions of years and has witnessed many great changes in the land, atmosphere and occupants. He has seen alien visitors arriving to exploit the resources of Earth, but has also observed a greater number coming to heal and restore the natural balance. We tend to forget that the Earth itself is a spiritual project. Humans are a recent addition to the mix, but we consider ourselves to be the most important part. We are not. Our presence on the planet is not very beneficial to the other inhabitants. Once Lasaray began incarnating, Bob joined as my closest guide. The first lifetime was some 400,000 years ago in the "ape-shape", as he calls the early, hairy hominins. During the intervening millennia, there have been many branches on the hominid tree, and Bob has participated in some of those modifications. He has watched civilizations advance and decline as their technology and spiritual understandings have changed. But most importantly, Bob has an intimate knowledge of how a soul may overcome the challenges in the karma program. Therefore, we would be unwise to overlook the depth of wisdom from which he speaks.

The Earth is only one of many destinations for spirits. The third chapter is a collection of Bob's travel adventures to the planets of Etena and Tiddle, as well as messages from entities who reside there. Neither planet is in our Universe. We introduced Etena in *Volume 1*. It is a center of learning in fish tank four, which is adjacent to our Universe, fish tank five. In the spiritual dimensions (the second, and the fifth through twelfth), libraries and museums are very important repositories of records. When spirits are occupying form in one of the fish tanks, the resources in the spiritual dimensions may not be accessible. So the libraries and storage units on Etena serve a comparable function for those spirits who have blended with a body or have materialized a body.

Bob describes Etena as being similar to Earth, with plants, animals, forests and water. The residents dwell in small, cozy homes which are interspersed among pyramids of various sizes, where the collections of knowledge and patterns of life forms are stored. They live there in manifested bodies on a somewhat permanent basis and serve as custodians of the records and caretakers of the planet. Setalay is one of those who communicates with us from her home on Etena. When spirits are created, they are "born" into different groups in different dimensions, each with specific duties. Both Ophelia and Setalay belong to a group on the seventh called Shea. Etena is a location where Shea can reside once they have progressed from incarnating in human bodies on Earth, or on another similar planet. They are more fully presented in The *Spiritual Design* series. The other planet Bob has visited, Tiddle, is in fish tank two and is home to a group of spirits from the second dimension, known as the Taffles. They also have materialized bodies and live on that planet permanently. Bob has traveled to Taffle and explored the society and the planet, and those adventures are found near the end of Chapter 3.

Bob's stories about teaching his students are gathered within the final chapter. Education is a mixture of lectures, role play, field trips, independent study and group activities. He is currently tutoring twelve students. Six of them are from the sixth dimension and will be incarnating on Earth. They have been paired up with another six from the second dimension, who will join as personal guides during each life. Bob is often invited to be a guest lecturer to young spirits on the fifth who have yet to undertake lives on Earth. He is given quite a bit of freedom to improvise situations and methods of instruction, which he does with great enthusiasm. Students are not graded or subjected to negative feedback, but are questioned about their understanding, similar as with the Socratic Method. Although it might be tempting to read these stories as mere curiosities about life in the spirit world, there are messages embedded in each one that can illuminate the path of our own spiritual development.

As you may recall from our previous books, spirits may interact with Earth by using one of three methods. A spirit can project its awareness from the spiritual dimensions to our planet, which is an advanced form of remote viewing. Spirit guides use this method to monitor incarnations or observe situations. The second method requires the spirit to project a portion of its soul energy into the fourth dimension surrounding Earth, and then create a manifested form that is partially materialized from the elements of the Earth. These forms are not biologic, although they mirror the human form in certain ways, but take on the shape of the spirit who is manifesting the form. The spirit can also vary the amount of matter they activate within their traveling form. A human body is about 98 percent activated on the third dimension. The Anunnaki, who were spirits from a group on the sixth dimension known as the Elahim, manifested forms which were about 80 percent materialized. They were able to maintain those bodies for thousands of years, which appeared solid to the humans of the time. Spirit guides also materialize bodies when they need to interact with their incarnated person, although in most instances the degree of materialization is quite low, meaning that they remain invisible to the human eye. Whenever I incarnate, Bob also materializes a body that he sustains the entire time I am alive. He told me his body is about 20 percent materialized. Even though I cannot see him, he is able to interact with material objects on this plane, which he occasionally does to make me aware of his presence. The final method to interact with a third dimensional reality is by attaching to a body from birth to death. This is known as incarnation or blending. Souls do this by sending part of their spiritual energy into the fourth dimension and energetically attaching themselves to a Coat of Karma and then attaching to a body. Based on what we have been told, on a planetary basis, incarnating is not nearly as common as manifesting.

There are no precedents for the information the spirits give. Some of their descriptions about the spiritual world and the journey of the soul are similar to conventional ideas, but most go far beyond any known beliefs. It can be challenging to understand some of the concepts, but the spirits do a remarkable job working around our mental limitations, and they do that while using our language, which is also very restrictive. When Bob tells about doing things with his students on the fifth dimension, for example, he cannot send a thought bubble with the actual picture and story of what happened. He must describe a non-earthly environment using terms we are familiar with. One of the clues that he has converted the story in this way is when he says "if you like". He means that what he just said is the best way he can present an idea, even though it is inexact. Knowing the lessons and spiritual

6 Notes from the Second Dimension

guidance were artfully embedded in a story we can relate to, it is easier to appreciate the beauty of their gifts.

With that brief introduction, we now allow Bob to continue where we left off in *Volume 1*.

Bob's Projects

The second dimension is home to the spirits who oversee animal and plant life on Earth and all living planets in the universes. They come in many shapes and sizes, depending on their role. They may be tiny atmospheric dots, fairies, gardeners, or those that care for animals and aquatic life. In addition to their normal duties, some of them are also selected to be guides to spirits from other dimensions when they incarnate on Earth. All spirits are born on one of the spiritual dimensions, where they are cared for and educated before being sent out on excursions. *Notes from the Second Dimension, Volume 1*, contains some of Bob's stories from when he was a sparkle (a young spirit), his education, travels and the steps of his advancement prior to joining one of the councils on the second dimension. Part of Bob's early training involved coming to Earth in his spirit form to tend to animals and vegetation. He first journeyed here just after the time of dinosaurs, he said, during a period of heavy rains, when clouds filled the atmosphere and animals coughed. That puts his arrival here at the end of the Cretaceous, in the early Paleocene, about 60 million years ago. Bob and my spiritual self, Lasaray, were paired up after he started coming to Earth, but long before Lasaray began incarnating. Our mentors put us together so he and I could learn from and assist each other. Bob comes to my lab on the sixth dimension to study the creation of form, such as planets and stars; and he follows me as my closest guide whenever I incarnate on Earth. He stays in close proximity to my physical body, from birth to death, during every lifetime.

All activities in the spirit realm involve progress and growth. Time, as we understand it, doesn't exist in the spiritual dimensions. That should not be misinterpreted as the past, present and future all occurring simultaneously, –that is not accurate in the least. It's better to imagine the spiritual realms being in perpetual afternoon sunshine, where there are no clocks or reference points to delineate "time". Nor is the spirit driven by biological demands for periodic food or sleep. If a spirit is called to attend a lecture, everyone assembles and there is a beginning and an end, and at the conclusion, each spirit has collected some knowledge. The cycles of learning and experience are spiritual "time", and it is different for each entity as it progresses from the moment of being created to the moment of its final ascension. Souls, no matter how advanced, continually seek to take on more demanding and complex activities. Since Bob and I have reached the end of my incarnation program on Earth, he has advanced to the next stage of spirit guide occupations. Those activities include planning lives and supervising other guides. Bob describes many of the decisions that each soul makes prior to entering a new life. The newest of souls to Earth have little input, since their mentors do all the planning. After a number of lives, the incarnating soul assumes more of the responsibilities for the preparation work. There are always guides involved, and Bob explains some of the work that occurs behind the scenes.

Becoming a Council Secretary (Oct 14, 2018)

In *Volume 1*, Bob described how he was invited to joint a council on the second dimension that is led by Ole, who is Gergen's mentor. Gergen is Bob's mentor, so Ole is similar to Bob's grandfather. Each dimension has councils that are assigned responsibility to oversee different aspects of creation within the fish tanks (the twelve universes of form). No council acts in isolation, as there is constant coordination between groups on different dimensions. If, for example, the Earth (a living entity) sends out a signal there are problems in its atmosphere, groups who monitor these signals from the fork will route the information to councils on the fifth. To solve the problem, this council might consider various options, perhaps shifting weather patterns, moving mountain ranges, or adjusting heat flow to different areas of the crust. Any of these options will affect life forms on Earth. So Ole, a member of higher councils, will have the council Bob sits on review the options and make recommendations. Bob's group is comprised of spiritual entities from the second dimension who each possess a unique skill set and knowledge about plants, animals, water, atmosphere or geology. After Bob became a council member, Gergen and Ole both noticed he was not fully engaging in some of the deliberations. He was pulling his energy away while other members were debating issues in which he had little interest.

Since Bob is being trained to take on more responsibilities in their group, Ole told him that he had been selected to take notes, because he was so good at it.

D. So, what else is going on? (*Bob had been talking about something else earlier.*)

B. Ohh, there is council work.

D. Are they keeping you busy?

B. I have been put in the position to journal. I feel I am a secretary.

D. Did Gergen do that, or did Ole? Did they say, "Why don't you take notes?"

B. Indeed, that's how it was. It was not put forward as a punishment, it was put forward that I had a great talent of journaling, and wouldn't I be interested in journaling our meetings? And I said, "Oh, fine." I felt complimented and I was a little bit rubbed behind my ears, so to speak, and I gladly took the assignment. But after a while, I felt like a secretary.

D. Do you wonder why they did that? Is it because you were backing out and just leaving a passive particle, so they got you to pay attention by taking notes?

B. Ah, so now I need to pay attention, I can't fall asleep because I'm journaling all these meetings, so I have to pay attention. I cannot drift away. So in some way, maybe it is a punishment.

D. It's not a punishment, it's a way of teaching.

B. Sometimes a way of teaching can be experienced as a punishment. Like my first experience of self-study, –that felt like a punishment–, even though afterwards, indeed, I was grateful for the opportunity to listen to the silence within my own being. And maybe this also has some kind of reward, a treat, –because I believe in treats! So I'm pretty sure that there is something to be found. Maybe I will stumble across something that is gonna be highly interesting. At the moment, I have not encountered that; I'm mainly taking notes.

D. Since everyone has had different experiences before joining the council, perhaps you'll be able to absorb some of the knowledge the others have acquired?

B. I actually said, "If you want me to be a secretary, why can't I come and be a secretary at YOUR council meetings?" –like with Ole and his old buddies, because they are probably meeting somewhere. I said, "Maybe I can take notes there?"

Huhuhuh, then I learn to listen and take notes, but I also get excited and enticed! At this time there is a lot of discussions about geology and movement of land mass and how to, – especially in the South American region, they're talking about the spine in that country–, to maybe move it a little bit. And if they do so, if they start to move things, then indeed it's gonna change life forms, and even the ocean bed is gonna be different. But they're trying to look into how to help the fossils in the water north of there, and in order to do so, a trick, they said, is to change the continents nearby. So that's what they do, and since I am not a continent kind–of–guy, I feel like I am just writing. But I'm pretty sure there is a treat here. (*He began to laugh.*) I actually asked Ole if he wanted to have a personal secretary, maybe to help him write his journals. If he gets tired then he can just talk out loud and I can write down his journal! Gergen, he laughed about that! Oh, he's always nearby, he never misses anything, he's always nearby.

D. That's funny! Did Ole laugh too?

B. Gergen laughed from the toes all the way up, his whole being bubbled, whereas Ole, he smiled and he said, "Oh, Bob, you're always trying to do things." Huhuhuh

D. He must appreciate your sense of humor.

B. Ah. He said, "Try to have the same enthusiasm, even if it's about continents." Huh huh, ohh. But I'm thinking maybe I'm being trained in this secretary occupation, then once I master this, then indeed, I might offer my services to other beings in other councils—like Jeshua! "Jeshua, do you need like a secretary?" Or maybe you (*Lasaray*) need a secretary when you go places? Because I have training, –now I am a certified secretary! Huh huh huh huh, oh, I don't know. Ophelia just shakes her head. She says, "Sometimes it's good to appreciate to just be in a relaxed state of mind and just write things down, and not necessarily come up with everything yourself." She says, "Appreciate that you can sometimes get a little rest, but still be in the puddle of knowledge, but you don't have to come up with all the ideas yourself."

D. Maybe that is the lesson here.

B. Because I do know how to write, so that can't be the lesson.

D. Perhaps, because your mind is so active, they're trying to get you to be more like a sponge.

B. I'm gonna be like a sponge. Ah, and if I don't do this correctly, they might put forward that harp, and then I would be a sponge! I just go to sleep. Nay, I'm gonna take this assignment of secretary occupation with no judgment and hopefully, quietly see that there is a treat coming my way after this. (*Ophelia uses a large harp in her lectures, in classrooms on the seventh dimension, to put her young students into a meditative state.*)

D. Before you started doing this, when you were in the council meetings, were you just shooting off thought bubbles, or were you intently listening to the others?

B. Nay, I wasn't just listening. I engaged, I had opinions.

D. Now that you're writing, do you find you're not sending out as many bubbles?

B. There's bubbles coming to me, I have to just maneuver them and get them down into this record thing, so there is no way for me to shoot off my bubbles. Probably some sort of an insight here, lurking behind the bubbles. So anyway, I've been doing that, and Ophelia says it's gonna be a short one today, saving energy.

D. Do you have any final thoughts before you take off?

B. Ah, only maybe that I do understand that everything goes through these phases of learning, and even this one (*Christine is always identified as "this one", the one through whom they are speaking.*) needs to know that, to appreciate being the sponge and being still. She and I can be sponges for a while and maybe sit and relax. But it's in our nature to somewhat try to engage and move ahead. So it's kind of tricky to be in that sort of reverse state.

D. Well, I really appreciate your curiosity, I think it's a wonderful thing.

B. Ah, maybe the other ones want to have their bubbles heard. I came (*to the council*), but we haven't really talked that much about my expertise yet. We're still talking about precipitation, continents shifting, and the soil and the fossils (*reefs*), –and that's not really my expertise. So in that sense, I should probably just sort of reverse my bubbles and try to blend in and show appreciation of other's understanding and level of knowledge.

D. It's like going to lectures in some way, because they are probably giving you the best of their knowledge.

B. So I'm gonna expand my knowledge bank by being a secretary for the moment. Ah, so there you go. Okay, okay, I'm gonna go now, so that will probably be it. Be–be–be–be–be be it!!

D. (*Laughing*) Well, it's always nice to hear your voice, my friend.

B. Yours too. Sounds different though, than at home.

D. What does it sound like at home?

B. It's more like little dots. But because of the pickle of language, if you like, you actually talk in pictures to me. I like that.

D. And how do you respond?

B. With pictures and emotions. We have trained you in shooting off emotions as well.

D. It's not natural to my being?

B. Well, it's natural to your being, but it's that part where it has to travel through the mists of translation that I don't understand. But it's not like you don't have happiness or love or gurgles, stuff like that, but the receiving end has to understand it, meaning me.

D. So I can transmit it now, and you can pick it up?

B. Indeed, you transmit now. Before you gurgled, now you can transmit happiness in a different way. In many ways it comes as colors. So I know when certain colors come that you're happy.

D. I'm sure I'm always happy when you are around.

B. Indeed. We're always happy. So anyway, I'm gonna go now. Ophelia is pulling my arm, kinda.

D. Well, thank you all, Ophelia and you.

B. And me. Anyway, I'm gonna go. Okay, bye bye.

Updates on Bob's Planet and Individual (Oct 14, 2018)

Bob explained, in our previous books, how he created a new species and placed it on Earth. It was a very intelligent and gentle creature with soft fur, looking somewhat like a little red panda bear. Gergen was aware that humanoids were about to be introduced on Earth, and he also foresaw that Bob's animal would be hunted for its luxurious pelt. He did not want the animals to suffer, or Bob to witness the suffering. Therefore, Gergen removed the species from Earth (it became extinct) before the hominins were created. Bob was very despondent about the loss, so Gergen allowed the species to be reintroduced on another planet. Bob had studied how planetary bodies are created and already made his own solar system, complete with a living planet like Earth. It is there that his species was given a new home and now resides. Even though there are many of them, he still refers to the entire group in the singular. He calls them his "individual" because when it roamed the Earth, it was a solitary creature. Bob modified it before it was relaunched so that it now desires to be in a group.

Reality, as described by the spirits, disaffirms much of what we believe to be true in physics, ancient history, astronomy, religion, biology, geology, evolution, and the nature of the soul. If we examine astrophysics, for example, the collective assumption among the academic czars is that the Universe is 13.787 billion years old. To reach that precisely incorrect conclusion, a host of ill-founded theories were employed, piled one atop another. Scientific misapprehensions are intrinsic to the theories of relativity, space-time curvature, singularity, the big bang, the properties of space, electromagnetism, gravity, and the use of red-shifting and cosmic background radiation to estimate distance and time. According to the spirits, our Universe, fish tank five, has been around for trillions of Earth-years, and will continue for trillions more. There are twelve universes on our Wheel of Creation (see *Wave 2*) that are separate, distinct and isolated from each other. Fish tank five contains our known Universe plus the parallel realities, about which we know nothing. All the fish tanks rely on an external energy to exist. The fact that the Universe is not a closed system invalidates most astrophysical theories because it introduces an unknown number of variables that cannot be measured or quantified. These other fish tanks and parallel realities have physical and non-physical properties and functions that are different from our third dimensional reality. We used the age of the Universe as an example, but a similar disconnect between belief and reality permeates most areas of science and philosophy.

In *The Spiritual Design, Wave 1* and *Wave 2* books, the spirits explain that everything which appears tangible to us has an origin from an invisible energetic level. The first dimension is related to the frequency of the elemental building blocks of matter, including electromagnetic and gravitational energy. The second dimension is the frequency of living form, beginning with water and extending through all structures of DNA and RNA. The third dimension is the manifested frequency of our Universe, and is the only vibrational field we can perceive. The first dimension is, in certain ways, a polarity to the Creator. The energetic patterns we identify as quantum particles arise from the vibrational field of the first dimension, the aether that fills all space in our fish tank. The building blocks of matter are cosmic light energy, which is constant or linear, and cosmic sound frequencies, which are patterns of wave forms. There is a third element that holds the pattern. The element creates what is considered a vacuum, but it is, in some way, what we identify as gravity. To create a living being, which is anything with DNA or RNA, the first dimensional elements are bundled together by another set of patterns created within the vibrational field of the second dimension. This form is then blended (infused) with a living spiritual energy from either the Master Mind, or an individual soul, as found in a human.

Bob created his solar system by building an energetic model in our lab. Design work is done outside the fish tank, usually in the sixth dimension. When all is ready, the patterns are inserted into the proper fish tank, where they coalesce the first dimensional energy into the intended forms. When any new solar system or galaxy is created, the designers will select an appropriate template for the star and planets. Bob was given a template for his solar system. He had to adjust the core size, gravity, and elemental composition based on the properties of the sun he was using, as well as the orbital location and purpose of each planet. On his living planet, as he called the only one with life forms on it, he added the patterns for plants and animals he wanted to have. Once Bob had completed the design, his patterns were embedded within the energetic field of our fish tank. Like seeds, they grew into a sun and planets, beginning their life cycle. This doesn't imply that objects appear instantly, but rather, matter emerges from the aether and grows into celestial bodies during linear time. These basic concepts of spiritual design apply to all matter, from a single hydrogen atom to a sheet of galaxies. Knowing that, it is easier to understand how the many and varied organisms came to be on Earth. Spiritual entities create patterns and place them on the planet, and those forms then manifest as a living being on the third dimension.

Bob mentions a map in the following session. He is talking about maps of energetic highways or passageways that connect different locations in our Universe with other fish tanks and the spiritual dimensions. This network is in a parallel reality that is invisible to humans, but exists within the vibrational spectrum of our fish tank. These highways can connect to a celestial body through a portal, which is a link between the two realities. The portals can be created by those who have the technology and understanding to do so, but some natural ones also exist on some planets. The parallel reality can be visualized as a thin sheet of energy that hovers over a location on Earth, and the portal between the two is like a stationary tornado where the two blend. Alien visitors shift into this adjacent energy field at their home planet and travel on highways to the Earth node, then alter their vibration as they move through the portal into our reality. Humans cannot stumble into a portal and be transported through a wormhole to some distant planet. That's a complete misunderstanding of the idea. The physical body is not energetically malleable in that way.

D. (*Bob came in but didn't say anything.*) Hello?

B. That took a long time!

D. Did you see who was talking?

B. No, Ophelia was blocking the view. Ophelia, she asked me to give a report today. I said, "Do we really have to do it now?" and she said, "Yes, let's do it now." So I gave a report on a couple of assignments she had given me priorly.

D. Well, it was an interesting talk, but very complicated, about the fish tanks and how they move through different realities and different types of learning.

B. Ah, I guess that's where my bubble is gonna go. (*He then looked to the left, towards Ophelia.*) We'll see about that, Ophelia says, we'll see about that. Bubble is not the same as a fish tank, and the bubble doesn't belong in every fish tank, she says. But mine is specially designed by Jeshua, so he might have created it to be able to travel, and one might not know exactly where it's allowed to travel to.

D. You don't want to find out when you're inside.

B. Nay, I think I'm gonna study up on that outside the bubble, so I don't feel like I shoot off somewhere into the unknown, and I have no maps to navigate from. This one says it's all about having maps, and since I don't feel like I have been given maps, I am not sure that my bubble is gonna go places that I have selected; and I'm not even sure if I'm gonna go by myself, –I'm actually not very interested in going by myself.

D. I wouldn't think so.

B. Nay. But this one said it's all about having the correct maps. If you have the correct maps, he said, then you're never lost. But I said, "I feel lost, because I get manuals, and that's not the same as a map." And he laughed and said, "No, that's not the same as a map." And I said, "Can I maybe borrow your maps?" He laughed about that and said I would not be able to read them anyway. So I said, "If you come with me and translate it to my understanding, maybe being inside the bubble with me?" But he said he doesn't travel inside a bubble, neither of you do, but I have asked both of you if there is, in the ladder of learning, if I am going to map school, if I'm gonna get my own atlas. And you said that we can create an atlas—you're very accommodating, I must say. So you gave me another book, which is an atlas, indeed, with pictures and images, like that, –but it's more like an energetic view into it, so it's not like changing, moving, in that sense; you look into the book, you open the book, like a box, and then it just creates different—you said "It's like an atlas, I give you one similar to what I have." And then I looked into it, but there are no roads, really, so I don't know how to navigate here. But it's a small one. I have actually seen, briefly, your books—not open—but I have seen them, and they are much bigger than my pocket book. But you said it's not to be confused. You gave me a pocket book and said, "This is like an atlas of where your individual is." So I looked into this little box, you open it and you can look into it, that's sort of how it looks.

D. How's your little individual doing? Has he manifested yet?

B. Indeed, a couple of them. They are gonna colonize in different locations. So there are three groups that have become family units, and that's what I wanted them to be. I actually designed them to be in a flock, I didn't want them to be lonely. Before, here, he was by himself, he didn't colonize with others. But now, I implemented in his awareness the sensation of group activity and to long for that experience of joy with others. So those who woke up from their sleeping pattern (*on his planet*), they actually had that in their awareness that they wanted to seek a mate, and they wanted to seek a mate not just to make another individual, but to actually remain with that mate. So now there are three groups located around a continent that has actually started to progress. There are others that will start to join, but they're not woken up yet. They actually enjoy being in group. They're playful!

D. Stomping all your foliage. (*His planet, where the Individual is now located, is also a greenhouse planet where he grows plants.*)

B. Ah. I have actually, in the center of this continent, I have created an outside greenhouse area where I plant herbs and other things that are beneficial for the soil, to help connect the grid underneath the soil. And here, nothing is gonna come and disturb my web in the soil.

D. It's going to be perfect.

B. It's gonna be perfect indeed. And Ia, I actually showed Ia, so Ia has also been looking at this.

D. Did she like it? (*Ia is his closest friend on the second dimension. They were created together in a big energetic egg, which separated into about 100 spirits.*)

B. Yes indeed, she complimented me. I brought, –well I can't say I–, but we brought her to watch the screens in your lab. She's always been invited, but she's busy with the little ones. But she was curious to see where my individual and my system was, so we're watching on big screens. (*Bob is able to observe his solar system from our lab on the sixth.*)

D. It must make her feel really proud of your accomplishments.

B. Ah, she said I created my own egg. My living planet is like my own egg.

D. And it's located in a nice, safe place.

B. It is indeed. There is a couple around it, other systems. Maybe you made them. They're kind of mirroring mine, so maybe you created similar ones, so they can become a family, like a system family. Maybe they want to be a family as well, like my individual.

D. Well, I like your ideas for a peaceful, harmonious environment. You might have come up with a better pattern for living planets.

B. Ah. Might be. And you might have put similar systems around mine, because they look kind of similar, they have the same song. I know that I didn't create them, so someone did, and I'm pretty sure you might have had a finger in this, because you know what I like. And you probably cushioned mine, like crash cushions around my system. So they are maybe gonna become a star system family. Even though my individual's not gonna be able to leave and go off somewhere, but there might be other entities that might come and visit, friendly ones, that come and visit mine, and appreciate the individual.

It is worthwhile to clarify the difference between dimensions and parallel realities. Since we can't measure spiritual vibration or energetic frequency, using these words does add to our understanding of the concepts. The dimensions are related to the changes in the spiritual vibration, more or less. The parallel planes are related to changes in the energy fields of matter. A spacecraft, for example, does not move into the mental realm or the fifth dimension. Material objects remain in the confines of the third dimension. They sometimes can transform and move into parallel realities, but that requires a change in the molecular structure or frequency of material. The human senses are not adapted to see or hear into the parallel bands, and the body is not capable of traveling into another atomic structure.

In the remote past, humans were able to create conditions where they could move their consciousness, similar like an OBE, up into the vibrational field of the fourth dimension and access information related to the Earth. Some shamans were able to travel even further, although the risk of inducing physical death was quite real. Within the fourth, if a soul manages to rise high enough, it will find itself above the timeline, and will be able to look forward and backward, in limited ways. Robert Monroe was able to document ways of doing this through brainwave modulation. The ancients had their own methods that involved altering the properties of the atmosphere, allowing their soul consciousness to have direct access to this realm.

The Velvet Purse of Notes (April 6 and 14, 2019)

Spirits from the second dimension are the ones who launch and nurture life on Earth. Over the eons, they have observed the coming and going of entities and travelers that visit the planet. The activities and creations of visitors—and that includes humanoids—have often been disruptive or destructive to other life forms. As a result, Bob often feels confused about the purpose and direction of evolution, and worries that similar interference may occur in his solar system. During our time together, he was made aware of an Evolution Group, which is affiliated with the Council of Nine. The Evolution Group also has a close relationship with the Eye, an extension of the Master Mind. As intermediaries between the councils and the Master Mind, they plant the seeds of change within life forms, planets, solar systems, galaxies, and even fish tanks. Not surprisingly, Bob decided it was important to meet with them so he could share his ideas and maybe discover their intentions for Earth and his living planet. As described in *Volume 1*, his request was granted. Ari, Isaac, Ophelia and Lasaray were going to escort him to a meeting with the Evolution Group so he could voice his concerns. To keep the meeting focused, Lasaray asked Bob to bring only five questions, forcing him to select the most important topics. He placed these questions in his velvet purse, as he calls a small purple bag given to him by Lasaray.

Bob has given detailed descriptions of my office on the sixth dimension, where he and I work together. We have covered an entire wall with notes on ideas and observations he wants to transmit to humanity during the course of this project. He has thousands of notes, and we have arranged them in some sort of order. Before each trance session, he and Lasaray review how well previous ideas were understood by Dave, the incarnation, and then decide which ideas are next in line to convey in upcoming sittings. He carries those to our meetings in his backpack or bag of notes. Even though it may seem his talks are somewhat scattered, there are continuous lines of teachings and profound wisdom embedded within his dialogues. I would also remind the reader that Bob has a unique way of conversing, often violating the latest rules in the *Chicago Manual of Style* (as do I). He will occasionally, for example, say "is" when "are" would be the appropriate verb. He also uses "so" with great abandon, but it is seldom followed by a pause. Therefore, I normally do not insert a comma, even though the rule-makers yearn for one. To maintain the purity of his voice, we only meddle with his sentence structure or choice of words when it becomes confusing to read. Sadly, the written word fails to capture the full glory of his personality. Lost are the linguistic inflections, as well as the enthusiasm and pure joy he radiates while speaking.

    D. Did you bring your little bag of notes today?
    B. I did indeed. I have several notes at my disposal.
    D. That's nice. I was hoping to hear a couple of your ideas.
    B. Well, we'll see how many a couple is, but one of my notes are actually that I am preparing my visit to the Evolution Group.

So a lot of my notes are actually for that specific trip. So if you like, we can go over them and see if they fit, and you can say if I can bring that note (*to the Evolution Group*).

D. Okay.

B. Huhuh. SO, one of my first notes is: "Are you fully aware of the occurrences within the species on Earth? And if so, when is the current upgrade gonna happen? And, my sparkles that I am training, will they get a new model, or an old model?" (*He wants to know if his students from the sixth dimension will get the next version of humans, possessing greater mental and spiritual abilities.*)

D. That's a really good question, or set of questions.

B. It is indeed. It's a crucial question on how I will continue my coaching. Will I get a new model of human? Or will I get an old one? The soul inside is pure, I do know that, but what sort of vehicle will they have at their disposal? Otherwise, I'm not gonna be able to train my sparkles fully. So that is the question I want to ask, "When they are ready for departure, what vehicle, what events, will they face? How can I train them? Am I training them for the propeller plane, or am I training them for a jet plane?" So that is one of the questions. Can I bring that one? (*I laughed, because he forgot he wasn't talking to Lasaray. In Volume 1, Bob compared the future human body to a jet aircraft, while the modern ones are like a propeller plane.*)

D. Absolutely.

B. Okay, so we put that one in my new velvet bag that I'm gonna bring.

D. A smaller bag?

B. It's a smaller bag, because I can't bring this big thing. They would go like, "What is this? What is all this?" So I'm removing certain things.

D. You have to be focused.

B. Indeed. I'm on high alert. I hope I understand them, but I have no hopes for that. So that's why Isaac is gonna be with.

D. Ah, yes, Isaac will be able to translate.

B. Isaac will translate. I hope that you translate my notes correctly, so that you don't miss any of my questions, you know, because I've been told that I'm not gonna be allowed to bring any notes in except in my velvet bag. It's more like a purse. It's kinda small, it's not like I was given a huge backpack. (*He will not be allowed to bring in his big bag of notes to dig through during the meeting; he has to prioritize.*) You gave me this bag which is dark purple, similar like your robe. You said, "They will understand that you and I are buddies if you come in the same color with your little bag." That's a trick, to know exactly who you belong to because of the purse you bring.

D. Are you going to have a purple robe too?

B. Ahh, that would be nice if I could get like a purple travel robe from you, so that we look the same. At the moment I only have my purse—that is a little velvet bag that you made for me—that I can put some Post–its in, you said. Huhuhuh.

D. What's your next Post-it question?

B. I'm not sure if I'm allowed to ask questions about other places than Earth, but I do want to know the grand evolution and the plans for where my individual is, that system; if and when they're gonna strike with evolution and what that would mean. When evolution comes in that region, what would that mean? Does it mean that certain areas will be shut down, or is it gonna be like blossoming and flourishing? What does it mean? So I would like a little bit of a sneak peek on plans of the grand evolution where my individual is.

D. That's a perfectly legitimate question, since you are in charge of your planet. I think you need to know that.

B. So that's also one of my questions. I also would like, another note is—and this is not just mine—but there has been a concern in the second about the seas, the oceans, because there are mammals in the oceans that are feeling anxiety, and there is great distress among my friends. They (*his friends on the second*) want to know how to best tend to these big mammals; and how to increase the light in the plankton; and if they are aware of those problems; and if so, what their intentions are and how they will fix the problem? I also had a question about a reboot, –if indeed nothing would work, what does it take for a reboot to take place? I'm not sure about that one! You looked a little bit concerned about that note.

D. What about Ophelia—what does Ophelia say?

B. Ophelia and everyone was like, "Hmm". And I said, "How long does evolution have to degrade for a reboot to take place?"

D. The Evolution Group is not the Creator.
B. But they are an extension of the Creator.
D. If they're operating from their own opinion, maybe you can influence their opinion.
B. Ah. So, maybe if I leave this little velvet bag with them, they can study my questions when they have their own meetings. I simply would like to know how long, or what has to take place, before a complete intervention takes place, a reboot, because that will help me understand where we are at. But this wasn't...
D. It wasn't received as warmly as the other questions?
B. No, it became a vacuum, it became silent in the group. I'm putting that one aside, I put that one here. (*He set his ethereal note down on an equally invisible table to his right*). But it's still a big question, because of the fact that if I train all my sparkles and "Whoops!", ten years down the line a reboot takes place, then they are gonna be disappointed and they're gonna say, "You didn't say this, Bob, you didn't tell us! Now there is no place to go to, everything is gone, it's in hibernation. We did all this training, what did we do wrong? What did we do wrong?" And then I'll say, "You didn't do anything wrong," and they're gonna ask me all these questions, like, "Why did this happen? Why, why, why, why?" So I'm moving that forward to the Evolution Group, "What is going to happen, and why? How can this be avoided?"
D. Well, there is a third option, and that would be for a partial reboot so you don't completely eliminate the species, but you thin them down considerably.
B. Or you bring in the consciousness from Siah's place, –that is what Ophelia says. (*Siah, my rescued pet, lives on the planet Etena, in fish tank four.*) "We're bringing in the light, and we're sharing the light. Because that is what you do," she says, "when someone is suffering." She says, "It's similar like if you have someone who has depression, –how do you cure depression? You embrace it with light and happiness and joy, because that is the strongest force, combined with love, –you do that." And she said, "It's the same thing; it's like Earth is depressed, so we are bringing in light from all different directions, –from all spiritual dimensions, from souls incarnating, and from Siah's world–, all to embrace this sad planet. And because the planet is sad and depressed,

everything and everyone on it will sense that." And that is also why certain events take place, because they don't feel their host is happy. It's like being in a family when there is someone with "Ohh" in the head (*he meant mental illness*), then everyone suffers. Or if someone is suffering from alcoholism, then everyone suffers. It's the same thing if the planet is depressed and everyone feels that, then it's hard to hear your song and it's hard to hear the tuning fork for the environment. But the humans are also struggling with finding their light because they feel the environment and the air around them, so to speak, is feeling depressed. So we need to increase the light. But I said, "I just don't want there to be sadness along the way."

D. In the future, are more souls going to be incarnating from six and seven than from five, where most are from now?

B. And even eight, because the eighth is gonna come back a little bit. "Not many," Isaac said, but it is to balance the depression, because there's no depression there! (*Snorts*) There's no depression in the spirit realm at all! So, that's also part of my notes that I have in my velvet bag. We're all gonna go, and kinda soon it seems, since I'm in that phase of putting notes in my velvet bag. But indeed, I do hope that I will get a robe so that I look like I come from your place.

D. What color robe does Ophelia wear?

B. She sometimes has really light blue, but also light yellow, and gold sometimes.

D. What about Isaac?

B. Blue, light blue, a darker light blue.

D. Is Jeshua going with us?

B. Ah, Jeshua is busy. He's patching holes, he said. He has great council work to do, so he might not go, but he said that he will come and have a listen afterwards. Zachariah's gonna come.

D. What color does Zachariah wear?

B. It's like green, dark green.

D. And then Ari, he was going too, wasn't he?

B. Ah, he's like you, he's wearing dark purple. And then there is me. I normally like red, but I don't want to stand out like a strawberry. They will go like, "Oh, what's that?" I want to blend in better. Anyway, that will be it for today, Ophelia says. But any–who, I'm ready to go!

D. Are you happy with the book? (*This was just after Volume 1 was released.*)

B. I am indeed. It is all my words, and some others, but I feel great happiness! I don't like to be cut short. So now, even though I've been participating in the other ones as well, but now it's mine.

D. Yes, very little dialogue, except for you and I talking.

B. It's a book about soul-to-soul communication. Anyway, I'm gonna go now, Ophelia says.

D. Thank you so much for coming, my friend.

B. Anyway, I go. Bye bye.

The next week, Bob brought up his preparations for the visit to the Evolution Group. What I didn't notice, until I began putting this book together, was that Bob immediately picked up where he left off eight days earlier. He had presented two of the questions he wanted to ask the Evolution group, but I diverted his talk onto another topic, so he had not finished his list. Once again, this shows how incredibly precise they are with the information they send through to us.

B. Ah. I'm still preparing a little bit for the Evolution Group.

D. How many notes are you allowed to take?

B. Five. I have three more, and the third one is, "Is it possible for someone like me to—maybe in disguise—to blend and incarnate? And if I could participate directly, hopefully not forget as much on my journey?" (*Bob has expressed a curiosity about incarnating. As a spirit guide, he sees a lot of things he could fix, providing he doesn't have to forget or become trapped in the karma program.*)

D. I remember they said Zachariah came in as an adult on at least one occasion. Another Elahim came in as a baby and prepared the body, then he left and Zachariah came in and took over.

B. Indeed. So, my third question is, "Whether it is possible for me and my friends to also participate and maybe not forget that much? Because then we could operate in a grand group. And it would be easier if we take on vehicles, passive vehicles, but inside we remember more." So how would that mirror in the events and outcome? I'm a little bit curious also about the design of soul versus vehicle, "Who creates these vehicles? And what components do they consider for a soul journey?" So, I'm curious about the makeup in an incarnation and how it is decided, –the blend of soul versus body. I would like that to be discussed.

D. That's four.

B. Ah, that's four. I did have five. But I'm thinking that me going (*taking on a body*), together with the question about the grand design and the grand makeup of an incarnation, maybe that could be considered like one question, –like 1A and 1B. Huhuhuh! You said that I couldn't put like 3A, B, C, D, E, F, G on my note! You said, "You're tricky!" I said, "You did say 1, 2, 3, 4, and 5, I'm just adding A, B, C, D, E follow-up questions underneath! And you said, "No, you have five that will fit in your purse." No, I don't want to waste a personal question, because I can easily ask Ophelia, so I'm not gonna waste that one, so I'm putting that aside, –BUT I am curious. So my next question will then be, "Who creates the vehicles for the incarnations, and what do they take into consideration when a soul connects?" I would like to know that blend.

D. I thought you and your friends on the second were the ones creating vehicles?

B. No. Well the physical thing we do, but we don't necessarily create all the conditions within it. So, I would like to know the grand design behind incarnations, that's what I would like to know. I'm pondering still, because I was not allowed to have A, B, C, D. I did have a little pile here that I was gonna put in. Not a pile, it is together five notes, but I put together with a little clipper, A, B, C, D, E underneath, behind. And that was not approved. So I have to rethink this. Anyway, okay, that will probably be it.

Bob Plans a Life for Me (July 25, 2019)

We normally do not include personal instructions given to us by the spirits, unless it has a general usefulness. Gergen's talk includes several observations about the brain and the soul, as well as how spirit guides work with the incarnation. When Bob comes in later, he elaborates on a future life he is designing for Lasaray. It might confuse the reader when he uses past tense verbs as he describes his work. However, he is referring to the activities in the pre–life planning, not the actual life. Designing lives is the next phase of his progression as a spirit guide, and he jumped into the project with his usual enthusiasm.

> G. This is Gergen. Oh, huh huh huh. Just squeezing in a little bit here. It is indeed a separate occasion and Bob is eager to start the interviews, he said. I don't know why he calls it interviews—apparently, he must have some questions lined up. (*Bob was interviewing spirits who might want to incarnate and have roles in a life he was planning for me.*) However, we do, from all levels, from all councils, we wish to say the greatest gratitude for the effort that we see that you are both engaging in your journey. You are embarking on a little bit of a pause, and that is also something that one should feel welcome about. Your pause is more of a reflective one, where you will move into the sensation of Lasaray, the higher mind, the higher consciousness within your being. It is there, do not think that it is not available. You just have to somewhat sit still and let the signals come from the brain, –it's similar to see like you have two brains, and at this point, the human brain is not really confident that it has the ABILITY to receive the signals from the higher brain, from the higher mind. The higher mind within, my friend, is ready to—it's almost like a separate entity within you—and it's ready to send signals to the more...
>
> D. Mundane?
>
> G. It's more like, I would say, that it's lacking confidence. Mundane, one can say, but it is in some way like a child, and the parent, the higher mind, needs sometimes to encourage the child, the human mind, to open up for signals. You are in that phase where you are given a silence, a break, for you to hear those signals from your higher mind, who is ready to communicate with you. That is something that will be prominent in the upcoming weeks for you. So in that sense, just before this one returns with its own noises, then you can indeed enjoy the silence. And there is a good link hovering above, ready to communicate. It is good to somewhat be aware of when the receiver within you are more welcoming. Knowing the different flows of energy is helpful when these occurrences are at a peak. So just know the beginning of September is a good time for you to access information. Ophelia is also ready to assist, of course, never far away from her children when they travel. I would not say you are a child, as Lasaray, but

as an incarnation you do tend to appear as such, and we do care for you as children when you incarnate. It's somewhat of a struggle for a spirit helper to remain silent, to allow its children to fly and to sometime fall and trip as well. Fall and trip is nothing wrong, as long as one stands up again. It is within the being if it has a capacity and a will to stand up. EVERYONE falls; not everyone rises.

Gergen remarked, before he left, "The human mind is like a karaoke machine, maybe, similar like that." The implication being that the physical brain will transmit whatever signals are fed into it. We can, and should, train our human mind to seek and find input from the soul mind. Gergen then stepped aside and Bob immediately popped in. But before we continue with the July 25 session, this is a good place to include a brief overview of the cycle of learning which souls encounter on Earth.

The spirits have given very thorough explanations about why people are born and the meaning of life. They often refer to the Coat of Karma and the blueprint for a soul. The Creator creates souls to fulfill certain purposes, so the blueprint is the plan for the soul, from its birth as a sparkle to the moment it returns and merges again with the Creator. All spirits who incarnate on Earth have, as a part of their blueprint, goals related to Earth, which may represent only a small part of the blueprint. Prior to its first incarnation, those goals are imprinted into a Coat of Karma, which is specific to Earth and to that soul. The Coat is stored in the fourth dimension surrounding the Earth, and, in its original condition, is pure, holding only the intention from the Creator. A soul incarnates to fulfill those intentions, which may take several thousand lives to complete. Once a soul incarnates, the physical, emotional, and mental centers of the body can override the soul. When thoughts, emotions, or actions are not in accord with the soul, it demonstrates a failure to master certain lessons. The Coat of Karma retains memories of all experiences on Earth. When the soul returns in a subsequent incarnation, its Coat has its original objectives to accomplish, plus any lessons not learned, which must also be addressed. We were fortunate to be told about the actual lessons available on this planet.

We might think the steps of progress in the Earth school are similar to our own education program, where everyone must follow a standard curriculum to eventually graduate with a diploma. Apparently, that is not how the Creator designed the system.

Zachariah gave a brilliant explanation of the steps of learning, and even though it is part of Wave 3, we are including it here. The Earth school has general themes, but each soul has a uniquely tailored education based on the blueprint given by the Creator. When a soul has completed the steps in its program and resolved karmic impurities, the spirits say "the Coat is folded" and put in the closet of the fourth dimension. Spirits may continue to come to Earth, but it is for other purposes, such as to assist a friend, share knowledge, or fulfill an objective for a council. A fair conclusion is that some souls have fewer steps in their ladder of learning than other souls, before the Coat can be folded. Zachariah gave a lecture on June 23, 2019, a part of which is presented here.

D. I had another question. You said the souls from the fifth have, for example, twenty-some steps. Can you give me the different types of lessons they have to go through?

Z. The first, normally, in a karma program, the first, let's say, one to eight, the steps one to eight, relates to personal lessons. Level nine to fifteen enters soul purpose, mission, what the Creator and council intended with you. The last steps involves enlightenment, spiritual connection. These souls coming in now from the fifth, coming in directly in the middle—soul purpose, mission—will later address personal events, such as family bond, love. But love also is the end on your ladder in your program. Different love. The end step of love is love for all, a compassion. Love at the highest form is compassion, love in a lower form relates loving an individual, loving yourself, loving where you are at, –it's still love, but it's like saying Love 101. The highest form of love is stillness, appreciation and compassion. That is the highest form of love.

D. Wonderful, thank you for that. You said the Elahims didn't have as many steps, yet when I came in, I still had twelve-hundred lives?

Z. It has nothing to do with how many lives, it has to do with the amount of steps implemented in your Coat of Karma, your program, your unique karma program. Most souls, like I said, have about twenty-five steps in their karma program, that's the norm. Some come in simply programmed for a specific task, can come in with only six steps. Those souls come in and, from a human standpoint, they appear odd. They don't necessarily have the human, or emotional, steps programmed within them, –they do not necessarily relate to human emotions. Those souls coming in specifically designed for a mission appear, in certain ways, alien. In some way they are. They don't necessarily mirror human behavior in the same way, they stand out because they are more methodical in their approach. They are more plastic, that's a word, in their persona.

D. How many did I have?

Z. You had eight steps in your karma program. This one has twelve. Depending on the wish and the need the soul was created for, all karma programs are different, depending on, in this case, cycle, ability, and so forth. Souls coming from the fifth rarely have less than eighteen steps in their karma program. That's why they blend in better, they have wider spectra mirroring the destination, feeling more at home than other souls.

We will now continue with Bob's outline of a life he has been planning for Lasaray. The main goal for the life is to find a plant he is introducing in New Zealand. To fulfill the mission, he put together a map of where I would be born (Dover, England), my personality, how much soul energy I would bring, the spirits who would be the parents and wife, where I would go to school (Oxford, for a Ph.D.). He then organized a series of events leading to the moment when I am standing in a particular location in the forests of New Zealand, discovering his plant. He wants me to study how blood affects the brain. He wants humans to know how light affects and deletes negative patterns in the brain, which is adversely affected by dirty blood. His flowering plant contains chemicals that will clean the blood and restore health to damaged cells. The mother he found for me is a spirit from the seventh. She and I have had lives together, one of which was described in *Volume 1*, where she, as Josephine, worked in a tavern in an Irish harbor town during the early 1800's. Bob, when describing this future life, speaks about it in past tense, which is a little confusing. From his perspective, he planned and previewed the life on screens in our lab, so he has seen how it should play out. When he describes an upcoming life as something he has already witnessed, our minds balk because it no longer fits our linear framework. Therefore, I altered some of his words to a future tense to make it more agreeable to read. Lives are scripted, to a certain extent, but there is abundant room for free will and other influences to disrupt and alter the plans. The blueprint given to the soul by the Creator does not change, but the Coat of Karma is adjusted after each lifetime to reflect the growth and future obligations the next incarnation will assume.

B. (*Bob immediately popped in.*) HUUHH! Ah, Gergen came first.

D. Yes, he gave some really good advice. I guess you didn't have a door today? (*In an earlier session, Gergen had put an energetic door up to keep Bob from hearing what was said.*)

B. Nay, it was no door! I did overhear, I heard that he was revealing a little bit that I, –you did say that you might return later. And when I said, "What are your plans for later?", you said, "I don't really have any plans". Then I said, "You want me to help with your planning?" and you smiled and you said, "Sure, we can look into that." I said, "Huh!" So I took off and digged up all my notes that I had, and I have several lifetimes that in some way needs to be activated; meaning I create more details to them. They are kinda basic, but when you said we can absolutely talk about it, then I took some of my favorite ones and I started to color and add more details. And with that, I looked into where geographically we could go and who could potentially go with you.

D. I'd like to hear what you came up with.

B. I did think that you would like to go to New Zealand, because New Zealand is a friendly little dot and it's very close with nature and there's a lot of vegetation. So I thought you might want to be like a—not a water biologist—but that you would understand how to excavate and how to use plants, like a scientist because I do know that you prefer that. So regardless of where I put you, I make you somewhat of a scientist—but here we used plant life in order for you to excavate plants and combine what you extracted from them to create different potions. So you're not a doctor but you are medically trained, you're like a professor. I made sure you had gone to a good school, so I put you in a school where I thought you would also find somewhat of a cell memory, so I put you in Oxford, in England, because it resonates well, –the British Isles. I say well, but maybe I should say it resonates strong. Some lives is not resonating well in that region, but you prefer the British attitude and they are more silent, –you like that, you feel more comfortable in a tea and cookie etiquette. So you are actually, –in this specific note that I have been coloring–, you were actually born Brit. I thought that you could be born in the area around Dover, that's where I thought that you would like to be born because of the cliffs, because I know you like that. So I thought, if I gather different details that I know that you like, similar like a wife—if a wife wants to go on a trip, you know, a wife would cook the best meal that the husband likes, before she asks! So it's similar, I know certain things that you like, places and cultures and societies, so I thought if I color that in my notes, in my lifetime, then it is more likely that you will approve. And THEN, I can squeeze in different things that you would maybe overlook, and you would approve the whole thing. And the little things that you might not really want to do, maybe it wasn't your first choice, but the general journey itself looked good, so that you would maybe overlook certain defaults in the journey. (*Bob always has ideas about things he wants me to do while I'm incarnated, and is always plotting to slip his own notes into my life plan.*) So I thought I'll make you be born in Dover and you are born as a single child. Both of you Elahims prefer to be born as, and you normally are, born as single children. It's not like you don't necessarily like siblings, but you come in and the parents are normally more significant—and your friends to come—than siblings. You do tend to need a lot of room. When an Elahim comes, it takes more space. So that's why you prefer to be a single child in lifetimes. But with that also comes that you miss a family unit because you travel by yourself. BUT in this case, when I made you born there, your parents will be friends from the sixth and from the seventh. They are not here now, they are friends of ours, or of yours, and I know that you like them pretty well. I thought that they could be your parents. It's not Ophelia that will be the mother, and it's not Ari or anyone that will be your father, but they will come from six and seven, and you will be the only child. And I put in a lot of extra spice in your human brain. I wanted there to be a stronger connection to the soul mind, with the soul mind being much more aware of certain scientific progress that would come. You become very early on like you are now, you read a lot; not because you don't have friends, you do have friends, but you don't live in the city, you live outside; you prefer to be there. And the family had a little cottage farm and there were sheeps and there were goats. And you did like to just go out and be by the cliffs around Dover. I knew that you liked those, so I thought, "Let's place him there, it's more likely he will say yes to this." So you do study early on and you, in some way, –I mixed and matched parts of certain lives that you already had. You had several lives when you have studied the blood circulation and the brain; you always study the brain more or less. This time (*in the current life*) you don't study how it is constructed and how it is connected, but you study the end result of behaviors from the brain. So you always, in some way, study the brain. In this case, you will study how the blood affects the human mind. With a strong connection to your soul mind, being able to decipher signals on certain things, how blood affects the brain. You become very interested in this, and early on, one knew that you would be interested in medicine and science. You were not however, going in the direction to become a doctor, –you did not become a brain surgeon, let's say–, but you were interested more in the scientific area of the medical establishment. You understand how light affects and deletes negative patterns in the brain that sometimes can be affected by dirty blood. So, early, at the age of eleven in this lifetime that I created, you were mentally as an eighteen–year–old, and you were almost ready to go to Oxford. You did go early, I plan on getting you a little bit earlier in there so that you will start around seventeen, sixteen. You did skip certain classes, you became somewhat, –in some way in your teenage time you were considered a little bit odd. I knew you would be, that's why I put you a little bit outside the regular society so that you would be a tutored, –your father was actually teaching you at home.

D. I think you said I've been considered a little odd in most of my lives. (*Bob occasionally says anywho, instead of anyway, as below.*)

B. A little odd. But here, I wanted you to be directly connected to your soul mind in much more obvious ways. But you were home–taught by your father. Anywho, I made you go to Oxford, and there you just dove into the old teachings, and you read everything on the blood and the brain, and you were fascinated to see the different end results of different intake and different potions and how it affected the blood, and in the end, also the brain. So that life you got a medical degree, like a Ph.D–D–D–D–D–D, and that was good, but you never had an interest in working in—you got several offers to work in hospitals—but you were more interested in finding cures, so you were more of a researcher, a medical researcher I would say. Then, because I wanted you to have a really nice life, so you would meet someone, a lady friend, and that lady friend came from New Zealand. And that is how you came to go there; it's not a coincidence, of course, because I wanted you all along to go to New Zealand, because that's where the plants would be that I will lead you to. But you actually remained there and you never returned to England in that sense. So that was a really a colorful life, I thought, where you would be able to, from a scientific foundation, create connections on how the blood affects the brain and what different—I say potions—but it's like combinations of biological components that you connect and combine to delete grey cells and you could, by using it, you could increase or decrease the rhythm of the blood as well.

D. That sounds like a really good life!

B. It's a good life.

D. I have a question about the parents whom you have picked. If we decided to do that life, we all make the decision and then they commit to coming down first?

B. Well, when you start to create and you gather all the actors, then they have to go down first, because they might have their own agenda before taking care of you. So in this case, these two are very well familiar (*to Lasaray*). They did not necessarily have an agenda because they are gonna be simple people. Neither of them have a Coat. But they're gonna come down and start a community in this countryside. So it's not a boom–batta–bang–batta–bang life for them, but a lot of times when souls come down with no Coats, they just mingle and meddle in society and just their presence creates good foundations in different aspects. These two had a small agenda to create a community for farmers to work with the soil, and they create like a farmer community in that region, in the whole county. So like I said, it was not a boom–batta–bang–batta–bang, over the whole world that they create effects, but they start and they make a society that is self-sufficient, and everyone is friendly. When I see it, I see them coming and doing this before you come. The father already knew that he will teach you. But you are introduced early on into a society that is self-sufficient and that is not operating from manufactured seeds or influences in general. The energy is also different in this community and in this county. They use solar flares, solar wind for power and solar energy, so that's what they do, these two. I really like them and I know you do too, so I thought if I pick nice parents, maybe you will come. So I did that. They are not here now (*not currently incarnated*). But in preparing, I did ask around if anyone would be interested in coming down. And I kinda showed the map, the outline of my intention. I first went to Ophelia, because the mother is important, so I first went there, and Ophelia said, "I'm not going to go but I'm always following him, following Lasaray, but there is another one here that will come." And this one that comes is not a stranger to you, this one was the one that was Josephine. But Josephine has not come back in a while.

D. Oh, her Coat was folded?

B. Coat was folded. She took that life in the harbor just to somewhat help the other women there. It was a shift, women needed to regain the power of their own bodies in some way, and their own power—similar like she will do here in the farmer community. I like her! I don't know why we don't travel with her more. Normally, I ask, "Why don't we pick that one? Why can't Ophelia come?" And this one (*Seth*) is like, "Oh, I ask that all the time why Ophelia can't come."

D. Ophelia doesn't want to come back here anymore?

B. Ophelia doesn't, she hasn't been here for, –I don't know when she was here last. Some early AD, she says, she was briefly here. (*She must have sent him a thought bubble with the information.*)

D. When was she here last?

B. In the early AD.

D. I know she was my mother once, in Greece.

B. Ah. And she's been with this one, mother to this one as well. And you do like that, you like to go with her in different constellations. But she's always present; so even if she's not in physical, she's always very highly connected to you when you travel.

D. Gergen said something about you doing interviews. Was that related to this?

B. It's this! I'm interviewing actors that might come on the journeys ahead. So I have been around asking questions; I have been showing outlines of different potential lifetimes that could come for Lasaray, and I'm seeing myself as somewhat of a manager for you.
D. I'm sure you're a good one.
B. Ah. Like a manager—you look around for what stage your person should go to. So as a manager, you do the negotiations on certain things.
D. Hire the roadies.
B. Indeed. So I see myself as a little bit of a manager in that respect. I conduct a little bit of questions, inquisitive as I am, and I show different outlines. I do like her, –we can call her Josephine because she's like you a little bit, she doesn't change names that much, she says, so she's similar like that. She's a little bit younger in soul evolution than Ophelia, a bit younger.
D. A little older than…who's the one you're friends with?
B. Julia, older than Julia. But Josephine, she said, "I can absolutely come down and be the mother, and I would absolutely, in my own way, like to help the society to become self-sufficient." So she was gonna go down and help with more of the soil, so to speak. So, –check on that! And then I thought, "We need a match for Josephine, someone that SHE might fancy." So it's not just about you! I asked Josephine a little bit about her preference in a mate. And then I thought (*after hearing what she wanted*), "I already thought that I was gonna go to the sixth."
D. So who did you find?
B. I went to the sixth and I looked around, and from those that are mentors for the three little Elahims, I asked them. And one of them were the best pick as a mate for Josephine, as well as for you. It's not as hard to make you happy with a father, but I wanted also for Josephine to be happy. That's important if you are a matchmaker. So I showed him what my plan was and what I was planning on doing, and he said that he would come down then and he would make this community, –it's a whole county, it's not just a village, it's a whole county that became self-sufficient. He said that he will come down and help them only be relying on certain energy

resources, like wind power and solar energy, so he was gonna come down and he was gonna help with that. So that was their mission, what they were gonna do, Josephine and him. He calls himself Nelo...Ne...Nealon. I like him! I do like him. I'm sewing the whole family together in a combined story. I'm highly happy with Nealon and Josephine, because who doesn't want to live in that community? It's very, –all of them live in cottages–, it's very British though, they drink tea and they have a tumbola thing (*he meant something like a farmers market*) where they meet and they sew and they sing.

D. That doesn't sound like a time in the future.

B. Sometimes time stands still in certain places, but there is nothing wrong with that, and that's what they show. They show that sometimes future progress is not necessarily to aim for change, sometimes the good thing has already been. And sometimes the simpler things are the ones to strive for, like here in this county. So, anywho, I made my rounds in creating different interviews on your behalf, as a manager for this specific life.

D. You put so much effort into it, it might be hard to say no.

B. It's hard to say no now, because now I, –and I did come to you and I showed you after (*making the rounds*), how my whole outline was now colored with different individuals. So you were very surprised of how ahead of myself I was. I was not so surprised. Ophelia was not so surprised. But you were like, "Oh, you already have everything set and done? So what time should I come down? When will I be born?" Huhuh, so I said, "I think that you should be born 2173 to 2175. Then (*after consulting with the Astrological Council*), I thought you could come down in 2178."

D. That's a nice time, I'm sure. Hopefully things will have settled down by then. There's a lot of crazy stuff going on in the world now.

B. Yes, I thought if I wait a while, it's more likely you will agree. So, I made interviews with that. I also looked into location and geographic preference that I know that you prefer. And I said, "You will travel to, and you will have your life in England," because the parents would actually not stick around all that long after you were self–sufficient, they had no intention to stay. So they were gonna leave anyway, so there was not gonna be any remorse. I didn't want there to be a feeling, –

because you were so close with your family, with your father and mother–, I did not want you to feel torn when you were on the other side of the planet. So I thought about it and I asked, it's not like I killed them, I asked, "What do you prefer when Lasaray has finished his education, and I will put him to find my plants and so forth in New Zealand, and he will find his lady-friend, what would you prefer then?" And they said, "Well, then, mission is done, so we can leave." So there is like, it's a little bit of an accident, but not a harmful one. Well, harmful in that way that they died, but not harmful that it was a trauma for the souls, –simply an exit.

D. It's kind of fascinating how souls plan all that down to the very fine details.

B. Ah, especially if they have a manager like me, who is very detail oriented!

D. I thought you didn't like the details?

B. I do, if I come up with them myself. I don't like details if they're forced on me. But if I create the details, then I'm highly interested.

D. That self-study paid off then. Thank you for that information. I may take you up on that offer for another life.

B. Ah, you don't really have a choice, it seems, since I have activated all these actors. I've activated, –we'll talk about this more, because we have the lady-friend and you have a male friend also that you're going to really like. But maybe I should have that as a surprise, like a treat, who they are. It's sometimes good to make that a surprise.

D. Bring Seth.

B. HUHUHUH. We'll see if this one wants to be female again, otherwise this one might want to be your companion friend. We'll see if Ophelia approves. We'll see, but I make my rounds and I make interviews.

D. That sound wonderful. Good luck with all of that. (*Little Seth, whom Bob mentions next, is one of the young Elahims that Bob is preparing to begin incarnating, as detailed in Volume 1. He gave him that name because he has a personality similar to Seth, Christine's higher self, which is very adventurous and bold. Also, the spider web refers to the Cell, the cartel that want control of the planet.*)

B. It's like, how can one reject such a fine proposal? And this is something that I want, because at this time, –yes, Ophelia, I will come–, but at this time, Little Seth and everyone will probably be down, and they will be implanted in the spider webs, if I have any say. So I thought maybe more can come down at the same time. But how many Elahims can be down at the same time? Well, we'll see. Anyway, I'll go now so I don't get dragged away.

D. Thank you so much for all that really good information. It was really entertaining and informative.

B. Ah. Okay, so you said yes now, I guess, with that. (*He took my statement of "that sounds wonderful' to be an agreement to accept his life plan for me.*)

D. Lasaray has to say yes, I can't speak for him. Alright my friend, talk soon.

B. Ah. Okay. See you. Bye bye.

In this session, Bob's offhand comment about solar wind as a source of energy may be quite prophetic. He does not say solar and wind, he said "solar wind" and "solar flares". While it is beyond the scope of this book to tackle the topic, I am quite sure that it is only a matter of time before cosmologists and astrophysicists finally admit their theoretical models of the Universe are fundamentally in error. As the truly brilliant Nikola Tesla said of the theories developed and published by Henri Poincaré and later plagiarized by Einstein, "Einstein's relativity work is a beggar wrapped in purple whom ignorant people take for a king." And, "A mass of errors and deceptive ideas violently opposed to the teachings of great men of science of the past and even to common sense... the theory wraps all these errors and fallacies and clothes them in magnificent mathematical garb which fascinates, dazzles and makes people blind to the underlying errors." While cosmologists drool over singularity, big bangs and black holes, which exist only as mathematical ideas, the true structure of our Universe is based on principles which have yet to be identified. All planetary bodies operate within electrical fields, which are carried by plasma in the aether of space. The aether of space is actually the basal energy field of the first dimension, and is the polarity to the Creator. This field contains cosmic light and cosmic sound energy undetectable to those of us on the third dimension. If we look at Earth, the electrical nature of the Aurora Borealis was identified by the Norwegian, Kristian Birkeland, in 1908. His theory is being inadvertently validated by NASA and other researchers, although they refuse to believe that electricity flows through, what they assume to be, the vacuum of interstellar space. The ancient visitors to Earth understood and used the electrical potential in the atmosphere for free energy, and future scientists will follow the lead of Tesla and figure out ways to harness energy from the vast electrical field surrounding the planet. This is the project the next wave of Elahims will work on when they start incarnate. If you find the topic interesting, you can investigate the Electric Universe Theories and Birkeland Currents.

Presenting the Life Plan to the Council (Sept 26, 2019)

Mentors are always responsible for designing the upcoming lives of their protégé. As souls advance and become more independent, they take over much of the preparatory work. Once a mission is defined and the intricacies worked out, the entire blueprint is brought before a council for approval or modification. The spirit world is structured like a highly efficient organization. Clusters of spirits are guided by a first-line management group of older spirits who share a similar specialty. The specialist groups are assembled under the larger umbrella of a higher council of older spirits who help steer the management groups. That council, in turn, is given direction by higher councils, who collaborate with councils on other dimensions, and so on, all the way up to the Creator. Because any given life intertwines with spirits who are incarnating from other specialties and dimensions, the coordination among the councils is extraordinarily sophisticated.

Bob has walked beside me through about 1200 lives. As a reward for being such a faithful companion, Lasaray and Jeshua turned over the entire process of planning my next incarnation to him. As described in the previous section, he was allowed to select a mission, choose the souls who will be my parents and wife, the geographic location where I will be born, my personality, where and what I will study, and other intentional undertakings. Once he felt ready, he and Lasaray took his plans to the Council of Nine, who preside over the Elahim incarnations. Bob uses "peer" and "mentor" interchangeably when he is referring to the older spirit assigned to guide a younger one. In his terminology, my mentor, Jeshua, is also my peer. Normally, once a spirit has folded their Coat, they only return to Earth for special projects. Bob decided he wanted to bring Josephine, who agreed to help with his project.

B. Josephine doesn't have a Coat, but you don't have a Coat either. My story is different, because I didn't ask your peer, I didn't ask Jeshua what we can do with you. I had my own agenda and presented it. I have presented my ideas, because you said, –you accommodated me with this (*his planned life*)–, you said, "Let's go to the councils and see if it's a good idea."

D. Which life are we talking about here?

B. The one, my life with you in New Zealand and England with Josephine. So you pushed me, you said, "Have you colored everything correctly? Because now we're going to go and show it."

D. To which council?

B. You said we were gonna go to the Council of Nine with Jeshua and Zachariah.

D. Did we?

B. (*He began breathing nervously, as he recalled the anxiety he felt about going in front of the council.*) Ah, ooohhhh.

D. How many were there?

B. Ten. Some I did not know.

D. Did they make you give a presentation?

B. I was giving a presentation, and you were beside me. Jeshua and Zachariah and Isaac were on the other side, on the panel, but you were standing next to me. I had my bag and you helped me draw an outline of the intention. I somewhat, I could not talk fully, but I rolled out my script and Zachariah and you and Isaac and Jeshua, you all talked. The other ones looked. I wanted to fill in with my own words, my own observations, but it was kinda hard, so I told you to tell them.

D. So how was it received?

B. It was received with caution, and with a "Hhmmmm." I heard that, it went around the group, "Hhmmmm."

D. So it IS being considered?

B. It is being considered as an option for a future life. HOWEVER, and here you shushed me, because I said, "Should I also roll out my scroll about me borrowing two percent? Should also show this?" (*He turned to the right and looked upwards, towards where I must have been standing during the meeting. His idea about borrowing some of my soul energy to animate a body, which he will then control, is presented later under the "Cells of Enslavement" section.*) And you said, "Shh. This is not the time and the place." (*Here he mimicked me with a dry, professor-like voice, while looking down and to the left.*) And I said, "When will that be? Is that another council? Is that not here?" You said, "First we take this step. Now we're going to look into your plan. You have drawn an outline of a life. This is good enough; we will begin here." That's what you say. And I say, "Oh, okay." So at this point, this specific note is being left. I might actually put that in my velvet purse for the Evolution Group, maybe that is what you meant. Because you said, "It's another council." So I'll put that in my velvet bag. But anywho, it's been in review. I put in great efforts and great detail in calculating who will be with you on this trip, and not ONLY focusing on you. Because that seemed a little bit selfish, you know, because here comes me, your spirit guide, and I just think about you. It doesn't look very mature; it doesn't look very almighty and considerate about others. So I had to, in my investigation, I had to ask what everyone wanted. I asked Josephine, for instance, "What do you want to come down and do?" And I asked Nealon (*a friend of Lasaray's from the sixth, whom Bob wanted as my father*) also, "What do you want to come down and do?" So there were two and I put in great effort into making sure that was also part of this journey. But the Council of Nine, they just went like "Hhmmmm, hhmmmm." So I thought, "Maybe they don't get it," so I wanted to jump in and assist. Huhuh. But you said, "That's not what we do here. We wait."

D. Do you think that's how a lot of lives are planned? Like with the little Elahims, is it a council that decides? (*When Bob next talks about suits, he is referring to the Coat of Karma, which gets modified for the mission and intention prior to each incarnation.*)

B. With the suits, you know, you have the suits, and from the suit your peer, –in your case, your peer is Jeshua–, so Jeshua assisted you, combined with your suit, he created—I don't know if he did it by himself or if he had help from others, if it was like a teamwork—but he created different places for you to go so that your Coat would be activated, so that your Coat would fold eventually; when and where certain things in your Coat would be activated, and so forth. But in this case, we do not have a Coat, we only have a mission. I do not have to think about a Coat, on or off. BUT the thing is that you will come in contact with those who have Coats, and that is also something that I need to be considerate of, you say, and Ophelia says as well. Because I can't just put in all sorts of progress and goodies in you, –that I find are goodies–, if you will come in contact with someone who needs help. Because it's not just to follow a purpose, to follow a mission. I wanted you to extract from plant life a potion that will help heal the blood, so it will eventually heal the brain, –so that is the purpose. But it's also that when you come down, your environment, your surroundings, should benefit by your presence. So I also have to think about that, you know, all those people in Coats that you will come across. Because it might be that someone in a Coat is the one that can make it or break it for your discovery to become something! So I have to look into that. And then I thought, "If I'm gonna have someone who's gonna approve for this discovery, then I wondered if maybe Zachariah wanted to come." Zachariah said, "It's just because you know that I would approve." And I said, "I don't know if you would." Huhuh. So I have presented my journey with you and it is in review. But, the important thing is that at least you kinda said yes. You said, "If the Council of Nine thinks this is a good idea, then why not? It's all for the higher good." And I said, "Here we have the general intent, the general idea." And you said, "Don't put other notes in the pocket when I'm departing, you know I can't really detect the notes then." That's what I kinda do; if I show notes before you go, then you see them. BUT, if you're already down, it's easier for me to—" (*he then leaned forward and blew towards me*), whoooh, I sort of, you know, whisper to you, send in a thought, like a wind in your ear when you sleep. And then you wake up and are like, "Oh, maybe I should just go on a little exploring today." And then I'm like, "Huh huh huh!" That's what I did when you didn't want to engage with people (*as John 54*). I went like, "whoooh", and I blew in your ear and I said, "Don't be such a crab!" And when you woke up, you actually had that sensation of feeling that, "Maybe I should just go down to the harbor and have a beer tonight. I will do so, indeed." And I was like (*he gave a little snort and a big laugh*), Hehehe! And you didn't have a Coat then, so once you're down there, you're kinda under my spell a little bit. Oh, not my spell, because Ophelia and everyone is always supervising, but I can whoooh!

D. Puppet–master. (*His plan to borrow 2 percent of my soul energy and then he would control the body, like a puppet master. In his next response, he mentions John 32. He simply numbers my lifetimes, as I seem to pick the name John over and over. They are sequential, so John 11 was in Morocco around 330 AD, John 32 was in the Catholic Army around 1380, and John 54 was in an Irish harbor town with Josephine in the 1700's. With the John 32 life, I only brought in about two percent of my soul energy, and was there to monitor activities in the early Catholic army for one of the Councils.*)

B. Oh, that's not been approved yet. Everything tends to take a lot of cycles. "Sometimes," I said, "it's like on Earth it takes such a long time for a new legislation or a new thing to change." And Ophelia said, "No, it's not the same, it's just that sometimes the deliverer has also to come up, reach a certain point, to be able to deliver certain ideas before it can be reviewed AS an idea." So I understood it as, "Am I evaluated? Am I under somewhat of a review whether I can pop ideas of that sort or level yet?" That was a new angle to it! Then I ask, "Is that the case?" And Ophelia, she smiled like she always does. She says that my mind tends to be a little bit faster than some of the rest of my development, sometimes, and she said it's just because I'm allowed to travel around and I see things. This idea (*to borrow two percent of my soul energy and use it to animate a body, which he would then remotely control*), it started as a seed when I saw John 32 (*in the Catholic army*). And I said, "Hmm, what are they doing over there? Doing something, not engaging, but still operating and collecting data." And she said, "Sometimes, when you have someone down with only a couple of percentage, like John 32, it's merely to collect data, and that is when it is a physical life. So in that sense," she said, "in many ways we just collected data about the Catholic army and group behaviors." They didn't intervene through John 32 to make changes, like I want to do. So she said that my idea developed from the John 32 level of collecting data to monitoring and making interactions, influencing. She said, "We did not influence John 32, we observed John 32 and we collected data." She said I took it to a level that would be from the Creator's standpoint. She said that sometimes my ideas are ahead of my development. It's not like I think that I will ever be like the Creator, because how would someone be able to pop ideas out to the councils if you are in the center pole? I have heard, through your discussions, that there is a way to operate like those mole people, looking the same in suits, but the spirit realm not only collects data but intervene. So I have seen that, but I have not seen WHO is behind the intervention, and Ophelia said it's not her, and it's not Isaac, so it's someone else that operates when it's like that. So she said, "I can collect data, but I'm not intervening in that sense. There are others who do." And I asked, "Who are they?"

D. And she just smiled.

B. She smiles. And then I said maybe I ask you (*Lasaray*) instead. So I said, "If you were to come down as John 32 again, not just collecting data, if I wanted to move you into the spider web, if I wanted to go there, who would that be that can intervene directly and not just collect data, but look around?" I'm not so interested in just looking around because I have been on all sorts of places, I don't need to look into the spider web. But I wanted to make changes in the spider web. You went like, "Uh, ah." (*The spider web is the Cell, those who control the governments behind the scene.*)

D. Maybe I don't know?

B. Then I thought, "Maybe we can ask Ari or someone?" But there are others; "They don't communicate," Ophelia says. They do differently, they can communicate through spirit guides. No one seems to want to tell me.

D. It must be up in eleven and twelve.

B. Indeed, and we have not gone there yet. I'm wondering who they are, if they are the ones that can go in and change things. When people think about when there is like magic happening or things that are way beyond what could happen, interventions that have taken place in a distant past, and occurs day-to-day in smaller settings. But the big ones, when someone wants to come in an observe and make direct changes, –who are they? And I asked you about this council here, the Council of Nine, the "Hhmmm" council, "Am I allowed to ask questions here?" and you said, "No, here we listen." It's a lot of listening. And we stood there and I left it in review when I went back, –bowed out, so to speak.

D. You know most of us, so it couldn't have been that intimidating.

B. I only knew three and you. I only knew Zachariah, Jeshua, Isaac and you. There was like six more there.
D. They said it's not just nine, there are representatives from all over.
B. There are several coming here and looking around the council here. So anyway, I wanted to stop by and just say that. I will return because I have more information to share. But for now, Ophelia says that we take a step back.
D. Well, we wanted to have a separate session because we've been anxious to hear you again.
B. Ah. Story continues.
D. Maybe you would like to talk this weekend?
B. Ah, I would like that, and I am available if someone wonders. So anywho, I step aside.
D. Alright, I'm happy to hear your voice again and get back into your story.
B. Ah, it continues. Alright, I go now. Bye bye.

Refining the Life Plan (April 5, 2020)

Several months passed before Bob resumed his musing about the efforts he was putting into designing a future life for me. After visiting the Council of Nine, he was encouraged to include others who still have a Coat, instead of bringing an entire team of those without Coats. So Nealon, the Elahim from the sixth, was replaced with a spirit from the fifth, who will benefit from his association with Josephine. In addition to making a return visit to the Council of Nine, Bob also has to confer with the Astrological Council and the Evolution Group, where some of his questions are to be addressed.

Bob came in during this session after the Council of Nine and Ophelia had talked for 40 minutes. Ophelia, knowing Bob can be quite sensitive about being pushed aside, suggested we do a separate session later in the week, when Bob would have adequate time to present his notes.

B. Separate session! I heard! I heard!
D. (*Laughing*) We can probably arrange that. (*Which we did.*)
B. Ah! Because you're not supposed to step on someone's toes. I'm not saying that they stood on mine or something—but I could feel that there was a vacuum, I could feel the distance.

I could feel like—I was not ignored—but on pause. And I'm not in quarantine! I'm not the one who should be on halt, I did nothing wrong! So I don't need to be on pause like everyone else. (*He's making fun of the hysterical, tyrannical government response to the flu virus.*) Oh, Ophelia laughed about that. She said, "There is going to be a really hard time to put me in quarantine!" Huhuhuh. Nay, that's not gonna work. I don't respond well to that, so it's not a good solution for anyone, I think. But I have been gathering my notes. And I have carefully selected some of my notes that I was gonna bring to the Council of Nine for evaluation. But then I heard—I don't know if they're busy, or if it's just to not make me come. But I said, "I'm not in quarantine, I'm gonna come. You can't just put a stop on me because it's my notes. And what if someone translates it wrong?" So you know. Zachariah said—you did not say, you shook your head when Zachariah said this because you knew that this is not gonna fly really well with me—but Zachariah said that there had been a suggestion that I could leave the purse, my velvet purse, with the two of you and maybe get the answers later. But later is vague, and you know that I don't like vague. So when Zachariah said that he could take the purse to the Council of Nine for evaluation, I said, "You might not give the right color to my question." Huhuh. Zachariah, he laughed and he poked me and he said, "Well, why don't you color it, and then I can just deliver it?" And he laughed, and you laughed. You knew that I wasn't gonna be satisfied with that arrangement.

D. It seems they have agreed to have you come and present your questions.

B. Ah. Because I have some and I had more. You said we were gonna begin with five questions. At first you said I could have more, but then you said it's better to come little by little if there is gonna be a discussion about the notes. And then we have gone through different questions that I've had along the years, huh huh huh (*laughing about his use of years*). You know, I've had some.

D. I thought we were taking your velvet bag to the Evolution Group?

B. Well, we are gonna go to the Evolution Group, but the Council of Nine apparently is part of this, so I'm not sure. They seem to be buddies is some way. The difference is, you say, and I think that's why you wanted to divide my notes into five and five, in different purses. I cannot, you say, ask the Council of Nine about the general evolution on my system, like in the fish tank and so forth. You say I should ask more down to Earth questions, huh huh, to the Council of Nine. So I have two purses—it's the same purse, you just divided them because you saw that it was a lot in the purse. So you say, "The Evolution Group and the Council of Nine work together but they work with different topics. It's like you can't go to the bank and try to buy eggs, and you can't deposit eggs in a bank, so it's similar, they have two different expertise." So then you say, "Why don't we start with the Council of Nine?" and the Council of Nine is actually gonna be communicating to me about my idea of designing a life for you—because Jeshua is there, and I'm friends with Jeshua. He knows that I follow, but the problem is—and he knows that I want the best for you and for the environment and the entire planet as a whole—the problem was that I had to calculate a life that was not just benefiting you or making you look good. Because if you look good, then I look good. Then you say, "You can't go with that plan to the Council of Nine, because they're going to say, 'Go back to the drawing board and make everyone look good, alongside with your person.'" So that took a while, how to make ME not look bad but not glow like a star either. You will still sparkle a little bit, but I have to make others to be like the leading actor of that idea, and to not just make YOU shine. Because if you shine fully brightly, then it mirrors on me and I get like a medal. Every time when you have done really well, done good lives and so forth and had good lives, I was rewarded as a participant. And all those little medals, all those little rewards that I received along the way, are stored in my office. And underneath each of them there is a little note saying what you did, –and then a lot said about what I did!

D. Well, you're very important in all these lives, especially this one.

B. Ah, ah. BUT once you start to design lives for someone without a Coat, –because you already shine–, so how can I make you come down and make others shine? At first, I was like, "Is Lasaray not gonna shine at all?" And then you say, "Once you don't have a Coat, you're not supposed to steal someone's thunder. You're not supposed to steal the light, you are supposed to ignite light. You're not supposed to steal the light and put yourself in that light." And that is something that you can see, if someone is promoting others instead of oneself, that could be an indication that that person is actually not having a Coat. Because once you have no Coat, you are there to make others shine. And that's why this took a little while, because when I said, "If Lasaray is not gonna shine, if you're not gonna shine, why do we need me? How is this gonna be reflecting on me?" And that's why this took a little while, because I had to create a new whole scenario with others.

D. Is this the life you had planned for me with Josephine?

B. Ah, indeed. And then I had to modify it because I took in just the best actors. And then you say, "But these are already shining," and I said, "Well?" You said, in general, this is about me advancing to the level of spirit guide where I can promote a journey by myself, combined with, in this case, Jeshua, for instance. But in order to do that, I have to bring in those who are a little bit dimmed, who could need someone to ignite them. And Josephine, she's already self-sparkling, but I wanted Josephine because I know you like Josephine, and if you like someone, then it's more likely that you say yes. But I had to change the father. I have Josephine, but the father that was one of the little Elahims' peers. So I said to him, "Thank you for your interest, but I have to go with another candidate." And that candidate was someone from the fifth, who needs to understand the prosperity of agriculture and the wind power and the solar power. So we bring in a father from the fifth. It's actually someone you've been working with before, but it's merely to make him ignite, because he's gonna go creating new trails, creating new footsteps of advancements in solar energy and wind energy and agriculture, and he's gonna be helped by Josephine. So as I did that, it became a little bit more acceptable as an idea. Because I don't get any credit from this person from the fifth if he succeeds. BUT I get credit for setting up such a good scenario where someone else can shine. But I'm gonna make you at least find the plant. Because your father is interested in plant life, you will get the interest and understanding from him, but you will carry the understanding on how to fully extract the potion that is existing in the trunk of the plant. Not in the leaves so much, but it's in the trunk and in the roots. So it's a functional scenario overall.

D. That sounds really great.

B. So I'm bringing that to the Council of Nine, that's one of my notes, to show that. Anyway, I'm gonna be short, apparently, because I have a separate session later on.

D. Okay. What day is good for you? How's your schedule look?

B. It looks like I'm gonna be available on either Wednesday or Thursday.

D. (*Laughing*). Alright, that sounds good.

B. So I'm gonna go now, but I'll be back, and I'm gonna organize my notes. But one of the notes is that one. And I'm still gonna make you sparkle a little bit, I just had to make you sparkle less. That was the thing that I was told would look better as an idea to the Council of Nine, if I didn't make you come in and look like a sun, like that (*he made a full circle gesture around in front of his face*) because if you were a sun, like that (*repeated the gesture*), then that indicates that I also am a sun, a baby sun, because I made you shine. I help you shine and you help me shine. Then everyone says, "Once you don't have a Coat, you have to make others shine," –so I did that. And I said, "Thank you," to the father I originally had in my plan (*Nealon*), and then I took one that needed a little bit of a push. Needed a little bit of self–esteem and confidence in moving forward—had lives that did not really blossom. And I said, "If I give you Josephine and Lasaray and you can't blossom in that surrounding, then, you know—", and then Ophelia came in and did this (*he clamped his hand over his mouth*), put her hand on like that. So that idea never came out. So, you know, some are not as receptive to a little bit of humor and a little bit of teasing. I tease you all the time, so I know that you are receptive to teasing, –but not everyone is.

All Life Plans Involve Astrology (April 18, 2020)

Once Bob settled on a personality type for my future incarnation, as well as picking the other participants in the family, he had to submit the plan to the Astrological Council. They are the ones who fine–tune the moment of birth based on location, personality, intent, and life path. The role of astrology is revealed to be a requisite component of setting up the life. It's hard to say whether the modern ideas and beliefs regarding astrology are accurate from a spiritual perspective. However, the location of the planets in the sky does have a direct and significant role in activating certain characteristics and situations at the time of birth and during the incarnation. We are influenced by both the energy grid of the Earth, which Bob calls the fork, as well as the external energy grid that connects all planetary bodies. We exist within, and are unknowingly affected by, this communication grid.

B. Ah! Ah, ah. Ophelia says to be brief. I don't know what that means.

D. A half an hour is brief.

B. Ah, I'm just warming up here. I mean, why say to me to be brief? Why not say to the other ones to be brief? Maybe it's better that I come in first...oh, Ophelia says it's harder for me to stop. So in order for someone else to come in, I might be more reluctant to step aside. She said, "There is a plan with this," and I just have to cope with it, I guess.

D. So what have you been pondering, since last we spoke?

B. I'm kinda working on creating and designing this life that I'm planning for you. So I thought I would invite the one who is gonna play your father for a preview on things that we have done in the past, so that he can feel the greatness coming his way. Even though you're not supposed to shine, and I'm not stealing anyone's thunder, I'm saying, "This is your time to shine, but you're gonna have extra resources to shine more fully." So I've invited him to participate. We kinda met in the Library, Zachariah was with—Zachariah tends to be with me when there is an activity or an exchange of knowledge between levels. So we were sitting there and you also came, of course, and I said, "We're gonna look at certain episodes where Lasaray was down before," so that he can get a sense of the son that is gonna come. Josephine and him have already been acquainted and they seem to get along. And now I just have to introduce the mission. I mean, it's not like you are the purpose of the mission.

D. It's the flower, isn't it?

B. The flower is the purpose of the mission. I just want to make sure that he understands the effort that he needs to put in to be a great father in order for you to be ignited in that mindset to even go and find the flower. I don't want you to become a bum, I don't want you to not have an interest in reading, for instance. I put in great effort picking out the best schools for you to join and so forth, so I don't want him to miss out of his role in order for you to become interested in studying. If you don't fancy to study then how will you EVER come across my flower? So I'm looking into that, and I'm showing different lives where you have been before, and we're talking about different things that might happen. So it has progressed pretty well. I put in great effort in showing different details of what it could entail once one fulfills this mission of finding this special flower, in order for certain diseases to be eliminated. It is a way to bypass the general pharmacy industry, and with that he has to understand to also keep his mouth shut about certain things. He can't reveal what you, his son, is doing. So there is a little bit of secrecy that he also has to sign up for, so there are documents I wanted to show him so that he's fully aware it's a secret mission. But you will be working under the radar so there is not anything going on that will disturb this mission. Josephine knows, because Josephine and you have traveled before. And then, when that was done, I went with you and we're going through some of the notes I wanted to bring to my meeting. I have two meetings; I have one with the Evolution Group and one with the Council of Nine. It seems like I'm gonna go to the Council of Nine first and you are kinda prepping me, on not only what sort of clothing I should wear, but what I should say, when I should listen, so you're prepping me like I'm going to a work interview, of sorts. And we're somewhat polishing my CV a little bit! Huhuhuh. I'm sort of getting myself ready in that sense.

D. You know about half the people on the Council, don't you? You know Zachariah and Jeshua and me?

B. Ah. But you said to not be fully comfortable that they will be there. You say that I should be prepared that there might be other members that will take my case, because otherwise I might be too familiar and trust too much that it will just fly by in a very approving way to me. But I am going through and I am being a little bit selective of my notes, as I'm polishing this little purse that I'm bringing with. And you're also telling me that sometimes it's important to listen, it's not me having a monologue, but it's actually me having them providing questions—you say there will be questions—so you're preparing me for that.

D. If you're bringing a little handful of questions to the Council of Nine, what have you decided to talk to them about?

B. Well we have been working on my purse, it is the same purse, it's just gonna be different questions, because the Evolution Group is a little bit different but that seems to be the next level, –if I master this first interview! Huhuh, ohh. I have like three to five questions to put in my purse. One of them is not a question, but it is a map of this life that I have been preparing for you to start somewhere in the mid 2178–ish, somewhere there. The planets seem to be in a very favorable position around the year 2178. I'm thinking that you might be born somewhere in May. As I have picked May, it is the fact that you will be a Taurus, and I'm thinking that if you're born there then you will be more stubborn, but not as stubborn and still as you are in this incarnation. You should know that I have been consulting the council that look into when an individual is born based on the positions of the planets in your system. So it's not just to design like, "Ohh, here he comes and he picks a flower," and "Ohh, he understands what to do with this flower because he's a doctor and he creates this new potion to heal certain cells and delete and bypass certain restrictions, like man–made restrictions that is not AT ALL spiritual restrictions or spiritual ideas or blockages." But, when you have designed a life—and this is what Jeshua told me because he's normally involved in designing your lives and so forth—I just sort of get a little, "Phtt, time to go, Bob. Let's go." And then I get a quick preview. BUT when you are traveling down to Earth, and the life has been selected, the purpose has been selected, the physical and the suit—the karma suit and so forth—has been selected, THEN the council of solar planets, –the positions–, creates openings. Normally there are three options when a soul can be born. So they normally provide three different options where certain lessons are more likely to be stumbled upon, or restrictions to be stumbled upon, and so forth, to trigger not only purpose lessons but karmic lessons as well. But since you don't have a karma, you don't have a Karmic Coat at this point, we are looking into the best positions for the planets as it relates to the purpose. Like when you were born now (*in this life*), you might wonder, "Why were you born when all the planets were positioned in Capricorn, and you were born when everything was congested around the point of your foundation and your home?" It was because you were not supposed to be mobile, you were supposed to be still. And the reason why you were supposed to be still is for your soul to fully know where the body was located. If you had been moving around too much, your soul being would have problems, not finding the body, but it is harder for it to blend. When you are in a life where you're supposed to be able to dim the soul, Jeshua said, then that is the reason why we made you not move. You know those stone pigs that they put out to block traffic and so forth?

D. Yes, a concrete barrier.

D. Indeed. So it was suggested that you were supposed to be that stone pig up till the age of 50, and it was so the soul would be able to find the pig and it would be easier to come and go. So it was merely considered like a pole, like a connecting point to Earth, to the body. And it's a whole science behind the incarnation verses the positions of the planets, and also the transitioning planets that moves and creates certain lessons. BECAUSE as we approached 2009, the planet Pluto started to approach this stone pig, meaning the stone pig started to shake a little bit in its core, and eventually the pig tilted. And that is when the whole soul purpose started and you were not a stone pig anymore. I'm not saying that you are pig, but it's called like that, it's like a stone cone of sorts. And now you're not that anymore, and now you're not dimming your soul and you're not coming and leaving. So this stone pig has tilted and it's not there anymore. So if you were to take off, it would be a little bit more tricky, not impossible, but a little bit more tricky to return—and you're not supposed to come and go anymore. As you were picking this life of being less mobile, and when I started to see how the Council of celestial bodies, like the planets and so forth, and how they put in great effort into making you almost immobile, I can understand that my idea of having you traveling to all of these places would not have been possible. It wasn't approved and it wasn't beneficial for the purpose as a whole. It would never have crossed your mind to take off because you were not supposed to take off. HOWEVER, I said, "If I'm gonna put him in 2178—and it appears to be favorable—2178 to 2183 is a five year window where the planets—and this one can look into that—but the planets are quite in favor to bump up the level of general consciousness when it comes to health issues."

D. You've really put a lot of thought into this plan.

B. Ah, and of course there was more, because we are gonna go to the Council of Nine and I have my purse. One of the notes is about this life, and also that we're looking into the positions of the planets, like I say, when it is beneficial for you to be born. And this council, it's a brand-new council for me. They seem to just emerge everywhere, new councils, and it feeds my speed and it adds more questions to my ever expanding bucket of knowledge.

D. I am curious about astrology; how does that affect the incarnation?

B. We can call them the Astrological Council, in the sense that they are connected to incarnations on Earth. So the astrological cycles are not the same everywhere. But if we call them the Astrological Council, they are very much aware on how the planetarium locations will affect, and when they will affect, the Karmic Coat and the journey that the soul takes on. This involves, number one, when it should start; when certain lessons will fall in; whether you are male or female, it's also involved in the decision on when you are supposed to be born. So there are several components that are part of this equation in order for fulfillment of a mission to reach a possible outcome that one seeks. There are times when, like a mole, when a mole goes down, they can have an astrological chart—and you can look for that—either the astrological chart when that person was born is very spread out, so it becomes a chameleon from a human standpoint, it can adapt quite easily to its surrounding, it's not affected by different choices and surroundings that this person encounters. OR, they have a chart similar like you had this life (*most of the planets are congregated around the Imum Coeli in the natal chart*) like a stone pig, meaning they are simply there, they don't have a lot of options to move around. Like you, you were not, –what I'm saying, your chart was a stone pig because you were not supposed to have different exits, entrances, choices and so forth. You were to stay put, so to speak. Like when you were John 32, that person also had a similar chart, because you were not supposed to have options, you were simply supposed to have this option of becoming a military person in the Catholic Army so they could observe the activity. But if the Master Mind and the councils want to investigate a specific expertise, area and so forth, like the medical establishment, for instance, then someone can come down like a mole with a very assertive chart, meaning a personality that will blend and be able to be a chameleon in the human play. But it's merely whether you are supposed to have a lot of options and blend in—and I'm talking now about those who don't have a Coat—if you have Coat, then there's a completely different design and conditions on where you are supposed to be born. But know that it is based on the soul's purpose, when it's supposed to be born, but it's also depending on the parents. So that all three in this wheel, that all cups are clicked into the right position.

D. Huh. That's pretty complicated to organize all of that.

B. I did not take this class, but I can see here, I saw them and you showed me a little bit on how the Astrological Council are operating. They come in sort of in the end before incarnating, when everything else is stated, you know—body is picked, players are picked, Coat is established, what the specific Coat should be focusing on in that life—THEN at the end, someone like Jeshua is presenting this to the Astrological Council. It's gonna be continued to talk about that, because this is important to understand, that there is a gradual development creating a life. And now when I am creating a life for you, I just thought, I want him to be more assertive, I want him to go around. But then they said, "His only focus is to go and find the flower. We're focusing on also the parents." The parents are more important for you in that life than let's say, this life, because you were only supposed to be a stone pig, until 2009 when it started to tilt, and then tip, and then fall, and then there's no stone pig anymore. But the human you still has sort of a memory and a fondness of being a stone pig, so just know that when you feel like a stone pig, it's just the human, because the stone pig isn't there anymore, it's tilted.

D. *(Laughing)* Alright, I'll keep that in mind.

B. So you don't have to identify yourself with a stone pig because it's not there anymore, it's just a memory. Anyway, I'm gonna go now.

D. Alright, my friend. That was an enjoyable and fascinating talk, so thank you.
B. Okay. I'll be back. I have to go the Astrological Council and just see—they come in later, so first I have to go to the Council of Nine and have this approved. But you're prepping me and we're polishing up my CV, so to speak. And also my personality, you say. Polishing up my personality so I listen as well.
D. You'll be like Ole.
B. Anyway, I go now. Bye bye.

Notes on the Human

The Spiritual Design series of books and this series, *Notes from the Second Dimension*, are interrelated and not intended to be studied in isolation from one another. The *Notes* are more personal accounts of Bob's travels and observations, but he is an integral part of the other series as well. Sometimes, after he delivers a very insightful talk, I will ask if he wants to put it in his book or in the other series. His response is usually along the lines of, "I don't want to be selfish here, but I think this will probably be in my book, this specific discussion." He definitely has a sense of ownership of the *Notes* and wants it to reflect the best of his teachings. As in any conversation, Bob and the other spirits change topics during a session. Some topics go into the *Spiritual Design* books, some into *Notes*, and the rest remain private. Those parts for publication are then organized by subject matter and date of delivery. The first half of *Wave 3* includes a lengthy chapter on the challenges of being a human. It would have been easy to move these following talks by Bob into that book, –and some were. But we also want his books to reflect the fullness of the knowledge he has collected while over the millennia as a spirit guide during my incarnations. Although this is a brief chapter, the advice Bob shares are important and unique contributions to spiritual literature.

Reluctance to Accept Change (Dec 4, 2018)

This is an interesting talk, because Bob explains why fear of change and of the unknown may be one of the biggest obstacles to spiritual growth, as they lay the foundations for many undesirable behaviors. Greed, for example, can be considered a fear response. We associate greed with those who are financially successful, but nearly anyone can cling to something that serves them no purpose. A mundane example would be to work tirelessly, year after year, earning fiat currency, which is then exchanged for objects stored in or around the dwelling we occupy. This gives a sense of security, of solidity, to our existence. But nothing in the third dimension is permanent. Nor do we really own anything, especially the earth.

Humans share the planet with all the other creatures, but we do that poorly. When confronted with the unknown, we often react with fear, even if there is no reason to be anxious. Bob likens this to walking to the edge of a patch of ice and over-analyzing the risk before we take another step. Fear of the unknown, he says, also manifests as hoarding tendencies, which can include emotions or ideas. We cling to old ideas the same way we accumulate old clothes. In doing so, we do not make room in our minds, our storage unit, for new things that would aid in growth. In late May 2020, while Christine and I were talking on the phone, he bumped her aside (she noticed his presence and invited him to speak) to add a few ideas about the topic. He said that clinging to negative ideas or emotional issues from the past is similar to not taking out the garbage. The mind is soon littered with waste, causing people to become restless and unpredictable, as their thoughts jump between the accumulated bags of trash. A clean mind is able to move around freely and calmly. When someone has not taken out the garbage, there is no way to cover it up with perfume, or to disguise the moldy energetic residue that is always present.

As a spirit guide, Bob journals his observations about humans as he follows me around. The life which inspired this teaching was a narrow-minded professor in the late 1300s, He tells about this life in Germany, later in the session.

- B. Here I sit.
- D. Patiently waiting.
- B. (*He delivered this most mournfully, sounding quite sad about having been left out of the previous session.*) Sitting on the bench where you left me last time. Sitting, waiting on the bench. Waiting first for someone to be finished, then waiting for my window. Sitting on the bench, waiting, like I do. I brought my notes, my journals. I have plenty of journals and I'm doing research in them, and I go back and forth to see what could be valuable for you, you know. So I'm going back in my journals, not necessarily only what we've been talking about, but my journals over time.
- D. We felt bad that you didn't get to speak last time. Is this for your book?
- B. Mine as well as ours. I have discovered certain things that I think is important that the leading mammal might know a little bit about. And that is how to not be so against changes, because changes always come. You think that this is maybe

the peak of who you are, and the peak of the animal life that you have, and the peak of the trees that you have, –but you have no idea what was before you or what is to come. It is this sensation within your species that comes from, or is somewhat of a side effect, to the power of choice. From the power of choice, another side effect is a reluctance to change. Because change, for some, can indicate fear for the unknown. Not all (*humans*) feel positive about the shifts of the seasons, so to speak. Not everyone is very enticed when winter comes around; they just sort of salute summer and spring, but forget to appreciate and understand how the cycles are actually creating a better spring and a better summer, potentially. So changes, evolution in that sense where some will be removed, and some will be revealed as a brand-new shining star, so to speak. You were like that one time. You were like a brand-new shining star, at one point, when there were only other kinds of creatures that moved around. And you were actually welcomed by the others that existed here at that time. But they didn't have the same capacity in their logical realm within.

D. These were the ones with fur? (*The early humanoid was the new shining star.*)

B. The ones with fur, yes indeed. They were curious about the smooth ones, they were not hesitant to them and they didn't hunt them, because they did know how to hunt, –well, after a while they did. But they didn't hunt them, they thought of them like something like a brand–new car, something shiny and interesting. But the current model that you are has a little bit of a struggle within your mental capacity, that is where you struggle with changes. Changes might indicate that you have to go out on a lake of ice, and you don't know if winter has gone long enough for it to carry you. So you try to calculate, "Oh, how many days did it snow, really? How many days were under freezing?" So you try to calculate before you enter (*walk out on*) this lake that is clearly frozen. But before you do so, you calculate and you try to navigate before you even know what it is you are supposed to navigate. Maybe you're not supposed to navigate, maybe this is not a big lake, maybe it's just a puddle. Maybe it's just like one step, so you will never sink even if it's like no ice at all, because it's not deep! So you calculate with things that have no relevance—because you don't know!

D. I like that! It's a good analogy.

B. Ah, so it might be that what you consider to be a lake is actually a puddle, and when you put the foot down you will sense the ground instantly. But you have calculated and gone around and measured this little ice puddle, created it into a lake, which it is not, at all! And that is because of the fact of the reluctance to change.

D. That is a very common human trait.

B. It is indeed a sadness when certain species disappear that you have become accustomed to, but that is part of evolution, and it doesn't mean that, within a cycle of a hundred thousand years, this individual that you cared for might not come back in twice, it might have split up into two beings, and they might be more suitable to fit into your surroundings. Like the elephant, for instance. I'm not saying the elephant is going anywhere, but it is big, it is the biggest thing that you have, and man seems to be very territorial. In that regard, you are more territorial than other animal life. It's like you piss, urinate, on your little spot, but you remain in that urinated spot. Whereas other species, other animals, they urinate, indeed, "I was here," but then they move on. But you remain in your spot where you urinate, and you urinate again, maybe. So, you know, it's a dysfunctional way of operating, because you can't really claim an area as your own. You are only here briefly, and you have no idea what this specific region that you have urinated on, if that is a part to be changed, if that puddle you are trying to protect is actually meant to evolve to a lake.

D. Humans have a culture based around property rights and the accumulation of possessions.

B. We do not approve, and we do not necessarily—and when I say "we", I'm talking as the voice of the council and I'm the voice of the second dimension—we move around freely, we do not urinate on spots, claiming it to be ours. We assist, let's say, on a spot, making it as lovely as possible because we know that a friend of ours will come later on, and we invite others to walk on our spot that we have taken care of. This is how gardeners operate, they place seeds and light in the soil, so that others who come from our level will feel invited and have a sensation of continuing and improving even more. And the first one there doesn't proclaim it to be his or her spot. They are like, "Okay, you come in with a different angle, what would you like to do with this place?" And it's a constant communication of improvement, instead of urinating and putting up signs, "Don't Trespass. Keep Out," –it's different. You cannot own, you rent. So in many ways if you are a house owner or you rent an apartment, it's the same thing. Even though you might have bought it, it's still never yours! Huhuh, you still rent it, so it's the same thing, you rent the spot you are at.

D. Yes, a lot of people have trouble letting go of stuff.

B. Ah, and that is a sensation of, –it's like having too many clothes, it's the same thing like if you are hoarding things. You pile up clothes because you anticipate that winter is coming. So it's like, "Oh, I need to have this sweater, and these gloves, and this scarf, and this hat, and maybe I should have ear muffles," so they just overdress, because they anticipate it's gonna be a cold winter. But it's still September, so they don't know, but someone might have said or mentioned, "A warm summer will provide a cold winter," so a hoarder person will start to overdress, even in September, and complain about the heat, because they are stuffed! So it's the same thing that you anticipate something to come. And with hoarding things, it's also to anticipate, "Oh, I might need this, eventually." What one should do, when one is in that capacity of holding on, –and holding on can be holding to not only physical things, even though those are more obvious, because you can see their storage unit and you open the door, and you can't even put a stamp in there–, but you can have the same action, really, or way of operating, by storing memories, or storing emotions, or ideas. One should think of, regardless if it's a physical storage unit, or an emotional storage unit, or if it's a mental one, "Is this something that made me happy?", number one. They look at this thing, this memory, this feeling, and ask, "Did this make me happy? When I got it, how did it make me feel?" And then they think, "Oh this is a gift. This specific chair, my father made me, that has great sentimental values." So that one can be kept, but maybe not in a storage unit, maybe have a specific place for it, you know, not an alter, but a specific place for it. But the reality is, that most of the stuff is not of sentimental value. They are in that thick coat of "What IF I need that specific chair? What if my chair breaks and I need to have a backup chair?" If you think of an emotion, like someone has a sensation of tenderness. Tenderness is a lovely feeling, if it comes from the right spot. But if you have sent out a sensation of tenderness to someone, and that did not return in the same manner, then that sensation, tenderness, has a bad taste to it, to you. It's like how this one thinks of celery! HAHAHA, spit it out! So, you will think of this feeling, that specific sensation that you are holding on to, if it doesn't anymore bring you joy, or if it never in the first place brought you joy, then you should let it go. It should not be in your storage unit anymore. Same thing with ideas, you know, like certain ideas that you had and when a human thinks of ideas, they always think of, "Invention! Something I invented." But you don't invent that much! So it's not necessarily, when I say idea, it could be something very plain. Like, "Should I take this class, or that class?" and you are faced with that sensation of choice and change, you know, "I'll play it safe, I'll take this class," but something within you felt like, "Ohh, maybe that one was even better, but let's play it safe, change might not be very good, because this is a brand new class, I'd be the first one signing up for it," so fear of change comes in and you take the one that has been going on for centuries, instead of taking a new class. But you constantly remember that you had a choice and you did not necessarily act on it in the way you might have hoped for or wished for. So, it's the same thing, how did that choice reflect on the rest of your life? If you were happy with the outcome of your life, why ponder about which class you took? Let it go, don't think of it any more. So, it's the same thing, it's like cleaning out the closets.

D. That's really good advice. A lot of peoples' beliefs are like that, they're afraid to move into new territory.

B. Ah. It's because they have that storage unit that doesn't fit a new stamp. So they have a stamp, a teeny-tiny little stamp, that provides somewhat of an insight, BUT, they open their closet and are like, "Oh, there's so much stuff in here, where is this gonna fit?" Or it's like having a puzzle and you think, "Oh, the puzzle is complete," but what they fail to see is that there are pieces in the puzzle that someone has drawn, that doesn't belong there. So the puzzle piece that you have in your hand, or the stamp that you tried to fit in somewhere, might actually be the right one. And in some way, and this is part of change, you have to be in the sensation of removing—we are back to removing again—so you look in your storage unit, or you look at your puzzle, and you identify, "Hmm, I don't want that anymore," or, "That puzzle piece doesn't seem to fit," so you remove it. That's what you do.

D. That's really good! Did you find that in your journals?

B. It's part of my training, it's part of my thought process, and how I encountered—after following you, I saw different things that occurred and I journaled. And I journaled sometimes for you, when you said like, "I'm gonna go in and I'm gonna go in with a very narrow minded personality, and I want you to take notes on how I interact with those who try to provide a new puzzle piece, because I'm going to be narrow minded." It was like that one time when you were a scientist and you didn't have a very nice personality. But you informed me of that, so I wouldn't be surprised. You said, "I'm not going to have a very nice personality, I'm going to be very narrow-minded, but I'm trying to see if my soul receptivity will be able to break through this wall of narrowness. I'm going to encounter others who will provide new knowledge, because I'm representing the old school, so I want you to take notes on how I behave and how I interact. You will be able to see both me, Lasaray, and you will see this person." And this was also around the Germany region.

D. What time frame?

B. This was 1385. So, we were there in Germany, not flat, there were hills and there were rivers, –down south, middle south–, and you worked with astronomy, but you also worked with plants and detecting new species and how they operated in different soils. And there was a younger scientist within your establishment, –you were in the region around Heidelberg, and there was a school there and you were a teacher. This was near the end of your life, before coming home. You were a teacher and this new one, very friendly, came from the seventh (*dimension*), and talked about the lights within the flowers. It was a discussion about sunlight and the amount of, and the impact of, the atmosphere and surroundings. And this young student, he had an idea on how to increase light in the soil if it was not exposed to sunshine. And you laughed at him, which wasn't very nice, and you didn't recognize that this was a friend from the seventh. I paid attention and I was well prepared, because you did say it was gonna be tricky, because you picked a really stubborn personality. A lot of it had to do with your personal life, because of the fact you didn't have a family, you didn't have a partner or children, so you were like a lion that had a spike in its paw, so you were just grumpy of life in general. So that is a lesson! You said when you have a life that makes you grumpy, then it's even harder to detect the light. And the light, in this case, was provided from this little student.

D. Do you remember the name of this professor?

B. Uhh, Heinz, Hanz, Blumenberg.

D. Heinz, There's probably no record of him, since that was a long time ago?

B. 1385. You died 1387, in December.

D. How old was I when I died?

B. Like 72, 73. You were really old.

D. I've had a lot of lives where I was by myself, haven't I?

B. Yes, but this one, you added in the mix a grumpy personality. But other lives you were also lonely, but you were happy in your solitude. But this one you added several components into your personality and into your life that would make it even more tricky to embrace new ideas. But that is what you wanted, and I took notes.

D. I must not have done very well, I guess?

B. Well, you didn't deliver forward your good ideas that you had when you were younger, –so what you should have done in that life was to have pondered about when you were as young and as eager as this student was, and returned to that sensation. But you were stuck in the closet where your mental ideas had overlapped the ones that were of light and happiness. So you didn't clean out that closet, but you knew that beforehand, and you said, "I want you to take notes on how the body, Heinz, reacts." There were certain times when Lasaray shined through, like when this young student, he had brought a box of plants that he had worked on at home, and he said, "These specific plants," –there were several in the box, like four or five–, "they have been in complete darkness." But he had provided light in different ways to the soil, not only with the power of his intention to care for it, and the plants were doing really well and they were blossoming. And he said, "It has not seen sunlight at all, it has been in the cellar in complete darkness," and you were actually surprised by that. And that was a little, shining moment when Lasaray shined through and you appreciated how dedicated this young student was, even though you were not very supportive. You actually saluted that and you said that he should continue on the path that he was on. It was a window that came, and I, present as I always am, took note of that, "What made Lasaray come through in this thick outfit?" And it was because of the fact that this young student didn't provide a threat to you, he only provided a level of his own doing. He didn't push it on anyone, he just wanted to show you. So, a lesson learned is that if you push too much then you might encounter this professor Heinz in life. So it's a better outcome, sometimes, depending on the way you deliver it.

D. Those are really good notes. Was I, at that time, still working on my Coat, or did I just come down to investigate?

B. No, you didn't have Coats after like 235 AD, you didn't have Coats. So you came down to try to experience your surrounding and how you would be able to function in different kinds of personalities. You were interested in human personalities, and how much that would color your inner light. This one (Seth) picks lives that are more mobile, and more in motion like that. So even if it is a very opposite attribute to its soul, it hears the soul better, because it is in motion. So again, you pick lives that were more in stillness, but it was more tricky because you were more influenced by other surroundings, impacts, behaviors and so forth, because you were more still. This one moved around more, so it is that part of being in motion, and you can be in motion internally as well as physically. This one (Christine's current life), what we talk about here, is physical motion.

D. That's really good. Do you think we should include this information in your book?

B. Indeed. Include as general enlightenment.

D. You've come to Earth a lot and witnessed human behavior for thousands of years, so it would be nice to share that.

B. General enlightenment is always appreciated.

D. We'll include this as part of what you observe when you are following me on Earth.

B. Following, taking notes. But it is the fact of that flower, if you think of yourself as that flower, even if you are in complete darkness, you, yourself have the ability to create the soil where you have your feet, so to speak. And the soil doesn't mean the physical soil, but it is that connection to who you are. So even if you are in complete darkness like that flower, you still have that possibility to blossom. So that's what I wanted to say about that. And that is what I tried to come and deliver when I was waiting on the bench. And more to come, indeed. I will rest my case for this evening, but this is what I tried to deliver.

D. Well, like I said, whenever we run over, we will try to make another session during the week so that we never ignore you.

B. I don't respond well to that.

D. We didn't feel good about cutting you off last time.

B. Neither did I! So that makes two of us. But Ophelia did say that it's gonna be a window to come that is not to share, so I knew it would be only mine.

Self-Healing (April 30, 2019)

Bob gave a teaching to his students about self-healing using harmonies, sunlight, or being in nature. Souls from different dimensions have an intrinsic ability or preference for using one of these three methods. The little Elahims, his students from the sixth, have a natural preference of using music or tones. While it isn't a surprising observation, he points out that aggressive, discordant or turbulent music will have the opposite effect. Souls from the seventh can use sunlight to heal and balance the body. Those from the fifth prefer the silence and sounds of nature. The remainder of his talk is included in the next chapter under the same date.

B. I have a little bit of stuff with me!

D. Oh? What do you have?

B. I have a flute. I have a squeeze box. I have an accordion, that's what you call it, and I have my—(*then he makes a high pitched sound*).

D. What's that?

B. The thing that you play with your mouth. (*He then makes a few random notes.*)
D. A harmonica? That's actually a pretty good imitation.
B. And I have introduced in my class...music experiences. Because of the fact that certain times when they come down and they're doing things, they might feel overwhelmed. And this is a way that I'm teaching them, that certain musical tones and melodies will trigger them to retreat into the light capsule, even if they are in an incarnation. You told me this, that it's important that when you are in an incarnation that might feel dirty and that might feel like one is trapped, that there are ways to move beyond the sensation of entrapment. And music does that. Nature is another thing, but that's sort of a given. But with music, we are looking into certain melodies and how the incarnation will respond to different melodies and tones. If there is like a mish-mash of tones, it will do the opposite. It will create anxiety within the being that would even mirror down to the core of the soul particle. Tones that are more in harmony, or like wider apart, a slower melody and sensation, have the ability to heal the vehicle. So, –like animals, they know how to self-heal in nature. When an animal is feeling ill, they can self-heal themselves by eating certain roots and so forth. What I'm saying here is that you can self-heal your mental, especially, because we are very much in the mental reality, –my people here, these six from the sixth–, so the mental reality is highly sensitive to different melodies. And, like the flute, it is very—unless you just blow in it, then it's not very harmonious—but if you sort of sway back and forth and slowly use the flute, then it's very comforting to the inner being, and that can heal the experience or the anxiety that a physical can experience.
D. Native Americans used the flute a lot.
B. Ah. It's to bypass the activity of bad signals in the mind. There are others, like Ophelia's harp for instance, she shoots directly for the emotional levels within the being, which is different. But I don't have a harp, I did not get one. Ophelia helped me to collect all these different instruments in my (*he leaned forward and looked towards the floor by his feet*), it's like a little carriage I have with me, with stuff. Different tools that can be highly useful when one travels. It's not like they can take these, but I am imprinting in their being, in their

mind, to look for tools like these if there is ever a sensation of anxiety. There is a concern in all realities that there is a higher frequency within your being that is connected to anxiety, and it radiates through all levels. Souls that come from the sixth are best suited to work with music and tones. Some others work better to self-heal in silence. And some others work better to just be in sunlight. So those from Ophelia's reality, when they feel a little bit anxious, regardless if it's a mental anxiety, or emotional or physical, they tend to be drawn to just be in sunlight. Whereas those from the fifth, they like the silence. And like you (*from the sixth*), you can work with tones, with sounds.

D. Well, the music that people listen to then, must have a big effect on them?

B. Indeed. And everything is speeded up. Music is faster, information and influences are faster, your technology goes faster, and it influences the beings. The problem is that you might not know what sort of soul type you are, or where you can find your self-healing pool to access. All three provides a comfort and self-healing for the inner being, then the inner being, the soul, has the possibility to extend that into the physical. But the physical cannot be healed first, and the soul second, so you have to heal the soul first in order for it to radiate out into the physical. So that is why it is so important that more and more come in contact with their inner being.

D. Hmm. Is there any way for an incarnated person to know what dimension they are from?

B. Well, one easy thing is like, if you are very much drawn to just be in direct sunlight, that it feeds your being, then you are most likely in some way connected to the seventh. The souls from the fifth, they want to hear nature, they want to hear silence, so they feel best when there is silence, because they are programmed to be in direct connection to the environment and nature, –and even us!

Mother's Return Home (July 25, 2019)

One of the most remarkable benefits of being married to a gifted trance channel is being able to ask unusual questions and get immediate and profound answers from the spirits. A few days after my mother died, I asked Bob about her progress through the fourth. Even though it is personal, we are including it because his answer reveals so much about the process of dying. We had been talking for a bit when I inquired about what she had encountered on her way home to the fifth dimension. My mother had a great compassion and kindness for animals, which was acknowledged as her soul passed into the Mental Realm. Bob teaches that the transition between Earth and the spirit realm is divided into two parts. In the first part, which is about thirty-five percent of the way up through the vibrational field of the fourth dimension, the soul is still attached to the Coat of Karma. Until the Coat is released, any experiences are interpreted through a human mind perspective. This is when the dying person will think they see deceased relatives, pets or religious figures. This is the main reason for the unusual accounts found in many near-death experiences. The Coat is released once a soul goes through a review of the life and accepts their death. The soul will then move into a higher vibration and perceive only the spirit bodies of their companions. One way to think of the fourth is like the entire keyboard on a piano. The lowest octave is the vibrational field closest to Earth. At the other end, the highest octave is very close to the spiritual vibration of the fifth dimension. The Coat of Karma is stored in the vibrations below middle C, and this is where memories related to Earth and past lives can be encountered. Once a soul detaches from the Coat, it moves fully into its soul awareness and eagerly ascends towards home Later in the book, under the section titled *Transitioning through the Fourth after Death*, Bob explains the transition in captivating detail.

- D. Did she run across anyone that looked like Jesus? I ask because she was religious, in a Methodist kind of way.
- B. She saw light-beings and she saw animals. She saw several animals and she saw like stars, like a light. That's what she saw. There were like dogs and cats and also wild animals that she had encountered during her life in different ways. That also provides comfort that everything is as it should be, because the soul remembers these encounters.
- D. The animals, I've often wondered about that. When people say they see their pets, how are those re-created?
- B. In the fourth.
- D. When the Master Mind leaves the animal, doesn't it go back to a common awareness?

B. It's the same thing like with a human, you don't look like that, –it doesn't matter if it is a soul from the fifth, sixth, seventh, it doesn't matter, because they portray who they were. Or, if it's a piece from the Master Mind that is out operating in a pet, that has the same ability to transform and portray itself as that pet that the human recognizes.

D. Ah. So that's kind of like a general pool of Master Mind awareness that can show itself as something the person remembers?

B. Ah. A soul particle, a soul energy, regardless of where it comes from, –if it's from the Creator and the Master Mind, or if it's an independent soul from, let's say the fifth–, will portray themselves as they were in that life. So those humans that showed themselves for your mom when she left, they portrayed themselves in a manner that she recognized. And the pets, they tried to mirror what the human mind remembers. The soul mind, –if the human mind is completely deactivated, then the soul mind would not recognize, let's say, your father, how your father looked. But as you transition through the fourth, the human mind is still activated. That is why souls show themselves as a prior incarnation or a prior animal or pet. When the transition moves to the far end of the fourth, you can see that the human mind is shut down, and at that point, soul meets soul, so she doesn't see them anymore as humans.

D. Huh. So the human mind would be attached to the Coat, the memories?

B. Ah. It's like, if you see the fourth reality, every time someone sees a loved one, a pet or something, or a person—even if it's an OBE, a near-death experience, or a full-death experience—that is what occurs. Let's say the fourth dimension is ten centimeters, that occurrence, when they see a loved one looking in a certain way, occurs up to like three to four centimeters into the fourth reality. As we are moving further to the center, moving through to the end, there is no looking like Jesus or looking like a squirrel or a dog, you know. But as long as the soul transitions from (*within*) the first two, three, four centimeters, then indeed they will encounter and they will see Jesus, if that is what they like. And many times, that is also designed before departure. A soul will say, "When I return, I would like to—"; because a soul can remember that the last time they transitioned it wasn't very pleasant, perhaps they didn't feel very comfortable—and it depends on how they die. So a soul can ask before they leave into an incarnation that "When I transition, when I leave my new life, I would like to have the encounter, in the first three centimeters, of Jesus," let's say. Sometimes when they don't ask, a spirit guide can still make that happen, just because they have a greater picture of the whole, of all journeys that this soul has been on. So let's say that your mother really had a NEED to see Jesus in the first two, three centimeters, –there was no need, the need was simply to feel the presence of family and animal friends–, but if the need had been, then she would have seen that and experienced Jesus in that space.

D. She loved her animals.

B. There were animals, and not just pets, there were several that were wild, like squirrels, there was a badger, even a snake came.

D. Yes, she had snakes that she took care of around the house. (*Mom lived alone on a rural hill in West Virginia, surrounded by nature.*)

B. Ah, there were snakes that came to pay gratitude, there were snakes. Even worms came. And butterflies, a huge amount of butterflies, they were almost cocooning her; so butterflies were there, and snakes, and a badger. There was a badger in early life that she saw that she wanted to help; the badger understood. So all of them, they were there. But now she's singing, it's a choir. She has a lot of, she's like a female energy, even in spirit, and she feels more comfortable in female energy. She picked a life to grow to be with only male incarnations around her. That was one of her lessons in this life, because she was too comfortable and became too dependent and too much in the female energy. So she was asked to move into more of a male family unit and learn how to embrace the male energy in some way. (*She had three sons and no daughters.*)

D. I always thought that Dad died early and she was forced to live a long time without him because she needed to become more independent?

B. Well, that was maybe part of it too. I'm not involved, I don't look at her life review, but I know that there was a need for her because her soul group is very female, the energies are very female; and coming to Earth you come to learn, and she came to learn how to be independent, to be feeling a little bit like an outcast even in the family, because you were males. So that's a teaching. She's in a very big soul group, females, a lot of them. So it's a part of the development. I think I'm gonna…Ophelia says we're running out of time, I don't know what time that is…

D. Well, is there anything you or Ophelia would like to say before you take off? I guess we are going to have one more session before this one goes to Sweden.

B. Ah, that I hope! I'll have one more, thank you! So, anyway, I'll go now. But just know that your mother is doing just fine, and she is singing. But one of her lessons was to be in a male environment and to learn how to be comfortable with male energy, because there is a cell memory, a soul memory, of feeling put down in male environment. So it was a part where she took the life to acknowledge the kindness in a male environment.

The Inner Calling (Oct 13, 2019)

Ia is Bob's closest companion on the second dimension. She was created in the same cosmic egg as Bob, and also has Gergen as a mentor. Since Bob and she are so close, she takes the stage occasionally to inform us about her work with the very young spirits on the second. Ia offered a lot of invaluable advice in this brief teaching, which we are also including in Wave 3. She gives direct instructions on how to tune in to your inner self and make decisions that resonate with your soul's intention. With all the distractions, noise, and activity that surround most of us, it is easy to forget that we have two minds. One is the human mind, the other is the soul mind. The physical mind is easily captured by the input related to the emotions, thoughts, and sensory interactions with the third dimension. The soul mind is the intelligence of your spirit. It is more of an observer and remains relatively unaffected by the emotional state of the body. By learning how to tap into the soul, daily life becomes more accepting, harmonious, and spiritually focused.

Ia. (*She began singing like she was warming up for an opera.*)

D. Well, if this is Bob, your tone has changed.

Ia. Hahah. No, this is not Bob, he has a different tone when he sings. If I'm a harp, then he's a trumpet. (*She looked left towards him.*) Oh, you have a beautiful voice, Bob—just teasing.

D. Hello Ia, how are you?

Ia. Oh I'm doing well. Thank you. I just wanted to let you know about the progress of the classes that are now heading into understanding the work that lies ahead. It is one of the eggs, these little sparkles would be considered nine-year olds. As a nine-year old, they have understood that they are an independent unit, a separate sparkle. They are placed in chambers, if you like, similar as how they started, to contemplate, to meditate independently in a cocoon. It is a way for them to hear their inner being, to hear that calling that we have already, in some way, deciphered and detected. Still, it is important for each sparkle, for each entity, to find one's path before one starts to travel into the world, let's say. How they merge with themselves is best done in complete silence. That is why you, as humans, struggle. You are constantly bombarded with sounds, either loud or silent noise. This makes it impossible for you to create that cocoon that you are given as a shield every time that you travel. Each soul has the ability to return into a replica, a copy of the cocoon that you were given as a child (*young soul*). This nine-year old sparkle is sitting in this cocoon, which is created in tones and colors, depending on that specific soul's blueprint. Once they have figured it out, they can always re-invite the shield around them, meaning that they will always know who they truly are, even though they might be far from home. You are far from home, but you feel separated from home because you have not the ability, you have been stripped of your hearing. Your hearing has been hijacked by those who don't wish you to hear your shield, who wish you to remain ignorant, to not understand your home. This is why humans feel lost. They do the most odd activities, due to the fact that their hearing has been hijacked. That is why, since we see that, that we advise you to listen to your heart. The heart is a different receiver of the connection to home. Since we see that mankind, humanity, has been stripped of their hearing, we direct humanity to listen to their heart. In many ways humanity, at this point, is deaf.

D. If someone grows up in relative isolation and isn't around noise or many people, would they have the ability to detect themselves better?

Ia. Oh, yes indeed, yes indeed. But humans are drawn to the big cities, and that is where the problem lies—not in gathering with others, but the fact that you have no separate sensation of who you are. You become a cluster. If you were to hear who you truly were, then you will connect differently with others, you will seek out your friends differently, you will create partnerships differently. Due to the fact that you are, in many ways, deaf, you make choices as you are stripped of understanding and finding the right match. Those cases creates confusion in the human being, making it harder to navigate in the mission and the purpose that you have to come. How to find your soul companions in blind? The heart is closer to the solar plexus area, the center point, making it easier for you to find your mates.

D. We were going to talk today (*in one of our discussion groups*) about soul contracts, is that deafness affecting people's ability to follow their intended path?

Ia. Yes, yes. They make choices that comes from a mute brain, instead of fully having all your senses activated. You are left with your heart and your center point, but you are given, as a species, more than just two sensors to find your path, to find your mate. Meaning that choices can be made that don't resonate with your blueprint or your mission, and you might prolong your own development, meaning that certain things in your Coat that you planned on addressing falls aside, due to the fact that you have not heard your soul, heard your calling, heard your mates.

D. What advice would you give to people to hear their soul?

Ia. Since in many ways your hearing is out, a way to feel the true connection to a mate is either to look into that person's eye, – the iris is a portal to each soul's origin. However, it might appear odd to stare into someone's eyes, and that is not a common behavior in your species. Another way to do, is to focus on the area in your chest which is close to your heart but more center, and THINK of the person. You don't have to be visually close. Think of the person, close your eyes; don't expect the understanding to come in your head. Withdraw your understanding and awareness into your chest and think of the person that you want to investigate, whether that person is a mate of yours. You will feel a color moving forward. Whatever color comes, see how that color resonates. Each soul has a different color pattern. Some will love the color brown, some will not, will feel that brown is dirty, whereas another soul will feel that that is the true connection. Wait for the color to come. You don't have to look into someone's eyes, but you can close yours and move the person you wish to investigate, visualize and place that person in your chest area. Think that you activate your heart and your center point, making them pulsate. Visualize this, –this is an exercise how to recognize your mates. As you feel your heart pounding, your center point rotating, then ask this individual that you wish to investigate to merge with you in your center point. Allow that energy to come in and become part of you, and see if you welcome this entity, or if you feel like it is invading you. If you feel like this person belongs in your chest area, then ask this person to give you its color. When the color comes— and silently just wait and accept the first color that comes— see and ask yourself, "Is this a color that resonates with me?" Some belong in the same color, such as you two, but you have friends who have a different color, but you feel welcomed to invite into your chest area, into a secret chamber where you can decide whether this person is a true friend. So even if you see a color and you see that that color is not your color, it might still be a friend. The way to decide is the sensation you have as you invite this person to step into the room, the sacred chamber that you have opened in your chest area, alongside the beating of your heart and the rotation of your center point. If you feel that this person is someone you would like to have in your sacred chamber, then that is a true mate. There you go.

D. That's really good advice, thank you so much for that.

Ia. So that is what we are teaching, to understand and to invite different experiences. Because the sparkles are different, they are gonna feel if the experience resonates with their true calling.

D. Is this before they decide where they are going to go and study?

Ia. They have been on field trips to different places such as the 4–H farm, the greenhouse planet, and so forth. But this is part of their training, to understand that certain conditions will be placed upon them as they travel, and they might indeed experience what you do, –based on the conditions of the destination, they might feel like they are stripped of, let's say, their eyesight, such as you are stripped of your hearing. Similar, they have to retreat into the sensation of having to understand the events and the surrounding circumstances to make sure that it is following their path. So, I'm not gonna be too long in the tooth, and Bob will just briefly pop in. He has requested, he said, a separate session this week, and Ophelia has granted this. The separate session will be conducted on either Wednesday or Thursday, and that will be his stage alone, since he had things to share.

D. Thank you for that. It's nice to hear the update on the sparkles and also nice to hear your voice.

Ia. Oh, the sparkles are full of light, they're sparkles!

D. Is this the same group that was dissolving earlier, or this is a different one?

Ia. This is a group that did not dissolve just recently, they have been dissolved for a while.

D. You've got your hands full.

Ia. Yes, always new sparkles! Hahaha. Bob wants to pop in. Okay, I'm being pushed.

D. Thank you Ia.

Ia. You are much welcome.

Inner and Outer Hobbies (Nov 17, 2019)

This is another humorously wise talk from Bob, as he instructs his students to be both internally engaged and externally active. It is unfortunate that we assume spiritual pursuits to be only emotional or mental endeavors. Happiness is an important part of spirituality, and it is easier to feel joyful when one is engaged in living. When a person is passive and disconnected from their life, it is much harder to connect with the soul. Ophelia said we should ask ourselves, "What sort of footprint do I want to leave?" and then act with those goals in mind. Some spiritual practices emphasize prayerful living and doing good deeds, but the spirits advise that positive physical experiences are equally important.

Bob recently explained that spirits have perfect memories. Once something is learned or experienced, it is never forgotten.

Bob can easily quote things he said years ago, and often does. His mention of baseball is a reference to a story he told 18 months earlier. He is Tom's mentor and Tom was all excited about fixing problems on Earth by telling his incarnated spirit friend what to do. Bob used a baseball game to demonstrate the futility of sending ideas where they would not be accepted, explaining why both the recipient and the environment must be ready to receive a new teaching. The full story is in *Volume 1* under the heading of *Shooting off Balls of Knowledge*, and was delivered in June 2018.

B. Ahh! Hmhmhmhm. Here I am!

D. You made your presence known?

B. I made my presence known. There is no need to be hiding or be invisible, because I DO want to be seen

D. No wallflower here.

B. No, I don't respond well to walls, I don't do that at all, and Gergen knows that and Ophelia knows that. That's why Ophelia muffles my ears sometimes, –but it's similar like a wall, it actually is. And I told her that this is also like a wall, and she said, "This is not to confuse you, Bob." It's sort of been a theme throughout my development that I—you people must think that I easily get confused, because it has been constantly up for debate whether I'm confused or not. And me, on my side, I say, "I'm not confused; please continue, tell more." And then on the other side of the table where you sit, you're like, "Little–by–little, in cups."

D. The measure of confusion is probably reflected by the amount of questions.

B. Hmm. Ha ha! Touché. Are you saying that if I ask less questions, that I will be brought more information? Ah–ha!

D. But then again, the colors you radiate indicate whether you understand.

B. Ah. I might want to put on a hat again. Huh. Anyway, what I wanted to tell you is that I'm preparing the six from the sixth and the spirit guides with another occasion, another scenario, about what is needed as you enter the vehicle of the humanoid. I have told them and I have dressed up here and I'm wearing a baseball suit.

D. Why a baseball suit?

B. Because it indicates I have a hobby. And I told them, "It's extremely important when you get to Earth that you develop somewhat of a hobby, something that is personal happiness and amusement within your being. If you do not occupy a hobby–," and that's what this is about. I have a helmet, I have my bat, I have my ball. Tom, he recognized this because we played before, you know, baseball, and he recognized this. So he said to his person, "Maybe you want to be a sports person, maybe you should do sports," and the one from the sixth is like, "What is sports? What is that?" And Tom said, "This is physical activity." In general, what is suggested as you come into a humanoid is that you have at least one physical hobby and one internal hobby—that is suggested. What we see at this time is that some lose one of these and some actually have none. As they have NO either physical or internal hobby or interest, they become numb, they become passive. And that is also what we are trying to move forward a little bit, that it's important to have an interest that is not related to making money or making a living, to do something for your own wellbeing and for your own amusement or just for your own relaxation. A lot of those who have dropped the internal hobby are simply focusing on doing an ACTIVE hobby, and there is an imbalance here. It's like this, the internal hobbies promote and assist mental and emotional wellbeing and relaxation. The other one promotes more of a physical adjustment and happiness. As more and more are having less time, as you call it, for their own personal being, they just say, "Oh, I have to take away something because there is no time, because I have to be at work more hours now. Or I have to do this and this and this, I have to fill out all this paperwork all the time, over and over and over and over again, so, "I just keep this one where I play baseball with my friends." There's nothing bad to play baseball with your friends, like me here in my suit. I have a number on me.

D. Ah, what's the number?

B. 2.

D. Why 2?

B. Because I'm from the second dimension (*which made me laugh*). It's to show where I'm from.

D. What colors do you have on?

B. My suit is white, and the number on my belly is red and blue. And my helmet also has a 2 here (*as he turned his head to the right so I could see the side of his invisible helmet*), and also on the top, if someone sees me from above (*he then leaned way forward so I could see the top*), because I'm smaller, so I wanted to make sure that someone finds me. So I have a 2 on the side and I also have a 2, like you can see, on the top, because it's kind of hard to find your person if everyone has the same helmet. So you want to make sure that from a spiritual level, as a spirit guide, it's a good idea—this was my idea—I said, "From a spirit guide's perspective, I think the upcoming vehicles should have a number on the head." You can imagine like those who play your football, who just falls all the time and get hurt, and the spirit guides observing that—you can imagine all the hustle because they all look the same! Huhuhuh. Ah, well, they kind of find them anyway.

D. That's funny. Lost in the pile.

B. You know when you were John 32, Ophelia said that there was somewhat of an imprint on you.

D. So they could track me?

B. Like a device to find you. We should also mention, when we talk about your history a little bit–, before we do that, this game, I'm returning to that so I'm not losing my thread here. It is important that you find an interest so that you do not feel passive. However, the most important one is mainly to have the internal interest or hobby established. Because that is to be with you, to be with who you are. The other one is just to be with you as a human, to be with the Coat, which is also good. But you have to find that little thing that makes you tick, that makes you step aside from the mundane and the day-to-day activities. And what we see is that more and more lack that personal sensation of, –I'm not saying duties because duty indicates the things that you have to do all the time. But you actually have a duty with your soul, and your soul needs hobbies in order for it to be comfortable in this setting that you are placed in.

D. So what would be an example of an inner hobby?

B. It could be reading. It could be just sitting in your own space and working on things creatively. It could be like reading, painting, singing, playing an instrument, –those are highly triggering inner happiness and amusement, and that would be considered an inner hobby. The other ones (*the outer hobbies*), I'm portraying here.

D. What about hiking, weightlifting or woodworking?

B. Hiking is more of an internal one because if you hike by yourself, then you are in some way moving into an altered state, a mediative state, and you are pondering about things. So it's similar like reading, it's just that you don't have a book, but it triggers the same centers within your being if you are just hiking by yourself, because you are reading within.

D. Even though it is still a little bit physical?

B. Ah. If you are hiking in a group, it's different But if you are hiking by yourself you are actually doing inner reading, even though your physical is moving around.

D. When I was doing woodworking, then that was an inner activity?

B. It was actually inner. To make you understand what the physical hobbies are, it's what I'm portraying here. It's easier to portray a physical hobby because I have an outfit, than if I just have a book.

D. So it's more like an activity you do with others?

B. An activity. It could be going to the gym, it could be like, –I would say sailing, but then again if you are sailing by yourself, you have also the time, similar like hiking, to read your inner book. But it's like playing basketball, playing baseball, curling, badminton, roller blades.

D. All those things with other people?

B. If you go on roller blades, one might think, "Huh! Isn't that just a faster way of hiking?" No, it's not. Because if you hike, then you have the ability to move into an altered state. I would not suggest that someone rollerblading move into an altered state, because you are not capable to navigate from dangers and pebbles, or even craters. So I would not say that roller blades is in the category of an inner hobby.

D. I follow your logic (*laughing*). Thank you for explaining.

B. Ah, there's a logic in everything I say. Sometimes it needs to be explained here, but there is a logic here. I told them this, "You're gonna be extremely gloomy and extremely passive, and if you are passive and gloomy on Earth, you are highly likely to be influenced by things that goes on over your head, so to speak, that is not for your higher good." So in order for you to not be passive and, like Ophelia said, "put in a cubic box", if you start to really focus on having a hobby that provides you a sensation of wellbeing, then it's less likely you will be encased in a cubic box. And because more and more are dropping, especially the inner ones, and exchanging them, and just keeping one, –and they keep the one that is more of a physical one–, then it's easier for you to be put in a cubic box.

D. Even bingo would be a physical activity?

B. Bingo, I would say, is not an inner hobby, it's a physical hobby. All these older bingo players–, but that serves a purpose because they are meeting others who are also old and about to depart. It's about just finding someone in your own genre, so to speak, that can relate to certain activities that took place in your…

D. Distant past?

B. Distant past. So it serves a good purpose for those that play bingo.

D. That's funny.

B. Anywho, what I would like to say about that is that it's important to have that sensation of the things that really makes you feel that you blossom. You rarely have that sensation, do you, in your office?

D. No.

B. Nay. And there are few that actually have an occupation where they feel like they blossom, –but the majority does not, and their occupation is a cubic box by itself. That's why it's important that when, ding!, 5 p.m., time to leave, that you don't just go home and put yourself passively in front of the TV; that you actually feel the joy that 'now I'm gonna do something that really makes me colorful inside'. It's about coloring the insides, really, and what we see at this point is that more and more become like—the colors are not as bright within, one can say that. That's why I'm teaching in my class here the importance of these hobbies; and I show great examples of those who sulk here and who are just passively observing life as it passes by. I say, "Why do you want to come if you're just gonna observe life passing by?" And they said, "We're there to teach others and to learn things," and I said, "Does it look like this person here is learning or teaching someone something else? What would you do with this person here who feels a little bit passive inside? Yes, we will give them a hobby. What do you think this specific person would do best with?" Then you have to look at what is suitable, you have to look at what is suitable for yourself, maybe I'm not cut out to roller blade, for instance. If I have bad eyes, if I don't see that well, maybe I should not roller blade. Maybe I should do like bingo instead. So it's about finding that unique pocket of enjoyment. So that was my class about that.

A Holiday Message (Dec 12, 2019)

We are often reminded that there are multitudes of spiritual entities and councils who observe and monitor our sessions. Even though Bob is given a lot of latitude to deliver his personal notes, he is in constant communication with Ophelia and other advanced entities. During this talk, he was getting input from Zachariah and some of his companions from the second dimension. The spirit world is aware that many people are alone or lonely this time of year, so they gave a really beautiful teaching about how to enjoy the holidays.

- B. (*He gave a little laugh but didn't say anything.*)
- D. This must be Jeshua! (*I was teasing him.*)
- B. No. I come with gifts.
- D. Oh, what sort of gifts did you bring?
- B. I have a huge bag of gifts that I would like to deliver to the human consciousness. As we are in the season of holiday spirit—or at least you are—we are always in spirit. And some in more merry spirits than others, one can say. But what we would like to say is that when you are in the energy of giving, you have to, or we ask of you, that you ponder a little bit about what it is that you give as a present to someone, and if it is really necessary, –and what is the intent BEHIND the gift, Zachariah says. Not just give something that is the more pricey, the better, because it's all about the intention. So what intention do you have with the present? Sometime the less pricey gifts are considered the greatest ones, such as kindness, spending time, putting all your gadgets like phones and computers and so forth away; shut them down and show that you are present in someone else's life. That is a greater gift than to give someone a pricey watch, for instance. So as you are in that energy flow where you are thinking about giving and receiving, think a little bit of what you yourself would like to receive, and to not be so stingy with what is

considered gifts, to be more present and soulful of needs and wishes, and don't be afraid to speak those needs and wishes out loud, –that's also important. So here I come and I'm showing this because it is also a fact that there are those who don't have anyone to give and receive from and to. And the spirit guides are well aware if their person has picked a path where they are in solitude, let's say, or are being a little bit of a hermit sometimes, and how that affects the consciousness. The human consciousness colors the soul, but if the soul is strong enough, it will actually not be affected in a bad way by solitude, it will actually see it as a gift. But the human consciousness tends to see it as a punishment, especially around those times when you are supposed to be with others. But if you don't have others, what do you do then? What you could do is go into nature—because the fact is that the spirit realm are well aware that there are a huge amount of people who lack a connection and a presence of family members or friends. So what they do is that, around this time, they activate animal life and nature. So if you take yourself on a walk, for instance, it is more likely that you will come across someone (*an animal*) who is trying to show kindness or presence that is just for you.

D. In the animal world?

B. Animal and nature world, yes indeed. So those who might not have family members or friends nearby, just be aware and know that in nature outside—and don't just be stuck inside and sit there, you don't have to walk that far and you don't have to necessarily find a magical mountain, like here (in Colorado)—but even if you just go around the corner to your park, the spirit realm is more on alert to show you their presence, even if it's just a small park bench. If you sit there, the senses one can use are smell and just the feeling. It doesn't have to be heard or seen because most people don't tick like that, so they might not hear. But what the spirit realm is conveying more strongly now is using smell and regular feelings.

D. That's good to know.

B. We are talking about that with the spirit guides, training them for the ones from the sixth (*who do not travel in groups*). I said, "You don't know if your person is gonna pick a life where it will be feeling sad and lonely, and they might be highly affected when there is a constant energy and reminder that you should be with others, and you should be so happy, and you should be so merry, and you should give and you should receive. But if you don't have anyone to receive from, or give to, then you can absolutely just receive and give to yourself. And that is acknowledged from the spirit realm, if you just give something in nature. If it's possible, for instance, one can plant a seed—it's wintertime and not everywhere will that be possible of course—but maybe just feed the birds in the park and feel the presence of the birds, knowing that they will give their gratitude to you. And that might not come then and there as an awareness, but it might just be a sensation of peacefulness, and that is something that a lot of people will lack around this time. I'm showing the spirit guides here what can happen if someone is alone. You did that! You picked a lot of solitude lives where you had a family but you didn't want to engage with them! That's been a lot of occasions, I must say. We give you family, and you don't want to engage. (*As he said that, he leaned backwards and looked upwards and to the right, perhaps imitating a gesture of disdain.*) We give you friends, and you don't want to engage (*He again repeated the haughty gesture.*)

D. Kind of like this life.

B. Ah. That's why this one came in, to sort of poke you, because this one is in your face and you cannot ignore. Huhuh. This one was like, "Oh, I'm gonna push him. He's not gonna be able to ignore me!" Huh huh huh. This one is funny when it comes to that.

D. That is true, I can't ignore her!

B. But what I would like to say is that the biggest treat that one should give this year is to oneself—it's important also to give like a gift to yourself—so what would be the Christmas gift you would give to yourself, if you could? And I will leave you with that thought. What would be something that you, to yourself, could give in order for you to feel content, to feel joyful, to feel perhaps relaxed, to feel empowered? There are different things that each and every one would like to have, and you can give that to yourself. You don't have to wait for Santa, so to speak.

D. Not necessarily material things?

B. No, nothing material. It has nothing to do with, "Okay, I'll go buy myself a new car," no, it's not the same, that's not what we're looking for. We're looking for what, on a soulful level, would give you the greatest satisfaction? And satisfaction could be different for each and every one of you, and it could be different each year. Maybe this year, Santa's sack is for you to travel. Maybe next year the greatest satisfaction for you is just to be able to sleep. If someone could just come in and magically give you something that you, on an inner level desire, what would that be? And then visualize how that treat comes to you. It is your spirit, your higher self that gives it, but you can always visualize that it comes from a magical being. Anyway, I'm gonna go now.

D. Alright, my friend. That was a really good story. Thank you for coming and sharing with us. It's always nice to talk to you.

B. Ah. Always nice to be acknowledged. Okay, I go now. Bye bye.

Fatness is not only Physical (Dec 15, 2019)

The grasping nature of humans leads to many of the problems that exist within individuals and societies. On a personal level, people who eat to excess will often become obese and diseased. But someone can also cultivate a mental gluttony for material possessions, wealth, admiration, or power over others. These behaviors can have far-reaching consequences, especially when embraced by large groups of people. Corporations frequently manifest the very worst of mental fatness, acting with a complete disregard for the planet as they exploit and destroy nature, all in the name of quarterly profits. However, as you release these tendencies and begin to appreciate the gifts of the Earth, that will be acknowledged by the spirits.

B. Ah, huhuh. La la la la la. Oh, we need to stabilize a little bit here. Huh huh huh huh (*He then sang for a bit.*) Oh, it's not as pretty as when Ia does it. I take another one. Oh, we all live in a yellow submarine, yellow submarine. (*He continued singing for few moments.*)

D. Do you like singing in a human body?

B. It's fun! It's more obvious, and I cannot be ignored and I cannot be missed. It's like, "Oh, what is that noise?" and there I am! It's almost like having a trumpet, it's just a different trumpet. But I do like to sing, and using this one, I can make myself heard, and it can travel differently to the human consciousness than if I just try to hum. Because I hum next to you all the time and you don't seem to hear me, which is somewhat unfortunate.

D. Is there any way you can adjust my hearing so I can hear you better?

B. Well, I'm not in charge of upgrading or downgrading your senses—because I asked, "There have been occasions when I don't feel like he hears me that well. Are there adjustments that can be made in order for him to fully hear me?" But Ophelia also says that with that comes a great responsibility as a spirit guide, because you want to make sure that you pop the right things into your human. And I said, "I never pop anything bad." And Ophelia says, "No, but you can pop things in that are way ahead of its time." Because I have somewhat of an understanding of other occurrences, and Ophelia says sometimes that I'm not fully aware of your mission. And I said, "If you were to tell me a little bit more beforehand, then I might not bother you." But that's why I also put notes in your pocket when you had a Coat; it was my contribution of how I felt like things could have gone better. And a lot of times, what it had to do with was that I wanted there to be an understanding of how nature is like the biggest resource, and how that could be used like a big pharmacy. And I wanted you to just create this big pharmacy and leave little clues for maybe a next visit. I wanted there to be a theme that went through all generations and all visits that we had here. And my personal wish was for there to be an understanding on how to maintain your physical vehicle by simply using what exists in nature. There were several lives where you were a shaman, and you did quite well. And I said, "Leave a little bit of a note now, so next time you come back you just pick up that note."

D. Humans used to live much closer to nature.

B. Ah. And they used different leaves and herbs and also from the tree, the bark, the skin on the tree—but you have to ASK the tree. And that is the thing here, people don't ask, they just grab things in general. It's like...(*He suddenly stopped and looked to the left.*) Oh, Ophelia says, "Gently, gently", but what I was gonna say, –if you have a big smörgåsbord, there are those who just pile up on their plates and just grab because it's free; and then there are those who only take what they are really gonna eat. And that is the thing, in the past there was not all this grabbing. If man knew to use the skin on the trees, the bark, and that the inside of the bark is actually really good for, let's say, different skin problems like psoriasis, for instance. So if you take the clegg underneath the skin of the tree, the bark, and you use that and put that on burn wounds and so forth, it heals. But if that were to come out, the current group might go and strip the skin off ALL trees with no consideration whatsoever. And that is NOT what you do. You ask if you are allowed to take a little bit and you tell the tree what you are gonna use it for. We don't want nature to be a big smörgåsbord where big fat people are just piling up and just take! Ohh, uhh, (*Ophelia must have said something.*) VOLUMINOUS individuals pile up on their plates, –that was better, wasn't it Ophelia? I tend to be sometimes a little bit blunt. BUT before each session, Ophelia says, "What are you going to talk about, Bob? What are you going to say?" And then I say, "I think I want to talk about this," and then she says, "How are you going to tell this story?" And I do (*tell her*). Then she says, "Why don't you smooth it out a little bit and just say something a little bit different?" Because my personality, similar like this one, tends to be a little bit blunt.

D. I like the blunt version.

B. Ah. But she says, "The blunt version is just for you and for here." Talking in public, you sometimes want to smooth things out. So I'll say, if the voluminous individuals who tends to overeat, if they just grab everything, –and here it doesn't have to be physical, you can be a voluminous grabby person and be thin. You can be as—I'm gonna be blunt now—you can be as oversized and fat in your mental as in your physical. It's a way to understand that there is this grabby, needy behavior that tends to go overboard. So it has nothing to do only with physical volume. If someone finds something that is good, then a mental fat person can just grab that and put like a stamp on it, a patent, so everyone is like, "Okay, you took it and I have to pay for it, because you found it first." That is why I am HIGHLY looking into who finds what.

D. Do you block people from finding certain things?

B. I do indeed! And we all do. That's the trick from the second dimension, you should know. If we find someone like, "Oh, you're mentally voluminous, you're not gonna do anything good if you find this flower." Then we can make like a bird—if someone is about to stumble onto something—then we can make one of the birds fly by, and the person goes, "Whoa!" and then turns and goes the other way. That's what we do—you're not gonna go there! Or sometimes we can release bees.

D. That's a good one.

B. That's a good one. Ophelia, she said we're being blunt today and she allows it to some extent. But she says that sometimes the only way to shake the whole system in the right direction is to be a little bit blunt. And this one is like, "Oh, I can be blunt, it's no problem. I take the blunt one, I take the blunt personality." And Ophelia says to this one to be blunt with care. "Tender bluntness", she said to this one. Huh huh! It is a problem though that it has moved into a sensation where people feel like they are victims of everything. So bluntness sometimes doesn't really fly. But if you are bluntness with care, it's a way to disarm but to still shake the consciousness. So that is what you are here to do, you are somewhat here to shake the consciousness, you know, put it in new lane. It's like, "Stay in your lane!" Oh, Ophelia says I'm allowed to be a little bit like that today. Even me, as a spirit developed individual, can have opinions about how things can be made better. Sometimes just shake things into the right lane.

D. It must be very frustrating because of the way people act and the way they are?

B. Ah. But that's when we also do adjustments, not just sending off bees, but we create a nicer diversion. Say someone is walking on a cloudy day and then suddenly, in order for them to stop and change directions, and it could be a personal change of direction that is needed in that person, but it has to do with making people stop and sort of pause and change lanes, so to speak. And what we can do for instance, if it's a cloudy day and someone is just gloomy and passive—and you know what the spirit realm thinks about that—then we can sort of briefly open up the cloud and let some sunlight come in so the person stops and goes, "Oh, look, there is a patch of blue and there is the Sun," and then we close it again.

D. That's like when we went down the river this summer. (*Christine and I rode our motorcycle down to the South Platte River on a cloudy day. When we stopped for a picnic, the clouds parted like they were cut with a knife, and we enjoyed over an hour of perfect weather, while it was overcast all around where we sat. It was too obvious to be a coincidence, so we accepted it as a gift from our friends.*)

B. Indeed. And you paused and you looked and were like, "Oh look, there's clouds all over but just here, right above where we are, it's a patch of blue and we have sunshine." And you appreciated that and you noticed that. The more you start to appreciate and notice what happens around you, the more you will be given. BUT, if you are voluminously grabbing things physically, mentally, –and some people can actually feed emotionally on others, taking others' emotions to feed themselves. This behavior is like overeating but on several levels: emotional, mental and physical.

D. What would be an example of emotional fatness?

B. An emotional fatness would be that if someone is happy and joyful and let's say in love with someone. Another person who lacks those sensations, they can try to take that and feed on that, and almost draining the person who is emotionally heightened. That's not what you do. You don't take other people's ideas. You don't take their happiness and their love, because it's about sharing. And you probably don't go and take someone's food on the plate either. It's similar like that, it's more easier for a human to understand that if you stand next to someone who has the last piece of the cake on his plate, would you grab that and take it just because you were without? And normally they say, "No, that's not what you do. You can't go and just take someone else's cake. I'll take a bun instead." That's what a normal person would think. BUT, it's the same thing when it comes to mental and emotional, but it's not as obvious. You don't take someone else's ideas and create it into your own; you don't take someone else's love and happiness just because you don't have that. It's the same thing, you don't take from someone else's plate just because you don't have that cake.

D. That's really brilliant, my friend.

B. Ah. So, ya' know, that's what I wanted to come and talk about today.

Teachings from Etena and Tiddle

If you were drawn to read this book, you are probably aware that the search for truth is an individual effort. Every person has their own spiritual intelligence which grows and changes during their life, based on their perception and interpretation of the world around them. This spiritual IQ is often at odds with the mainstream ideologies taught in universities or theological institutions. Scientists are very careful to avoid the fluffy world of the transcendental. If you isolate your knowledge to what the academicians sanction, you "know" that intelligent design is part of the imaginary world created by religion. Organized religion, on the other hand, is an emotional pursuit that minimizes logic. They require the believer to accept "the truth" in their gilded book, which contains words purportedly revealed by a fanciful or contrived prophet, messiah or demigod. Both the scientific and religious worldviews are flawed and misleading. The teachings from our spirit friends require the reader to move beyond the commonly accepted ideas of how the Universe came into being or how it operates. The complexities of creation are beyond the reasoning abilities of the human mind, but they do their utmost to give us a simplified outline. As of this writing, six years and 1.2 millions words into our project, I have yet to uncover a single error or inconsistency within their teachings. When I have difficultly with a topic, they always go back and explain it differently. Even so, there will always be things we do not comprehend, such as multiple universes and parallel realities, and we have to be content in our unknowing.

In *Notes, Volume 1*, we introduced Etena, a planet in the fourth fish tank with grand pyramids that contain libraries and cashes of genetic material. It is also home to Siah, Lasaray's rescued pet, and Setalay, a spirit from the seventh dimension who lives on Etena. A handful of spirits live there on a somewhat permanent basis and oversee the libraries and pyramids of life forms. Setalay and Ophelia manifested as Shea as recently as 3000 BC in South America, although they were there much earlier. The form the Shea manifest is very tall and magnificent, so the natives perceived them as godlike or angelic beings (which they are). Prior to that, the soul of Setalay went through the karma program and folded her Coat. It was, however, eons ago when the human vehicle was different. But because of her involvement with Earth, she has given many insightful talks. Some are in this Chapter, others will be included in Wave 3.

Etena is a planet where patterns of life forms are archived in large pyramids. It is also home to a library that has copies of information from the main Library on the fifth dimension. The fifth is a spiritual vibration, but Etena is a planet, so physical or manifested entities can travel there to study and learn. A traveler would be able to go to Etena, for example, and obtain a replica of an animal or plant they wanted to introduce on their home planet. The pyramids contain a vast treasure trove of DNA patterns from life form on planets in most of the fish tanks. Etena is also a teaching center for visitors from many distinct realities within the fish tanks. When Bob and Lasaray travel there, Bob manifests a solid form and can experience what it is like to have a body and bump into things.

Bob divulged some of his early travels to Etena in *Volume 1*. In this Chapter, he continues to tell about his friendship with Siah and how he recreated his female counterpart, Tess. He also tells about classes he attended and what he learned about the Big Eye. Later in this Chapter, another group will make an appearance, whom Gergen calls the Tiddle-Taffles. Tiddle is the name of a planet in the second fish tank, and Taffle is his word for a caretaker from the second dimension. They are a joyous group, and Bob tells us about his travels to their planet.

Bob Reads the Soil at Etena (April 21, 2019)

Spirits who are occupying a form travel to Etena in a craft, normally through a parallel reality. From the spiritual dimensions, a soul visits by projecting their soul energy and adjusting the frequency to match the planet. The manifested form can then interact with all the other objects and beings on that reality. Bob enjoys the experience of manifesting, saying that it is similar to incarnating, but without having to enroll in the Karma program. On this trip to Etena, he and Lasaray went to a class where students were learning to read and identify the stage of life that different soils were in. Soil, at any localized point on Earth, is a conglomeration of the first through fourth dimensions, and goes through life cycles like any other entity. Bob was taught, and is telling us, that we can read and communicate with the soil on a soul level. Ancient people had a much greater sensitivity to the land, but modern humans also possess the ability to detect the signals from the earth. We should, therefore, try to determine the intent of the soil and its stage of life, before we disturb or interfere with the land.

When Bob talks about listening to the solar system, he is referencing a story he told in 2018 when he was working on a project to identify the sounds or signals emanating from a model of a solar system he was studying. That story is in *Volume 1*, under the section titled A Healthy Sleep, or Dead?

B. Ah! I have also been visiting!

D. Who have you been visiting?

B. Siah!

D. Oh, you've been back?

B. I have indeed. Together, of course, together with you.

D. Did you get to spend time with Siah?

B. Stopped by to chit–chat a little bit, but I am indeed in classes.

D. In our little temple?

B. In a little temple, not the big one. Everything is like a village, like a temple village with certain pillars. So even if you see like a cone, it's still like a little city, and there is a grand hall with pillars where we met before. It's like a campus, and I've been in a little pyramid.

D. Oh, so what were you studying in your little pyramid?

B. I was studying the effect of noise.

D. Oh, was it quiet in there?

B. (*Whispering*) I had to be very quiet. (*Then resumed in his normal voice.*) And you said, because you were with, you said, "You have to be silent in the mind." It doesn't matter if you are silent like this (*sits for a moment without moving or speaking*), but if I'm not silent in the mind, then that will be considered like a little bit of (*makes a noise like a mosquito buzzing around*) in the classroom. You were with, of course, so we were way in the back because I'm brand new. I don't want to be sitting in the front. I'm sitting here in the back with you, and I'm looking at all these students, and you said, "Pay attention. Can you sense any activity in here? Focus on the waves that comes from each being in the classroom, and compare it to yours." (*He laughs and gives a little snort*) And that was a difference! I said, "I listened," and you said, "No, you need to listen the same way like you listened to the solar system, –you listen with you center point, you don't listen with your ears, kinda." (*He uses "ears" for our benefit, but spirits don't have auditory systems like humans, but rather pick up vibrations around them in their entire body.*) So I did, and it was indeed, I would say, in the brain, or in the general receivers in there. And then you said, "Now turn this grand, big inner ear to your own being." And it was like blup blup BLUP (*continued making loud noises for a bit*), like that. And you said, "If you want to participate in these classes, then you have to adapt to this environment, you have to make your receiver quiet. Otherwise, you will not hear the teachings. If you go blup blup blup, and the others are more like huuuuummmmm, then you're going to miss everything the teacher is telling."

D. So how do you turn off your blup blup blup?

B. I took a long, deep breath, and tried to mirror what I encountered in there. I don't want to stand out, like someone who is a disturbance in the back. I don't want to be the 5G here, at all! So I said that, "Do you think they will experience me like a 5G mast?" And you said, "If you go like blup blup blup blup, then they will! We can do a little bit of training." There was a break, and I didn't need that much of a training, but when I got back, I could hear the teachings.

D. Can you share any of those teachings?

B. Oh...maybe some, Ophelia says. The class is about detecting wellbeing, or not, based on—you don't listen with ears, you listen with your center point, you listen with your being. And they were taught different exercises how to connect—but then again, this is a very harmonious place, so I don't know where they're gonna find differences, really. You can't move around too much, so you silence not only your inner being, but also your physical being, and you can detect the occurrences around you. And this was to detect the waves in soil, where they have their feet. So I took off my sandals, because everyone was barefoot, and we put our feet in different kinds of buckets. The teacher had put it out, and this was a great teaching—maybe I can use this in my class! Oh, nay, nay, don't confuse (*Ophelia must have said something*), I'm training incarnations, that's not the same (*he sounded rather disappointed*). The teachers put in different tones and different, it's like they have a flute thing, and they activate the soil differently. This is highly skilled, I must say, but based on the instruments that they are using here, the teachers, they put in different teachings in the soil. So me and these students, we are barefoot, and it's not buckets, because we can walk a little bit, so it's a little spot and you stand there. We are actually in groups, –they're really friendly, they invited me right away. So I'm standing there with two other ones, and they're kinda a little bit taller than me, and they were like petting me on my head! And I was like, "I hope I don't disturb!" and they were like, "No, no, you're doing well, you're doing just fine." And the three of us were standing there, and first we were standing by ourselves in this three–unit, trinity. Trinity is extremely important here. That's what my new friends told me about. They told me the trinity, everything with three, it's a holy number. Trinity, working in like a triangle, you can, from there, you can develop portals, they say! They are way ahead in this class! I'm just sensing the soil with my sensors in my feet, kinda. Oh, let's see. It's tricky. But they're friendly, and they said, "What do you feel?" and I said, "I feel sleepy. Is it good to feel sleepy?" And they said, "Yes, this specific spot we are standing on is becoming, it's brand–new, like baby soil. So if you come across an area in nature and you put your feet there, and you start to feel a little bit sleepy, that could indicate that specific spot is waking up from hibernation. It's about to become." So I said, "Could it be the other way around? Could it be like an end result, like it's dying, falling asleep?" And they said, "Yes, it can. But at this specific spot, we are on a rebirth spot. You will sense a difference if you fall asleep differently, because you will detect it in your being, it's a different melody you will detect in that spot if something is dying, or something is being born." I don't know how I can implement this in my classes…I'm not allowed to, Ophelia says, "It's not part of their training." I'm being trained here to detect in a physical reality. I mean, we do this in the second all the time, but this is a physical reality. It's a place, it's not a spiritual reality, but they (*his new friends on Etena*) know how to be in resonance with, in this case, the soil. These lessons are to be established here.

D. So that would apply here, on Earth?

B. It would indeed. So I said, "Do you have to be barefoot?" and they say, "It actually helps if you are. And you can communicate directly to that spot and ask for permission, if they allow at that particular point for you to grow things there. That's what the ancients did, and they did that, they said, when they were here as Shea. They said, 'We don't grow, unless we have been given permission.'" So they listen to the soil, and if the soil feels like, "I'm still waking up," then they wait a while. It's about honoring another life form.

D. Does that have to do with the seasons, or is it more about where the soil is in its developmental cycle over a long period of time?

B. Both, both. Mainly the last. You ask, for instance, "Would it be okay for me to grow vegetables here on you? Or do you prefer that we grow flowers? Or do you want to be left alone for a while?" The ancients did that. Shea taught about that, how you want to make sure that it's a joint effort, because your growth affects that spot. Like S— (*friend in Sweden*) and her greenhouse, she started it and kinda, within her being, asked to start this little greenhouse, and the result was tremendous. Everything was growing hugely and fast.

D. She has a little bit of help, too. (*She has a gardener from the second, named Truls, that follows her.*)

B. She has a little bit of help, but she honored not only the soil, but the second dimension, within her being. Even if the computer (*brain*) didn't register, but she is programmed within her being to constantly ask for permission. It's the same thing here (*on Etena*), so they taught about that when they were here (*on Earth as Shea*), and they want that to be moved forward to humanity. If you ask for permission, they will normally grant you that, but they want to be acknowledged—the soil and the elements. The elements are living entities, similar like you. If you just put in bad seeds (*GMO's*), first of all, you have not asked for permission. It was a different time, I must say, when you honored each other; not only the space and silence within the species, but also where you were. You could communicate with the eighth, asking for rain and so forth. It was a chain of communication that went on. You are stripped from a lot of these sensations, and the thing is that if you only knew that you could actually activate all this again—you are not deaf, you are not blind, you are not crippled, you simply are asleep. That's what they say.

D. Was some change done to humans that caused them to disconnect?

B. Ah. A little bit.

D. The ancients might have been structured differently, and had a better connection?

B. Ah. Better connection, indeed. The last wave, because they were overusing the resources. You can ask, you know—even your profession (oil and gas exploration), do you ever ask before you start digging a hole?

D. I'm sure most don't, but I did when I was drilling.

B. No? And what I say is about up in Alaska, and even in the seas, pumping—you don't ask, you just take.

D. That is true. That is the way humans do everything.

B. It's the same thing. You will see better results if you act a little bit kind and not like a grasshopper, like someone said before. (*Ophelia said humans act like grasshoppers.*) So, I'm here in class and I'm given a lecture on how they operated here before (*on Earth*), but also how they operate here on this planet (*Etena*). I've been here in class and I've been listening to what they say. This is a very peaceful group, it's very much like Ophelia's footprint, I would say. It's very lit up and bright.

D. Do all the students live there on Siah's planet?

B. I would say these are 12 to 14-year olds. Everyone is wearing white and they have different golden adornments, based on the classes they have taken.

D. Did you get anything for taking the class?

B. I got like a button. It's a button that I can put on my belt, my first visit here.

D. How was your travel there, when you go through the dimensions in your peanut suit? (*When Bob began traveling from the spiritual dimensions to Etena, he learned how to create an energetic bubble around his spirit–body. He calls the energetic bubble he travels in a peanut suit because he thinks it makes him look like a peanut. This was described in Notes, Volume 1.*)

B. Oh, it's okay. I kinda like it. It's like going to an amusement park, it's fun, it tickles my being. But I also like it because I know where I'm going, and I do respond well to knowing a little bit in advance where I am going. I knew that I was gonna go and visit Siah. I didn't know that I was gonna participate in the class here. But they do a lot of tuning or like mantra things, and that's how they can connect with each other. And if someone feels a little bit tired or maybe left behind, then everyone assists. All classes begins with everyone connecting in a little bit of like chanting. And I, being the new one, was allowed to sit in the middle of this. And I said, "Are you gonna be in the middle too?" and you said, "No, this is just for you. Enjoy. This will give you a feeling of belonging." And it actually did, and I felt extremely welcomed. It's not at all like being glanced at like, "Who is this person?" So they welcomed me and they're curious about me. You are really close by all the time, so I'm not sure if there are rules on what to say here. But I've been traveling, and I also looked after Siah a little bit.

D. What did you do with Siah?

B. I brushed him a little bit, because he tends to be a little bit dirty sometimes when he moves around, so I just tended to his fur a little bit. I sat down and told him stories about what you and I do, because he wondered, when you're away, what you are doing. So I sat down and told him about certain things, and how I follow you, –and he also would like that (*to follow me during incarnations*). And I said, "It's probably not possible, but I can come and share and we can sit here and talk like this, if you want to." So.

D. Did he want to?

B. Ah, he likes that. So I sat there and communicated a little bit. And he also wants to show things, so he's gonna take me places. He wants to show the surroundings. I communicate with him differently, he doesn't talk, so I communicate directly with him. It's really easy, it's similar like communicating with everything else from the second dimension and animals, so it's no problem with him, –it's easier, actually.

D. Does he have a lot of Master Mind in him?

B. Ah. He's full, he's full. And that's also why you removed him and put him in this nice shelter. This is a nice shelter, I must say, he's gonna be tended to forever here. But he said he's gonna take me away, go places around—not only be here on campus in the city—to make me look at things. He said there are grand spots, he likes to go places where he can recharge, in some way. There are like craters where you can recharge, he says, and waterfalls.

D. Have you ever seen any trees?

B. It's not so green in the city center where I am now, but he's gonna take me out, and he said it's different. So I'm gonna do that, but Ophelia says, "Now time is up." We've been talking a lot today.

D. It was really nice.

B. Ah. More to come. So, anyway, I'll go now, but this was nice to go and visit and just see another civilization and how they are doing and being so welcomed. They like strangers. Here (on Earth) you say, "You don't talk to strangers." But on Etena they say, "Oh, a stranger, let's talk to that one!" Very different.

D. I'm sure someone that had ill intent wouldn't be able to go to that place.

B. No, because the birds will stop that person, they would not get through. So, I'm a good stranger. That's also what I want for my Individual, I want good strangers to come. (*Bob had to be granted access by guardians when he went to Etena, which he perceived as large birds. The Individual, as mentioned in Volume 1, is the species he created on Earth, and later put on his living planet in his solar system.*)

D. Well, you probably hold the keycard to that.

B. Ah, or you do, because I was extremely clear on that.

D. Only good can come.

B. So anyway, I'll go now, but I'll be back.

D. Very well! Thank you for coming today. I appreciate the information.

B. Okay, okay, I go. Bye bye.

Beekeeper Bob (April 28, 2019)

This is another amusing story from Etena, when Bob was invited to join an excursion to collect honey. Etena is a physical planet, but the vibration is higher than Earth. They have plants and animals, some of which do not go through life cycles, –meaning they do not age and die. But some do, apparently. Since they feed Siah greenery and collect honey from the bees, other plants and insects must regenerate in some manner. The description he gives of Siah getting his face stuck in the little bucket of honey is very endearing, since it shows how hard Bob tries to blend in and be

Teachings from Etena and Tiddle 99

accepted by others. He begins his story by describing how students on Etena are taught outside in nature, which is a practice, he said, that would benefit children on Earth.

B. So, it's my turn now, so here I am!

D. Ah, hello, my friend.

B. Hello, indeed. Huh. I have been visiting more, –I do like this place where Siah is, because I get teachings outside, outdoors. They are actually, most classes on this reality, are not in the cones because they know that if someone is enclosed, meaning in a room or in a pyramid or similar, you don't learn as well. We see that schools here (*on Earth*) for little people place them inside classrooms, where they don't learn as well. In the fifth (*dimension*) even, there is no roof, there's no ceiling. There might be walls around classrooms to muffle the wisdom that flies within the classroom, BUT there are no ceilings. So, the Creator and the atmosphere can hover above the classroom. And it's similar here (*on Etena*), and they said that, "We are outside, normally." I don't know if they have a lot of weather shifts, really, it always looks the same here. But they say they do.

D. They must get rain?

B. They get rain because they said on the back, maybe not the back of the planet, but on the back they said that's more jungle-like. So this is just a spot where they seem to live. But they say that an individual learns best if they don't feel trapped, and trapped might mean just sitting in a classroom. So here I was in the cone (*Bob refers to pyramids as "cones". The ones on Earth, he identified as "stone cones"*), but it was just a gathering, we were not supposed to stay there. So, I have now been following some of these other students and we are indeed working with different insects and animal life.

D. Does this explain the outfit you showed this one? (*He had appeared the day before in a beekeeper hat.*)

B. Indeed. I am wearing a hat and a net, and they do too! So it's not just me that needs protection.

D. Are there a lot of insects?

B. Indeed. And we are currently working with, I mean, there are bees, because we are taking honey, –Siah LOVES honey. But because Siah cannot be covered in a net, then he cannot participate. He is standing at a safe distance, because he knows that everyone will give him a lick in the jars afterwards. He knows exactly what's going on when these students are going here to work with the bees and the honey. But the teachings here, first of all, is out in nature. If little ones here (*children on Earth*) could be having their classes, once in a while or more often, in an outdoor scenery, they are much more likely to be calm and better receivers. The receivers within your being doesn't operate as well if you are sitting in a box in a classroom. It's even worse if there are no windows, like some here (*on Earth*). It is hard for a receiver to be motivated TO receive. In the spiritual dimensions, where it never rains, there are no ceilings, really.

D. That makes a lot of sense. People are calmer and more relaxed outside in nature.

B. Indeed. So one of the teachings that they would like me to bring to this plane is that little ones, up to the age of twelve to sixteen, before they become an adult, they are those wide-open receivers and you are responsible for what you teach and how you teach. And teachers should know that there is a better outcome of their effort to provide knowledge to smaller ones if they are in an outdoor environment. There's no need to sit inside if it's not raining. You could potentially sit in a park next to your school under a tree and have the same teachings. You don't have to sit inside all the time.

D. Like the ancient Greeks.

B. They did indeed, they had classes outside. They were very much mirrored from the spiritual experiences. But I am also here attending to insects and to the bees, and making sure here, –there's a whole ecosystem that they are tending to. It's similar like the 4–H farm, but we didn't really tend to insects. Here it's very much that they are tending and adding light to insects, because they will fly around and they will merge with solid objects, such as flowers and trees. So there is a great emphasis on insects here.

D. Do you know more than they do about the insects?

B. I do indeed, in some ways, indeed.

D. So do you help teach?

B. I do indeed. I say, "I created that one, similar like that one." Huhuh. So I kinda know a little bit of the background of all the insects. So that's why I'm highly welcomed here to participate. But Siah, he's waiting for his little treat. They say that he always does that.

D. He's very observant.

B. He is indeed. He knows exactly, when they put on the outfit, then he knows exactly that a treat is coming soon. So I have been observing how they are operating and working with the level of insects and bees, especially bees. And there are other things that you might not know that don't exist here (*on Earth*), but it's a different ecosystem (*on Etena*). It's important that you tend to insects as well because they are part of the great eco–chain and, similar like the little plankton in the sea, they are all part of a great chain. And if you start to disturb this great chain, then in the end the bigger mammals will feel confused.

D. The poison that farmers spray on their fields kills so many insects.

B. It's killing off insects, and bees are like on the highest level in the pyramid in the evolution of insects. So they are extremely important. They are not necessarily, you know, created for birds to eat. Siah's place is very much about birds, there are a LOT of birds here. It's a bird planet, almost.

D. It does resonate with the seventh.

B. But they (*the manifested spirits*) communicate with the birds, because they are on the same frequency, so they understand each other. I mean they look like humans, almost, –almost the same. No one is chubby, though, everyone has the same physique. They don't eat meat, they only eat a lot of root vegetables, –beets, potatoes–, those types of root vegetables. Not all exist, I'm saying potato because you know what a potato is, but I haven't seen a potato there really, but I'm sure they are there. But there are root vegetables that they eat, and they eat the whole thing, even the leaves on top of the soil. They boil that so nothing goes to waste. Well, some do because Siah gets a lot of green, but it's not like they are throwing it away, it's not composting, but they give it to Siah. But they can also, some things that they don't use, they bury it in the ground, so they give it back to the soil. And the soil is a living entity, so the soil receives that. So I've been here a little bit and having training.

D. Well that's a better way to live. Do I come with you?

B. Nay, nay. You said you had engagements elsewhere in the pyramid, so I'm on my own.

D. I mean as far as traveling back and forth?

B. You travel back and forth with me. I guess it's because you are concerned that I don't go back.

D. Did you give Siah any of your honey?

B. Ah! I gave him all, I didn't need it anyway, it's not like I can bring it home. So I had like a little bucket that I had collected the honey. I asked how much I could take, and I was given, in my mental being, an image of how much I could fill up my bucket with. And I did not take more than that, because you're not allowed to. You should honor that someone gives you something, and not grab more. So I filled it up maybe like a tenth, in my little bucket, and all of that I put down in front of Siah and I said, "Here's some treats for you." The funny thing was that he was almost stuck in it, his nose, and he lifted it up with my little bucket around the nose, and he sort of took off. And I was like, "Oh, that's not good." So I trotted after, and I fixed it. But he was kinda icky after that, and then I thought, "Maybe it's better the way they did it", because the other ones, they used a spoon kinda thing and just fed him one at a time. And now he was just all sorts of icky. And because of that, other dirt was stuck on him. And then I thought, "Everyone's gonna see that I made a boo-boo. Everyone's gonna know exactly who did this to this lovely creature." I stand there with my bucket, and everyone else has spoons, and then everyone knows it's me. So, next time, I'm gonna do different, I can still have a bucket, but I'm gonna give it little-by-little, provide it in cups, so to speak.

D. So the people on Siah's planet, they still need to eat, even though they are manifested?

B. Indeed. They are manifested. They look exactly like you, you would not see a difference. The only thing that is different is that they are, the soul is completely filled inside. They don't need to think, "Oh, where is that signal coming from? Oh, uh-oh, I hear something from below here, uh-oh, something up here is saying something else." They're just constantly in connection with the soul particle, there's no mixed signals there. (*He is comparing the human mind and soul mind confusion faced by those who are incarnated on Earth.*)

D. That would make a better planet.

B. Ah. But there are no challenges, –but there is not supposed to be a challenge, you say. That's why, when I'm on my training camp (*with the students he is training for Earth*), you said, "You're training them to undergo certain challenges." And I said, "Ah, ah, clearly." And then you said, "There are much more rewards for you as a teacher if your student manages a challenge, than if someone just manages to hear their home base!" Huhuh. And then I said, "Maybe I'm gonna be a little bit rewarded! I'm gonna take credit for their advancements as well." Then I really dived into what tools one can need on one's journey. (*Spirit guides are considered part of the incarnating team, so if the incarnation does well, the guide gets to take some credit for their achievements.*)

D. (*Laughing.*) You do seem to like Siah's planet.

B. I might stay. But there are certain conditions and terms, you say. You don't want me to be too, –you want me to be influenced by this place so that I can teach certain things to my sparkle students, those now in training with the sixth dimension souls who will come down. I'm sure Zachariah has a lot of these teachings from Siah's place in his classrooms, because the souls from the factory, they can actually take all these teachings and just plant a seed here. Whereas mine might not necessarily do the same; they are here to work on communication, those from the sixth, the three Elahims and the other three from the sixth. They are here to establish new communication patterns, and they are also gonna assist in the seas, some of them.

D. The communication patterns between humans?

B. Indeed, because it's gonna change within your computer being (*physical mind*), and doing so you kinda need someone who is a role model and trying to operate this new brain. So if you're gonna have a new brain increasing the receiver for light, then someone needs to be, similar like you did when you came in, you know, in the furry one, and tried to upgrade the computer; they're gonna do the same, the three Elahims. But the other three, they're also gonna come in and work on scientific shifts. So I'm teaching them somewhat similar. None of them are planned, it was said to me, to work too much with the environment and so forth. They are gonna come in and be more hands–on when it comes to: number one, the computer, the receivers, and similar like you, to operate and see whether it fits to have a greater upgrade, –like a Window 10. (*He's drawing a comparison between the brain and Microsoft Windows operating systems.*) We're aiming, you said, for them to be like Window 20. So if a Window 20 exists, then the physical also needs to have the wires correctly connected to that Window 20. This is similar to what you did before (*with the early hominins*), you came in and they (*the councils*) were like, "Oh, we're gonna have a Window 1," HUHUHUHUH, ya' know. Now they're doing similar. But the others from the sixth, they're gonna work on scientific advancements as well, so they're a little bit different. But this experience and excursion here to Siah's world, that's just for me, for my amusement and—to—tell—you—to—tell—everyone else on this plane. That's why you sent me.

D. (*Laughing*) That's a good note. Early on Ophelia said that this was going to offer us quite a bit of...(*Bob began trying to open Christine's eyes, and it completely threw me off.*) Are you practicing looking? Do you think eventually you'll want to walk around and look at people?

B. I do indeed. I do, I do, I would like to move around a little bit more (*during our trance sessions*). But I'm sitting here and I'm stuck! But my training program is proceeding with great results. Everyone is paired up. Tom is not given Little Seth. Tom is given, if Little Seth was like number two in this group (*of the three little Elahims*), he (*number one*) was the one that popped in his head, way back, and said, "Tell me more about Earth." And number three is a little bit similar to Little Seth, but number one is more still. And because Tom is not very still all the time, I thought it would be a better match if he was matched with number one. (*The story of when Bob first met the three little Elahims, whom he has since been training, was presented in Volume 1. Bob calls one of the little Elahims "Little Seth" or "Seth Junior", because he has a personality similar to Seth, Christine's higher self. Tom is a young spirit from the second, whom Bob is mentoring. Tom will act as a spirit guide to the little Elahim who is more still, and will follow that Elahim through all his upcoming incarnations, similar to how Bob has followed me.*)

D. Is this like you and me?

B. Similar like you and me, indeed.

D. This one, Seth, is always complaining that he didn't get you.

B. Nay. I'm pretty sure it would have been a rumble through the Wheel of Creation, if we were together! And Ophelia says, "No, that was not going to happen." I said, "Who really had the final say?" I'm not complaining, but I'm wondering a little bit, because Seth and I are more similar, so you might think, "Oh, we should be paired up." But now, sitting here and me, myself and I are creating all these pairs, comparing all these different souls together, I do see that there is a greater evolution and a greater end result if there is a balance in the friend–couple. So I'm aiming for that. Ophelia said, "Look for balance, look for balance. Similar like light and sound, they balance each other. Light and dark balance each other; similar here, you are here to train them to find a balance counterpart so that both can grow in their separate being at home and away."

D. So Tom didn't get one of those that went on the ship? (*As described in his King Henry the Eighth play, in Volume 1.*)

B. No, he got number one. There was only number two, Little Seth, that went on the ship, and he is paired up with a student that is gonna, a little bit, hold the reins; make sure that the pace is suitable to the general intention. So those two are paired up. Everyone is paired up, and the other three, all six from each side, all twelve are paired up. And we are, I'm having them now—because it was somewhat of a shock to self-study, so I am introducing self-study a little bit earlier. I am telling them first, "Two-and-two, you and your spirit guide, write down a combined experience journal of what you experienced."

D. In your plays?

B. In my plays. Sorry, no, the opposite. First, they sit, everyone is scattered and they sit and write down their own experience. If we take Little Seth, he sat and he wrote down his experience on the ship, and if he had the ability to hear his spirit guide. His spirit guide is doing the same journaling of the same experience, "Did Little Seth hear him?" We can call him Seth Junior, "Did Seth Junior hear him? What signals did he send?" Seth Junior on his side is writing down, "What signals did I hear from my friend?" So they are sitting there and then they go together and they compare the notes, and that will be delivered to me.

D. That's a nice way to introduce self-study.

B. Ah. Because no one wants to be in shock.

D. Sitting there with the dot language.

B. Dot language. And I'm pretty sure that all souls here from the sixth, they are probably programmed to self-study from the day they hatch from the egg! Huhuh, but we are not. I'm gently introducing this idea of collecting your thoughts, earlier, and then I sit, huh, in my study and I welcome the couple in—the spirit guide and the one from the sixth—and I said, "What is the report of the experience?" And then I have the proof, because I have the film here.

D. So you have screens?

B. I have screens, and then we try to mirror exactly what happened. I say, "Here is what happened up here on my screen (*he turned sideways and looked to the left, at something only he could see*), and what does it reflect here on your notes? I want to know, first, your independent notes, and then I want to know the group notes." So we look at the notes. And then I turn on my screen and I say, "Let's see what happened here. How can we improve, if we are in this setting, live?" Huhuh, so that's what I do.

D. I had a question about the notes in general. We talk about notes all the time, but how do you actually store them? You talk about writing notes, but I know you don't really write.

B. I store them like dots in my being, and then I sort of spit them out, I mean I don't spit them out, I release them from my being and I store them in like an energetic image, in a tank.

D. I know it's hard for humans to grasp this type of information, but I appreciate the fact that you put it in simplistic terms.

B. Oh, it's important, because no one wants to feel stupid. So if I say "a written note", then everyone understands what that is.

D. In our book we are ready to publish, your *Volume 1*—

B. I could go on more!

D. Do you think the description of Uranus is important to keep in there?

B. It's important to understand that there is a receiver and a counterpart, the Sun versus the stabilizer, so the general idea is important to get across. But some of it—to just make it more simple—it's a general idea that we are trying to portray. Even if it's a solar system, or if it's just a regular note to be friendly or have sunshine in the head, it's still that we're aiming to make it as easy as possible for the current Window 10 or Window 8, or some are still on Window 5, so we have to be somewhat wide in our teachings! Let's even include Window 5! HUHUHUH (*snorts*), no one wants to feel stupid though. (*He is saying that some are more mentally capable of understanding their teachings.*)

D. There probably won't be too many Windows 5's reading our books.

B. Nay. It's mostly Windows 8 and up that we're hoping to reach. But Window 8, they might know someone like a Window 5, and if a Window 5 feels very comfortable and relies on a Window 8 person, then gradually it will spread. But a Window 5 might not hear what YOU are saying, but they might listen to a Window 8. It's like rain, it drops down and it lands on the ground and it can create new foundations for the feet. Ophelia says this is probably it for today with teachings, but we might do a separate session, she say.

D. Oh, that sounds nice. When would you like to do it?

B. I'm available on Tuesday.

D. (*I was laughing at that remark.*) Okay, Tuesday it is then, my friend.

B. In between I have classes! So I'm gonna go now, but see me soon.

Other Worlds for Advanced Spirits (April 30, 2019)

Spirits who incarnate on Earth come from various specialty groups on the fifth, six, seventh, eighth, or ninth dimensions. There are other planets where only souls from specific groups can go to live. Etena is one such planet. Spirits from a small group within the seventh, known as Shea, can become long-term residents. However, unrelated groups are free to travel there to teach or conduct research in the pyramids. There are other planets in fish tank five where souls who have graduated from the Karma program on Earth may incarnate or blend with a body, each having its own type of learning.

Bob and Lasaray have made many visits to Etena. Bob and Siah have become friends and walk together in the forest. All spirits communicate telepathically with thought bubbles, so there are no barriers between them. When Bob returned to the second, he would regale the students with stories about his large, lion-like companion. In retrospect, he realized he should not have opened the door to their curiosity, because most of them will never have the opportunity to visit Etena. In this session, when Bob talks about casting, he is referring to interviews he conducted for young spirits from the second to become guides for the three Little Elahims, who will soon incarnate on Earth. After Bob began going to Etena, he thought it would be more pleasant for his students to follow someone on Etena instead of Earth. Zachariah told him there was no reason for spirit guides on Etena, as the residents are all fully in touch with their souls. The potato reference is about a very dense reality he visited one time, where the inhabitants looked like tubers with feet and a head, but no neck. Their physical shape is due to the high gravity on that reality.

- B. We (*certain spirits from the second*) work directly with souls from the fifth, except for me! I got someone completely different, and I'm not complaining, I'm going on all sorts of adventures that many might not ever go on. (*Bob studies with Lasaray on the sixth, but most of the spirits on the second do not travel like he does.*) And I'm not gonna tell, because blowing my horn sometimes backfires, so I have been a little bit resistant with sharing lately—because I'm not sure! Like for instance, there was someone (*one of Ia's students*) who came and said, "We went to your lecture, when you talked about that grand being that looked like a big lion." And I said, "Oh, I don't remember. I don't know what that could have been." And they were describing Siah, and I was like, "Hmm. I don't remember. I've seen so many different creatures. Maybe it was something from the dinosaur time." And they were like, "You said it was a very nice being that was rescued." Then I said, "I'm sure that being is doing just fine." And they wanted to know if that was Earth, and I said, "Nay, but there's gonna be other animals that you can connect with, similar like that." And then I showed pictures of a hippo, I showed a picture of a lion, and I said, "This is what you might encounter."
- D. You didn't want to tell them too much about where you are going?
- B. No, because of the fact that they will fall under the spell of having too many choices, and there is actually not a choice. I wasn't given a choice. I was given Earth. I asked if I could instead do a casting for Siah's place, but Zachariah said,

"They don't incarnate. They are placed there and they have gone through, already, most lessons that is involved when it comes to a physical experience." And a physical experience is not just being a potato, because they would say, "Oh, look! I'm a potato, I can go and be at Siah's world, I can be a potato over there." It has to do with that you occupy and carry within that experience the (ability to make) choices within the emotional, mental, and physical; three different choices. And people might be like, "How can physical be a choice?" Well, physical is how you execute the signals that come from the other two. And those on Siah's world, they have already gone through those lessons and mastered, with a BIG golden star, I would assume, since they are upgraded to this lovely reality. I'm not sure if all of them have been to Earth, I'm not saying that, I don't know if they have been there, but they have been to a similar reality. There is also a sister planet, Ophelia says. Similar like Earth.

D. What galaxy?

B. Oh, it's nearby here. It's like operating similar like Earth. It's a little bit bigger.

D. Do souls incarnate there, as well?

B. Ah. But not at first. I wouldn't say that it's a backup plan, but it's almost like a dual reality, based on choices. If you do certain choices here, on Earth, if they reflect and mirror the other planet, then you have the opportunity to incarnate there as well. It's considered like Earth.

D. Is it a slightly more advanced location?

B. It has less beings there. There's much more water on it, so the continents are less. Fewer people on it. Technologically, they are maybe not as far ahead, but spiritually, emotionally, and mentally, they are WAY ahead. Ophelia said they learned the lessons of overusing energies, so they are using the resources that exist on this planet—water, actually—as their main resource for energy. They don't need big towers and poles and wires. They use all their energy resource from the ocean. That must be like a big wheel! That's the one I showed you. (*In one of my past lives, I developed a water wheel for energy, but Bob was the one who put the idea for it in my mind, so he takes full credit for the advancement.*) Oh, Ophelia laughs about that, "There's no wheel in the ocean," she says. But they are aware of how to only use resources from the sea in order to create, not only water for them to drink, but to use for electricity and energy. They learned the lessons of technology on this plane (*Earth*), and some of them were moved, Ophelia said, to the other one.

D. I remember someone said that Earth is the only place souls incarnate from birth to death, so do they have a different system?

B. It's a little bit similar there. They live longer there than they do here. If someone can top or reach a hundred here, they can, over there, reach about two hundred and fifty, Ophelia said. So they have a longer lifespan over there. But they are born, it's not like at Siah's place where they just sort of seem to emerge.

D. They just show up?

B. They just show up, I don't know how. You say to not bother so much about how things move between certain places and how they pop up. But I do know there is a chain, so I'm wondering where they come from. And they have a spiritual home as well, and you say, "Yes, but they are in constant connection." On Siah's place it is like having fifty percent there, and the other fifty in their home base, and they can sort of mentally move in-between. It's just the physical manifestation of the soul that I see.

D. But they don't really have bodies?

B. They have a body, on Siah's place.

D. Is it like a manifested body?

B. A fully manifested body. It's not like half-and-half, it's not like they don't have legs.

D. (*Laughing*) But they aren't born?

B. They just are. I haven't seen that many children here. There are some but they're not very small. They are like nine-year olds. And you said that if someone manifests there as a nine-year old, then they will have about seventy percent in the spirit realm and thirty percent manifested as a nine-year old. If they are an adult, if I see an adult there, then they are like fifty-fifty, you say. And they just move in-between freely, there is nothing really that prevents that.

D. That's a nice way to occupy your time. And they are working, too, aren't they?

B. They're working a lot with farming and how to really honor the earth, the soil, and how to make the soil come alive again.

D. They also maintain the records?

B. Indeed, and that's in the pyramids. I have been only one time in that big one with the pillars. I might try to sneak in more times, but I'm pretty sure that I will be detected. I don't look the same. And I said, "Maybe we can manifest myself like someone like them?" And you say, "No, you come as you are. There are conditions, Bob," you say.

D. Rules everywhere you go.

B. Always rules.

The Pyramid of Life Forms (June 2, 2019)

On one of Bob's trips to Etena, he describes a pyramid containing collections of life forms that have existed on innumerable planets within the fish tanks. For each pattern, they maintain corresponding records about the host planet, atmosphere, gravity, sunlight and other vital characteristics. The patterns are available for replication on another planet, if oversight councils approve the introduction of the species into a foreign ecosystem. Since there are dissimilitudes within the soil, atmosphere, gravity, solar radiation and energetic frequency found on every planet, most patterns will require fine-tuning. The patterns themselves are an energetic form of DNA, as expressed within the vibration of fish tank four. When placed within a reality, the blueprint will grow into the third dimensional form of a specific plant, animal, fish, tree, or other life form. When we think about the many billions of species that live on Earth, and the billions that have gone extinct, it is comforting to know that nothing is ever lost. The Creator has a complete memory of all creations.

Bob tells how Siah takes him to some of his favorite spots out in nature. When Bob mentions a couple, he is talking about Setalay and her companion, the ones who take care of Siah. Bob also gives information on collective karma on Earth and a 10,000 year cycle, which is nearing an end. The human body is going to be altered to be more spiritually engaged, and many of the souls who are currently here will not be returning.

D. And he's back! (*He had bumped Ophelia out earlier.*)

B. (*He makes a sound like thua–thua–thua.*) An. I have been with Siah.

D. Oh, you have?

B. I have indeed. I have been collecting information with the couple, –very tender I must say. I don't mind if they adopt me. I can be there like Siah maybe, manifested like Siah, manifested like everyone else. I kinda like this, to be more manifested, because that's sort of what happens here is that you travel like your soul, in whatever peanut suit you have, but when you enter this reality, you are solid and you are what you are, the preference that you have. It's not like you can change. I thought I would try to pick a form that was looking like you! I tried to blow myself up like a balloon, and I thought, "If you can just pick whatever form you like, then I might try to just look like Lasaray." But that did not work, so there are conditions, indeed. You said, "What are you doing, Bob? Why are you blowing yourself up like that?" And I said, "I'm trying to create a form," and then you said, "You have a form, what's wrong with the form that you have?" Then I said, "If you can just create whatever form you like, then maybe here I would like to be a giant, maybe look a little bit like you!" And you said, "But you don't have that in your makeup. Everyone, depending on where you belong, has a makeup that you can, in some way, manifest or de-manifest. So you kind of are what you are. Why are you not happy with the way you are?" And I said, "I am happy with the way I am. It's just that I thought if this is a place where you can almost be like an incarnation, then I also wondered if I could change on different travels, like an incarnation?" And you said, "No, no. You manifest here as the pattern and makeup that you have at your disposal. So you cannot just use another ones makeup, you come as you are." SO, I am Bob, I am a little bit smaller. Anyway, I came here to somewhat take care of Siah.

D. What did you do with Siah?

B. Siah actually took me for a walk.

D. Outside of the city?

B. Outside of the city, so we went sort of that way (*nods to the right*), in that direction, and we came to, –it's like waterfalls. And Siah goes here, it's like that big one?

D. Niagara?

B. Umm. But there are smaller ones too, and there are things flying in the air here, similar like fairies, but also birds. But we went there and it's somewhat of a jungle area. Strangely, it's not as loud as Niagara or other great waterfalls on this plane. It is because of the fact the atmosphere is different here, so even if you have the same conditions, like a waterfall, it changes the sound level. It's soft, it doesn't have a rumble, and it's because of the atmospheric conditions that exist here. You will also understand this, the couple said, that the noise levels are increasing on Earth in many different aspects, because your atmosphere is in some way dissolving and changing. So things have a different sound when the atmospheric conditions are different. So here we sit by the waterfall, me and Siah, and it's remarkably, –it's not silent, but it's not rumbling in the same way, it's more pouring.

D. Do you like it better?

B. Ah. It's nice. So Siah took me here, and also, we went into the vegetation, the jungle, and he showed me different creatures (*he wasn't sure how to describe them*), it's like, if you think of a hedgehog, but they're walking like a prairie dog stands, so they can stand up. And they have nests under trees, and Siah showed me different ones. They're like a prairie dog, but they look like a hedgehog. I can talk with them, everyone talks here.

D. Do they live forever, like Siah, or do they live and die?

B. They don't die, nothing dies. They come here, –maybe they come from the 4–H farm or something, who put them here, one might wonder? But it's a life form and you can communicate with them, and they don't seem to, –the couple said that even though things don't die, a capsule can still go to sleep and it will appear as a species or an individual died. But it's more put in a state of rest, they said, So it's not dying, so they don't bury anything, they just put it in one of the pyramids. That's where they put the individual, or species, or even plants, –plants also can somewhat die–, so in one of the pyramids, they have cocoons where sleeping individuals or species reside. And they are taken care of by, –it's like nurses, you know, walking around taking care, taking measurements. So I was allowed to go inside one of the pyramids here to see the cocoons, and they're placed on top of each other.

D. Stacked up?

B. Ah. And I can see flowers, and I can see certain creatures sleeping in there, so in some respect they are dead, because some have been here for a while, it seems, but they are not dead in the sense that they can never be brought to life again. That's what the female said, Setalay, she said that you never toss these away.

D. Did she say if any of them had come back to life, after a rest?

B. Some of them have, but I'm looking at those who are still resting. And then she said, "Some of them have been here for a long time, but we honor them, similar as our living friends who are out and about. We care for them and we nurture them, because when we get called, there is some sort of receiver that comes in, information comes in from different councils, and they can actually use some of these little cocoons, and they can actually go places."

D. It sounds similar to a greenhouse planet and 4-H farm collection center, all in one?

B. It's a storage unit and some can come here, –and they seem to do that–, and they can have a look, and if something is missing in their flora and fauna, they can use one of the cocoons here; they can take a sample from a sleeping one here. I would assume there's also a collection of those who are out and about, like the hedgehog I saw—but upright hedgehog—and communicating similar like Setalay. Little bit different tone, I must say.

D. What did it say to you?

B. It said that I was welcome to come in and have a look in their home under the tree, –but I was too big! That was a nice experience to be too big, to suddenly don't fit, because here I can't merge with the tree because I am not energy, I am a manifested form of my preference. I am ALMOST like an incarnation, and I kinda liked it. This is like warming up, maybe. And I said, maybe we should send all my little students here, to warm up to the great adventure on Earth. And you said, "They don't have a peanut suit, and they have not reached that level." And you said, "Just think how long it took before you could get your peanut suit. We can't just give it to the little ones, they would just be completely confused." So that was different, that I couldn't get in. But I laid down on the ground, because there was an opening at the bottom of the tree where this hedgehog went in. It's a happy little creature, I must say, and it was completely different to not be able to just move more freely, like I'm used to. And you said,

"This is similar like an incarnation, now you will feel how it is to be limited." Because I bumped into things.

D. Used to walking through things?

B. I just walked right through things, and suddenly I bumped into things. And you said, "Bob, you're solid. Stop! You're going into the rock; you're going to hurt yourself." And Siah laid down and did this (*he put his hands up over his eyes, as if he couldn't watch Bob crash into things*). Siah came here in one of the cocoons at one point, when you moved him here and then he was woken up here. So we will probably see if we can get information about that, how someone comes into the cocoon in the big storage unit, in the big collection of life forms that exist. It seems, however, that this big storage unit of cocoons, are not just from species on this level, on this reality at Siah's place, this is a storage unit for several different realities. So someone can come and say, "I have a planet located in fish tank two. I seem to lack a little bit of flora and fauna. I might want to have a little bit more roots and vegetation on my planet. it seems that I have a lot of droughts." So someone can help them to get access to existing forms that will work on his planet.

D. Do they just take the patterns? Do the cocoons stay there?

B. If you see it like a glass cocoon, and let's say for example we see a flower, you don't take the flower out, the flower is still there, BUT one of the nurses, one of the caretakers here, they will extract the pattern from the flower and put it in a little glass jar almost, for this visitor who has been allowed to get some of this flower to establish on a planet or reality. Because it might be that the pattern is not on the planet, it either went into hibernation or it died, or you can kick-start an ecosystem with things from this storage unit that might not have been there, the pattern from the beginning. I learned, when I created the solar system, that I had to think of EVERYTHING that I might want to have on my planet. But suddenly it seems that there is exceptions from the rules here, that you can actually get assistance from these helpers.

D. Did you have to go down to the individual plant types that you wanted on your planet?

B. I DID, and you said, "This is how it's done." But clearly you can, because here comes people, all sorts of different looking individuals—that's how they manifest themselves, and I don't judge.

D. Strange looking people?

B. Ah. One is kinda round in figure, with a small head. Like a big, not a bug, but like a big beetle-shaped form.

D. That's not very attractive either.

B. So this specific individual is here in his preference of form, and I don't judge, to have help for his reality. So he has made the journey here to get access to something in the pyramid, in the storage units, in the cocoons, that is helpful for his reality. And it's not a store, at all, you can't go in and say, "I wanna have one of that, and wanna have two of that, some of those," it's not like that. You have to have somewhat of an approval from your home base. It's council work here, you say. So you give a little bit of information when you come into this big storage unit, that you are on a mission from a specific planet, which was given the approval to have an extract from the plant.

D. So are most of the entities that come and go, are they council members or spirits working for the council?

B. It can be like a scout, it can be like a messenger, but they have to have approval from some council that oversees the reality where they come from. So let's say that you have the approval, then you can come here and pick out what you need. And I say, "Maybe we should go shopping for Earth? Maybe we should do that." And you said, "Oh, I knew that you would say that, Bob. We still have to have approval from the council that oversees Earth."

D. Which council is that? Where are they located?

B. It's a council on the fifth.

D. So they are the ones in charge of what is on Earth?

B. What finally reaches Earth, yes.

D. Is Zachariah involved with that?

B. Zachariah is there. But they communicate with six, seven, eight, nine, and probably others too. But there is a council on the fifth that is responsible for sending down the great manual, probably, into the cloud, so it reaches those like me who work on the second, related to Earth. So it is a chain. (*The cloud is what he calls the location for the manuals given to those on the second to create or modify life forms on a given planet.)*

D. I've always been curious who was given the keys to the kingdom.

B. It's not a store, this pyramid, and there are sections, so you can't just look around and say, "Ohh, that's a nice plant. I want to have that one," because it might not fit in your reality. The storage unit is also categorized and divided into fish tanks, so if I, let's say, come from fish tank five, then I will be directed, gently, if I am allowed to go shop here, I will be directed gently to the section where the cocoons and different physical things that have already been on Earth, or in this fish tank, that are available for me to potentially use. BUT it all follows a greater evolution, and, you know, I'm outside of the evolution. That's why you have to have clearance. You say, "Okay, I come from Earth," and you come here with a paper that says you can only shop for Earth. But once you're here, if you want to do something on the planet on the other side of the fog band, it doesn't fit. So there is an order here.

D. How much of your soul energy did you take to Siah's planet?

B. I have about fifty, because I manifest myself. So it's a lot, I almost feel like I have overeaten, I feel like I'm in a food coma. That's how it feels to be in physical. I feel a little bit heavy. And you said, "You will learn how to navigate, in a little while. But this is similar like being in an incarnation," you say.

D. Are you similar to Setalay and the other ones on that planet, about the same density?

B. Same density, but I don't know if they have the same percentage, like you say.

D. So you can hug Siah?

B. I can hug Siah, I can poke Setalay, – but I don't! I can touch Siah's nose, everything is solid. I am solid I bump into things because I didn't understand that I was so solid.

D. When you are home on the second, you're also solid, aren't you? Can you bump into things at home?

B. Ah, but I don't hurt myself. I feel a resistance, but I can power through. Here I have a resistance, but I cannot power through.

D. So is this kind of the way the Elahim and Anunnaki traveled?

B. Ah. They just manifested when they were here. They used the same modality of travel, like I do now when I go to Siah's place. I've been here and I'm fascinated with this big store and I'm walking around. Since I have been in fish tank five, whatever exists here, I can look at those cocoons. It's like glass cocoons and I can see things, and some of them I remember; I said, "Ohh! That's a friend of mine! I remember that one." An interesting aspect here is that there is a smaller model, a version of the dinosaurs. But they're not in the regular size.

D. Do you think your individual is stored there?

B. Probably. But I did not know.

D. Did you look around at any of the other fish tanks?

B. I tried to, but I was kindly and gently assisted elsewhere. They said, "Oh, are you lost? Let's see, we're going to go back here." And they just smiled—they're like Ophelia, they just smiled—and they just escorted me back. So, that's what I've been doing.

D. What else did Siah show you when you were out and about?

B. We went through the nature and looked into that. He has somewhat of a path that he normally goes on, and he communicates and talks with other friends. So he has sort of a daily routine, it seems, where he strolls around, making the rounds. So this hedgehog family, for instance, they're friends, so he called for them and they come out, and were like (*then he makes a chattering noise*) and smiling and jumping a little bit and looked at me, and I was like, "Ohh!" They wanted to invite me in, so I said, "Okay, I go and see where you live." But since I couldn't go in, I laid down flat on my belly and I looked in like this (*turns himself so it looked like his cheek was on the ground*), and I said, "Oh, that's cozy! I would really like to enjoy coming in there, but it seems I am limited here." That's different! So, I'm not telling this to my students at this point, because they are still a little bit concerned about karma. We are entering karma classes where we try to understand, first of all, the collective karma that the civilization will go through, that none of them—and neither of you—are able to just skip. You're all part of a collective karma as a group and as a society and civilization, and it has nothing to do with a lifetime, it has to do with the cycle that you are occupying. A cycle can be like, in human years, like ten-thousand years. So everyone

who comes to Earth in that specific cycle will fall under the collective karma and the collective intention that the Creator has for that specific group.
D. Can there be smaller groupings? Say you have the whole world, then you have Europe, and then a country?
B. Indeed. It can be that too. But there is one big one for everyone who comes in. It is the sparkle dust (*from the eighth dimension*) that somewhat creates the foundations for group and collective karma; but if you break it down, then there is like for regions, for countries, all the way down to people and individual lifetimes. So when you navigate from the fourth, you can see all different collective karmas, it's like a cloud that you can see when you travel and navigate in the fourth. It's spirit guides' work, it's not for just anyone. But, as a spirit guide, you can look through this tunnel on the fourth and just look at different collective karma that has existed prior to the civilization that you are currently monitoring. The current one will be more lit up, but you will still be able to see the general cycles of group karma and group expansion in their awareness and their progressive development over time. You can navigate in the fourth as a spirit guide and access information from all civilizations that has existed. I'm pretty sure that you can also look the other way and also see what might be coming. I cannot, I can only see here and backwards. Ophelia, I'm pretty sure, and Isaac and Jeshua and everyone else, I'm sure they can see upcoming collective karma. It looks like a cloud is stationary over a specific spot. So we have ours here, it's located here, and it's for about, it's been present here for about the last 10,000 years, because it's from like 8000 BC. So it's that sort of group experience we are still under.
D. Is this drawing to a close?
B. It is indeed drawing to a close, we are in the end of the cloud, but it's still active. Because there is so many events that go on, it's lit up, the way I can see it, it's lit up so I can look down on the Earth from this perspective, but in the cloud, because here in the end of the cloud there is a lot of lightening going on. There are changes and it's moving frequently. If I look back in this cloud, then I can see it's more still, because it has already somewhat occurred, even though time doesn't exist. But time exists on the planet itself, but it does not exist here

up in the level where I am. (*His position in the fourth dimension as he looks over the timeline.*)

D. Well, what about when you are back in the spirit realm? When you come and go, to visit us during our sessions, do you have a sense of time?

B. I don't necessarily travel through the fourth because I'm not an incarnation, but I can move around here and have a look-see.

D. Like when we go from week to week, do you see our sessions in a linear order?

B. Not linear, it's more like on top of each other. So it's like creating a cake. So it's not linear, it's like I'm adding on top of each other.

D. Adding notes.

B. Adding notes, adding layers on top of the cake. Well anyway, we're going to save energy, Ophelia said. But it's been a privilege to go into the big store and to see what exists and the purpose of it. I've been around.

D. That's amazing. I wish I could remember that place.

B. You can't remember as the one you are now, but you remember in your being. I don't need to forget here, you say. I was concerned about that, that I would forget, like if it was a dream and when I left, I would forget. But you said no. I might not want to incarnate on Earth. I might do this instead. There is a very open society here, open to the level that I am allowed to see, of course. I was not allowed to just move around like, "Oh! Fish tank two, what's over there?" And then these kind helpers that work here, –they smile, they're like Ophelia and Julia–, they show up.

D. It must be a really large pyramid to hold all that stuff.

B. It's huge. And it's not just on top, it actually goes below, –and below, I have not been going there. But they're so friendly, so even if you are misplaced, or you try to be misplaced on purpose, you are kindly assisted elsewhere.

D. Maybe you have a little tracker on you, too.

B. Maybe I might have, we don't know that. I might have. Anyway, so I'll go now. I'll probably like to go back here and look. Ah. I'll go now, Ophelia is dragging my arm.

D. Alright, my friend. Always a pleasure.

B. Always a pleasure. Okay, bye bye. See you.

Ia brings Siah to our Session (July 13, 2019)

As most practitioners of psychical abilities will attest, repetition is one of the keys to perfecting their skill. When Christine moves into her trance state, she always returns to a place in the fourth dimension she created many years ago. During the transition into full trance, the identity of Christine is dropped, and her higher self, Seth, is the one who ascends the mountain towards a temple and the white marble bench on a cliff overlooking the sea. It is quite common, during this journey upwards, for Seth to be joined by the spirit who intends to speak first. In this session, Setalay glided along with Seth as he climbed upwards. What was unique is that both Ia and Siah, my pet from Etena, were also tagging along, observing. Setalay began the session and gave a brilliant talk, which will be included in Wave 3. As Setalay pulled away, Ia moved in to take over, but she allowed Siah to blend briefly to observe the surroundings where Christine and I sat. Siah and Lasaray are very close companions on Etena, and he knows I have gone somewhere, but doesn't know where. Although Christine never opens her eyes, all the spirits "see" me quite clearly. From their perspective, our physical bodies are bundles of energy that are immersed within the first, second, third and fourth dimensional reality of patterns, colors, sounds, thought forms, and energetic structures.

- Ia. So, this is where you live. (*Ia made the comment on behalf of Siah, while looking around, studying the room through Christine's closed eyes.*) Umm. We are here with Siah, and he indeed climbed the mountain when you began this journey. Butterflies and squirrels and chipmunks were sitting on him as he was climbing up to the temple. This is the first time he actually is very present. He cannot communicate; however, he sends his longing for you, his question about your journey and when you will return. He has things, he says, that he wants to explore with you. You asked him to guard a gate, a cave, and he has been doing so. There are things in this cave on Etena that are treats, your notes, personal notes, that he guards.
- D. Is that why he sits next to the pyramid?
- Ia. Indeed. Well, the pyramid is your office. There is also a cave in the nearby environment, in the forest, where other things are found. There are toys here as well. He says that you play with him, and he wants you to pick up the toy; he wonders when you will come back and pick up the toys in the cave. So

there are toys and memories in this cave that he takes care of, that he guards. But he also follows you around when you make trips around (*Etena*) with people. He says that it's his honor and his duty to make sure that you move around safely, even though there is no danger. But he is a close companion to you. But the biggest question at this point is when you will come back and play with him again. The toys, he watches over the toys.

D. I'm sure I'll be back before long, because I'm getting pretty old.

Ia. Siah is missing you. You visit him as you dream and you do play with him. But in many ways, he is like Bob, he doesn't understand why things have come to an end and why it cannot just continue.

D. What does Siah think about Bob when he comes to visit?

Ia. Oh, he likes Bob. Bob sits and he reads about the adventures the two of you are on so that Siah feels more that he belongs in the story and in the travel. So Bob puts great detail and effort into making sure that Siah is involved. And they indeed go out on different excursions in the surrounding as well, where Siah gets to show him different things.

D. When Bob and I travel to Etena, I also play with Siah, don't I?

Ia. Yes you do, yes you do. Then you have to leave. Bob has been allowed, a couple of times, to remain, to be with Siah. He didn't beg, but it was a desire, I would say, that he had to be with Siah and to remain. So, yes indeed, a couple of times he was allowed to remain. He did…(*Bob obviously said something to her, because she then began speaking towards where he stood, to the left.*) Okay, Bob, you can say it by yourself, I don't have to tell him everything for you. Yes, I know you have your own voice, there's no need to be grumpy. You always have your time, Bob. Okay, I will let you say your piece, it is your story. (*She then turned back to me.*) Anyway, I just wanted to pop by.

D. It's so nice to see you again, Ia. Thank you for bringing in Siah and sharing all that with me.

Ia. Oh, you are much welcome. Just know that you have a lovely being, a lovely creature, waiting for you to come and play with him.

D. I will return as soon as I can.

Ia. There you go. Okay.

B. (*Bob came in right away, letting Ia know that he could talk for himself.*) There is no need to take ALL sunshine. I mean, it's not like I don't have a voice. It's not like I can't speak for myself. Huhuhuh.
D. Well, thank you for taking care of Siah. Ia said you almost begged to stay with him?
B. I do like to, –I feel a need to stick around there because I feel appreciated. And maybe not everyone has time for Siah, but I have all sorts of time because I have nothing else to do there. So I volunteered to take care of Siah. I'm reading stories, telling him about different things that we are doing, so that he knows that you have not just left him, but that you are doing things. So I am showing him pictures, I'm sending pictures from my chimney to his chimney, to just show him where we are at. And I don't think anyone has done that with him, so I feel a great responsibility to make him a part of this journey.
D. Thank you so much for that. That's really kind of you.
B. Ah. Because no one wants to feel like they're left behind, and he doesn't always know when you come, so I'll tell him where we are at, so he can see what we are doing. And he doesn't see days, he has not the ability. Spirit guides can see the soul, a Coat, and a human, and they can see, let's say, "Oh, now it's just human activity, now the human has taken over." But for Siah, he only sees you, he only sees Lasaray, so he doesn't see the capsule that you are in.
D. I have a question—since only a few percent of me is down here, why can't the rest of me go visit Siah?
B. Well, you are in other fish tanks that I am not invited in. I don't know why I'm not invited. You said that you are over in seven and eight and do things.
D. What about in the lab, are we still—
B. We are in the lab occasionally, yes indeed.
D. So I'm just so spread out that when I go to Siah's planet, I need to take more of my energy?
B. Well, when you go to Siah's place, when you fully manifest, – not in your dreams, but when you really go there–, then you will draw a lot of your traveling energy from five, seven, and eight, and you go there. It's to really BE there, you say. You don't really have to do that, you can go with a couple of

percent, if you like, to manifest still, but you really see it as a place, –it's like an oasis, you say, it's where you just sort of gain energy, it's a holiday almost, like a relaxation. You do a lot of maintaining in the pyramid, and I have volunteered to go with you in there, to see what it is that you are storing in there. And you smiled and you said, "Well, I know you volunteer, Bob, you always volunteer. You don't have to say that, I do know that you are ready to go, and eventually we will go. But for the meantime, to not confuse you, we will just be here for play and fun."

D. That's a good objective too.

B. Sometimes you also have to be just in play and fun, not everything has to do with work. So when you are here (*on Etena*), you really want to be here, so you kinda withdraw a lot of your energy from other places. In general, that's a mindset that you should be in, that when there is, even down to the smallest understanding of a human, –let's say a weekend–, that you withdraw everything that has to do with Monday to Friday, everything from work, that you somewhat take all that and you withdraw it, and you move yourself into a holiday kind of mindset and spirit, which would be like Saturday and Sunday, then you can move back into your work environment again. So you can be the same. It's a healthy way of being, "Now I'm on holiday; now I work." Rest—work. Receiving—action, so to speak.

D. That's really good advice for everyone, because a lot of people can't do that. My current job is not demanding, so I never think about it when I'm home.

B. Ah. But some do, and they never move into the holiday spirit, the resting and amusing, to just have fun, because they don't know, necessarily, what fun is, because they are so in the mindset of Monday to Friday. And it's unfortunate that it's not a balance, that it is five work days and two holidays. If it had been more fifty–fifty, then people might have an easier way to be on a peak, both in their work capacity, as well as in their personal capacity.

D. That's so true. That's really good advice.

B. You might want to promote that, since I'm not able to, because I'm not engaging in the karma program so I can't make that note, but you might say that. You can begin by adding a couple of other yearly holidays, that's what you can do. You could, just send a note to someone, someone who is in the fine room of decisions, –since you did not want to go into the fine room of decisions. (*Bob amusingly calls the dictatorial organs of government the "fine room of decisions".*)

The Song of the Creator (October 6, 2019)

In this talk, Setalay reveals a surprising link between the Master Mind and the incarnated soul. She said that every creature or creation has a little bit of the Creator within. The soul within most animals is all Master Mind. I had always assumed the human incarnation was independent from the Creator but she advised that a tiny particle of Master Mind awareness joins with the soul during each incarnation. Therefore, a soul is never alone when it travels into the universes of form. It is a beautiful concept and a remarkable bit of information about the grand process of incarnation. In the past, the Master Mind of the Creator occupied all bodies on Earth. Gradually, souls were allowed to join with the Master Mind in a blended mix. The current humanoid is designed such that the incarnating soul has full control, and the Master Mind awareness is only an observer. However, this union creates a direct link between the soul and the Creator, which can be used for communication. Upon death, the Master Mind assists with the life review, never judging, but always present.

- S. This is Setalay, here with the council from Etena. We are here to provide information and light to your species, to your host, to your consciousness, and to your heart.
- D. Welcome, everyone.
- S. We are here to bring divine understanding on how to connect with Source, how to connect with the Creator, meaning the inner you. The inner you is a song from the Creator, placed within you as a gift. In each soul, as they travel, the Creator will follow you through helpers such as Ophelia and even myself. I have indeed followed a human on Earth. This soul is known to you as Josephine. Josephine now travels, taking education on Etena. We work with melodies, tones, to refine feelings within beings. As we increase the light in the emotional aspect within an entity, it has the ability to expand into the mental realities as well. What we see at this point in your consciousness is that fear has a grip, meaning your heart, your center core, your soul, struggles to make itself heard. The veil is primarily over your mental aspects. The way

you seek information has changed, it has shifted from a sensation of higher knowledge within you, to what someone states or tells you. This is the veil. The veil over human consciousness. As we see progress in souls coming in with a higher light, we feel comfort for your evolution as well. You are here to lift the veil over consciousness, over the access to knowledge. Others are here to kickstart how to channel emotions. Two different realities struggle uniquely. Your planet struggles in its feelings, if you like. Too much karma needs to be addressed on your planet. Karma primarily is linked to the mental.

D. I always thought that emotions were a stronger carrier of karma.

S. It should be, shouldn't it? Here (*on Earth*) it's different, karma here has a bigger debt when it comes to the mental. More efforts need to be addressed when it comes to the mental aspects of karma here. Different. If you choose to work with emotions, then a lot of mental karma will be erased. But here it's somewhat looked down upon if you FEEL knowledge. Humans are expected to KNOW knowledge, you have to know your path. If someone feels information, steps, insights, it's not considered science, it's not considered valuable, fully. That is why karma here is more mentally inclined.

D. I remember Zachariah said one time that people shoot karmic arrows into the future, and emotions create a bigger crater. How does that correspond to what you are saying?

S. Emotions has a stronger hand, indeed. It creates both a bigger crater, but also a bigger salvation. You have a tendency as a species to send those arrows, as you called them, primarily as mental arrows. If you were to focus on sending emotional arrows on your path, then indeed some will create craters, as you call it, because, as a species, you are not comfortable with feeling. That will be experienced as an abyss. The difference is that the emotional abyss is welcomed, it's welcoming in your progress if you dive into it. A mental abyss leads you nowhere. An emotional crater or abyss has a treat within it. The higher order is feelings, but nothing can be felt and understood completely without the counterpart of mental. As you balance those two, you understand that neither is you. Both are lessons of how to operate, both are choices of how to navigate through teachings, realities, –regardless if you incarnate as you do here, or if you visit other locations such as Etena. We have, in that respect, mastered to balance both. We do not become either side, we lean on both, connecting mental, emotional, becoming us. We do not dress in an experience, we observe and we transform teachings, placing them objectively into a box, if you like. We never become fear. We never become love. We ARE love. Here you become sensations, and it's easier, for some reason, to lean on your mental aspect because you have to understand, and man thinks the brain understands. The brain is merely operating as a central (*organ*) to collect data, to make sense of your surroundings. The largest brain, if you like, is in your center point. That is why it is easy to say, "Understand with your heart." If you say, "Understand with your center point," many will be confused, –even those who proclaim to be empaths, as well as those that proclaim to walk a spiritual path–, they might be confused with relating to the center core, the center point, as the greatest brain, the greatest central (*connection to Source*) of all, within you. The Creator has placed a particle of itself in each soul. That part is the connection to Source, it is not a connection to your higher self, it is a connection to Source. Each soul, in the center point, has a sparkle of the Creator. That means that if you see the center point as a big sun, somewhere in this sun exists a light dot that is different. That is the Creator.

D. So the Creator occupies a body along with the soul energy?

S. Yes, as it travels, yes.

D. I did not know that.

S. Hmm. Yes, you do.

D. Not as a human (*laughing*).

S. As a soul travels, it feels lost, regardless of destination. That is why it is provided companionship, as a small percentage, if you like to call it like that. If you see the sun, the soul, departing the spiritual reality, as it moves out into experiencing different realities and fish tanks, it feels lost. In many ways, it feels disconnected. That is why the gift from the Creator is to accompany the soul. So if the soul, let's say the sun in your center point being a hundred percent, then the part that is the Creator is, tops, one percent. Normally it is 0.3 to 0.7 percent that travels with each soul.

D. Is that the same as the Master Mind?

S. Indeed, because the Creator travels and experiences, but also brings comfort and guidance to the soul. As the soul returns home, it can communicate with this small particle of the Creator, who might indeed have a different life review, but never judging, simply coloring, simply bringing the awareness to the soul as a life review takes place. The soul will never know that it is speaking to the Creator; it appears as a thought bubble, an idea, but the Creator brings forward its knowledge of the travel into a life review.

D. At what point does the Master Mind join with the soul energy? As it puts on the Coat, or once it is incarnated in the body?

S. Normally as a soul dresses, indeed. Because the particle, the Creating particle, the Source within each experience, is silent. But the soul knows as it departs that companionship will come, but not in what color or in what area in the Coat. The Source particle moving into the Coat will have the first preview of the journey itself, and it will place itself and read the Coat. It will place thereby itself in the specific area mostly challenging for the soul. If the greatest challenge of the mission is to work on, let's say, anger, then the Source particle will spread out its 0.3 percent in that part of the Coat, to assist, to help, to warm the soul, to welcome the soul to find it, to assist a challenge. Even those who do not come with Coats, as they travel, they still have companionship.

D. That's fascinating. That makes me think about in the Bible they talk about the Holy Spirit being with people, would that be a similar concept?

S. It could be in the same concept, indeed.

D. So the person is always not only in connection with their higher self, their remaining soul at home, but also the Creator?

S. Yes. But the Creator indeed can be silent, so the soul might not understand that it is discussing with the Creator. It does not matter which way the soul feels it is communicating. Sometimes this little light, this little particle from Source, will take over as a spirit guide, normally when a soul has progressed for a while. When spirit guides take a step back, when a soul chooses to go into a life with no companionship, such as companion souls or spirit guides, then indeed the Source particle can act such a spirit guide; but it acts silently.

It is somewhat like a clairaudient signal, but the soul will not hear it, this will simply be felt. It's different than communicating with a spirit guide; this will more resonate with intuition, if you like.

D. Has the percentage of the Master Mind that joins with the soul changed over time?

S. It never normally reaches more than 1.2 percent, that's the most that it sends. And indeed, we monitor this as a group on Etena, as we are in direct contact with the life reviews and collecting information and data from different locations that we store in our hub. So in many ways we collect information from this particle; not the whole soul journey but the particle's experience.

D. Does it focus on different aspects of the incarnation than the soul would?

S. It can indeed. It can operate as a single unit in some ways, indeed. This is why individuals, as a human, can sometime experience a huge shift in, let's say, their personality. That means that the original path led nowhere. The crater that one was headed for was perhaps not intentional, or better yet, it might not be suited for the continuous journey. I'm just going to say this, that this happens after a soul has been around for a while. In the beginning, you are supposed to navigate a little bit by yourself with spirit guides and so forth. But as a soul can sometimes feel a shift and being a completely different person, then this particle can, in some way, take over and lead the journey into a different path. So it's a living entity traveling along with you. See it as you see the hippo, and on the back of the hippo is a little bird, and the little bird, it travels along on this big hippo because it trusts the hippo and it is always in symbiosis with the hippo as they travel together, –so it's similar like that. So the little bird would be considered the Creator, this particle, and the hippo would be you. So there, I hope you understand.

D. I do. That's a beautiful teaching.

S. And we do tend to Siah, who is more wild than tame. When he came, he was quiet, he suffered trauma. You should know that on Etena, we work on healing the different parts within beings. We took great care, and attention was made to heal this big animal who came, who suffered sadness. It took a long time, oh, time and time here...efforts were made over a period of cycles to embrace this being. He was missing his companion and he didn't know where he really was. He was sad and we provided different ways to lift his spirit, to embrace him with light and warmth. We early on understood that he responds well to sweets! So we had friends coming over with honey. He has a great fondness of honey, and it never ceased after sadness disappeared. The craving for honey increased, which was merely supposed to have been an embrace to remove him from this state that he was in. However, as we saw his fondness for this yellow sweet, then indeed he was provided it more frequently, even though it doesn't serve a purpose more than, –well, it serves a purpose in that he feels happiness with the sweet. But after a while, he felt reassured that he was taken care of. You were there frequently and sat with him, talked with him. He didn't understand the shift that had taken place, wondering when he would return to his home, which was not an option. You were present during this transition for him, and you talked with him about that this is a new home and so forth. The problem that you knew was that he would be alone here. There will not be a companion in the same way. So we all, including you, put in great effort in showing different companions that looked different than him. So in this great effort over cycles, he collected and gathered new friends. As his spirit increased, his appetite for honey as well increased.

D. I have a question about his spirit. Because I guess he was an animal, is he all Master Mind?

S. All Master Mind.

D. I appreciate that you take care of him.

S. Oh, we all take care of him. And even your Little Friend (*Bob*), who has come to visit, takes great care and attention to his wellbeing. But I also see that there is a little bit of another side of this coin, and it is because your Little Friend wants to be shown around. So a lot of times when your Little Friend is here, they go out on long excursions. Your Little Friend always has a little box, if you like, with honey, because of the fact that Siah tends sometimes to drift off and your Little Friend wanted to have somewhat of a tool to lure him back, so he wouldn't be lost in this great wilderness. And he always comes back. They have established some sort of unity, these two, and your Little Friend seems to really care, and the two of them have bonded in way that we did not foresee, that it would increase to such a level of mutual love and understanding.

D. Since he's from the second, he understands animals very well.

S. He does indeed. So there. If there is nothing else you wish to ask me, I will now resign.

D. You've given me a lot to think about, because I had no idea about the Master Mind connecting and participating.

S. Always participating, just differently. In Siah, fully participating. To go back to the percentage of the sun, the Master Mind, it's not a hundred percent of course, because it is still a separate soul, a separate unit, but it's filled up to eighty percent or even eighty-five percent of Master Mind.

D. Then what is the other twenty percent?

S. The other part is unique spirit.

D. Can you explain how the unique spirit is different from the Master Mind?

S. You are a unique spirit, you are not completely Master Mind. Each unique spirit is born into a frequency band in the spiritual realities. They are not completely black and white, like five, six, seven, eight and so forth. So in this case with Siah, he has somewhat of his own spirit that resonates with the frequency and vibration of the second. The 85 percent that is the Master Mind, is coming from, –to give you a picture since you like numbers and you like the ladder–, more from twelve and thirteen, the Center Pole, so to speak.

D. Hmm. I'm just trying to picture how this works, because I had always been assuming that animals were 100 percent Master Mind?

S. Oh, they are filled up, but they still operate as an independent spirit, more or less.

D. Is Siah ever going to cease to exist? I know he won't die, but—

S. Here nothing dies, nothing ages, everything remains the same. But if, let's say, Siah would ask to resign, to merge back into Source when someone is filled with this high percentage from the Master Mind, it simply absorbs back. But each spirit, regardless, has a specific part that is unique spirit.

D. So even animals on Earth have a unique spirit?

S. A little piece is still a unique spirit. It might be mute, so it appears the Master Mind is operating the animal, and that is what you consider to be filled up with the Master Mind, but the unique spirit is still present.

D. So when an animal on Earth dies, what happens?

S. They don't have a life review, in that sense, because the Master Mind experiences everything within the animal. So it's almost like it's reversed. If I said that the Source particle traveling with a human soul is 1 percent, the other part is the unique spirit. When it comes to animals on your plane, then it's the opposite. It could be like 99 percent is the Master Mind, the Source particle, and only 1 percent is the unique spirit (*of the animal*).

D. Then when an animal dies, what happens to the unique spirit?

S. It returns to its destination, normally in the second dimension. Because it doesn't have a life review, it doesn't experience, it simply holds the experience for the Creator. Do you understand the difference? It's mute. But when Siah existed on the other planet, his separate spirit was not mute. That is why he remembers and he experiences, and that's where the sadness was located. So in this case, on that plane, about 15 percent was his unique spirit, whereas 85 percent was the Master Mind. Here (*on Earth*), it's different, the mathematics and the combinations are different. So here it's 0.5 percent that would be considered a unique spirit in an animal, and the rest would be the Master Mind. The 0.5 percent in an animal here simply holds the experience for the Master Mind. It's like a tour guide for the Master Mind.

D. So when that animal dies, its small percentage returns to—

S. It's like a group consciousness on the second dimension.

D. But yet it still holds a bit of its individuality?

S. In some way, but you cannot draw the same comparison to your own soul. It's a group consciousness.

D. So when a human dies, do they meet their pets that they had, as they travel through the fourth?

S. They recognize the 0.5 percent.

D. That actually makes a lot of sense to me.

S. It's hard to fully provide numbers and pictures so that it makes sense in a human ear, in a human consciousness, especially since you have the veil. But we try our best, and this has given you a lot to ponder about, Ophelia says. So there we go. Thank you so much.

D. Well thank you. It was an amazing lecture.

Twelfth Dimension of Healing (Oct 6, 2019)

This is the first time any spirit has commented on the function of the twelfth dimension, the vibration closest to the Creator. We know from other discussions that the tenth, eleventh and twelfth are increasingly less individualized. The spiritual beings that occupy the twelfth still have forms, but operate collectively as a group with one mind. Because of their mastery over light and sound, they work to restore balance and heal energy patterns in all the spiritual dimensions and the first through fourth dimensions in the various fish tanks. On planetary bodies such as Earth, one of the ways they transmit healing vibration is through water. Water, as we have discussed in previous books, is the base of the second dimension. No living being exists without water, which they describe as a form of light. On Etena, there are pools of water that were used to help Siah recover from his trauma, as Bob explains in the following discussion.

B. (*Bob came in making tones, not really singing, but clearly trying to bring the vibration up to his level.*)

D. Is this Jeshua? (*I was teasing him.*)

B. Hahaha, nay! Nay, it's ME! I've been on excursions again.

D. Where did you go now?

B. You took me because—I wanted to say that I asked, but I must have repeatedly asked to go—because you and I have been exploring, first of all, Etena. But also, we've been on an excursion on Earth because I wanted to know more about the activities in the mountains over in Tibet. So, two excursions have been taking place with me—I did not bring anyone else because I felt like there was gonna be enough questions just with me. So, we went to Etena and I was joining you as you were introducing me in, –it was a teaching, a classroom, where you say you meet and contemplate. And I said, "Can we contemplate out loud, or is it like silent contemplation?" And you said, "No, we can do both, but because you are here, we're probably gonna talk out loud." So we were contemplating about the effects of healing, it had to do with my ability to enhance my skills as a healer. So the class was about healing waves being a separate element. Here we talk about, you know, there's light, and light heals and so forth. But the higher science of healing is that you connect with a different source, a different element that taps in directly from a healing source that normally, you say, originates from the twelfth. The twelfth is a healing pool, of sorts. This is where entities reside that operates as great healers in different fish tanks, and also heals WITHIN the spiritual realities. So it's like a grand hospital, the twelfth, you say, and they carry the teachings on how to combine its energy with light, and from that point this combined energy source has the ability to rejuvenate, remove, clear organs and cells.

D. So like when a soul passes, leaves Earth and returns home, I know a lot of times they describe being in a shower of healing light—

B. Indeed, and that originates, that comes from the twelfth. It's like a big healing source. You showed me because I wanted to know about this place, and I said, "Can we go?" And you said, "No, you don't really go there, they come to you. In their presence you feel like you're standing in a shower almost, with light. It's like being bathed in light." But you also said that water is an element here related to them. That is why there is concern about the water, because the sea, the presence of water, is the twelfth experiencing here. So the seas and the water is linked to the twelfth and when they feel like they cannot provide the intentional amount of energy and source of healing that they are supposed to do, which is the case here, then it sort of becomes an imbalance. Each dimension is also connected, you say, and these people say, to different...OH! Words, ohh. (*He gave a long sigh, as if exhausted from not finding appropriate words to express himself.*) Like the planet, each dimension is in charge of experiencing and being connected to your planet. So the seas are connected to the twelfth. The atmosphere and clouds are the eighth. Sunlight is the seventh, and it goes down like that. Six is connected to, actually, movement on the planet. So when there has been shifts on landmass and motion, that is the sixth experiencing. And this is not you experiencing, these are the higher councils on each, on six, seven, eight and so forth. Nine is connected to...oh, you did not say...what happened to nine and ten?

D. Ask Ophelia, she knows.
B. They are more connected also to motion, but not motion of landmass, like you (*the sixth*). It's motion of, oh, the tenth is motion of thoughts and consciousness. The planet has consciousness as well, so it has to do with that motion, not just motion of landmass. Nine (*he pauses and listens to Ophelia*), is about something with sound waves, Ophelia says. It's very vague. I might want to say, "Raise your voice, Miss!" But here on Etena they know about these things, and they teach me that each dimension is present in various amount, it seems, on living life forms such as Earth, or a planet like Earth. I wanted to go to the twelfth, since I, myself, am considered to be a healer. I thought I might go there, but you say, "You don't go there, they come to you," and I say, "How will they appear? How will they come?" And you say, "You can't speak to them, so you might be confused." And I say, "Why would I be confused?" and you say, "Because they don't communicate, they simply are and they will have a presence more like an energy, like a light pole in some way. It's like experiencing the Center Pole, but directly."
D. There might not be as much individuality on that dimension.
B. There's not, you say. You said that I cannot expect like "George" to come and talk from the twelfth, it's not like that. You say it's a group consciousness. But I'm learning here that elements are combined with the different amounts of energy from the twelfth, usually light. But there is a huge connection on this reality through waters. So water and light are two elements that are used to channel the twelfth. And in this case, on Earth, you suffer with water, meaning the twelfth, the healing capacity that is yours by birth, this planet, it struggles. As you start to change, you say, the shifts of the atmosphere, the conditions of sunlight also changes. The way the twelfth channels, they use water and light. And when those two elements are not in balance, the twelfth cannot spread out, you say. So that is why there is a huge effort going on in understanding and raising the awareness of, –primarily here we're talking about the seas–, and that's why my little friends, like Tom and so forth, are going (*to Earth*) from the water world, because they are highly connected to water. And the second dimension, since you did not ask, is considered here as, –if you (*the sixth*) are landmass–, we are in charge of

the entities, from the smallest little particle, all the way up to the largest form; that's what we are in charge of, meaning the higher councils on the second. (*The second dimension oversees all living life forms.*) So this must be a council that Ole might be a student in, so we're talking about high, high, high councils. So I can see here that there is a long way before I'm gonna dissolve. I'm now in one council, but I see that this is not the council that communicates with the healing puddle in the twelfth, so I think that is Ole and his friends. (*Ole is Gergen's mentor, and is similar to a grandfather to Bob.*)

D. Well, that's good that you have a long, long way before you dissolve.

B. Because that was concerning, but I can see now that there is a long road ahead for me to go there. We all, in some way, more or less, operates and channel with the twelfth, but differently. And all dimensions in this project Earth—that is why this is considered a project—because all dimensions have an interest, a unique interest and a unique specialty, when it comes to your planet.

D. That's some great information.

B. So, I've been there. Siah and I have also been on excursions, he takes me places. Because we have bonded in a way that maybe not everyone bonds, and it's because I communicate with his unique spirit, and you say that I should do that because the other part is just experiencing within the reality where we're at. So I'm communicating directly to his spirit and he takes me—he communicates with me, of course—and we go places and we have been, –he likes to swim! There is a big waterfall and at the end there is a big pool, and he likes to be there; he likes to be weightless, he says.

D. What about you?

B. I swim too! I float.

D. Just like you float with me in the ocean. (*He enjoys when we go to Crete and swim in the Mediterranean.*)

B. I float. I float here (*on Earth*), but here (*on Etena*), I get wet! When I float with you, I don't get wet. So this is a unique experience, and here, since I know now that this is the twelfth, then I'm trying to connect with the twelfth dimension in the healing puddle, just floating with Siah. And I KNOW that when Siah went into his healing phase when he came here (*when he was relocated to Etena*), he was bathed a lot. He did not bathe as much in the other place, so that was a new element that he encountered, and he could feel the presence, you said and Setalay said and he said, from a higher source, –he doesn't say twelfth, but I know it is the twelfth–, but I don't have to explain it to him. I understand now that when we are swimming in the puddle, we are indeed in direct contact with the twelfth, because there's no pollution in our pool here. But if someone tried to connect and be healed and feel the connection to this healing puddle in a lot of waters on Earth, it's not operating fully. The intention is about cooling down the planet, it's about bringing healing to the planet by itself, but also everyone who step into the water also gets this treat from the twelfth. That is the gift.

D. That's really fascinating. Yes, Setalay said you have been bonding well with Siah.

B. Ah. And I try to be there a lot, but I do have a lot of assignments that I cannot just leave. But sometimes I also want to be a student, and this is like leisure/student time.

D. Setalay said you carried a little box of honey around with you.

B. It's because sometimes he takes off on his own path that he knows, and I don't, and since I'm a little bit solid here, I move around like he does. So I send out a call for him, combined with I open the lid on the box of honey, and he smells that and then he comes right back. So I've been there and I've also been on an excursion with you (*to Earth*), as we silently monitored the activities that took place in the mountains, because I've been really curious about that. And you said that they are receivers, and I see boxes located strategically in what appears like a line. But not all boxes are in a line, some of them are a little bit to the sides. They are not that big; it's like a metallic box and some of them have light dots on them and they operate. You say that they are remains from visitors that have an interest in keeping an eye on the spines (*the mountain ranges*), and they are from the sixth. So these boxes reads activity from landmass and, like I said, the sixth belongs with motion of landmass and spines. So even if me and my council, we have been sitting and talking a lot about moving a spine, but nothing will move the spine unless councils from the sixth, that actually are in charge of motion of landmass, gives a thumbs up. But you say these were placed here by visitors in an ancient past. And I said, "When was that?" and

you said, "Around one hundred million years ago they were placed there."
D. That was early, I'm not sure how old the Himalaya are, but they are not that old.
B. It was a long time ago, and at that time when you say they were placed there, it caused motion and rise. And it was somewhat of a turmoil, you say, as they were placed in a line and it caused a shift in that region; motion.
D. So the receivers actually do something other than record information?
B. It's not just recording, it actually does things. Now it's recording, because it is silent, you say. Now they are just collecting data. If I see them now, there is no activity, but you showed me how they were different in the past. You say, "Look, Bob, now the boxes are mute. They don't have any lights going on, they just silently collect data. Before," you say, "here you can see that some of the boxes started to light up, different colors, buttons, lit up." They are connected in somewhat of a wire, it seems, in this line. And you say, "At this time, motion took place." (*I must have shown him what happened in the past, a little holographic movie.*)

Once again, Bob displays an awareness about topics which Christine has little knowledge or interest. And even though I have a second B.Sc. degree in petroleum geology, I had to do a little research before commenting on Bob's observation. As most of you know, the crust of the Earth is broken into tectonic plates that move in different directions from one another. When the adjoining plates push together, pull apart, or slide against one another, forces are generated which create mountain ranges, deep ocean trenches, volcanic activity, faults and earthquakes. About 300 million years ago ("Ma"), a lot of the current plates were conjoined in a landmass known as Pangea, which broke apart some 200 Ma into two main blocks called Laurasia and Gondwanaland. Laurasia would later break into North America and Eurasia, and Gondwanaland went southward and became the source for all the continents of the southern hemisphere, which we know as Africa, South America, Antarctica and Australia. However, what is currently the Indian subcontinent (the bulk of South Asia) was also part of the landmass in the southern hemisphere. It is estimated that around 130 Ma the Indian plate, which was located near the South Pole, separated from Gondwana. At that time, it was far, far away from the Eurasian continent, which was located on the northern edge of the ancient Tethys Ocean. For some unknown reason, beginning 80 to 100 Ma, the Indian block began moving rapidly north at a rate that has confounded geoscientists. Normal tectonic plate movement is around 3 to 6 cm per year, but the Indian plate moved northwards at an estimated rate of 20 cm per year for at least 30 million years, ending with the collision that produced the Himalayan Mountains. Several theories have been put forward to explain this anomalous movement and speed, such as double subduction zones or hot spots in the mantle, but it remains a controversial issue in geodynamics. If we accept Bob's statements, the true explanation for why the Indian subcontinent made a 6500 km journey is much more mysterious than anyone imagines. Various spiritual councils planned and executed the motion by having visitors (also known as aliens) strategically place these physical boxes in a line along the Eurasian plate where the Himalayan range was intended to form. In later conversations, it was explained that the boxes interacted with and influenced the living energy field that the spirits call the "fork", and set in motion the rearrangement of the Earth's crust as the new pattern manifested in the lithosphere. The Indian plate was pulled north, as on a conveyor belt, until it collided with the Eurasian plate and shoved the Himalayan mountain range into existence. The spiritual entities who are in charge of the Earth project must have needed a massive barrier at that location for atmospheric, biological, or other reasons. Similar boxes have been activated and placed at other locations as well, either to monitor the fork or to stabilize the Earth grid. Bob mentions elsewhere that boxes were placed beneath several of the ancient pyramids to stabilize the grid, although there is not one beneath the great pyramid in Egypt. The ones around the poles are mostly for monitoring purposes, although they can be activated if needed. What we assume to be natural geologic processes are, in fact, directed and controlled by intelligences from outside our Universe, and certain visitors to Earth are here in physical or manifested form to assist these higher councils in executing their intentions. One of Bob's friends from the second, Joel, actually observed the visitors installing the boxes, and he became very curious and concerned about the purpose.

    D. Those boxes were put there by travelers?
    B. Travelers, indeed, not looking like a human.

D. But they must have been working with the sixth?

B. Ah, sixth, they come from six. This is like the motion guys that came and did things. But before changes took place in motion, these were placed. But it's not like you put boxes, you say, everywhere, just to make things move, but it was important with the creation of what was supposed to become the mountains in that region. So it's not like there are these boxes everywhere, but they are more present, you say, when it comes to certain land masses. When I see the map you showed me, there are more boxes in that region than there is in that spine in South America, there's not the same amount of boxes there, and there's no light in the boxes, because they are not activated, you say. It has not started to happen there yet. So we've been looking at that. And I asked, because I was not here at that time, this was before (*Bob came to Earth around 60 Ma*), and you say that you did not do this, it was uncles, you say. And I said, "Was it Ari?" And you smiled and you said, "Ari knows them, but it wasn't Ari." Huhuh. They were like uncles, you say. This was when I was a child, but we learned about this in our school. I asked if I can take your classes from when you went to school, like a big documentary, a big recap—but you say that it's not allowed. You said, "I'm not allowed to learn everything on your level, am I?" And I said, "No, because you don't understand, and you're not vibrating in the same frequency. It's not like it's a secret...is it a secret?" And you said, "Well, we can call it a secret." Then I said, "It's not like it's a secret on the second." And you said, "Yes, it is, because that is not available for me, so it's the same as being a secret!" Then I said, "It's not a secret, it's just not available for you!" So whenever I ask, "Is this a secret?" you say, "Well, it's just not available for you." Huhuh. And then we laugh.

D. Do you share what you and I discuss with your friends on the second?

B. No. And you say to not share left and right. I learned that lesson, because if I blow my horn, I have seen the end result of me talking too much on things that are not a secret. If I were to tell about the boxes in the mountains, for instance, I know that one, at least one, would come and ask more questions, and that's Joel. Because he saw this, Joel is older than me and he saw this.

D. He saw the boxes being placed?
B. Saw the boxes coming in. He said there were individuals putting things in his mountains, moving things around. So anyway, I'll probably go now, but I've been on excursions and I have collected my own information and I'm now compiling my notes, separating them so they don't slip out to those with ears that are not supposed to hear them. I have two books, and I have two journals; one that is for my ears only and one that is for sharing. This was suggested by Gergen, to have two different systems of journaling, and that I should move in between those. He said, "Change the way you communicate. When you communicate to students, move into the energy of the collective journal, the open journal." He said, "It can be like an open journal and a closed journal, so you just shift your mindset," he says, "so that when I am as a teacher then I move into my open vault, my open volumes. Then it's less likely that something would fall through. So that's a step–," he said, "now that you are older, you move in between, you have to separate the way you are: Just you—or the tutor." So I'm shifting my energy and as I do it's like pulling down the curtain on the other one so it doesn't slip through. I close that window. "It's easier for me to operate," he says, "if I close that window—it's a mindset." So anyway, I'm gonna go now.
D. Well, that was really good information, my friend, so thank you for that.
B. But Joel with the mountains—he also has things to say. He's not really content with the explanation about visitors in the mountains. His personality is like that, –if you do not answer immediately, he does not go away. Back home, he follows me and he goes on and on and on about the visitors in the mountains. And then I say, "I have not met them, I don't know." And he says, "Well, you have a friend who has met them. So maybe you can ask him if they are gonna return? Are they gonna mess up my mountains? Are they gonna return and mess up my mountains?" That's what he said. And I said, "Okay, I'll ask Lasaray." So I did. I asked, "What about the visitors and the mountains? What about the boxes?" And then you said, "No, there's not going to be anyone coming back to the mountains at this time, so you can tell Joel not to worry." Joel can see the effects, because he is working on a project where they are planning on moving spines. And he

said that he's not very interested in moving spines if there is gonna come someone from outside and mess up the project. So he wants to know if there is any agenda or any plans of someone coming into that region where the boxes are in his mountains. There is gonna be some sort of activity over in that region, like north India, Pakistan, Tibet, there is gonna be a little bit of motion there, and that is why he is very inquisitive of knowing if there is gonna be disturbances and interruptions, he say, by someone who might not know anything about this.

D. You said those boxes were placed there about 100 million years ago?

B. There are boxes placed in the mountains, but the boxed on the North Pole, they are more active. When you showed me these boxes, the boxes in the mountains, they are asleep.

D. They were at one time active, weren't they?

B. Ah, indeed they were. There is more activity at this time, you should know, on the North Pole. And there are some boxes reciprocating that signal on the South Pole. So there is communication going through the fork, and it has to do with motion and to move the land mass and so forth. Ah. Okay, I go now, so we'll see you another time. I'm always nearby, of course. Hmmhmm.

D. Thank you for coming and sharing with us today.

B. Sharing is caring. So, okay, see you. Bye bye.

The Washer (Nov 9, 2019)

When a spirit travels from the spiritual dimensions out into one of the fish tanks, it must pass through different energetic barriers and frequency fields. Bob described in *Volume 1* how he first traveled in a protective bubble that Jeshua made for him. Later, he learned how to generate his own energetic shield, which he refers to as his peanut suit, because his resulting shape was peanut–like. When he travels to Etena, he goes in his peanut suit. If he wants to visit realities in fish tanks on the other side of the wheel, such as eight and nine, it requires a different mode of travel, where his spirit pattern is rearranged to match the frequency band of the destination. Bob likens this process to going into a washing machine, where he will be subjected to unknown forces and turbulence. Not surprisingly, he is very apprehensive about committing to that process. He commented once, about spirits from the second dimension, "We don't necessarily like new, until we know what new is."

B. Ahh! Ahh!

D. Welcome.

B. (*He began rubbing Christine's face from top to bottom, over and over.*) Feels differently.

D. Maybe there is still some residual energy.

B. Ah, there is something that is not just Ophelia. It's a little bit like asleep. We'll see here, but Ophelia is present, she said that she is sending like, you know, heat. So she's present, of course, like always. So I'm back, and I'm kinda curious about what's been going on above my head.

D. Oh, in what way?

B. There are indeed discussions that goes on in the lab of the sixth. And I did overhear that there were visitors that was gonna come to the sixth. Visitors that you say belonged in another fish tank. And Seth, he was like, "Oh, I know them, I know them. They're friends of mine, I go there all the time." And there was like a meeting that was gonna take place and I was kinda curious, like, "Who are they? Where do they come from?" and so on.

D. Did you get an answer?

B. Seth was about to, but then you shushed him. And then I said, "Seth, do you want to go for a stroll? Maybe we can go look at your maps...?" and then you said, "No, session is out, session is over." But you did say that I was gonna meet individuals that were coming from another place, but I was not gonna go there. And I'm fine with that, because if it's not the same as going to Siah then I'm not sure I wanna go. And you said that this specific reality is on the other side of the pole, and I said, "How do you get there?" And you said, "You rotate," and I have not taken that class yet to rotate. I said, "Like rotating around the pole? Like rotating up and then just spit out somewhere? Like a merry–go–round and just spit out somewhere?" And you laughed about that, and then you say, "No, but it's a different suit." There are so many places I feel like I would like to go to.

D. Ophelia suggested you were being shown that for a reason, so maybe you're going to go?

B. Ah. But you say I have to conquer my fear. And I said, "What fear is that?" And you said, "It is to fully, in some way, dissolve, but not dissolve like the end result dissolve (*the final ascension*)," But I have to be content that my being—as what I understand my being to be—will transform. But you laughed about that and you say, "It is similar like that. You put someone in like a washer and it rotates, and then you open the lid and spit something out. But when you spit something out of a washer, it's clean. It's not like the object, a sweater for example, has gone anywhere." It might have got a different color if you put a red sock in it. So if I'm like a white sweater and someone put in a red sock, Huhuh, I might look different, but I'm still the same. You compared it to the rotation and you said, "It's like you go into a washer. You open the lid on the front and you put me in there, and it starts to rotate." And then you said, "This is where you have to conquer your fear because there is a sensation of letting go of the idea of who you are. Because if you're going to travel," you say, "to the other side, which is a different existence than I'm used to, then I have to go through the washer." And you put me in there and you say, "On the other side, on the back of the washer, there is an opening, so I'm not coming in and out the same way." You say, "You come in from this side of the pole, you go into the washer; close the lid," –and this is where you said I have to conquer my fear, because the lid has to be closed, and I'm not comfortable necessarily with closed. And you said, "As long as you're not comfortable, you will not be able to travel to the other side of the pole. If you want to travel to the fish tanks and realities on the other side of the pole, or of a band, and it can be different. It doesn't mean you travel through the pole, but between different realities." And you said, "You go into the washer, you have to close the lid, and then someone starts the button and you begin to rotate. You have to be in the sensation of transformation." Then, at a given point and time and for whatever someone is looking for, a lid, you say, is opened on the back of the washer and it spits you out.

D. Are there other spirits who are controlling this?

B. I was asking that! "Who is pressing the button? And can you hear me in there? Is it similar like my bubble as we were traveling, or is it different?" And you say, "It is somewhat different. You will not hear us, but we will have full view on you. So that is also part of conquering your fear, because a great traveler has to go through this magical washer with two lids." And I say, "Okay, what do I need to prepare to do that? And can we maybe go in the same washer if we are going to the same destination?"

D. What was the answer?

B. Oh, you laughed and you say, "No, Bob. We all have different washers, similar like you have your different portals when you go to see Siah. But this is different, this an instant travel between."

D. It does seem like it would be similar like when you go to Siah's place?

B. But you say it's a longer process. When I go to Siah's place in my peanut suit, it feels like I'm in motion forward, but I'm sort of rotating around my own axis, spinning through like this (*as he turns sideways in the chair*), but I'm still me in my peanut suit. You say, "You will be you when you are spit out, but you have to do a transformation in the washer." It's not like a mile-long washer, it is a washer and I'm rotating, circling, but I'm not moving forward in the washer. So something happens to me where I, in some way, –you know I don't like the word dissolve–, so you call it that I transform. You rearrange me. And you say, "You have to be prepared," because when I was in my peanut suit, I was still me, and in the bubble I was also still me, but you say, "you have to drop the sensation of me and understand that when the process is over, when you are spit out, you will still be 'me', but in a different version." So when Seth came back (*after traveling via the washer*) he said, "I'm still me, I'm just more dense." He was bigger when he came back than when I see him sulking back from Earth.

D. (*I laughed at that*) Sulking back from Earth!

B. Ah, he does that sometimes.

D. So he was bigger than he normally is, at home in our lab?

B. Ah, he was bigger, and if I poked him, it was like he was rubber. So when he comes sulking back from Earth, he's not like rubber, he's more like cotton. Both of you are more dense, so that's why I said, "Where have you been? Why do you look like rubber?" And then I poked him and I said, "You feel differently. You look differently." And he said, "I've been on another vibration in another reality on the other side, in a parallel reality that Earth doesn't belong in." And then I asked, "Oh, where was that?" because I was curious. And he did start to say that he was gonna take me, but then you shushed him. Both of you said, "In order for you to be like this, you have to travel in another way." He said, "You have seen me on Earth and you know how I am in physical vibration, and you know when I return how I appear to you. So now you can see that I appear differently. It is because I have been in another physical experience where the conditions are different and where I bring more (*soul energy*)." And I said, "So are you basically made out of rubber? Is that what you're saying?" And he laughed and he said, "Noo, I'm not." So the thing is, the teaching in all of this is that I will come out of the washer and I will be Bob, similar like Seth is Seth, but he's a different Seth.

D. Do you think he came through the washer to get back?

B. I asked if he came back from the washer and he said yes.

D. But he still had a residual energy?

B. Indeed. He must have come back differently. Maybe he didn't come through the washer completely. But he said that you all travel through this transformational washer. So you put in this detergent in there and you are spit out as something else. Maybe I'll become like a rubber ball.

D. You'll be bigger.

B. I will be bigger, I asked that, "Is it possible for me to grow, to be bigger?" And you said, "Yes, in your molecules you will appear bigger." But that is the whole thing, I have to be okay with becoming a different kind of me, because Seth is different than when he comes back from Earth. I said, "Okay, maybe before we go there, what is 'there' like? What can I expect?"

D. It must be nice because Ari said we go to Vlac all the time. (*Vlac is a planet in fish tank eight, occupied by the Tallocks. Both are explained later in the book.*)

B. Ah, he likes to go there. He has friends there, he say, and they are like masters of engineering. Maybe they are the ones creating the dishwashers. Ah, anyway, that's what happened. There's gonna be visitors coming, guests from fish tank eight and some from fish tank nine even. And I say, "Maybe I can join and just have a look?"

D. There was one here a little bit ago. That's why you felt funny. (*He felt their residual energy when he merged with Christine.*)

B. Ah, they do feel funny. If that is what it's like, it is tickling. It's not as soft as Setalay. She's more in motion. This one is more rock solid. I don't know if I pushed it, if it would move. You say I'm not familiar with that high density. Earth here is also high density, but you are trapped under mental density. Whereas, you say, "In fish tank eight we are solid, but we are free and move around easily within our mental capacity." You say it is a MENTAL reality, but you travel there in a high physical dense form. Whereas like Setalay, they are also solid, but not as solid. And they are very free when it comes to their emotional centers.

D. But they also have a lot of mental, don't they?

B. Indeed. But it is predominantly an emotional feel. When Seth came back—it's like the communication is different between the two of you, it's like you are completely transformed into that dot language. When I was close to Seth, it dropped off on me and it felt like I had put on a really heavy hat. So my mental was just really heavy, my head, so to speak.

D. That was an introduction to where you are probably going to go, at some point.

B. Ah. I think I would like to go there, even though I have to go through this washer, but we'll see. Anyway, we're not gonna be too long in the tooth here. Maybe separate session coming?

D. That would be nice.

B. Maybe separate session on Thursday? We'll see what Ophelia says...she smiles, so it's an option. So, I'm gonna go now, but the option, the suggestion and idea has been put forward, and we will see what Ophelia says.

D. We've lost a few weeks here.

B. Ah. I'm gonna go and have a look at this washer, first of all. Maybe there are different brands to take into consideration. But there is a lid on the front and a lid on the back. I'm not traveling in the same way as when I'm traveling in my peanut suit. You say the lid opens and I'm spit out, and there I am in the right spot. And that is probably created by those who do the laundry detergent and press the buttons. They direct my washer exactly to the right location where I'm going. That's what I think. But the questions clearly come, you know, "Who are they? What is it that they put in?" And I say, "I wanna make sure that if I go in there in my light blue travel suit that someone doesn't accidentally put in a red sock." I don't like to be pink—Ia likes to be pink. You say that it's not you managing the washers.

D. It must come from a higher level.

B. Ah. You say they are hard to see, they don't show themselves. Which, again, means I have to conquer my fears of someone invisible who might not talk, who might not hear me. Oh, they hear me, you say, but I would not hear them, so there's gonna be like a ghost managing my washer.

D. So on dimensions where we hang out, there are spirits who are less dense or have a higher vibration?

B. Indeed, indeed. Appearing like a ghost. You say, "It's the ghosts that manage the washers." Again, you know that I feel most comfortable if I have a discussion and I can communicate and feel warmth. "Here," you say, "this is a different way of travel."

D. Maybe they will show themselves so you can see them.

B. Maybe that. Anyway, I have to think about this. But I did feel like Seth came back from somewhere HIGHLY interesting and he was really happy and really powerful. So I felt like, "Oh, wherever he's been, that must be great! He's not that enthusiastic when he comes back from Earth!" So I was like, "Oh, where have you been? Where is that? You don't look this enthusiastic when you come back from Earth." And he said, "No, I've been in a more complementary energy and understanding." And I said, "Can I come?" And he said, "Sure!" and then you say, "Shush." And then the whole discussion about the washer came up. So, you know, I have to think about this, but clearly, he came back from something interesting. In the meantime, I think I'm gonna go and relax over at Siah's place, because I do feel comfortable there. And Siah created a nest and we sit there and hang out. It's a secret nest.

D. In the forest?

B. It's like in the forest, but there is a little bit of a cave. It's where we sit and contemplate about things. I tell him stories, and he tells me stories where he's been. He's been around, he has thoughts and feelings about certain things. But there's a treat coming his way. (*The companion that Siah lost on his original home planet is being recreated.*)

D. Oh?

B. You say there's a treat coming his way, but I'm not being told yet because you don't trust that I don't tell. But there's a treat coming his way. So Okay, okay, I go now, but I'll be back.

D. Alright my friend. Thank you so much. It was a really good story.

B. I do feel tempted to go into the washer.

D. That's the first step, I guess. You have to want to do it.

B. I said, "Maybe the back lid can be a little bit opened when you closed the first one, because you know I don't feel comfortable if I'm trapped. Maybe a red sock in there would be good, because I like red.

D. You don't want to leave the door open because you might fly out in the wrong spot.

B. Ah, and I don't want that because what if someone can't find me and I can't communicate with the ghosts? Nay, nay, we have to think about this—long and hard, you say. Seth said, "Have you thought it through? Are you ready to go?" And you said, "No, we're still thinking—long and hard. There's all sorts of things to take into consideration." Anyway, I am inspired by Seth and his travels.

D. I'm sure you will go at some point.

B. I can't see, really. I have to go through the washer. Okay, I will persevere (*as he raised his right fist about shoulder height*). Okay, I'm gonna go now.

D. Thank you again for coming. We'll talk later in the week in a separate session.

B. Ah, separate session. Okay, bye bye.

Bob Recreates a Companion for Siah (Nov 13, 2019)

Siah, a very large, intelligent, and agile herbivore, once lived on a planet with a female companion. The female had been killed by the inhabitants, who encroached on the mountain area where they resided. Lasaray, seeing Siah's plight, took him from that planet and moved him to Etena so that he might live in peace among the Shea. Bob realized Siah was lonely and missed his female counterpart. Since Bob had wandered through the pyramid where the patterns for life forms are stored, it occurred to him that Siah's companion could be recreated. He then began lobbying Gergen and Lasaray to allow him to give that gift to Siah. His wish was granted and he was given a copy of her DNA. He took it back to his work area on the second dimension and replicated the body of Siah's partner, whom he named Tess. The patterns for life forms are fine-tuned for the conditions on the planet where they are introduced. Fortunately, the planet where Tess previously lived is similar to Etena, so Bob only made a few adjustments. Tess's memories, which exist in the fourth dimension around her original home planet, were recovered and implanted in the new body. When Bob and the other entities were done with their work, a new version of Tess existed that carried all the memories, emotions and behaviors of the former body up to the point of death. In later sections, Bob tells how that was accomplished.

Bob invited his students—the six from the sixth and the six spirit guides from the second—to come and witness him merging with Christine. Just as the session was about to begin, Bob moved aside to organize his students, and Gergen took that opportunity to blend with Christine and begin the session. Once Gergen stepped out, Bob came right in and began his talk. Midway through his lecture, he blocked them from hearing what he was going to say, which he called "shutting the curtain". He had not shared with them his travels to Etena, and he didn't want them to hear about Siah and start asking questions. The portion of his talk about creating a companion for Siah is presented after Gergen's introduction, but we moved the earlier part of his lecture into the next chapter.

G. Hm Hm Hm, this is Gergen.

D. Well hello, Gergen.

G. Good evening, indeed. The Little Friend stepped aside to fetch some notes, so I took the opportunity to step in and say some words. We have been indeed progressing with the council work with Bob in it. He has been progressing, I would say, in his role as a council member and has been able to reveal the way he communicates through this one here, and also about his travels. Some of the other members have been to Etena, but some have not. It became a merry occasion where Bob indeed revealed the different species and sceneries that could be found, let's just say like that, and also the animal or pet, Siah. Bob has grown great fondness to this being and is in the making to design a replica; asking for manuals, asking to bring to life a pattern that is no longer existent in this specific region where Etena exists. He had been EAGERLY asking for the patterns of Siah. And after quite a long elaboration I must say, with me pushing for Bob; because I do indeed have the background, the knowledge, about Siah and I knew that he indeed misses a companion, someone who is similar like himself. So indeed, the pattern has been asleep. Bob, on the other hand, knows that ALL patterns are available to awaken if someone has been granted the key. So he has been asking for the key, putting forward the importance of happiness in ALL creatures; long speeches about Siah and his wellbeing, and how that will improve if a partner were to be reawakened, so to speak. So indeed, that's been a little bit what he has been doing on the side. (*The rest of Gergen's talk, and the first part of Bob's, begins on page 378. Bob eventually picks up the topic of creating a partner for Siah, which is presented here.*)

B. What I'm now planning and what I can talk about now with the curtains shut, is that I wanted to give Siah a companion. And with your permission—you had already thought about this, so who sends the thought bubble to who, you might wonder here?—but we wanted to, and I wanted to be a part of this—so I asked Gergen if we could create this. I wanted to re-invite the pattern of his female companion.

D. Oh, that's wonderful. When you mentioned last week that Siah had a treat coming his way, that's the first thing that popped in my mind.

B. It's a treat coming his way. I did ask and you said that you had thought about it, but it's tricky. I asked repeatedly, so you said, "If it's okay with Gergen and your council. If it's okay with Gergen then let's go and unfold the pattern in the pyramid here on Etena," because they exist there. There is a sleeping pattern there that I can go and use.

D. Is the pattern for a male or female, and do you have to manipulate it a little bit?

B. The one that is asleep that I'm gonna use, you say it's actually programmed as a female. But you say there is also those cases where it's neither gender, it's an outline and a form where you can use the pattern and modify it depending on where it goes. It might not even be the same reality, so it might need adjustments to go into another reality. Let's say the level of oxygen is different from one location to another, then it has to be modified within, with the lungs and the breathing apparatus and so forth. But here I'm gonna have this friend, this female friend on Etena, and I have asked Gergen for permission.

D. So how are you going to handle that? Are you going to personally introduce them?

B. That is my idea, that is my idea, to introduce this friend, his friend.

D. That will make him really happy.

B. So I am in the phase of working on it in my lab, because everyone agreed. We haven't said anything to Siah, so I'm working in my second dimensional lab. It was like I got a new manual in the cloud, a manual that was not for Earth. I was given access to the cloud where Siah was originally located.

D. Where was that? Was that in the fourth fish tank or somewhere else?

B. Uhh. I think it was in the fifth, but not here. Further in, I think. I can't really see.

D. Okay, that's alright. So the form that Siah has now, is it the same as what he held on the original planet, or has it been modified?

B. Indeed. He is the same. And I'm just gonna kick-start the other one, and modify it a little bit, because they're gonna be on Etena. So you might have done some adjustments on a cellular level so he would easier adapt on Etena, because it was different. Different atmosphere.

D. I would have had to have someone on the second to help with that, wouldn't I?

B. Ah, probably. It was not me, someone else. But you just moved him, so you didn't create him, so you might not have had help with that. You said that you somewhat dissolved the pattern and re-manifested the pattern on Etena, -maybe in that washer. In that washer something happened and he was more adapted to Etena. There is a higher level of oxygen available on Etena than it was on his old location. There was an outburst of volcanic activity that created the atmosphere, like a coughing atmosphere, and he was left behind. But he was also high up on the mountain and the other ones (*the human-like entities*) started to climb that mountain. So it was sort of—what I can see is that it just looked like the world was on pause, it just stopped suddenly. I see an image here of a movie with motion, and then suddenly it stopped, and then he was no more existent on that place.

D. I just snatched him away?

B. Took him away, put him in the washer, did something, popped him out there on Etena.

D. He's going to be so grateful to you. He'll know you were the one involved in this.

B. Ah. I wanted him to have someone like himself. But I'm working on it. I don't know how it will become there, but it involves the individuals on Etena.

D. Well, if Gergen and the councils have approved of this, I'm sure they will lend a hand.

B. Ah. So that's what I'm working on. And I have several ideas about my own evolution as well—where we can head with me and what we can do with me.

D. (*Laughing*) Gergen said you were making your own ladder. (*The intention the Creator has for a soul involves becoming progressively more knowledgeable in certain subjects, which the spirits call the ladder of learning.*)

B. Well, it's like, if there isn't any ladder—oh, Gergen said that there is—but I said, "Do you have to have just one?" I thought that maybe on my ladder I can add certain things in between the major events on my ladder; so I gave suggestions what we can do with me and what we can teach me and where we can send me, –for the higher good of others, of course.

D. Where did you want to be sent?

B. I want to explore the wheel, because I have seen the fish tanks and I have repeatedly asked about the other fish tanks, and I see myself moving through and getting new friends and learning and also teaching in different fish tanks. Because they might not have seen someone like me, for instance. So it's a win–win for everyone.

D. When did you first see the wheel? When were you exposed to that?

B. When we were in your lab and we created my individual and the solar system, you showed me the fish tank. But you didn't show me the full picture, so I did not see everything. But I suspected because I saw the pole and things on the other side, and then I saw and heard about those coming from the other side of the pole. So I kind of made a picture in my own being what that could be about and then gradually the image revealed itself. And as it did, especially now when I see that Seth is somewhat of a traveler–ambassador. He travels around in all different fish tanks, he say, and he just do a little bit here, do a little bit there, meet people probably there and here and here and there. So he likes to be in constant motion, because the wheel is in constant motion. He says that he prefers when it's—you both do—prefer where there is silence. There are different fish tanks that carry different tones that you are aware of, and some of them have a lower tone, and that's where you prefer to be. Don't prefer the high-pitched ones, like between 1 o'clock and 2 o'clock—those are lit up and high pitched. I don't know who wants to go there, I didn't volunteer for that; I volunteered to go with Seth as a travel companion if he felt lonely. He laughed about that, and you laughed and you say, "No, it's not lonely."

D. Would you be willing to travel with Seth all by yourself, or do you want me to come with?

B. I think it's better if everyone goes. I wouldn't mind if Ophelia and Zachariah and Jeshua also came, and Isaac. I like when Isaac is with because he's very—you all carry different personalities that are well adapted and well received by me. Like you, for instance, you bring me a lot of—I focus a lot with you—I think that's why I was given you and you were given me, because I needed to direct my thoughts, I needed to be centered and focused in my knowledge bank and my way to access knowledge. It was all over the place, like Gergen said to me one time, so he wanted me to collect my thoughts. That's what I feel with you, I feel very sure and very comfortable where my abilities lie with you. Zachariah has a similar sense of sending his presence to me, so that I feel very comfortable with my level of knowledge, and I feel very centered and sure about who I am and what I want to do. Seth, he's like that fun uncle that just comes in on Christmas and says, "Oh, here I am!" All sorts of fun, like charades—he likes to dress up in different characters that he knows I have seen, so he's the one that is funny, because some things are a little bit scary! It's scary to go through the pole and washer, so I might need Seth for that. It's not just to understand the process, which I would do with you, it's that I have to be somewhat diverted in my fear, and he's good with that. And then we have Ophelia, of course, oh, she hugs me when I feel that I'm far from home and I feel...she has the ability to, in some way, make me fall to sleep and to just relax. It's like being with Ia, and I like that. And then Isaac, he is the one, when my mind starts spinning and I start to question my abilities and what I want to do, then he comes in and gives extremely well-defined scenarios and thoughts.

D. I remember when he took you for a walk in the forest when you were worried about pairing up your students with new souls from the fifth.

B. Ah. So he always brings me additional perspectives. So if I can choose, then let's just rent a big bus and everyone goes. It could be like a grand field trip for everyone, –and who wants to steer the bus? Seth probably. I do want to have a window seat so I can see. Anyway, that's what I wanted to come and say today, I have things that I'm working on.

D. Well, that's wonderful. I really appreciate you making a companion for Siah.

B. Ah, so that's happening, I'm awakening the pattern of his companion.

The Pyramid of Light Bulbs (Nov 21, 2019)

To simplify complex topics, the spirits often turn to things we are familiar with. Here, the circuitry of the brain and energetic connections to the body and soul are allegorically presented as light bulbs and electrical sockets. Patterns for different light bulbs and sockets, which are unbelievably complicated, are stored in repositories on Etena so they can be reused. The physical brain of all animals, including humans, is a central processing unit with an operating system which interfaces with the body and the animating spirit. The body is built by codes programmed within the DNA by spirits on the second dimension. But the energy patterns embedded in DNA control much more than are physically observable. When animals act in certain ways, we say it is instinctual. But what does that really mean? We know that many behavioral instructions are coded into the DNA, but others are not. Plants and animals can think, feel and act with a certain amount of independence, and even coordinate actions as a group. They have a very open and pure connection to the Master Mind, but they still have individual responses to external situations. Humans are more complicated, because we have two minds. The physical mind is where decisions are consciously made, but the soul mind is located in the Center Point above the solar plexus. The connection between the two is tenuous, and the physical mind can ignore signals from the soul or the spirit guides. This is the essence of free will, where the conscious mind can elect to make decisions based on fallible thoughts and emotions, sensory inputs, or influences from the Coat of Karma. If the soul were in charge of the body, the challenges of the karma program would diminish.

Psychologists like to prattle about nature and nurture, but their superficial descriptions miss the supernal reality. Within the "junk" DNA are innumerable on and off switches that affect behavior, health, mental abilities, and physical traits (within limits). The genes of a fetus are edited by the incoming soul, according to the life purposes and karmic needs. Human nature, if defined properly, would include the control the soul has over the body, personality and health. The same applies to the idea of nurture. The soul influences how a body responds to external experiences, but it does so through filters. The sensitivity of the human brain to signals from the spirit realm and the fourth dimension has been intentionally impaired in modern humans. Our distant ancestors had a greater ability to communicate with the unseen world, and they were also more intelligent due to their larger brains. So when Bob talks about different sized light bulbs and matching sockets, it should be interpreted as various configurations of reasoning, emotional, physical and sensory abilities and the matching connections to the Master Mind or soul. As new models of life forms are created, there is a vast inventory of light bulbs and connections to choose from, all stored on a central location along with the patterns for the bodies.

The first part of Bob's talk was about the spirit guides oath, which is found later in the book. He then shifted over to telling how he had to select an operating system for Tess. In jest, I suggested he improve my brain a bit.

- D. I would appreciate more light, since I'm struggling to understand a lot of the topics.
- B. Ah. Well, I've been talking on your behalf with several councils on the second and with Ophelia. I'm trying to see if we could maybe just put in a stronger—

D. Light bulb?

B. Light bulb! Huhuh! One time I said, "I think his light is dimming. Maybe we need to switch?" and Ophelia said, "Okay, we can switch." So we did switch. But it hadn't been dimmed, it's just that you were not there, that was what caused you to dim, but the brain was the same. Ophelia, she's no fool, and everything has to go through Jeshua as well, and he's no fool. So I said, "I can go to the light bulb store and just find one." Because of the fact that there is, –and I did not know this–, but on Etena where there are all these pyramids that are storage units of things, there is actually one that carries different light bulbs, if you like, that you can plug into different entities. Ohh! And when I heard about that, I was like, "I might go to the storage unit of light bulbs," and there are like departments in there. There is Earth and you can see that there is a little teeny–tiny light, like a night-light there, and then you can see that it was a little bit bigger, like a volleyball; and then, at the moment, it's like a tennis ball. But you can still go and see (*previous versions*) in the museum. So I said, "Maybe I use a light bulb from another department?" Huhuhuh.

D. Find a brighter illumination.

B. Setalay took me, and you took me, on a tour in the light bulb pyramid, in the light bulb storage unit, and I saw all sorts of different lights. There was one that was only like night-lights, and I was like, "Oh, is this from the potato reality?" And you said, "Don't be confused about the size. This light bulb actually comes from entities occupying fish tank ten." But we don't know if there is more progress in ter., you did not say. But because of the fact of the way you said it then—because I said, "Oh, this must be for the potatoes," –then maybe size doesn't determine everything.

D. Is this a place that stores the patterns related to the mental?

B. Indeed. So I can see different containers where they have these—it looks like light bulbs, just to give you a picture, in different sizes.

D. I would be happy with a volleyball size.

B. Even if we could take the night-light from fish tank ten and put that in, but you say it might not mix and match, it might not connect. You say, "You can't just put in different lights, like an American plug into a European socket in the wall. It's the same thing." Ah, so I said, "Who creates the sockets?" You say, "That's a whole different council." Ophelia dragged me away when I asked that question. She said, "Come, why don't you and me and Setalay go and feed Siah." And I was like, "Uh?" But I remember! I remember my question because I wrote it down immediately as soon as I was able to. Because there is clearly someone who maneuvers and observes sockets.

D. Speaking of Siah, what's going on with his companion?

B. I am indeed creating, and it will be launched shortly. She looks exactly the same, I recreated the exact pattern. And I gave her a really nice collar. It's with crystals around. The crystals are pink and whiteish.

D. What about the memories she had?

B. It's the sockets. I will have to go in and get the light bulb that matches the socket in this being. So this is a whole new level of learning, because I never put in—since I left the work on the brain (*to travel and learn on the sixth*). But then this came up, that there is also somewhat of a switch of a light bulb situation, and the sockets needs to match the exact consciousness of this light bulb that is coming in, that you plug in. So when that discussion came up, because of the fact that I am creating Siah's companion completely, then I needed to know that. So I'm reconnecting not just the consciousness and awareness within the brain in this individual, but also the memory, because I want him (*Siah*) to feel that it is her—and it IS her—I'm just remanifesting her because she needs to be somewhere nice. The intention here that never came about, because of the fact that there was a snooze, a pause, is that they never got babies, and I'm making sure they're gonna have babies. They're gonna have several.

D. Oh, that's nice. We'll have to plant more greens.

B. They grow up kinda fast, you say. It's not like they are little long. They're sort of a hungry species, you say.

D. They won't have a life cycle, will they?

B. Nay. Well, they're gonna be babies and they're gonna become. But once they have become, they're gonna be a flock and they're not gonna reproduce more in that flock. They're gonna be just a big family. So there's gonna be Siah and the wife, kinda, and then there's gonna be six pups, probably, and that's gonna be it. And you said, "Not more, Bob, it cannot be more, and they cannot reproduce within the family, they're gonna be just like this, one big flock." And I said, "Yes, because they wanted a family and Siah never got to have a family because it was taken away." And I assigned myself to be like a caretaker. That was one of the criteria why this was allowed, it was that I would put in a lot of effort in being there and assisting. I might become a farmer just because of the fact to help with this growing need of feeding. Anyway, I'm gonna go now, but I'll be back the normal time.

D. Alright, my friend. It was really nice to talk with you. Thank you so much.

B. Ah. Thank you for listening. And thank you for taking me to the storage unit for all the light bulbs. I'm putting in a request to learn more about the sockets and the, huhuh, socket council!

D. When you figure it out, then you can come by and fix me.

B. I don't figure out things by myself. You have to help me, that is the trick. And sometimes you are not fully engaged. So we'll see about that. Anyway, I'll go now. Okay, bye bye.

Watching over Tess (Nov 28, 2019)

The record of Siah's companion, Tess, exists in the fourth dimension surrounding the original planet where she and Siah lived. Bob, with help from other specialists, implanted and reawakened most of those memories from the original Tess into the new Tess. As he is telling about this process, he jumps off on another topic which had sparked his interest. After he met a healing team on Etena, he thought it would be a good idea if they could go to Earth. And then he decided it would be best if they built an entire city, where people were healed in peaceful surroundings. He intends to propose it to the Council of Nine to see if they are interested. Such cities once existed on Earth during earlier civilizations. The Shea built a healing center on a small island northeast of Crete. The island sank into the sea about 15,000 BC from earthquakes and tectonic plate movement. Mythologies about Atlantis are related to those cities. In the next chapter, Bob gives a detailed accounting of the healing centers that once existed here.

B. I made progress!

D. On what?

B. On the being, Siah's friend. It's a pup.

D. A pup? Where is it located now?

B. With me in my study. Gergen said even if it looks like a pup, its consciousness is like an adult. I'm done with the modifications. It wasn't that tricky because I got the whole manual, so it wasn't like starting from scratch. I got all information because I was just restarting the pattern.

D. You didn't have to work on it too much then?

B. No. I just restarted the pattern and I observed the growth. It was like planting a seed, –but it's not like putting it in a pot with soil.

D. What is she doing? Does she follow you around?

B. No. The thing is, when I restarted the pattern, inside it is like an adult, but the physical hasn't caught up with the consciousness yet, so she is a pup. Inside she is as intelligent and aware and she remembers similar like Siah, but she is a pup. She was moving around kinda quickly in our labs, so Gergen said, "You made this, you have to tend to her, you have to take care of her." So I have been staying put. It's like having a baby, and this is my first baby, in many ways. I never had to care for someone like that. So I take her everywhere. It's a great responsibility. I call her Tess.

D. Tess. Does Tess eat?

B. AH, Ah. I have to tend to that. Inside Tess is similar like an adult, it's just that she has to grow up a little bit. She understands—I have actually not fully ignited the memory, because with the memory comes Siah. There is a healing team, you say, on standby on Etena as we are moving Tess there. Similar like what you did with Siah. As we ignite the memory—because we are not creating a new species, we are bringing Tess to life the way Tess was. So when Tess comes back in full consciousness and full memory, she will remember certain things, similar like Siah did. So there is a whole healing team on standby to attend to that as we later go to Etena.

D. What dimension is the healing team from?

B. On Etena they channel from the twelfth, they say. There is like a water they are gonna put her in. I say, "I don't know if Tess likes to swim." But they said it's a part of the healing, and

Siah did swim. Sometimes I see Siah kind of bathe a little bit and walk around in the water, but he's not like a fish. It's not like he dives down to the bottom, so I wasn't sure if Tess would like water because I've never seen Siah swim. But they said it's a healing water that exists there. It's a whole team of the best doctors you can find, like six that are gonna operate. Setalay is part of this group, she's a healer, she acts as this source of healing water. (*I think he means that Setalay is able to transmit healing energy directly from the source on the twelfth, which is also present in the water.*) So we're gonna use that later.

D. When Tess is wandering around with you—

B. Haha. Oh! Not wandering! Jumping or running, not wandering—that would be easy!

D. Do you let your students see her?

B. Ah. And that's the thing, that's the thing. They were like, "Is this your pet?" And I was like, "Ah," so everyone is really interested in Tess because she is very social. I can sense that once I push the button that consciousness and memories comes back, that she's gonna be HIGHLY inquisitive. She is probably more inquisitive than Siah, this lady version. But I haven't pressed that button yet, so in many ways she IS a pup. I showed Tom and the others.

D. Did they ask where she is from or where she is going?

B. I avoided it by saying this is just a project and it's a pet. But the problem is that later, when Tess is not here, they will ask, "What happened to the pet?" But it's a great responsibility; she is not on a leash and she jumps around kinda fast.

D. You're like her mother then?

B. Ah, I am indeed. But we are indeed about to soon gradually kick-start the memory, and the memory would be connected to a sensation of loss of Siah, in the beginning. She has to be healed herself first before we can introduce her to Siah, and that is sort of a border, a crucial phase where you have to heal yourself first and your own memories and experiences before you can rejoin. It's similar like when you leave this plane. You have to heal your actions and your thoughts and your perceptions about this plane before you can fully merge into the spirit realm. It's the same thing here with Tess, she has to heal her memory of the loss of Siah, among other things. And also, she will remember her home, where that was, and that also has to be healed and understood and left behind in order for her to surrender. As you surrender, that is when you transform. A soul surrenders in the fourth reality, in the later part, as it transitions into the spirit realm (*after death*). It's the same process, it's nothing different, really. So Tess has to go through that phase of self-healing, with a little bit of help from the greatest doctors and healers available! I said, "Why aren't these healers incarnating as doctors on Earth? Because there's a big need for them." I asked because I felt that, even though current doctors are capable of whatnot, this and that, but I asked if we could create a hospital, a healing center. I wanted to place it somewhere in Canada. It would be free and it would entail doctors who were incarnating from the doctor team here on Etena, similar like that, or only souls from the higher levels of seventh. So I wanted to create a hospital, almost like a city, so it's not just like a building. Saying, "I'm going to the hospital city" would be like saying, "Oh, I'm going to Miami." And everything would be free and there would be doctors operating directly from Source and having more connection to the puddle of healing energy from the twelfth. And there would be surgery that would be done with less harm, meaning that they don't have to—this is a trick—there are ways to operate, at least on Etena, where you don't have to put someone to sleep in order for them to fully be worked on and healed. A lot of it had to do with just putting them in the puddle, in the pool. So I drew a design and I wanted us to go to the Council of Nine with my drawing. It's like a city and there are hospitals, of course, but then when someone recovers and they don't need constant attention, instead of sending them home to some non-impressive location, then there are buildings and houses in this healing city where you can recover for a while, –so you are cared for there. And this is free! All governments provide a little of their total net worth and total income of the year, they provide about five percent to this new city that I created in Canada. I thought in Canada because it's less likely to be invaded.

D. The pharmaceutical cabal would have it bombed.

B. Oh, they're not there! They're still working in the little regular hospitals. But you can be granted to come there, and it's not just one hospital, it's a city, and I wanted that. Just so you know, that is on one of my projects. It has not been granted, which I don't understand, because this is helpful for everyone. I said, "I would be absolutely delighted to share some of the (*healing*) plants with this group, because they are not submissive to the pharmaceutical industry." They have their own healing resources in the pool and they have gardens and they have people working there, tending to the herbs and so forth. It's a completely different level of science. A lot of people can be treated not only in the puddle of water, but you can burn certain herbs and it becomes a smoke. That can also be used if you don't put someone in the pool. The extreme cases are treated with spiritual surgery which is different than the regular. You might wonder where this idea came from? Well, indeed, it existed way in the past in a smaller version—I just made it bigger!

D. Where was it located in the original version?

B. Ah, you know, outside Africa in the water, and then there was a hub in the Mediterranean for healing, a healing hub. So this is my new city, it's a healing hub. And I put it there so it's less likely that someone would just invade. It's like a neutral place because all countries give a little bit of their percentage, like five percent of their total yearly turnaround, and they put it there. So it's like Switzerland, it's neutral, meaning that no one has a need to invade; you would be invading yourself because you're part of this project. That's my idea. And then the extension of that thought is that all countries would be similar. If everyone has more of an interest, they are less likely to invade. This is a long-term project and at this time it's just on the drawing board. BUT what I wanted to say with that is that you cannot merge with a new reality, like Tess moving into Etena, unless she is fully healed; or a soul moving into the spirit realm, unless it has fully released and healed actions and thoughts and so forth in the fourth reality. So the process is similar, but at the moment she is just jumping around, we haven't pushed the button on the memory yet. Tom likes her.

D. I would imagine everyone likes her.

B. Ah, everyone likes her. The sparkles, because of the fact that some of them saw me draw Siah, so here comes questions. At first, they wondered if this was Siah because they never really knew how big he was, and I said, "No, this is just a smaller one. It's going to grow to the size of Siah eventually, but this is a girl." And then some were like, "Oh? Will there be more coming, like pups of them?" And I said, "Well, not here." They are really interested, and because they saw me draw Siah they wanted to tend to Tess. But a lot of times Tess is just sleeping. I have a basket in my office—it's not like I put her somewhere and then I leave. She has to be constantly monitored and if she wakes up, I have to be there. So wherever I go, Tess goes. It's like when you tend to a baby elephant that has been an orphan, it can't be left alone because it gets depressed, and I don't want her first level of feelings to be depression. So at the moment we are doing joyful activities here on the second. But she sleeps a lot too, but when she's not sleeping, she doesn't wander around, like you say, she runs and jumps around. We're introducing certain things, and little by little we are gradually igniting the memory. We're gonna go to gardens and see like birds and butterflies and different things, to gradually start to remember vegetation because there was vegetation at that time. I have been given a little bit of a manual from Etena on what I gradually should warm her up for, before we fully push the button on the memory—and then we move her to their care. And who wouldn't want to be in THEIR care? Siah was there (*with the healers on Etena*), you placed Siah there. It's a long sleep first, you say, where they just put—the first thing they do when they come there, you say, and what they did with Siah, is that you put a big blankie on him and he was just sleeping for a long time under this blankie. It provided heat but it also ignited certain cellular, emotional DNA—it warmed him up in some way. So I think that maybe he was frozen when he came, I don't know, like a popsicle. I don't know if he was frozen when he came. I'm not sure if I want to put Tess in the freezer, but you say it didn't travel in a peanut suit, so maybe they go through some sort of freezing. But I'm not sure I want to freeze Tess, I'm not sure she would like that. But I'll leave that to those who are more medically skilled. So that's ongoing here. I–I–I do tend to that and it takes a lot of effort. It's not just a walk in a park to have a pup, I'll tell you that. And Ia came and I said, "Do you want to be with Tess for a while?" And she said, "No, if Tess wakes up, she needs to see you because you're like her mother. This is what we do when we work with the egg—you have to be present; they have to recognize the same individual. So I stand next to the egg, and you stand next to Tess." So I said, "So this is like your egg!" At the moment she's just sleeping here in the basket. (*He leaned forward and was looking down at the floor.*) I have to be a little bit quiet.

D. This is like a teaching about how to be present and patient with something.

B. Something that is beyond my control in some ways. Like when I had my individual, he was placed somewhere and I just looked in on him now and then, traveled there. But now, here we are (*looking at the floor again*). So it's not the same, and it's very important that if she wakes up, she's not alone. You made that perfectly clear to me. But she's growing out of the basket, so I'll probably have to have a bigger basket soon.

D. You might have to have a bigger office if she gets as big as Siah before you move her.

B. Ah. I don't know where we're gonna be then, but Gergen said we have a room where we put us.

D. What does Gergen think about all of this?

B. Gergen, he kinda laughs. He said, "This is a part of growing up, Bob. This is you becoming a parent, a full-time parent." So it's part of my development, clearly. When I tend to you (*as a spirit guide*), when I go with you, in the beginning it was similar like a parenting thing. But like I say, I can withdraw and come and go. When you sleep, I don't have to just sit there and stare. I don't have to do that much, so I can tend to other things of my choosing. But here, I am constantly present with the same amount. It's like I adopted her. That will make me feel like I have great responsibilities on Etena, because she will miss me, and I'm already friends with Siah. But I will also, you say, once they are introduced, I will have to step back a little bit, because they have to reunite and connect their beings. I don't want to come back and just be like a grandfather and tend to little ones all the time, but I look forward to little ones coming because I have that in my manual here about the levels of what's gonna happen. So it IS gonna happen that they are gonna be a flock, and I do like that.

D. That will be fun.

B. Ah, that will be fun. But I don't know how I can tend to them all. But you say it's not like I have to tend to them all because

Tess and Siah are parents, so I can just be that fun uncle coming in.

D. You'll have to be the farmer that supplies the food. Didn't you say you were going to have to help raise greens?

B. I'm gonna be with Setalay and assist. It's not like a project that ends. I adopted Tess as my pet and I'm gonna make sure that they are taken care of. If Siah is your pet, then Tess is mine.

D. That's really nice that we both have similar companions.

B. Ah. So that would be it. I don't want to wake her up here, but just letting you know what's happening. Later we can talk more about my city. You said that's very futuristic and optimistic.

D. That's funny—futuristic and optimistic. At least for humans in their current state.

B. I don't see why not, just give a little bit of each economy and create this place of free medical aid. And also, sometimes some people just need to rest, to be in silence. There are zones here in my city that are just for silence.

D. It would have to be a pretty big city to accommodate all the people that will want to go there.

B. Well not everyone can go there. But it's kinda big. It would be like the size of Miami, that is my intention. It's not just a building with a pool in the back. There are several different functions here. You have the gardeners tending to the earth and so forth; you also have the accommodations for those who are recovering who don't need medical care but need to recover. And then there is also the silent zones. In the silent zones you are allowed to get inner recovery. You might not need physical recovery but you might need inner help, and I wanted to provide that. I don't see why this can't work.

D. I like the way you think. I know Edgar Cayce talked about light and sound being used for healing in the distant past.

B. Ah, ah. They used that.

D. Good luck with getting that set in motion.

B. Ah. In my futuristic and optimistic idea. Anyway, I'll go now because I don't know if she's waking up here (*looking towards his feet again*). She does snore a little bit. She's really delightful, she's really cute. She's like a small Siah.

D. You never had a pet before?

B. Nay. I mean, the Individual is kind of a pet, but I released him and I let him be. I didn't stay with him all the time and I didn't nurse him all the time.

D. What do you feed her?

B. Oh, she does like fruit, sweet fruit. Not apple because her teeth hasn't grown yet so there's nothing to bite. But like a raspberry for instance, that sort of melts when you have it on your tongue. And mango, those sort of things, sweet things. Ah, I'll go now, but I just wanted to let you know about my progress.

D. Thank you for doing that. Siah's going to be really happy.

B. Ah! It's gonna be a big surprise! It's like, "Shh," we're not telling yet. Okay, I gotta go now.

D. Alright, my friend. Thank you so much, it was a lovely story today.

B. Ah. Okay, bye bye.

Update on Tess (Dec 8, 2019)

After Tess has grown bigger and Bob begins to reawaken the memories of her previous life, the healing team is summoned to help her recover and heal. They work on her on the second and will continue to heal her once she is moved to her new home on Etena.

B. Ah. So, Tess has grown! She doesn't have a basket! Nay, she's the same size now as Siah.

D. What are you doing with her now? Does she still sleep a lot?

B. Nay. Nay. It doesn't help that I sing or hum, she doesn't sleep. I think it's because we have started to ignite the memory and she feels that something is up, but she doesn't know exactly WHAT is up, only that something is. So there are gonna come a group that will prepare the movement, you say and Gergen say. I see them, they're dressed in white here. They work gradually with her. She's still like a wild animal, so she doesn't respond that well to what is new. So I'm there. And these in white, we meet, –it occurs here because she is only familiar with here. They transform their energy and work on her here (*on the second*). It's to establish a safety and a trust. You should know that this specific species is very into trust. They give their trust easily and they trust and they give freely, but if that trust is broken it's not like they hold a grudge, but that link of trust to that specific source is gone, it's deleted. They don't hold a grudge, it just disappears.

D. I guess she trusts you?

B. She trusts me, indeed! So I'm going here to these transformation meetings, preparing her for the movement that is coming up.

D. Does she still run around?

B. Well, she rotates, she turns and looks at all these people because they're new. Eventually they are allowed close and they pet her and the trust is established. So I've been with Tess and we have started to ignite the memory, that's what we've been trying to do here. Gradually she's gonna remember Siah and when that comes, that is the cue to go.

D. Have you been over to Etena to see Siah?

B. Well, not really. I'm pretty sure, because Siah is very intelligent, and I think that he can sniff that there is something going on, and he might smell her on me, so I'm avoiding that. But I don't want him to feel like I have left, so I communicate with him like I do with you, with butterflies. There are butterflies there, so I'll send them to him and he knows that I'm with him, and I send to him that I'm just engaged with other things at the moment. Because I'm pretty sure that he would smell her on me in some way and just sense that there is something there. It's supposed to be a surprise.

D. That will be a nice surprise.

A Little Rocket Ride (Dec 12, 2019)

From the many personal accounts Bob shares, a general picture of life in the spirit world emerges. It is full of purposeful activities, intermixed with learning, teaching, and leisure. But through it all, there is a deep compassion for one another and a tremendous amount of joy. The joy sometimes takes the form of playful tricks, and Seth occasionally takes advantage of Bob's naiveté to introduce humor into a situation. At this point in the story of his life, Bob is aware of a device used to transport a soul from the sixth dimension to locations within certain fish tanks. It rearranges the soul particles to match the destination and then projects the soul to the desired planet. Bob calls it a washer (like a washing machine) for our benefit, because it causes a spinning sensation.

Since he wants to travel to these areas, he has no choice but to learn how it works. He was feeling a little unsure about these upcoming training activities, so Seth decided to play a trick on him to help him relax. Seth's purpose, aside from entertainment, was to let Bob experience a little bit of the vibration associated with travel. When Christine is channeling a spirit, they always refer to her as "this one". Depending on the context, they are either talking about the incarnation, or about Seth, her higher self.

B. You know what this one did?

D. No.

B. We were gonna go training for my washer activity, and I said, "I'm not sure I'm ready for the tumbling, as of yet." So this one said, "You don't have to tumble, we can do it in another way." And I said, "What is that?" And he put something on me, on my back. He said, "It's like a rocket," and he sort of taped it around me, put it on me like a backpack. And I said, "What is this?" and he said, "There will be like a big bang. This will make you sort of shwheee, shwheee, (*Bob made a circling motion with his head*) go around the wheel. You can just have a looksee and then you can maybe have an opinion where your washer should be directed and where you want to go." And I said, "Is that possible? Can I go like that, just around like shwheee, shwheee? And is this really safe to do so, and have you done this?" And he sort of mumbled something and I was like, "Okay, we'll see here." Then he put that on me and it started to ignite and I didn't leave—we were in a room, similar like the sphere room—but it made a lot of noise. It's like (*he then made a deep rumbling sound like a rocket lifting off*). I didn't leave, but I had lifted a little bit. And then you came and you said, "What's going on in here?" And this one was like, "We're playing." And I said, "He said that I can go shwheee, shwheee, go around the wheel before I put myself in the washer, just have a looksee and see if I wanna go." And then you said, "No," and you fixed it, you took it off really quickly.

D. He was just messing with you.

B. Ah. He does that, messes with me. He said, "This is like high-end cosmic engineering and cosmic travel, where you just sort of tumble." And I said, "I'm not sure about the tumbling," and he said, "Well, you know, it's just to get you used to the feeling."

D. That's probably why you're not allowed to hang around with Seth, he's not very safe.

B. He's not known as the safest person in this reality! But he is absolutely known as one of the most bold ones. And I like bold and I want to be bold! (*He gave a nervous laugh*) And I am! I am bold. But he does that sometimes to somewhat put a lid on my boldness, he says. He said he does that to make me think before I just take off in all my ideas about what I want to do. But he's quite bold and he's fearless, and I want to be fearless too! But it hasn't fully blossomed in me yet. I'm fearless but I tend to be a little bit cautious.

D. That's good. You'll eventually get to explore the wheel, just not like that!

B. Ah. But I did ask, of course, I said, "Did you go with a rocket on your back, just take a loop around before you decided where you wanted to go?" And you said, "No, not with a rocket like that; he plays with you. But you can absolutely travel." You said that you traveled remotely in your mind. You said, "It's not like my whole being took off with a rocket on my back."

D. That sounds a lot safer.

B. Ah. And I said, "Why didn't we try that? Why didn't we make me remotely travel?"

D. I would think you should be able to tap into different realities.

B. Well, it's the fact of the different vibrations in there, and I think that is what he wanted to try to convey, that I have to be somewhat comfortable with a little bit of turbulence, he says. Huhuhuh. You said the same thing when I went to Etena in my peanut suit; you said, "There's going to be a little bit of turbulence but you have to master it, you have to power through." And then Seth said, "There are other realities where you won't have like a crash–cushion of Lasaray, where you have to master the turbulence by yourself. So this is an easy way to see if you can even endure turbulence," with this rocket that he put on me. But I understand the purpose of the rocket. It was so that I settle down and not just stumble around and think that I can take off anywhere. Because now I'm not fully sure about that. I mean, I'm pretty developed in my travel skill set, as I have left now for Etena, but sometimes you have to also be content. I got a feeling that I am content, and I think the rocket helped me with the decision of being content. So sometimes he does that to make me take a step back—and you know that, so you allow it to happen. You tried to talk to me and I'm sometimes like (*he started whistling and looking around, showing he doesn't listen.*) But then this one has a different approach and just does things hands-on, and it becomes quite clear to me what the end result could be if I'm not prepared. The lesson was whether or not I'm ready for turbulence.

D. I'm sure we still have plenty to do on Etena.

B. Ah. But that looks nice to sort of glide in on a cloud!

The Big Sleep for Tess (Dec 12, 2019)

It may seem that descriptions of how spirits move from one reality to another, or how entities are transported, have little value to a human. But as we have previously said, they wouldn't tell us if they didn't want us to know. After the original Tess was killed, Lasaray went to rescue Siah. The pattern of Siah was instantly frozen, like stopping a movie. After the molecular action ceased, the pattern was moved to Etena and reawakened. The two planets are both physical realities, but when Tess was moved, it was from a spiritual reality to a physical planet. So she was put to sleep and relocated using some other method. Once she arrived on Etena, a healing team worked on her while she slept.

We know from NDE accounts that a person's entire life, down to the most minute details, is available during a past life review. The spirits have assured us the memories of all the successive incarnations of a soul are available within the fourth dimension surrounding a planet. But on a larger scale, the memories of planets, solar systems, galaxies, and entire universes are also recorded. Bob tells us the records are kept in cocoons within one of the pyramids on Etena. For those councils who work on modifying existing planets or galaxies, the information about the past would be invaluable.

D. You can travel to Etena pretty easily now, can't you?

B. I can indeed, I can indeed. It's not such a big thing. I do travel in my peanut suit but I simply sort of step out of it, if you like, when I arrive. I have been there because Tess is about to...she's sleeping now and she's not gonna wake up, you say, until she wakes up on Etena. I'm a little bit concerned about the inner organs, because you say, "It's like pausing. If you think of Siah and Tess, when Siah was moved, I paused the reality, I simply made it frozen (*instantaneously stopped*) in its molecules, and then I sort of collected the color pattern, the DNA pattern, of Siah and I removed it from that reality, from that memory. I shifted him to Etena using a different kind of travel, where you pause, you collect DNA color pattern molecules, collect them and reignite them somewhere else. You can only do that if it is a motion or movement between similar realities of life forms. Where Siah was, to where Siah went, are both physical realities." You say, "It's not like dying, because when you die your physical pattern dissolves and you transform into spirit. But if you want to fully remanifest a pattern and a life form, then it has to be compatible realities. And Etena is similar to where Siah came from, they're both considered physical realities. So if Etena had been less dense or more of a mental reality, it would have been impossible to move the pattern and re–awaken Siah there." But with Tess, she's coming now from the second dimension, so it's different. You say, "It's not like she is going to dissolve in the same way, like Siah did, because Siah went from a physical to a physical reality. Tess was patched up and awakened from an existing pattern in a spiritual home, before she will be reunited into a physical reality." So it's not gonna be the same, you say. Tess is not gonna dissolve—because I was concerned about that, if she was gonna dissolve—and you said, "No, she's not going to dissolve, she is simply going to move. It will appear," you say, "that she just travels on a cloud." This cloud is not just a transportation device, –I don't know why I didn't get a cloud, why I had to go through all this bubble training and spinning before I was put in a peanut suit! Why couldn't I go on a cloud?

D. Do you want to be dissolved?

B. Nay!

D. Do you want to be put to sleep?

B. Nay! And you said, "This is because you were not put to sleep," and that's why I had to travel differently. But it's a transportation device for motion. "It's just a different way to travel," you say, "and she's gonna be activated on this cloud but she's just going to be sleeping. When she arrives, she will be sleeping for a while in an energetic cocoon to help her adapt," you say.

Teachings from Etena and Tiddle 173

D. I'm sure that moving a living creature to Etena has been done before.
B. Ah. You say, "Everything on Etena has traveled there in some way." If you think of a greenhouse planet, but it's not just for vegetables; it's for life forms and manifested occurrences like crystals and so forth, and beings. So everything has traveled there, it is built as a gathering reality for all types of different life forms in different fish tanks," you say.
D. Would you guess it to be about the same size as Earth?
B. Nay, it's smaller.
D. Have you ever seen any water or oceans?
B. I've seen waterfalls because Siah took me. But I have not seen outside of this area where they live. You say, "This is like the central hub where those who are in charge and operate on Etena exist." But you say there are other societies outside of where I have been. They come there and they look the way they are, but they all need to travel there differently. Not everyone is allowed to stay, so it's not a place where you go and stay, –unless you are Siah, but that is different. You simply go there and you can leave off teachings or remains (*patterns of life forms*) from realities. You say, "In the storage unit, it is not just physically manifested forms, it is a little bit of everything."
D. There are energetic forms there too, aren't there?
B. There are, indeed, but I have not been allowed in there.
D. Kindly directed elsewhere. (*Bob told how he tried to go look around in the storage pyramid at forms from other fish tanks, but the ones who work there gently directed him back to the fish tank five area.*)
B. I sort of thought I could trick them by saying, "I'm looking for Setalay, I think she went in here!" Hehehe. But they always seem to know—I don't know if they can read my mind, those who tend to this place. It's like a vault, but a huge one. There's a lot of workers here. But I have seen you go in there (*into one of the storage pyramids*), and when you come out, sometimes you are different. You are very–, I mean, it's not like you are bouncy as a personality–, but when you come out of there, you sometimes look like your light capsule has gone away a little bit, you're very tired. And you say that you dock in there sometimes with different reality cocoons, where you can step

into and refill. (*I think by refill, he means that Lasaray supplied the energy to read the contents of the cocoon.*) When you do that, when you merge with different levels of understandings, you say it also wears a little bit on the energy flow. When you came out you looked a little bit—not drunk—but I stood there and I wanted to know what happened. And you said, "I need to be by myself a little bit. I'll be right with you, but I need to recharge myself again." And I said, "What did you do in there? Why are you like that? What did you find, and why did it affect you like this?" And you said, "It's just because I merged with different cocoons, I sort of step into them and I absorb the knowledge related to that specific cocoon, but," you said, "to compare it, it is like going into a library and opening a book, –but I step INTO the book." Then I said, "What sort of books would that be?" And this specific time you said, "I stepped into the book that related to fish tank eleven." And I said, "What did you read? How many chapters? And what did this specific cocoon entail? What did it say to you?" And you said, "You have to learn how to listen with your inner being, and you dock with the reality. But instead of going there, you step into the cocoon." And this exists here on Etena. I'm not sure if it exists in the spirit realm somewhere else too. So I said, "Instead of me shooshing around with a rocket, maybe I just step into the book to get a preview, just look before I tumble?"

D. Would the cocoon be specific information from a fish tank or the realities within?

B. Well, you said that you stepped into the cocoon that was related to fish tank eleven, and you were looking into a magnetic field that was healthy; you wanted to use some of the knowledge there for repair work. And I said, "Repair work where?" And you say, "It's repair work here in the fifth."

D. If only I could remember.

B. That's why you have me, so that's why I tell you! And you do visit these different cocoons here. It's like a huge, separate building that I have not been invited to, even though I have volunteered.

D. Are you going to help Tess adjust, or just turn it over to the healing team?

B. You said that I have to take a step back, because Siah is gonna teach her everything, and it's important the two of them establish a reconnection again, –and I shouldn't meddle, you say. Then I say, "Maybe what we could do in that sense, like if I take a step back but am still very present, we could go and look at the cocoons."

D. That's a good thought.

B. You did come out a little bit thoughtful. Like I said, you're not bouncy in your personality as is, but you were slower and more reflective in nature when you came out. And I was like, "Something happened in there."

D. It would be nice to know what.

B. Ah. You could easily tell me, I'm pretty sure you can tell me if you wanted to. But sometimes you say, "It's not to be confused." And I say, "I know when you say that, eventually I will not be confused and you will tell me." That's my theory. And you say, "It might not always be." So far, in my current understanding, if I'm just patient, then it will be delivered in some way as a treat. Because I believe in treats!

D. Do you and I always travel to and from Etena together?

B. Ah, even though I said, "You don't have to hold my hand, maybe I can go by myself." But you always say you have an errand anyway. Maybe I cannot go by myself and that is a kind way for you to say that, –that you have engagements there anyway. But it might be that I cannot go by myself even though I feel like I can. Sometimes I do feel—and that is part of the fact that I feel a little bit bold—that once I have passed the threshold of something new and I have come to terms with 'new is not new anymore', then I tend to be a little bit of a daredevil and want to do things by myself. I think that is what Seth tried to show me, that if I try to do things by myself, it will be similar to going with a rocket and the turbulence, and I am not comfortable with turbulence as of yet. And he said, "All thresholds are in some way related to turbulence." And you know that I am not comfortable with that, so it might be why you escort me.

D. We're good friends and we take care of each other.

B. Ah. So that is what I wanted to tell you about that today, so I'm gonna go now.

Previous Occupants of Earth (Dec 8, 2019)

When Christine and I hold a trance session, we never know who is going to speak. We have been told there are multitudes of spirits and councils who observe, but only a select few get to communicate. Ophelia occasionally invites guest speakers to convey specific information. Anna is a spirit who currently incarnates on a planet in the Andromeda galaxy. She incarnated on Earth during an earlier civilization that existed about 5 million years ago. A mix of Master Mind and soul occupied the humanoid bodies, so the Coats of Karma were different. Societies, at that time, were spiritually and technologically superior to our own. After her Coat was folded on Earth, Anna began to incarnate on another planet. When she says she is right next door in Andromeda, it highlights how little we understand about the Universe we occupy. Visitors to our planet can manipulate certain energetic components of the third dimension, and by using the interstellar highways located in parallel realities, they are able to traverse vast distances outside of the limitations we perceive as space and time. One of the concerns she voiced was the drilling and depletion of the oil and gas resources. The hydrocarbons are vital to the cycles on Earth. Even though we do not understand their function, oil and gas are called the Earth's blood, and are needed to rejuvenate the fork.

Although 'A' is normally an abbreviation for Ari, in this session it is Anna who speaks.

A. Hello there to you, hello there to you. Here we are, here we are. (*She sang for a moment, apparently testing out the vocal equipment.*) Neighbors, neighbors, neighbors invited by Ophelia. Oh, let's see, there are several here who wish to talk.

D. What is your name?

A. You can call me Anna.

D. Alright. Hello, Anna.

A. How are you on your planet? We are neighboring, we are from the galaxy next door, observing the activity that occurs—female polarity, friends with Etena but not in that space; you call it fish tanks, no, no we are not there, we are not there, we are next door, next door.

D. Like in Andromeda?

A. Yes. There you go, there you go, just next door. We are observing the activity because we have indeed experienced some of the same struggles as do you. Because we are in the same fish tank, we also fall under the spell of time. Everyone in this space, this box—fish tank that you call it—falls in some way under the spell of time. However, whereas you have one kind of cycle, ours is longer. So you have 365 days in your cycle, we have 525.

D. I think Ari or Eli mentioned a planet with 500 and some days in the year.

A. Friends, stopping by sometimes. We are similar as humans, looking quite alike. Our skin, to give you a picture of how we appear, we appear female on this specific location. Not everyone, of course, but from where me and my friends are sending signals to you today, we appear female. You would probably see us similar as those on Etena. However, we are in some way incarnating similar as you; we traveled here and we leave. It's a way to occupy space and grow projects that is not available in the same way in either the spiritual realities OR in realities only carrying energetic form. So we are practicing molding light in order for it to, –let's just say, we are the co-creators of snow. We like to play with light and form and, in some way, snowflakes are a residual gift that we enjoyed here. I wouldn't say that we have snow necessarily, even though we are fully capable of creating snow if we choose to. However, the climate here in Andromeda is quite different. When me, myself, wandered here on Earth, as many of us have—we simply prefer a more quiet experience at this time—yes, yes indeed, Coats folded on Earth. Coats open in Andromeda. (*Ophelia must have suggested Anna say that they completed the human cycle and were thus able to move to a different location for new experiences.*)

D. So, do you actually incarnate the way humans do, by taking on the body of a baby?

A. Yes indeed, in similar way.

D. Are you then stuck in the body?

A. Well, we have more opportunities, more options I would say, than do you. Here on Earth, after someone has folded their Coat, then yes indeed they can come and go a little bit, like you did—and we did observe that. We do observe others with no Coats who somewhat dim their soul. When you dim a soul, that indicates in some way a departure; but most souls coming here do not operate their experience in that way. They come in with one amount of their soul capacity and that remains until the mission is fulfilled. The experience in Andromeda is a bit different. We have the option to dim, meaning we can come and leave, but we do not fully exit. It's not like leaving an empty shell, but we can dim and also withdraw more light from our soul energy, if that is necessary. You do not have the same options here (*on Earth*) because you have not mastered the cycles within you that is needed in this atmospheric reality.

D. Does your body age?

A. Yes, indeed. I would be considered, in human terms, a very young 50 year-old. But I look much younger. I would say that I'm similar to a 50 year-old person on Earth, however, my appearance looks like I am 30. So we age physically slower, and we grow consciously faster.

D. When you say you observe activities on Earth, how do you do that?

A. Oh, it's similar like remote viewing, if you like. We have big screens that monitor activity, and what we are interested in is the shifts in your atmosphere, as that is something, myself, as well as others who came down to Earth at that time, were highly connected to. It had to do with the different waves, solar activity, that came to exist and develop on the Earth plane. So we were here in a civilization that is long gone. My Coat was folded, –you should also know that the Coat program, the karma program, has changed. It's not the same Coats now as when I was there, it's probably out of fashion at this time. But in human years, my Coat was folded five million years ago. We were there in a civilization that was highly intellectual, as well as we worked with biology and the elements and how to connect Earth elements to the upper elements, creating rains, if you like. We had the ability to, in more of a friendly fashion, manipulate weather phenomena. We do not necessarily approve of the way you try to mirror that project. (*Governments nefariously use microwave energy, geoengineering and high energy radio waves for weather manipulation.*)

D. How did you do it?

A. Huh huh huh huh huh (*she gave a very gentle laugh*). Well, we used the resources at hand and we used solar disks and we turned them to different—if you see a satellite, but the satellite was located on Earth, and it withdrew the solar energy, and the disk was shifted to work with the upper web that had a similar receptive disk. So we worked with satellites, similar as do you. We only used wind and solar energy in order for occurrences to take place. If we wished for, let's say, a spot to have rain in order for growth, then we moved the disks away from the sun and we only used the wind. It's a way to combine the elements that you possess but you use the disks based on the understanding of the web as a whole. The web below your feet, as well as understanding the power web that you possess in your atmosphere. Current man doesn't understand how to read the power web below them, simply dig around like grasshoppers in your resources. Even oil and gas were used in order for shifts—oil and gas is not just to make a vehicle move around. It is a way for the Earth to tell what...hmm...that specific location, whether it's a sea or a landmass, what it is in need of. The oil that exists under the sea bed is to stabilize the motions within the seas. If the seas are imbalanced, then what you see is the occurrences of weather phenomena above. You do not understand the correlation of that what you excavate and what you take from the resources below your feet have an impact on what occurs above your head. So there we go. I have a great interest, such as my friend here (*she must have projected her consciousness here, along with a friend from her home*) We kind of look human–like, and we have a great interest in Earth because we have all folded Coats here. Our Coats were quite different, I'm not sure I would even master a current Coat! I don't even know what it entails.

D. You're lucky you got out early.

A. Ya! Huh, huh, but we do work closely with the second dimension, and so did the entire civilization—all the Coats that were down at my time on Earth. That is the difference. The little ones, they will tell you when you are not supposed to excavate a mineral or an element, like oil or gas. You should know, and you should take great interest and pride that you have such helpful little friends that tell you what you yourself do not know! So what we see, let's say up in what is now called Alaska, we do see that there is...we send our prayers to that region because we see the ocean and the little beings in the ocean—physical as well as non–physical—are trying to send a signal to those above who master the machinery (*humans who are drilling for oil*) to be careful because it will eventually, if nothing is corrected, it has the possibility that the sea becomes angry and it will send a signal to the poles, and the poles are the masters of the whole planet, making it tilt or not tilt. And you do not want it to tilt because if it tilts it will manifest floods. So I'm just saying, listen to the little people in the seas and listen to the ones that you don't see (*spirits like Bob, from the second*) because they are fully aware of what goes on beneath the seabed. Do not excavate resources that are not meant for cars or for something else! Some are meant to just make your host operate or to communicate with the energetic web, the power web above. And the power web above can help very little to balance this because of the fact that it is somewhat in symbiosis with the lower web. What you see when you do all these changes—that you are not fully aware of what is the end result of your activity—is that the power web dissolves above you. And that is the end result of what later will make certain weather phenomena. You tend to be observant of those but it would be nice if you could observe it earlier, when it did not become a storm and it did not become a tsunami, when it did not become an earthquake, let's say. Some however are planned, like some earthquakes—it is to move spines and those have nothing to do with the Coats of you. I'm just saying, pay attention to what occurs below your feet because it affects the power web that is above. And the power web above has very little impact, it somewhat follows what occurs below. So the below web is the director of how the power web above functions. THERE! That was what I was supposed to say. Thank you, Ophelia, for inviting me. It was a true pleasure to talk to the current Coats. HUH HUH HUH. Oh, they work with different things, do they? (*Anna was talking to Ophelia.*) Yes they do. A lot of greed. Greed in Coats, that's strange, that did not exist before.

D. I have two questions, if you don't mind.

A. Yes?

D. Does the Earth naturally regenerate oil?

A. Indeed, but not in the amount used. If you take too much, it has not the possibility or ability to rejuvenate and restore. It is similar like your blood, if you give blood in the hospital, you later rejuvenate. It's not like you run out of blood, –it's the same thing.

D. And then my second question is, if you had an advanced civilization here five million years ago, are the archaeologists likely to find any remnants?

A. Oh, they can indeed. However, it has tilted a little bit. We existed in the North Americas as well as the South Americas. So what you detect is that there was no soul here. But that is not necessarily true, is it, since WE were here, the Coats were here. (*Anna means that a type of incarnation program was active.*) At that time a lot of the other continents were more asleep. Like the continent of Africa was somewhat asleep. We used it to absorb solar energy, we did not occupy the space. It was high in minerals here in the north Americas. So yes, this is where I was located. Have a great fondness of this country, and this is also what I said about what you now call Alaska, we did travel and we communicated with—there is a big puddle of resource under the seabed there that you should leave alone for the time being. If you disturb, it tends to create a ripple in the below web, it creates a crack in your below web, but you can't see it because it is underwater. The effect, however, can be tremendous and it can impact the poles as well as the power web above. So, your question about how and if it can rejuvenate—yes indeed it can. But it's like if you have a piece of land, you grow your carrots and you grow your potatoes but after a while the soil also needs a break, so you move and grow on a different location on your plot. It's the same thing here.
D. Okay, I understand that. Thank you.
A. I'm pretty sure we might return, but just know that you have friends next door that observes the activity that goes on. Me, myself, observes the activity of resources and the atmospheric shifts, and how you manipulate the resources, both in your elements and minerals, as well as the effect it has on the webs.
D. When you were here, did you incarnate the way that we do, by taking on a baby's body?
A. Yes. However, the filters within the human vehicle were different and we had...what I can see now is that the vehicles—if I compare the vehicles available in my cycle and the vehicles available now—it is that the vehicles now are more contaminated. They seem to be subject for pollution, both outside as well as what you eat. So it's harder, it's heavier. If I look at the vehicles available at my time, the vehicle wasn't as heavy, it was lighter and it was a pure joy, because you could maneuver your soul energy more lightly

than you can now. There were less contradicting energies exposing the physical body and especially the mind. What we see is that the mind is highly affected by the occurrences that goes on in the web above you. And since our web was considered a friend and we listened to the wind and the web and the friends from the second dimension who guided us, then our minds were clear and it was easier to maneuver the physical body than it seems to be now.

D. Well, I guess you must have had a physical form that was similar to the modern human?

A. Yes indeed, yes, indeed.

D. In what way was it different?

A. We had a stronger connection to the Master Mind. The Master Mind was more available in the mental capacity. As of now, what I can see, there is still a little sparkle in your solar plexus area where the Master Mind can connect to the entity if it chooses to. So you still have a little bit of a snowflake within you; however, we had a connection within our mental capacity. If you see a humanoid at your current time, the Master Mind is a light dot in the center core of your being. Whereas when we were here, the Master Mind filled from the solar plexus and up. Different. Lighter to move.

D. Wonderful. That's good to know and very helpful.

A. So thank you for listening to your neighbors and just know that we are there. Please communicate with us because we do appreciate it. We know the struggles that you go through and we have also been in the Coat program, so we somewhat understand, even though the Coats were very different.

D. It was so nice to meet and talk with you. I really appreciate the information.

A. I do like to have a human name, even though my spiritual name is different. It's a name I used a lot of times as I traveled to Earth, it's an Earth name. So there you go.

D. Thank you, Anna.

A. See you. Bye bye, bye bye.

D. Talk soon, I hope.

A. If allowed, yes indeed.

D. Okay. Bye bye.

B. Ah!

Teachings from Etena and Tiddle   183

D. You just popped right in?

B. Oh, I know those.

D. You know them?

B. Ah, ah. They were here when I was here. I saw them. Different. I saw them. I was not a toddler, I was all sorts of grown up. I saw their activity, I know. That's why I also say things to Ophelia, like, "I know certain things have been done, so maybe we can change, because I observed that it was done before."

D. How long did that civilization last?

B. Oh...fifty, a hundred thousand years, they were here for a long time. Ophelia says, "Longer. You did not observe them fully." But I saw them when they were moving around.

D. This must have been before I started incarnating?

B. You and I did not go, but you were probably here in a different kind of form, who knows? But I did see them and I know that they are friends. So I wasn't excluded, I was allowed to have a listen because I have seen them before, even though I did not engage with them in that sense. I observed Gergen, he communicated with them, showed them where to go and how to use elements. So he communicated with their elders. When I went with Gergen, I saw that.

D. That's fascinating.

B. I wasn't a toddler, but I hadn't gotten my own project (*as a spirit guide to me*), fully. So I was still learning. Maybe that was sort of a preview of what was gonna come for me because I did see that he communicated with them and I could see that they listened. They moved around according to the message in the wind.

D. In what way did he communicate? How did he do it?

B. Oh, so he communicated with fire. There was like an elder there, and that elder, he used fire. And he used it in a way to call for advice. So he sat by the fire and when the fire was alight, he could read how the fire was moving and that's how he got his messages on what to do. So it was like his pendulum. (*Bob communicates with me through a pendulum.*) There are a lot of those ancient shamans who just stared into the fire, and you think, "Oh, they're just daydreaming," –they were not. They were reading the fire and the messages because they could read how the fire moved and the sparkles sort of shoot out, and that meant different things. So Gergen, he sent in different ways, I could see Gergen like whooo (*he made a blowing sound*) on the fire, meaning that he communicated to that person that was in some way connected to him. So he gave information like that. A lot of the ancients used fires in a way to communicate and they could read all sorts of different messages based on how the fire moved and also the intensity within the fire, and so forth. You, you, you got stuck in the fire! Maybe you tried to read the fire, maybe that's what you were trying to do. It did not go that well because I did not know how to blow in the fire, maybe that's what happened, maybe you tried that! And because I didn't do what Gergen did, maybe that's why you burned. No one told me that I could do that, it wasn't established beforehand that I should do that, but maybe that's what you were doing.

D. That was at a later time, wasn't it? (*In one of my earliest incarnations, I burnt to death in a fire. Bob was off in the underbrush collecting a rare flower and didn't notice the danger. We tease each other about that incident.*)

B. A later time, indeed. But you had read up on things before coming so you must have been here looking into certain things, not just taking a body as a pickle to look into certain things. You used that technique that you send out an energetic bridge to something that you want to investigate. "So sometimes," you say, "I did not come in a manifested form, regardless of how that form appeared. I simply sent out my energetic bridge and I attached it to a destination that I wanted to experience. And also, I attached it to a being that I wanted to investigate." So you might have done that and then maybe you saw that experience with the fire and you thought, "Oh, okay, that will be the way that Bob talks to me." But Bob was somewhere else! Huh huh, because I didn't get the memo that we could communicate in the fire. If I had, I probably—I was very drawn to the flower—but I might have waited until you were safe. You sat very close to it, probably. Not what you do, especially if you have all furry clothes on you. It's like, POOF, and it's too late to communicate like that. I mean, I communicated with the fire, but you WERE the fire, so that's different. But there was no hard feelings, but after that I thought maybe that will be something that we do. But you said you're probably not gonna do that anymore. So we established our own way of communicating; I communicate with different animals like butterflies and so forth for you to recognize certain things. I also tend to communicate with temperature because I do know you are sensitive to that. You're more eager to listen if I send or I surround you with warmth when you are cold. I monitor your physical body to see where it's cold, like your feet for instance, tend to be a little bit cold. So it's easier for you to hear me and to communicate and connect with me if your feet are warm—that's why I say put them in socks or put them in a foot bath and it's easier for you to directly communicate to me. If there's a certain part of you that is cool or not tended to, then try to warm them up and then it's easier for you to hear me.

D. That's good advice. Thank you.

The Tiddle–Taffles Color the Worlds (Dec 22, 2019)

In this session, Gergen introduces the Taffles, spirits from the second dimension who live on Tiddle, a planet in fish tank two. These joyful spirits transferred most of their soul energy to Tiddle and became long-term residents. In their manifested form, they are solid enough to perform physical actions which cannot be done by spirits on their home dimension. The Tiddle–Taffles work with color maps, which are energetic patterns of light and sound that manifest as DNA and RNA on the third dimension. DNA holds more instructions than modern geneticists recognize. The coding dictates physical, mental and emotional characteristics, and DNA also holds information related to the soul mission, Coat of Karma, and any pre-programmed changes in health, for example, along the life path. The Taffles assist in caring for Earth and its life forms. They work primarily on improving nature, but they also want to assist humanity to be more colorful. The Tiddle–Taffles are only one group that work with color codes to improve or adjust life forms. Another group are the Little Greys, who operate an observation post on the Moon. The data they collect is shared with the Tiddle–Taffles and various councils. Humans, if they are aware of these visitors, are suspicious of their intent. However, the Taffles and alien visitors are here to help the planet and they work to improve the waters, atmosphere, land and organisms. Vacuous humans then see the refinements and call it evolution, failing to grasp the omnipresent spiritual design.

Spirits from the second are seldom involved in solo activities. The Taffles are no exception, and they came in as a boisterous group, but several spoke and gave some wonderfully uplifting advice about how to connect with colors and radiate your own rainbow. Gergen closed the session by saying that he planned on taking Bob to Tiddle so he could explore their outpost in fish tank two.

G. This is Gergen. We are here to introduce a new group for you, and it is my pleasure indeed to introduce the Tiddle–Taffles! Huhuh. The Tiddle–Taffles belong in the second fish tank but they are very close and connected to the second dimension. They are our ears and eyes, so to speak, on several locations. If you think of myself and Bob—and everyone else on the second for that matter—but in manifested form. So it is the second dimension manifestation on this planet where the Tiddle–Taffles reside. This one has seen the Tiddle–Taffles in dreams, –drew a picture and will remember, of course, the pictures. It's a highly playful group—yes indeed, yes indeed, you are all here and you are eager to talk—shh, shh! It's a lot of noise, they have been waiting eagerly and when they heard the bongs (*we begin each sitting by ringing our large Tibetan bowls*), they thought, "Oh, here we go, here we go! It begins, it begins! The show begins, the show begins!" And it became somewhat of a commotion in the group because there are several here and everyone wants to step into the first row, so to speak, and there is a lot of movement. We will see how this proceeds and I will stay present, of course, to somewhat organize this. But it is a place where some humans have a fond memory of. The reality is a physical form. It is highly colorful, the greenery, the textures on flowers and trees, and animal life is highly colorated in stronger colors than can be found here. The skies are normally looking similar like a sunset sky, always orange, red, yellow—very strong in colors. There are mountains, there are valleys, there are rivers, –there are no predators, so everyone living here feeds on vegetables and fruit. They work with energy—if you think of the second dimension and how it has been described—but in manifested form.

D. You said it was in the second fish tank?

G. Second fish tank indeed. It's not a silent world, I can tell you that. And here there is living proof of that, because there is a constant discussion and commotion among the Tiddle–Taffles. Before we try to see if some here wants to talk—and yes, there are several who wants to try this—we will just introduce them so there is no confusion, as this is the first time they have ever been allowed to communicate in this way. Bob is not aware of the Tiddle–Taffles, but has been gradually told about a manifested reality of the second dimension, but he thinks that it is in fish tank four or five. It is not. However, this reality is a small galaxy. There are several neighboring planets operating similar, even though this one in particular where the Tiddle–Taffles live is considered somewhat of a grand hub, if you like. They work with sound, so this is not a silent reality; it's a lot of music and tones, and they work with color a lot. These are the ones who operate and try to modify color maps. If you think of big bathtubs with different colors in them, that is sort of how their laboratorium looks—big bathtubs with different colors. And they dip little pencils, of sorts, to create, and they operate from that knowing. They are not simply manifesting color maps in fish tank two, they are actually looking into Earth as well. And one way they have the ability to do so is through your moon. So they can use moons, who are close to bigger realities such as planets, in order for them to see. It's like a peek hole, they say, to have a look–see. They use the moon because they have not been seen on Earth but they are close friends to the Little Greys; so the Little Greys have been seen on their behalf. They have not wandered here, but there are several humans that have fond memories in dreams from childhood visiting the Tiddle–Taffles. It is a very amusing reality, so we will see here if someone wants to try this, now that they have been introduced. It's a large group, it was not possible to invite just one. I'll step aside, but I will be present of course, if there is a need of translation. So we will see how this works. One at a time, one at a time!

TT. (*There was a lengthy transition while one of the Tiddle–Taffles made a lot of sounds and tongue movements as they practiced controlling Christine's body.*)

D. Welcome!

TT. Hehehehe. You see me! Huh Huh! Lalalalala–lalalala. We are the Tiddle–Taffles and we do like to sing and we are travelers. We like to look into the big ones through the moons and we look through peek holes—peekaboo!—and we look into certain things and we try to modify the color maps so that the animal life, in particular, and nature will have a better development.

D. When you first come into a body like this, how do you manage to communicate? Do you instantly pick up on all the words?

TT. We were told to connect with the, ah, emotional center, the solar plexus center where we sort of entered the being, and then we were told to find a large book of words available. So I'm looking around here in the top (*the mental area*) and Gergen said there would be a big book to look into, and I can flip and flop and he will be helpful in finding the right phrases to communicate. But–but–but I–I–I kinda feel like you're staring at me! Which feels a little bit odd. But you have been, you both have been visiting us, so it's not like we're strangers; especially this one is a friend who likes to come and lay down in the grass and sort of be tended to and smell the smells. It's a reality that is…next one? Oh, it was really short! (*Apparently the other Tiddle–Taffles were clamoring for a turn.*)

D. Maybe you can tell me what the difference is between the second fish tank and this one in terms of vibration and density?

TT. Ah, the density is different because there is more sound. The fish tanks are different, so when we travel here it almost appears silent. I mean, it's not silent, it's just that your tone vibrates in a longer frequency. Ours are faster, so it's quicker—and so are we! If a human have ever been incarnated and visited a reality in fish tank two, they find this reality (*fish tank five*) extremely slow. Me, myself, I have not been in human form or anything like that. But we have neighbors that have hosted souls such as yourself and those on other realities—mainly those who have advanced high on the fifth dimension—and they feel very comfortable here. If they have reached that level of travel, they normally like to come here because it's very similar to what they are experiencing with the gardens and so forth. (*He means the gardens on the fifth dimension.*) But there are close by realities that some souls here have visited. Our planet they have not visited, and neither have you, not in physical form. If you are in a human body, you can only reach our reality in your dreams.

D. Wow, okay. Do you have individual names you want to go by?

TT. Oh, there will be a lot here. We will have to think about that because we are several here and there has been somewhat of a commotion, so I'll step aside here. I was first in line to communicate and wanted to just say hi. We are closely connected with the areas of the second dimension that you are aware of—Gergen and such—and in many ways we appear similar, but in a manifested form. We—we— we don't like to take things so seriously and we feel like fish tank five is kind of serious. It's a little bit too serious for our liking. What we are trying to do is that we're using colors to try to change the color codes in the human vehicle. So we are part of helping to recreate the color maps in physical manifestation such as a human. It seems like you are a gloomy race, I must say. And perhaps it has to do with that your host is not fully happy. It must indeed rub off on you. So we have been looking into that. Okay, there is someone who will take on the torch here. Okay, don't push! Don't push! Everyone will have their turn, Gergen said. Don't push, I will indeed step aside.

D. Well, thank you for coming and sharing with us. I do appreciate it.

TT. Okay.

D. Alright. Goodbye.

TT. (*Another of the Tiddle–Taffles stepped in, making noises for a bit.*) Oh, oh, uh, what we do do is that we look at the gloomy race and we try to assist, and you can assist indeed by changing the colorations around you. So what we seeeee in many ways is a world that is sort of black and white, and that mirrors off on the being, the manifest (*he struggled to say the word*), oh let's see the word we can use...the manifestation available also makes them a little bit black and white. And as we are moving into a new era where the beings have to be a little bit more connected to the emotional amusement within them— (*His manner of speaking was very drawn out and deliberate, but when he had trouble with the "th" sound he began making it repeatedly.*) Th-th-th, what's that? Something feels like...oh, that was odd, I lost the way to say "s". Oh, la-la-la-le, let's see. SO! What we do see is a need for your race to become more colorful. We see this as we look through the moon and we send our little friends, the Little Greys, who are great companions, happy little creatures—but we are all concerned with the low frequency in general in the fish tank. We have not, of course, the mandate to upgrade the vibration in total in your fish tank, but what we can do is give a little color to this reality. Giving color to a reality means that you do not take things so seriously; that you try to see yourself in the light of a little play. It's just briefly, my friend, that you are here. And you have had several roles, several plays that you have engaged in. And if you try to find your path within and look for the inner adventure, you will have the ability to find more colorful events, current as well as past. From that point you have the ability, using your IMAGINATION, to create a more colorful future. But you have to first want to color your present. It's EASY to look back and see where and when and with whom you were most colorful, especially IF YOU ARE with a person or with friends that make you not shine in the full colors of the rainbow. The soul in a human are supposed to shine like a rainbow. We have friends from the rainbow land here nearby that try to help us as well when we traveled there, of course. Gergen? Gergen (*as he looks to the left*), do you want to say something about that? Yes, indeed. What we will try to say is that once you try and identify in your life where you lack color; it may be with people, or it might be with situations, or the profession where you are spending long hours (*he laughed about that*), huh huh, you might consider that to be a source where you might—huh huh, it's so obvious! Do I have to say this? What is not in color in your life, exchange it for something that makes you become the rainbow. Huh huh huh. It's quite obvious, but Gergen said sometimes the obvious has to be said because it might not be obvious in the containers, especially if the container is contaminated and not in color. But in general, the gift from the Tiddle–Taffles is to color your world. A way to color your world is also to put your hands and feet, touching things that is soft. That is why having a pet and petting that pet, stroking it and holding it and sniffing it, it colors your being. It is a gift as it triggers the color map within you. So those who tend to pets, to feel their fur and to communicate with them, easier becomes a rainbow. And with feet! You do not stomp on the pet, of course, with your feet. But you put your feet in, let's say, soft grass. And if it's a little bit wet from the rain the day before, it's even better. With that sensation of moist and wet on bare feet, then it is almost impossible to be a black and white person in that sense, you automatically restart the rainbow colors within you. If you struggle in finding this rainbow of colors within you or around you, simply begin easy. Gergen says sometimes this species has to take little steps. So what you could do, you begin with your first favorite color and you simply allow that color to become you. Don't make it too tricky for you, simply allow yourself to be, let's say, green. And then you imagine—imagination is the key to access not only your inner being, but your inner colors. So you begin with your favorite color green and then you think of everything you know that is green; and you go through the different objects that you notice around you that are green, and which green do you like the most? There is the stronger green, the lighter green and so forth, and after a while you can play with this color and imagine, "What if I was green?"

D. Like a big pine tree.

TT. Like a big pine tree. And then you play with that and you become the color green. The important thing is to be PLAYFUL, people, be playful and ENJOY this play that you are in. If you are in a drama and you would like to be in a comedy—create the comedy! Some who are in, let's say a mystery play, they are more likely indeed to be colorful, because if you are in a mystery, you are closer to the sensation of adventure. I would say that the ones we are most concerned about are those who find that they are just in a really gloomy drama. They don't make anyone have colors; they feel they have no purpose. If you think of the most depressing TV drama that you have seen, there is a huge percentage within your race that play their play in that respect—not knowing that you all can change the play. You can change it into a comedy, you can change it into mystery, and a key to do so is to find the vibration of colors within you. (*He kept having trouble saying "s".*) There's no "s", what is this! That would be it, Gergen said, from the Tiddle–Taffles today. But we will return with more magic and more treats. Just know that we wish for you to color your surrounding and change the play if you do not find yourself in a play that you enjoy. Simple, wouldn't you say?

D. Indeed!

TT. And you can change the actors in the show as well. So what you can do, for instance, if you are in that gloomy workplace, and you are kind of stuck there for a while—and you are fully aware of that, and you can't just take off and find a new profession—what you could do with the tasks at hand that makes you black and white, –color them! If you see, let's say, one of your co-workers that you do not get along with, dress that person up as your favorite cartoon and see the drama as a little comedy. Create the comedy in your head and you will see that the workplace that was black and white will start to have some color. So you can dress people around you in different costumes to your liking. Just in your head, of course, and to make that a part of your inner happiness when the outer happiness might be lacking.

D. That's really good advice.

TT. Final words from the Tiddle-Taffles.

D. I did have a question.

TT. Oh, oh, okay!

D. How do you relate to the other spirits like Gergen and Ole and Bob—are you a different branch on the second?

TT. Bob has not been introduced; we have not had the pleasure for Bob to visit but we expect him shortly. Gergen has said that there is someone, and that might be him, ready to join our group. We...what was the question?

D. Do you know them?

TT. Oh, yes, we know them all. Gergen comes frequently. We are in some way looking similar as Gergen looks.

D. But your mentors are on the second, or in the councils?

TT. The councils come and visit indeed. And we all, we are closely connected to the second dimension reality. We just manifested our full form here in fish tank two.

D. So do you have any working relationship with Earth?

TT. Only through the peepholes, the ones that we send out to gather samples are the Little Greys. We have not been here, we look through the moon and then the Little Greys—highly efficient, quick—we ask them for samples and they go!

D. So you've been working with the Earth for a long time?

TT. But not directly on it, my feet have not been on it.

D. Like Bob walks the Earth.

TT. Oh, he does, does he? What a pleasure...or is it?

D. I think so.

TT. Me, myself, I have never set foot on Earth. We travel differently, we never—how can one say—we are in manifested form and I do not know how one can be in not manifested form. But we are closely connected to the second dimension and we travel in sort of a cylinder object that we can move through the big highways—lightways—and we normally aim at moons.

D. So do you work with moons around other planets?

TT. Indeed. We like moons and that's why we are acquainted with the ones from the sixth because you create the moons. So we have met. This one travels a lot and visits a lot and shows us new highways to travel on. So indeed, we are always informed.

D. Okay, I follow that.

TT. I don't know if there is anything TO follow, but that's what I am. I don't know any other way to exist. So I am a manifested being saying hello from fish tank two. I don't know anything else.

D. Does part of your soul energy remain on the second dimension?

TT. Very little, very little. I rarely come home and when I do, it's to connect with the one percent that remains. We have decided to...let's see if I can find the word here...emigrate, that's the word. You have those here too; I don't know if it's the same. But we emigrated, meaning that we left one percent behind; it's a relocation that has been taking place. It's been so long that I barely remember not being in physical form, so this is just what I am. The Tiddle–Taffles, we emigrated, that's the word they want us to use, and we relocated to fish tank two. The connection to home is Gergen and Ole and the Council. They come, but we rarely leave. We are fully occupied having looks through the peepholes through the moons. So if we could just tell you to try to remember the colorations inside yourself as you were a child, because you were more colorful. You tend to become black and white and grey as you advance. You would think that you would add more colors to your being, but what we can see here, and the reports that we get from the Little Greys, is that instead of getting more colors you tend to move to grey. And that is a concern. So the gift from the Tiddle–Taffles is to color yourself and your surrounding and to dress people up. If you think of the game chess, you can in some way remove some of the players from your board. (*You can avoid some people.*) But some you have not solved, such as the equation on how to remove that tower (*the tower is the rook, which, I assume, represents certain difficult people you cannot avoid*), but you can color the tower and you can make it into a different suit, a different persona, making the game easier, even though you have not fully solved it. You should also be aware of that, if you think of life as a game of chess, not all lives end with a checkmate. Be aware of that, because if you think the end result of all your lives is to be cleaning out the house, so to speak, and to have a checkmate, you're going to be extremely sad as you return (*to spirit*). So just know that not all lives are meant to be a clean house (*capturing all the chess pieces*), you might simply be in the back row and your life might be to simply be able to remove the tower, not the queen or the other ones. So if you think of life as chess, you try to identify the player that you are playing against—which is actually yourself! And you look into how you can maneuver this human-self versus your soul-self; and if those two were playing chess, and the players on the board are actually those you have incarnated with, then you will see the game differently. Sometimes the soul wins; sometimes not. Sometimes it IS a clean house; sometimes not.

D. I love that analogy.

TT. Start to play chess and see your life and color it, and know that you have the ability, and also to WANT to have the ability. People feel like there is a ban over them because there is a ban on everything. You hear about it in that box you stare at (*TV*), that there is a ban here and there is a ban there, and you have to do this—I recorded what the two of you were talking about this morning—completely irrelevant! (*We were discussing how to handle the idiotic tax rules in the US and Sweden.*) So there is all these rules and bans and that INDEED creates grey in a very colorful intended reality. So I will leave, but I WILL RETURN! Oh, this was fun! So, from the Tiddle-Taffles, we will return, and until then, find your favorite color and play the game well!

D. Alright my friend. Thank you so much for that. You're welcome back anytime.

G. So, this is Gergen. There you go, met some new friends today.

D. It was a really good lecture.

G. They have been eagerly awaiting, there is a somewhat of a schedule, of course. The Tiddle-Taffles, because of their fondness of colors and happiness, when they see a reality that is sad or depressed, then they are eager to come with their brushes and their colors. They have been collecting samples through the Little Greys, remaining silently, observing in the moon. The Little Greys have somewhat been runners for them, collecting samples how they can improve.

D. How do they observe the Earth through the moon? What is the mechanism they use?

G. It's similar like remote viewing, that's the only way I can describe it for you. It's not a lid where you open it and look out! Huhuh!

D. So they can connect with the moon and then observe the Earth?

G. Indeed. They use the different moon phases for what they are trying to do. So when there is a full moon, they are more alert and you could actually sense the energy from them. So the full moon is when they are more wide-open. Normally when there is a new moon, they look more quietly.

D. Do they observe other realities than Earth?

G. Different moons. This moon is looking here. They travel to different moons, yes indeed. So that's sort of a hub they travel to, and using the different moon phases, based on what their operation is about. Normally, since they try to be a little bit in hiding, you can simply know that the new moon and the full moon, both of them are operating—I would say like this—when there is a full moon, their eyes are on full display and they send out their eyes. If you think of it like a big flashlight, like the moon is when it's full, their eyes have the ability with the help of the full moon to see more clearly. As the moon moves more into the darker side, then that's when they bring back the information they have found. They collect the data and they ponder about it. But they use the cycles because they are invisible as the moon is full; you cannot see them, but they can see you. We will talk about this more. So today, that was the treat. Bob is going to have a separate session, due to the fact that the energy has been taking a lot from this one. So Bob has requested a separate session on Wednesday. So on Wednesday there will be a separate session just for Bob and Ophelia.

D. It has been a real pleasure to meet the new friends.

G. It has indeed. The Tiddle–Taffles are really a joyful group that we were happy to introduce today.

D. Thank you so much for doing that.

G. Oh, you are much welcome. Bob was aware that there was someone else talking, and he requested then, since he still has a claim to this circle, that he will have his own. And he will indeed, perhaps with Ophelia, have his own session on Wednesday.

D. Are you going to eventually introduce him to that reality?

G. Oh, yes indeed. I'm putting it in cups to him.

D. He's not going to move there permanently, is he?

G. At this time he sort of wants to emigrate to Etena. But what he means with emigrate is not the same as with the Tiddle-Taffles. He means visit, and emigrate means stay. So we have to make sure he understands that. He's not in that position yet where he feels comfortable in his being yet to not be able to move, and emigrate means relocation, and that is not what Bob, my friend, is ready to do just yet. He would like to visit indeed, but it requires a different way of travel. And this one was very helpful trying to imitate the travel with a rocket. But we will see, and Bob is still not sure. So we are indeed introducing Bob to this reality. He will travel with me in a way that is unique for the second dimension, as it is related to this reality, so he will travel in that way first. As he does, he will be told that this is a place where you visit rarely when you move into the council work. You do not just come and go in the same way as you do on Etena. It's a place, one can say, where one retires. You have Florida, we have Tiddle. So until then, Bob is aware he has a separate session coming up on Wednesday and it has been approved.

D. Good. Wonderful.

G. There we go. I wish you a wonderful day, whatever that is that you are supposed to do. We follow you as always, and it was a great joy to invite some of the little beings on a different reality—as you try to connect the wheel—and that is the work ahead, that you are trying to connect the wheel in many ways.

D. Alright, thank you so much.

G. Oh, you are much welcome. Bye bye.

Siah and Tess are Reunited (Dec 25, 2019)

After Tess was taken to Etena, she remained in a deep sleep. A team was assembled who lovingly cared for her as her body adjusted to the new environment. Bob describes the joyful reunion that transpired in the forest when she was finally awakened.

Bob then describes a ritual he took part in that honored the fabric of life and the elements. The culmination of the ritual was conducted inside a pyramid when they all met and communicated with the Big Eye. The Eye is an extension of the Master Mind, and is something that prehistoric humans could connect with in the fourth dimension around Earth. By connecting with the Big Eye, they could move back and forth over the timeline, or examine other places in the universe. If the ceremony is analyzed, it seems reminiscent of the oldest spiritual beliefs in Europe, Asia and the Americas, where fire, earth, water, air, and spirit were honored. Because ancient humans could connect with the Eye, this suggests there is a universal truth in this understanding of the elements. Once the Eye was closed to humans, direct knowledge of the Creator was lost, and societies fell victim to superstition, ignorance and fear.

B. Deet da–da deet! And there he is! Huh huh huh.

D. The star of the show!

B. Ah, the grand finale. So, ya know, I was, I wouldn't say told because I don't respond well to being told, but I was given the opportunity to have my own show with Ophelia. I did not want to give that opportunity up, so I said, "Oh, okay, if I can have my own spot in the sun." I kinda knew that there was someone coming in that might take a little bit too much time, and that it would be not so much for me. So that's why I wasn't objecting.

D. Did you have any idea who came in? (*It was the Tiddle–Taffles from the second fish tank.*)

B. Gergen said they were gonna be friends that I'm gonna meet. And I'm all in favor of having new friends, so he said that I will meet some individuals, he said.

D. They seemed really nice, so I think you'll like them.

B. Oh, I probably do. Gergen, he tends to know exactly what I like and what I look forward to encountering and so forth. So I'm pretty sure he knows that whomever I'm gonna meet, that it is someone who is not only beneficial for me, but they might benefit from my visit as well. That's what I think.

D. I'm sure they will. We all do.

B. So I look forward to that. It's upcoming. What I would like to tell you is that Siah and Tess have now met.

D. Oh, that's wonderful! How did that go?

B. It went really well. We, me and Setalay and everyone, we were sort of walking Tess into the forest where I know that Siah has a secret hidey hole, and we went there. Siah was having a nap, just resting, and I told Tess, because it's sort of a little bit like a cave, but it's not in stone. It's like moss and roots, so it's a cave under a tree. The ceiling, it's not rock; the ceiling is roots from the tree above, and he likes to be there because he feels close to and communicates with the roots. You know, like the hedgehog that also had a home under a tree?

D. Yes.

B. It's something that they like, to have a nest or a hidey hole under a tree. It's just that the hedgehogs' hidey hole was kinda small and this, where Siah is, is much bigger. But it has the same modality, meaning that the roots sort of encases around this hole and open space where Siah is. I know about this place because he's been taking me there. So I said, "We should guide Tess there," and so we did. We didn't want to interfere, so I told Tess, "If you just go straight ahead to that big tree over there, on the back there is a big treat for you!" And she was a little bit groggy because of the waking-up ritual that took place where we established everything, but she knows that there is something that she is familiar with that is gonna come her way, so she's not afraid or anything. So we have awakened the memory, but we are waiting for it to have a full effect as they also meet. So I told her, "Just walk all the way over to that big tree. Go around the tree and look below, and you will find a big treat." So she did, she kind of waddled—she didn't run at this time, and I think it's because of being a little bit groggy after the waking-up ritual. So she was idling along to the tree. And then she disappeared because we stood way back, we did not want to interfere. I could hear sounds that I've never heard from either one of them before. It's like a language that I've never heard...how can I describe it? It was like a mixture of how lions roar but it had high pitch in there too, almost bird-like, so it was rising and falling in a variety of sounds. We didn't see anything because everything occurred behind the tree, and then after a while it became silent, and I thought, "On, what does this mean?" I was standing there with Setalay and everyone, and you were also there, and we were maybe 30 meters away just to observe that everything went fine. And then you said, "I think Siah and Tess have joined in a unified sleep, because that's what they did before. That's how they connect, –when they sleep." And I said, "How long is that gonna take?" And you said, "Where they were before, that is how they docked and their souls become one. So there were two beings but the way they connected was they lay down and they instantly fell into a joined dream, a joined sleep. And that is how they operated," you said, "it's similar like going into hibernation. It's important for them to do that now in solitude because they have a lot of catching up to do. So they are going to be in a long kind of hibernation for a while." I mean, not long like you think here, like go to bed and wake up six months later. You said, "It's not the same because there is no time, necessarily, but this is a way for them to reconnect in that dream. So they are going to be in a hibernation for a little while." And I said, "Do we need to stand here for the whole time of the hibernation?" And you said, "No, because it will be known to us when it is time to come back. If we don't come back, then they will idle back to the village and find us again. So this is good," you say, "because now they are in that familiar way of connecting. That's how they did in the other place where they were at before. So we have to leave them alone during that phase." I don't see anything, so I said, "Can I go and have a peek?" and you said, "No, we have to leave them alone. If you go and have a peek, you will interfere with the dream. It's not like they are just there, their awareness is occupying everything around them. So they are fully aware of us even though we are thirty meters away, because their consciousness, as they connect in this hibernation dream, expands. The physical is close, so they have the ability to dock, but their consciousness travels indefinitely." So you say, "They are fully aware that we are here and staring. So you don't have to go over there, because they have already detected you. And that is also how they started to detect the invasion of the other ones moving up the mountain. It's like, if you have the two eyes and you can look around, when they dock like this, they not only have four eyes, they actually dock to one common eye, like a big eye. Then they can see the whole reality where they are at. In this case," you say, "they have the ability to see the whole of Etena." And I said, "Well, that's magic, to have one big eye!" And you said that that is something they are designed to do, when they are two. The idea is for them to become a flock, and they will learn the little ones to dock. It's like taking all eyes and merging them into one big eye." You said, "If you were able to see this, you would see, at this moment, a huge eye, which is them. And this eye can see the whole reality; they can see the location where they are at, Etena, and so forth, but they also have the ability, if they prolong this way of operating, that they can see the whole fish tank, they can see whole worlds, if they connect with this big eye. And it's not just these two individuals, it's a design that exists from different fish tanks, especially," you say, "fish tank seven, fish tank eleven, and also fish tank four." You say, "It's just a way to exist, and they are designed to be able to connect to this big eye that can see EVERYTHING. It's almost similar like the Creator having this big eye, the Master Mind, –it's just that they become this big eye. They don't become the Master Mind, they don't become the Creator, but the Creator has given into these fish tanks—seven, eleven and four—the ability to manifest their awareness as one big eye."

D. What about Setalay and the other ones on Etena?

B. They can connect to this big eye. I did not know that, I did not because you did not say, and they did not say. And I said, "Is this like a big peek hole that you can see in all directions?" And they said, "Yes, we access this big eye in rituals." So Siah and Tess, they do it by docking in this dream, and they become their big eye. But it's not the same eye that Setalay and the other ones are connecting to. So they are connecting to this big eye with a ritual where they are doing chanting— there are bonfires—and I said, "Maybe that's what you were trying to do with the bonfire! Did you try to become that big eye and just became a little bit too close to the fire?" Huhuh! You laughed about that and you said, "No, I was just clumsy." Not everything is magic, not everything has a big magic purpose like I believe it does. But it is because I believe in magic and I believe there is a purpose to everything. Behind everything that I hear and see, I wonder about the preparation or background or the intent of it. So I always believe that there's gonna happen something extremely fascinating. But you said, "Sometimes it's just being clumsy and being burned in the fire. Not everything has a big, magic purpose." Hehehehe. But they connect to this big eye, Setalay and the other ones, and they do it with rituals. First, they have a bonfire outside one of the temples, which is one of the pyramids, and they purify themselves and they honor the element fire. "It's very much," you say, "that you have to honor the elements and not materia, but what exists in your reality. As you start to honor what exists and coexists with you, openings take place." That is why man is so numb, because they don't coexist and honor the environment and the planet; meaning the planet cannot give you any treats. I'm not saying that your planet and your environment will give you a big eye, but as long as you do not honor where you are at and the fabrics that exist (*the energetic substance from which matter arises*) in nature, in rocks, and also it has to do with honoring the fabric in YOU. If you only think that you are something that is here to just eat, then you are not honoring yourself and not honoring the fabric of plant life, atmosphere, trees, and so forth. That means that the Earth will never grant you a big eye or a grand treat. So what they do is they honor the fire, they purify themselves and they give thanks to the FABRIC, they call it, in everything that exists. The fabric is the web that is physical and visible but it's also to honor the life force that is the fabric within you, and in a human that means DNA and so forth. But man has problems with honoring something they do not see. They think, "Why should I honor DNA? Why should I honor the liver? Why should I honor my spine?" And as you are in that mindset that you are not grateful and appreciative, and if you do not recognize the different fabrics within you and around you, then there's not gonna be a big portal, there's not gonna be a big eye coming your way. So in many ways, what has happened here (*on Earth*) is that the eyes are shut. But on other places the eyes are open. And when they talk about open eyes, they actually talk about understanding and honoring the fabrics within life forms, as well as the environment and atmosphere. Someone might say, "How can I honor the atmosphere and the fabric in the atmosphere?" Well, the clouds and everything are visual evidence that there is a fabric and there is a web in some way. But if you do not honor this, then indeed your eyes are shut.

D. That's the way Native American cultures saw the world.

B. Ah. So what they do is that they do this ritual outside, and I was actually allowed to follow this ritual. You were a part of this and you said, "We're going to go into one of the pyramids where they store a lot of knowledge and we're going to observe this ritual as they connect with the big eye." When I worked with life forms on Earth, there was no one talking about a big eye and to connect with that. It probably would appear to connect to the Master Mind eye; if you think of it in that way, it's easier for mankind to have a visual of what's happening. So indeed, one can say that you are connecting to the Master Mind and the big eye. But like I said, here (*on Earth*) the eye is shut for a variety of reasons. So we watched the fire and we were supposed to sit there honoring the fire until the fire was done with us. That's different! It's not us putting out the fire, it's the fire saying goodbye to us. So we waited until the fire felt like it was done. And we were sitting around the circle around the fire, and I said, "You might want to skootch back a bit since you tend to burn easily!" HA HA HA! A little joke there. And you said, "Don't be so cocky, you're kind of physical too, you can burn easily too so you might want to scooch back!" Huhuh, Earthly humor. So anyway, we were sitting around the fire and everyone was silent, everyone was honoring the fire in their own way, including me. I was honoring the fire because it actually brought you and I much closer together and it started a beautiful journey. So I gave gratitude to the fire—not for burning you—but how the end result of that experience was actually a starting point to a beautiful journey. I'm not sure what you were thinking, because it's private and you do not interfere and you don't sniff around, but that was mine. Oh, I disclosed, I told—I'm not sure if I'm supposed to tell (*as he is looking to the left*)—I was not supposed to tell, okay. For the next time I know that, okay. So you sit there, and you honor the fire and what the fire has done for you and how you feel about the fire, and you communicate in your own special way—and apparently you're not supposed to share, but I'm sort of a sharing kind of guy, so it tends to be like that. But next time I'm not gonna share.

They said it was okay this time because I did not know, I didn't have the manual on how to behave in this ritual. So we waited until the fire burned out, and when it became ashes, we collected the ashes and we buried it in the soil in a hole that was prepared to dig all the ashes down. Everyone put the soil back on top of it. We put all our wishes and all our wellbeing into the planet. We put everything that we had prayed for and everything that we were grateful for and had been honoring—some silent, some out loud—in that hole, all the ashes, and then the intention was heard and sent down into the core of Etena.

D. That's a great ritual.

B. And then you said, "Now you have to be quiet, Bob, because now we're entering the pyramid of rituals.' So we went into the pyramid in a line. I was last. There was probably some sort of order. You were next to last and I was last, and we went into the pyramid to continue this ritual. And the ritual was to connect with this big eye. And we were sitting there in a circle, but now from the inside of the pyramid, lids opened up and it started to drizzle water. We were sitting on a circular platform and around us was a ditch, and the more the water fell—it was not a waterfall, but it was dripping—quietly filling up the ditch around the platform that we were sitting on. And this time I knew to be quiet because you told me, "This is a quiet experience." So we were sitting there and the circle around the platform was filling up with water. And they said, "This is a time where we are honoring the flow. The water is life, all elements are life, but now we honor the circulation and the flow in the fabric within us, which would be the circulation of blood in a humanoid, but also the veins of the waters that flows in each living planet. So we were sitting there just honoring the water in many ways. You said we honored the earth element as we were digging down the ashes. So we were sitting there for a while and you said quietly, you whispered, "The last phase of this ritual as we connect to this big eye is going to be connect to the element air." And that's when the chanting started, it's sort of a breathing exercise with chanting, and it was to fill up the space. During this, the water kept on pouring. So earth and fire sort of connected, and here, water and air were somewhat connecting. So we started to chant and do the breathing, joined breathing exercise, and suddenly at the top of the pyramid, it became an opening and what I saw was this huge, big eye, just looking down into this circle of us. And you said, "We don't go up to the eye, but now as you chant and as you breath, and in connection with the water, floating, now you connect and you ask the eye to take you there." So it brings you up to it in some way. I could see little flames rising from the other ones—I struggled a little bit—I came halfway but I understand the intention here.

D. What did the eye look like?

B. It looked like a big disk, a big shield over this opening, looking down at us. I could see the vibrations of all sorts of colors, and in the center was a black hole. You said, "This is the portal, this is how you can travel and do remote viewing without leaving the spot you are at." So when you are allowed up to the eye, –and I don't think I was fully allowed, I was allowed to observe the ritual but I didn't go up to the eye–, but you said I will eventually. It probably didn't recognize me! It has to be granted and you have to be invited, and I know all about that, so I was not sad. Everyone else went up—you did not leave me, but I'm pretty sure you can go up to the eye here. You said that I will eventually be able to ascend into that, and as I do, I will have an overview of not only Etena, but in this case, fish tank four. Once you have mastered this way of traveling, which is similar like remote viewing, from this big eye you can extend that and travel. It's like the eye sends you out remotely to investigate different things, –that's a treat!

D. Just in the fish tank?

B. I don't know, and at this point it's about this fish tank. But you said that this way of experiencing exists in fish tank seven, eleven and four, because the big eye is open there. There is not a big eye here in the fifth. You can see how many possibilities and adventures lie before me, now when I know this.

D. That's better than going in the washer!

B. I said, "I don't need to go into the washer if I can just connect and be invited into the big eye. But it's a different way because with the washer, your whole being goes, it travels, –but the eye is for remote viewing.

D. It would still be quite handy.

B. In some way it's connected to the big Master Mind, so it's a Master Eye, I would say.

D. Would humans be able to do something like that?

B. They did before. In earlier civilizations back, in Earth years, about two to five million years ago, the eye was open, you said, and there was a way to connect. They did rituals like that and they connected. But you said it's not just to wish to see something, like, "Oh, I'm spiritual. I have my eyes open." You have to honor the whole creation where you are at. And the creation is also you, so if you don't like yourself very much, it won't work. You have to honor the physical, not only honor the soul, you have to honor the whole connection of the fabrics. Then eyes can be open. But you said, "What was a remnant of that time was that there were shamans, later on, who had the ability to connect with the big eye. And in doing so, they could look over the timeline. On Earth it was different than other locations, because the eye existed in the fourth dimension." So different shamans knew how to do this, and you said that was actually available for some humanoids, shamans, all the way up to about 500 AD. But before, when you were here in the beginning, it was a common knowledge, you said, and everyone knew how to connect. Maybe they didn't travel on the timeline in the same way, but they connected to an overview, a Master Eye, and had the ability to see occurrences on the Earth plane, and also how the Earth itself was doing. The eye allowed them to travel and see the galaxies, solar system, and the fish tank by itself. But that was about five million years ago. The remaining understanding, up to 500 AD, only allowed certain shamans to connect to the eye; but the eye didn't leave the fourth reality, that was the thing. And now there are certain individuals that can connect in some way to the fourth reality and the eye that travels over the timeline, but they cannot leave and look at the Earth as a whole, the galaxy as a whole, or the fish tank as a whole.

D. You said two to five million years ago, so I guess there were civilizations that were here?

B. Indeed! Indeed. Looking kind of similar, but they were more intelligent.

D. Do you think they were occupied by souls, or was it the Master Mind?

B. It was also visitors. So not everyone looked the same. It was a higher intelligence in operation, you said. And the higher intelligence didn't look for the container, the physical, it was just the higher awareness in the intelligence that was present.

D. More like manifested forms, as I used to travel?

B. Well, there were humanoids that were like 50/50 with the Master Mind and soul, that existed. It was in the beginning of the reincarnation program in some way. When souls have memories of earlier, being here in the beginning, kickstarting the project, they might have been like a one-celled individual in the ocean, they were actually remotely experiencing. I mean, they occupied the form, like the little particle in the ocean, but it was not reincarnating. They may have memories of existing, but it's similar to remote observing and remote working and experiencing. That's what I was trying to say today, and I'm done. It was extremely interesting and now we are waiting for Siah and Tess to return after they have docked and connected to this big eye.

D. I'm interested to hear what you saw then.

B. When they came back?

D. Yes.

B. They were in hibernation. You knew, and everyone knew probably, that I would be a little bit impatient with this. So that's why they showed me and let me be a part of this ritual, which I really enjoyed. It was a magical experience! I was hoping the eye would see me fit to join and to have a looksee. Gergen is observing this from home and he is making sure I don't see more than I can handle, and so do you.

D. I would guess that Gergen is familiar with this process?

B. Indeed, indeed. When I told him about this when I came back—I was full of excitement—and he said, "Oh, I know about the eye." And I said, "Have you traveled? What have you seen, Gergen?" Then he said, "It's different for everyone. You will see when it's your time." And I was like, "When is that?" and he said, "Today you were a part of the ritual. Little by little you progress and break more ground," he said, "and you access more knowledge about the whole. It's just also to enjoy the little things and to not just be overwhelmed with everything. Now you have something to ponder about because you saw the big eye, and you saw the ritual and you saw the intent of connecting to this big eye, so that will give you

something to ponder about, won't it?" And I said, "Yes, it will." He said it's like a new project of mine, now when Tess is gone.
D. That's a good project.
B. So now I'm thinking about that, and I'm journaling my experience about this. I'm not gonna tell the little ones like Tom and everyone because there is no need to brag.
D. Well, Gergen didn't tell you.
B. Everything comes in due time. So anyway, I'll go now but, you know, I'll be back.
D. That was a wonderful story! It is so fascinating!
B. I thought so! And now I know that when I do this the next time, I will be quiet and not share everything, –it's a quiet experience.
D. It's really nice that you thought about us.
B. It was a great starting point and I wanted to acknowledge that and thank the fire, who initiated it in some way. Huhuh. Ah, anyway, so I'll go now, but I'll be back!
D. Alright, my friend, it was a pleasure to hear you again. I always enjoy your company.
B. Ah. I like your company too. We do things together and I like that.
D. You're a really good companion.
B. I tend to be a good traveler companion, since I'm full of excitement. If you go on a trip, you don't want to be gloomy! You want to be excited about the journey and where it's gonna take you and what you're gonna see. You're always gonna know more after the journey than before the journey, even if it's just a little thing. Now today, in this journey, I saw a lot and I learned a lot, and I'm pondering about this and I'm putting it in my journal about this big eye because it's fascinating to know that the Master Eye has the ability to observe and I can connect, –let's say with this Master Eye in the fourth fish tank–, my first graduation to be accepted up to this eye would be to see Etena, let's say, and then gradually be able to see the solar system where Etena is, and then the whole fish tank four. So gradually this eye will just open up more and more for me.
D. Do you think that along with being able to see it, you understand the meaning of what you are seeing?

B. Oh, indeed. That's what it is. Now I am aware of Etena and when I'm eventually invited up to the eye, I will probably be able to investigate Etena and just hover over it and connect with that planet and the intent of the creation on there and so forth. And gradually it will open up for me and so I will see where Etena is located. You say, and Setalay say, that after a while, I'll be able to join with them as they travel in a group and observe different parts of where this eye takes them. So they travel in a group, and they bring back information, and they talk about it and investigate what to do with it. It's somewhat to collect information, and they store it in this facility. But their physical is still sitting on the platform with me, –so I didn't feel lonely! It wasn't like I was left alone on a platform and everyone left. That wouldn't have been a fun feeling—being left behind—I don't respond well to that.

D. So I gather! (*Laughing*)

B. So in my mind we were all sitting there. I did observe some flames going up to that opening and to that disk. The disk was magical! It was like a big eye, but the core, the iris, was black. If you think of the eye color being green or blue, that was vibrating in all sorts of like purple, yellow, like flashing. I didn't see like an eye white, that's not how it looked at all. (*He had become very quiet as he described this, as if he were in awe.*)

D. It wasn't scary, was it?

B. Noo. And the center was just a still point and everything else was vibrating like a big thunder, but it was silent. And the color around the center was flashing like a big storm. And that's where they went up to. The center, that's magical, I don't know about the center because you don't go to the center, there's something in there. We'll see, you say. But they went up to the flashes and the purple and the yellow, that's where they went. Dark purple, black and yellow flashing, light purple, and I saw the flames going up there, even though they were sitting there next to me in the circle on the platform. And the water was filling up—but I didn't get wet! Ah, I was sitting there breathing and chanting. The funny thing is, the physical kept breathing and kept chanting, even though they were not there, you said. They left but the physical continued because that was the connection, you said, to home. The physical just kept doing what it did, the chanting and the breathing, but the soul wasn't there. And that was the connection to Etena to return to. So when the soul was done traveling up in the eye, the way to find its way home was through the chanting. I wanna go—I'm gonna go!

D. I guess we're going back to Etena then!

B. Ah. Okay, I'll go, but I'm fascinated by this, by what I observed.

D. So am I. What sort of chanting were they doing?

B. (*He chanted in a series of eight, without breaks.*) Like, Humm–uhmm–uhmm–uhmm–uhmm–uhmm–uhmm–uhmm–Humm–uhmm–uhmm–uhmm–uhmm–uhmm–uhmm–uhmm. Sort of similar. All of them had different, it's not like everybody had the same; that's how they knew how to return to their body. You don't want to return into the wrong one! Huhuhuh! Like you and I would switch! Huhuh. Suddenly you will be in me and I will be in you and it's like, "Ohh? How did this happen?" So you have your own personal chanting and that's how the container, the form, invites the vibration energy that has left, the spiritual energy if you like, that has ascended into the eye, and that's how that vibration returns into the right form. This was magical! I wanna do this again. Setalay said, "We're not doing this every day."

D. I'm sure we'll go back when they do.

B. Oh, I wanna come back. I said, "I'll sign up for the next class." Oh, okay, I'll go, I'll go. Ophelia laughs, she knows this was a happy adventure for me.

D. I'm glad you shared that, it's totally fascinating to me.

B. Okay, I'll go. It seems like everything comes to an end.

D. It was a pleasure to hear you again, my friend. Thank you and Ophelia for coming.

B. Thank you for listening.

D. And giving us such a nice Christmas present.

B. Ho–ho–ho. Okay, I'll go. But take me next time! Bye bye.

Preparing to Travel to Tiddle (Jan 13, 2020)

At this point in Bob's chronology, he is not aware of the Taffles, but Gergen is preparing him to travel to the planet where they reside. When spirits manifest a solid form on a remote location, it requires a larger percentage of their soul energy. Similar like the washer on the sixth, the second dimension has a device they use to assist the spirit to manifest on a physical planet. Bob calls those who operate the device Merlins because they wear tall, pointy hats. But they do not communicate with him, so it only adds to his concern about embarking on the adventure. When this session was held, there were huge fires burning in Australia. Bob tells us that many spirits from the second dimension, who were on assignment on Earth, were temporarily going there to help heal the animals, trees and plants.

B. And now the door was opened! Huhuh

D. Hello, my friend.

B. Huh! I'm here! I'm back. Nah nah nah nah (*He began singing a random melody.*) I've been in training for a new destination of travel.

D. Oh? Where is that?

B. I don't know. Gergen said it's going to be something magical.

D. Is it related to the second dimension?

B. I'm thinking so because I'm not in training with you. I'm getting prepared, he said, and I'm gonna go somewhere that is beyond beyond! Beyond beyond beyond it might be, because I know what is beyond beyond. But now I'm curious what is beyond beyond beyond! Huhuh. And he said that I'm gonna go somewhere and there are friends that I'm gonna meet.

D. I bet I know who they are.

B. I don't know. But it's a different preparation, because he said that in order for me to go there, and I'm supposed to take a form, my own form, so it sounds like I'm gonna be myself. But I'm taking a manifestation class. Meaning that it's not me going in a peanut suit, and it's not me going in a bubble, it is ME transforming into a manifested me. It's tricky! It's also scary, but Gergen says this is the only way for me to go. I'm gonna dissolve in the second dimension and I'm gonna reappear, it seems, somewhere else. And he said it's gonna be interesting. And he said that he will be there as well, and Ole will be there, apparently. I wanted to go talk to Ole after I had my training with Gergen, so I seeked him out and I said, "I'm going into the dematerializing and manifesting training program. I'm heading for a new destination." And he just smiled, –he's like Ophelia, he just smiles and you think you're gonna get an answer, but you do not. So I said, "Gergen said that the two of you were gonna be there as well?" And he nodded. So I stood like this (*looking expectantly*) and waited and he nodded and looked at me like I was gonna ask another question, and so I did. I said, "What can you tell me about this new location?" And he said, "It's going be a treat, Bob. You don't want to run ahead of treats, do you?" And I said, "I'm not sure. I might." Then he said, "No. Because if you do, it will not be the big bang, the big hoo–haa that it's going to be." And I said, "Is it gonna be like a big hoo–haa, a big bang?" and he said, "It might be. But if you run ahead of the treat you might influence the treat." And then he left.

D. You didn't get much help. But that was like a reassurance because both he and Gergen have been there.

B. They're gonna be there. The difference being that I'm gonna, in some way, dissolve and I'm gonna reappear in my manifested me. I'm gonna look the same, Gergen said, and everyone's gonna look the same, it's just that we will be manifested.

D. That's like going through the washer.

B. And I was wondering about that, how the transition would take place. And he said that it is traveling, in some way, in a tube; it will appear like a tube. It might be similar like the washer, and I think it is. Gergen said it's like a little washer but it will appear like a tube. And then I said, "Maybe this is like the first, my first experience with the washer before I go somewhere where I'm not familiar? But what if there's no one on the other side waiting for me?"

D. It's nice that Gergen and Ole are going.

B. Ah. They're gonna go, they're gonna be there when I shoot out of the tube, into my form. He said we will all look the same, it's not like we will look different, we will just be. It's like the second dimension but it's in a manifested reality. And I was like, "That's special!"

D. So if you walk around you will bump into things?

B. It's not a merging, and that is part of the theoretical teaching. That's not in the practical part of my training, but the theoretical part is that we don't merge with things. We are there and it has to do with some sort of assignment. There are others there that are from the second dimension, so in many ways I will see this reality similar as the second dimension.

D. I think the ones who crowded you off the stage a few weeks ago are from that planet.

B. Ah, humm. I might see what that is all about. So that is my personal agenda; that is what I am doing on my own time. I'm learning on how to—it is like shutting down your light capsule and move yourself into like a hibernation. But it's not like a regular hibernation where you sleep and then wake up and you are in the same spot. It is a transformation that occurs and it has to do with some sort of rotation. So you, in some way, you turn your eyes inwards, and it's like shutting down all your physical—I'm not physical—but all my conscious abilities, and I turn them inwards and I look for that Center Pole that we all have inside. Each spirit has that Center Pole, and as you see that with your inner eyes, focus on that and it will start to rotate. As it starts to rotate you will become first sort of sleepier, and you will feel heavier, and it will lead you to that hibernation. But it's just the form of who you are that hibernates; the Center Pole is the one (*part of you*) that goes into the washer or into the tube and then it reappears on the other side as you are coming out of the tube.

D. So someone else would have to control where you go then? Or do you do that internally?

B. It's an internal activity. But there are those who monitor and direct. I'm meeting them here; it's a new council and they look like us but they are different. They're not very social.

D. They're like the Moon People.

B. Like the Moon People but on the second dimension. They look like Merlins, like magicians. They have like a tall hat with stars on. There are three and they are the traveling engineers. They maintain and make sure of the motion through this facility, and they do things, these Merlins, and I'm not sure what. Gergen said I'm not allowed to talk to them—because I started to, I had questions about this process and how do I return. But this is not a place for communication, in that sense. I have to do my preparation and they will complete it. So that's what I'm doing here. I'm pretty sure the Merlins are friendly but I never met them before. Gergen said, "You were not ready to dematerialize and materialize in another way. You have now done it differently with going through the peanut suit and going through the bubble, and this is a way for you to travel." And then I think all sorts of opportunities opens up here. If I'm becoming really good friends with the Merlins then I might ask if we can direct my tube to several places. But then again, there's no questions here, so I don't know if I can sit down with them and find out if this tube only goes to one place or if they have several tubes, and where do they go? They are similar to the Moon People but they look like the Merlins, they have cone hats with stars on them. There are three, so I'm trying to detect if one is more eager to share, but at the moment they look the same. They maintain and assist travels when spirits, such as myself, have reached a certain level. BUT, it comes with conditions, you should know. The conditions for me traveling, because I was all excited about this, like "Oh, let's go, let's go." But Gergen said, "Yes, but in order for you to fulfill this new mission of yours, you have to be participating in council work." So I'm back being a secretary. Gergen knew and detected, he said, "You're not paying attention." I said, "No. I'm thinking about my training." And he said, "You're not going to go anywhere until you really refocus and take notes and participate in council work." So I'm doing council work, and the council work at the moment has to do with a change in the ecosystem. They're doing changes on different locations to upgrade the ecosystem. Some is on land, like over on the Australian island, so we're looking into that. There are healers heading that direction. There are a huge amount of spirits from the second dimension that are relocating from other assignments on Earth at this point. (*This was delivered during a time when great wildfires were occurring in Australia.*) I'm not able to, because I'm following you, but I said, "If my person can go to that location then I can also help." I thought that might be helpful for my progress here in my training, if I volunteered. But no one from the second dimension who follows a human are going. There are nature spirits from the second dimension, the healers, you know, fairies and those who look like little snowflakes—they're not snowflakes but they look like snowflakes, I would say, and they're gonna go. They are relocating at this point; they're leaving certain assignments. For instance, they're leaving certain assignments in Thailand and heading down. There are also several from the Amazon heading in that direction, and from Peru and Argentina, who are volunteering and relocating to that island *(Australia)* in need of upgrading its ecosystem. It's not like, I mean, if you were to go and I went with you, we could have done something hands-on, and I might have an input on that. But that's not gonna happen. I can't just make you go places, because you follow a plan and I have to go hand-in-hand with that plan. So I'm here following your plan, which seems kinda selfish one might say, because I might have a plan of my own. Huhuh. And you said that you will later follow my plan, so I'm thinking that my life that I have planned for you might come to term. Anyway, the council—I drifted off there—the council that I'm taking notes on and participating in—they are relocating, you should know and you should tell, they are relocating several nature spirits to that region because there is a huge need of upgrading and rebooting and healing and reconnecting ecosystems. It's similar like when a human has a cold, or you with your arm that I had to heal. I had to reconnect certain dots to help you heal your arm, it's the same thing here but it's a greater effort. That is why spirits that normally belong in other regions on the planet are actually, some of them, relocating at the moment.

D. Is that because of the fires?

B. Indeed, indeed. So they are relocating.

D. I keep thinking it would be easier to just get rid of the humans.

B. It has nothing to do with that, with the fires here. But I'm thinking, because we are talking about, in general, about the upgrade of the humanoid. The physical is one thing, but I also KNOW that Ophelia and some councils, like Isaac on the eighth, they are working on upgrading the consciousness. The emotional is quite fine, but the consciousness—and that is also why you are here to do your hands-on job—but later on it will in some way mirror how the development of a new level of brain will come in. And when that is done, then the rest of us will get new manuals from the cloud and we will then create a new physical humanoid able to carry a higher developed brain.

D. That will be good.

B. Ah. It's coming, but until then, you have to do with what exists.

D. I was going to ask Ophelia about something she said.

B. Ophelia is not here, I am.

D. (*Laughing*) Well I will ask you to ask her.

B. Ah. Ask me.

D. At one point she had said this would be a ten-year project where you would be communicating. Is it actually going to run longer than that?

B. It was intended to be a ten-year project, but it's gonna be longer than that. It's because of the fact that there is just this huge commotion on my stage, and maybe that wasn't known in the beginning how the project would develop. Maybe they didn't know that I would take such great interest in this and claim my spot.

D. I think they may have originally suggested you would only be involved with the first wave.

B. Ah. But that was not my suggestion, and it changed because of the fact that I felt a huge need to talk with you more and it was approved.

D. I'm really happy about that.

B. And I didn't feel like I needed to go. And I said, "Why should I go?" It was known that it was a great connection and a great opportunity for everyone. But then suddenly there were all sorts of new entities also craving time, and that's when I went and talked to Ophelia and talked to you and I said, "I might need separate sessions," and that's when separate session came about.

D. So this will run longer than ten years?

B. Indeed. It's gonna run till it's time to go home, but I'm making sure that you're not close to any fires—I'm making sure of that. And this one, also making sure this one is not rumbling. Don't want that. Making sure that this one stays put. Huhuh. But Isaac and Ophelia mainly takes care of this one, to make sure that this one stays in her lane. It's important.

Bob Travels to Tiddle (Jan 26, 2020)

Gergen begins by giving details about how certain fish tanks around the Wheel of Creation are related to specific spiritual dimensions. Spirits from the second dimension, for example, prefer to manifest in fish tank two. Souls from the fifth dimension are connected to fish tank five. Locations, such as Earth, are where learning and third dimension role plays take place. Fish tank one contains many of the patterns and intentions found in the other fish tanks, and has a strong affiliation with the Creator. Gergen calls it a warehouse that higher councils can access.

Bob describes his journey to Tiddle and his experiences with the Taffles. In order to get from the second dimension to this planet in fish tank two, the Merlins dusted Bob with a powder which put him to sleep. Then these second dimension magicians transported his center point to Tiddle, where he woke up. Once he was there, he felt right at home and, not unexpectedly, made a few friends among the Taffles. Several of them followed him to this session.

TT. Huh huh HA HA, do you see them? Oh? (*One of the Tiddle–Taffles came in and sang and just made happy sounds for a few moments before Gergen took over.*)

G. This, this is Gergen. We have to have some order here, we have to have some sort of control of the group present. We have Bob and we also have the Tiddle–Taffles, and there is somewhat of a gathering indeed, so we have to have some sort of control of what's gonna be delivered here. You should know that when this came about, it became a huge festivity, activity, and everyone was in a merry spirit as they were communicating and meeting for the first time. As of the fact that the Tiddle–Taffles have not really been home for a long time, Bob had several questions for them. And now he has secrets, he said, to reveal. So it became an interesting meeting, I must say, when they met. The Tiddle–Taffles, you should know, –as we merely visit to brief them on council matters and how to proceed with energy transmission–, are highly involved in fish tank two. They rarely have visitors such as a spirit like Bob, and in that sense, it became somewhat of a commotion.

D. You're also a spirit.

G. Oh, I have grown older in my ways. I am, hmm, less bouncy and enthusiastic, –I mean I'm enthusiastic, but merely on the inside. I tend to leave the surprising events and treats to him, as I know how much he appreciates the little blings along the way.

D. So did he travel there already?

G. We did indeed, and I'm pretty sure that he wants to tell you about the actual transmission of his being, because it was quite different than going in his peanut suit. He actually fell asleep and transformed and changed his energetic being and later manifested in his form, –and yes, Bob, you can tell the story, indeed. So today we are here with Bob and the Tiddle-Taffles and the disclosure of that first meeting, and also a little bit of a sneak peek up in fish tank two, to see the activity that these highly inquisitive little entities do on our behalf, who occupy the space working on energy transmission.

D. Do they work in other fish tanks?

G. The Tiddle-Taffles are not—you might think they are as eager as Bob to travel—but they are not. They are somewhat set in their ways and they prefer to be home. Even though they have traveled far and do not necessarily return in the same way to the spiritual side, they are not as eager to move around to other fish tanks. They are interested in exploring other realities IN fish tank two. Huhuhuh.

D. So that's where their efforts are focused?

G. Yes, yes, indeed. The second dimension has a tendency, when traveling and becoming manifested and parked, to do so in fish tank two. In some way, you should know, that the fish tanks correlate to the spiritual levels. So here, fish tank five is highly connected, and is why most souls from the fifth dimension belongs in this fish tank. So in some way, yes indeed it is a correlation. Don't be confused with the fourth reality, because that would indicate that fish tank four would be an illusion, which it is not. But you should know that in many ways the dimensions—yes, Bob, you will soon come in, we still have time. There is no need to rush or be grumpy, there is still time for you. What I would like to say is that most fish tanks relate to the spiritual dimensions. So here fish tank five, predominantly souls from the fifth dimension occupy space and travel to realities such as Earth. It's not a black and white science, as you, yourself travel here as well. But in general, as for the Tiddle-Taffles, they come originally from the second dimension, and they prefer to be in manifested form in fish tank two. Fish tank one—no, Bob, I'm not going to go through the whole wheel (*as he looks to the left*). He has his ways, but that's also why he was chosen to become the great explorer that he is, because he has a very pushy, yet tender, and a very persistent personality. I'm pretty sure that is why he was designed from the Creator to be the little happy entity that he is. I see myself a lot in him, even though I have become a little bit more still in my older days. But I can see myself and I indeed had some of his traits earlier in my development. But as you grow older, you tend to become a little bit more fond of stillness, don't you?

D. Does Ole have a mentor that is still around?

G. Yes, indeed. Yes, indeed.

D. And does his mentor have a mentor that is still around?

G. I am not aware, but Ole's mentor is still around, so it is a long way to be dissolved. Huh huh huh.

D. Where does Ole's mentor reside, mostly?

G. We're all on the second dimension, but he is in a collective council. Ole's mentor is in the overseeing council of the second, so he is supervising and making decisions for the presence of the second dimension, regardless of fish tank. I have not had the pleasure to communicate with him, but there are occasions where Ole comes back and sometimes brings a little bit of an idea, that I would assume comes from higher up. The big ones in that higher level, so to speak. But fish tank one, it is somewhat the initiator for the rest of the fish tanks, meaning it correlates, in some way, directly to the Center Pole. And the Center Pole is the connecting point, the solar plexus, the center point in galaxies, in solar systems, in fish tanks and so forth. So in many ways, fish tank one is not suitable for visits in that sense. It is merely filled, if I use the limited supply of words that we have here, if you can see it as the warehouse where all tools, all elements, everything that needs to exist in all fish tanks, originates from. So, light, sound, gravity, iron, all these different elements and keys on how to combine DNA and elements originates from this big warehouse in fish tank one, which is in some way mirroring the Master Mind. So one can say that fish tank one is the home for the Master Mind to, in some way, be able to, from that point, channel its energy flow or awareness through all fish tanks. And it doesn't have to go from one to two to three, in that way—and yes, Bob, we will soon stop this lesson of physics and the lesson of cosmology, but it is of interest.

D. Yes, it is.

G. So it doesn't have to go from fish tank one to two, going around that way. From fish tank one it has the direct connection to the Center Pole and can communicate to the Center Pole if, let's say, if something is needed or added to fish tank nine, it doesn't go the whole route around. It communicates directly to the Source, because the Master Mind communicates

directly to the Father and Mother energy inside the Creator, which transform and transmit that specific energy flow or awareness in the direction where it's needed. So in some way, one can say the Creator uses fish tank one as its warehouse for what to use in all the other realities. So when I said that this is not merely where you go to visit, there are those who are equipped in modifying and directing certain elements and awareness's to different fish tanks, who have access to fish tank one. But it's not a place one goes to incarnate. In some way it is not very open, fish tank one, and it is supposed to be in that way. It merely communicates with the Center Pole, and from that point, goes directly into whatever fish tank the intention lies. So, that's something of an interest, I would assume, for your teaching.
D. Yes, it's very interesting.
G. But then again, there are several here and we want to make sure everyone gets their time, so I'll step aside, and we have, guess who, first in line.
D. Thank you so much for sharing that information, I really appreciate it.
G. You are much welcome. So, okay, it is your turn (*speaking to Bob*).
B. AH! Ooooohhhhh! Do you know where I've been?
D. I heard a hint.
B. You heard a hint before me?
D. But I have no idea where you went.
B. Nay, nay. I've been around, not everything involves you. I have traveled by myself as well. And Gergen, he came in, like one sunny afternoon, and he said, "I think it's time to go and meet some of our friends who occupy another fish tank, another space. They don't come back here as often because they have somewhat emigrated." And I said, "Emigrated? What does that mean?" Then he said, "They are from the second dimension, but they have chosen to remain in a solid reality. They work as batteries and energy transmitters in fish tank two." And he said, "There are several realities in that region that are home to expats from the second dimension, who simply have gone and set tent and do not necessarily come back." And I said, "Uhh, I have still unfinished business, I can't emigrate at the moment." And he said, "No, you're not gonna emigrate, but if

you want, you can go and have a preview, you can go and have a look–see; and if this is somewhere where you wish to retire, you have this as an option." And I said, "Is retired the same as dissolving? Do they dissolve from there?" And he said, "That is not to be given at the moment, but we're going to talk more about that." Because retirement, I've have never heard about that, and I'm not sure if that is the same as dissolving. But he said it's not, and he says they are expats, so they go there and they don't come back. He says that he and Ole apparently go, and they go and give notes, he say, they give certain ideas and notes on DNA and energy. He says that sometimes those from the eighth also travel there.

D. Such as Isaac?

B. Isaac, probably. I don't know why no one told me. Maybe it's because I didn't ask, but it's hard to ask when you don't know. So now when I know this, then I can ask more questions, and I'm pretty sure that's something everyone looks forward to! Huhuhuh. But apparently, they have retired up there, the expats, and he said that they prefer to be there and they are stationed there. They work on the transmission of energy, and you should know that they are quite similar as myself.

D. Lively? Jolly?

B. Quite lively! I found plenty of new friends, and they say they have no need to return back at the moment. They're happy here and they seem to enjoy life.

D. Sounds like a nice place to visit.

B. You can't go there as a sparkle. In many ways it is similar like you retire to Florida. They are HIGHLY active and they're funny and they sing and there is always something going on.

D. Did you feel like you fit in there?

B. Ah. They took me around. Before we left, I wondered if I was gonna go through the washer. Then Ole came, because he apparently is buddy–buddy with the magicians, the Merlins with the washers, and he said that it gonna not be like the washer. But the Merlins are gonna come and put some sort of dust on me, like a sleeping dust. Then I thought maybe this is similar like the Evolution Group—so I wanted to know about the compound and foundation of this powder. I said, "I have seen powder, and that is what the Evolution Group did, and it was to speed up evolution." And I said, "Are you going to fast–forward me to retirement?" And Ole said, –because the

Merlins, they don't talk that well and you can't really ask them–, so I ask Ole and he said, "No, they're not going to transform you into a retired individual. And it's not like those up there (*the Tiddle-Taffles*), they will not appear as they are retired, it's not like all of them are seniors." He said that the Merlins are gonna come and put that dust on me and I'm gonna, in some way, fall to sleep. As I do, some sort of energy work is gonna happen to my presence and my being, and they're gonna, in some way, release my center point, my sparkle inside, and that is gonna go (*to Tiddle*). He said, "You're not going to be aware of the travel itself, but the Merlins take your center point and make it go somewhere." But I'm not gonna be in the washer and I'm not gonna tumble, I'm not gonna be aware; I'm simply gonna feel like I'm falling asleep. But here comes trust issues. You have someone who doesn't speak well—or at all, in this case—who looks like Merlins with big cone hats, and you have to trust that they know what they're doing.

D. I'm assuming that Ole wouldn't put you in danger.

B. Nay. Not Gergen either. I asked if Gergen could also be present, and he could indeed. So when this took place, it was not just that it came dust on me and I fell asleep, there was actually some sort of tunes, and it was to relax my so-called physical being, the body that I occupy on the second. But the spirit itself would move, but I will look the same because my spirit is unique and the blueprint will simply unfold as the body that I hold on the second dimension as well. It's simply a shift that takes place where you demanifest in some way and then remanifest somewhere else, but you need the Merlins, apparently. Ole said that the Merlins are not needed fully; he said you can do it by yourself eventually, he say. But Gergen still needs the Merlins, but Ole doesn't need the Merlins. He probably has a back door where he goes. But Gergen, who also has gone, he still needs the Merlins, he say. So I don't feel like I'm a rookie here because if Gergen also needs the Merlins then I'm pretty sure this is high tech and quite advanced. I can't tell you about the journey itself as I, myself, my conscious self, was not aware. BUT, when I arrived, there was Gergen, he traveled with me, he also went because I wanted that. He probably heard my thoughts. I don't know if I said it out loud but he probably heard my request from my being. But as we came there, OH, it was like being dropped into a mist of happiness! And everyone was just like greeting me. When I kinda woke up, it was like on a little platform, like a plateau, like a cliff, and I was laying down. And when I gazed up, when I came about, there they were! Just staring! And smiling and they were like "Lahdaalahlahl", something like that!

D. Did you understand them? Do they speak your language?

B. Ah, they speak. It's a happy group. I brought one, he's here. I got myself a friend.

D. So tell me about what you saw and what you did.

B. Well, first it was like—you know how you do those dances around the Christmas tree? You're sort of in a line and you hold hands and you run around the house, and you sing and run upstairs and go in one room and you go downstairs, and you go around the tree, and you open the door and go out in the garden, and you sing and hold hands—so I was just swept away in this little train of singing. They took me around like that. Gergen, he didn't come, he said he had business to attend to.

D. He didn't feel like running and singing?

B. Nay. He said, "Go and have fun, amuse yourself, this is fun. Have a look–see around. I'll catch up later, I have business to attend to." There's a library where he goes and he fills it up with notes. So he had some notes that he was gonna put in this library. As he went in one direction and I went in the other with—you know what they're called? Tiddle–Taffles!

D. I've heard the name.

B. Tiddle–Taffles.

D. Is that what they are called, or is that the planet?

B. It's the planet, and they are the Tiddle–Taffles. The planet is called Tiddle, and they are the Tiddle–Taffles! Taffles mean caretakers of Tiddle. So the planet is called Tiddle, they are the Taffles, you know, caretakers, so combined, Tiddle–Taffles. If they go anywhere else, like Earth, they would be the Earth–Taffles. Huh huh, so Taffle is a word for someone who is a caretaker. Ohh, so we continued this dance and we took off and they showed me around. They have little huts. They live in a little society. The climate is extremely suitable. When I woke up, they had put me in some sort of fine outfit. (*He looks down and mentally examines his clothes.*) It's very colorful, –almost like how your native Indians were dressed–, that's how they're dressed, a little bit. Not feathers but a lot of different colors. I got one of their suits, so I fit in. I don't want to look like an outsider, I wanted to fit in. This is what I woke up in. I'm not sure if I'm gonna be able to bring it home.

D. That sounds nice.

B. So anyway, we took off and we danced and ran around. I was in the back, and my friend here, he was the last one in line, and when the other ones were singing and I didn't know the melody fully, then he explained, when we passed different things, he explained what it was. And we went to their huts. They live in little societies, they don't live secluded to each other, they like to be close by. Apparently, they all share meals, all meals, together. There is no privacy that one can consider here, and they don't really like privacy, it seems.

D. What do they eat?

B. There is some sort of seeds, it looks like pumpkin seeds almost, and it looks like they have prepared it into somewhat of a porridge. They use seeds and beans, those kinda things, for everything. They have like cooks who prepare and everyone has, maybe it's not called like that, but they have breakfast, lunch and dinner together. They enjoy being together and no one is excluded. It seems like they really—my feeling here is—what they are all about is very much that they talk a lot, and they share. It's like flying with the Riddler, there are talks and stories and they share everything. It's a very active community. (*I had no idea what 'flying with the Riddler' meant. Apparently, it means having a barrage of questions tossed at you.*)

D. I have a question about eating because I've wondered that about manifestation. Why do they need to eat, and do they have internal organs?

B. Here they do. They are almost like a human, it seems. They have brought (*manifested*) all interior organs needed to coexist with the atmosphere here.

D. Are there animals there?

B. Ah, indeed. Birds! Birds, –you don't eat them. There are birds, there is somewhat of a cat animal, similar like a mountain lion.

D. Is there a sun in the sky?

B. Ah. There are more. There is three, three suns. The temperature is like 18 to 23 degrees (*Celsius*).

D. Are they stationary, or does the planet rotate?

B. Well, it seems like it's stationary, but they also have nights in some way, but it's not dark at night like Earth night. It's more like late sunset, that is night.

D. Do they sleep?

B. Ah, in their huts. Everyone goes to bed at the same time, everyone wakes up at the same time, everyone has breakfast at the same time in this little colony where I am. I don't know how big this is. They do like water and they communicate with some sort of entity in the water. They are highly connected with waters' oxygen. There is a laboratorium that works on the transmission of energy through waters and establishing...oh, they did not want to tell me that. But there are facilities and they mainly seem to connect and come from the sea, from the water. It's not like satellite towers at all. Their transmission system and their energy source is from the sea. And they say that the way we use energy on Earth—not we, you—is very primitive. They say you could have more supply if you went natural, if you went organic and used the resources differently. They say that it would be desirable if there would become new energy engineers who knew how to use water and also the wind and sun. They use the natural elements and actually say you can learn how to connect and combine these natural elements that exist in their world as well as here, even though they have three suns and we only have one. So they have the upper hand, –I say that because the Earth only has one sun. But they say mankind and the planet would have a cleaner and better and even a higher percentage of energy supply because the Earth will provide more if man knew how to excavate energy resources differently. They say at this time, the planet Earth is in some way guarding its resources, meaning if mankind has all these pumps and they drill and do all these things, Earth is holding back because of the fact it needs some of it to maintain its own circulation system and maintain the core of the planet. What the Tiddle–Taffles do is that they read the core and from that point, they know how to...oh, they take things away from me here. Maybe Gergen is doing something remotely from his

Teachings from Etena and Tiddle

library over there. (*Apparently, Bob was blocked from revealing certain information.*) He knows I'm curious. But just know that what they do, they are like your profession, not petroleum engineers, but they are energy engineers and chemical engineers and they know how to use and connect natural elements in order for—it's like an opening in the sea at certain times, and that becomes a source of energy that they tap into. It's not like electricity. You might think this is a high–tech society, but the huts don't look very high tech and the temple on the cliff and the facility doesn't look very high tech. They say they are little professors and inventors. Gergen and Ole bring notes from several councils, and they are modifying experiments and trying out different ways of generating energy. Apparently, the waters are a great source.

D. So what do they do with the energy they either collect or generate?

B. I have not been told yet, but the general intent here is that some of the energy remains within this system, the system they belong in and the fish tank. But they also are doing assignments for other fish tanks when it comes to how to generate and how to recycle energy. They say you don't recycle energy on Earth, you simply take it and it doesn't return, it's not a natural flow. So they have different tasks.

D. Do they share the information with councils or Ole?

B. Ah. It appears, because it is a foundation on several realities. They share it with council members that come, such as Gergen and Ole. And Ole, it appears, has someone above him that he communicates to. So in some way the Tiddle–Taffles, on behalf of several fish tanks and the second dimension, they work on their behalf. And because there are different conditions in all fish tanks, so their tasks and their assignments vary as well.

D. That's really fascinating. It sounds like very beneficial work.

B. Ah. So they're not lazy, they're not retired just playing chess or bridge, or sit and eat candy—they have that porridge, they seem to like that porridge.

D. Did you have any meals with them?

B. I'm not sure if it's good for me to eat. But then again, I don't want to sound ungrateful. So when we had our sit–down, when they shared the meal, I actually had a little bowl. It was quite tasty, it was kinda sweet. It was like a peach flavor. So if you think of seeds that exists in like a honey-melon, it was like seeds they made into a porridge. It was quite sweet. So I had a taste, I don't want to be like an ungrateful guest. So we went there, and then I said, "Oh, I wonder where Gergen is?" And he was in the library, adjusting notes, he said.

D. He's like Zachariah over there?

B. Ah. He collects notes, he collects information that he brings home to Ole, probably, but he also leaves new assignments that comes from the ones above Ole. They're like a little industry almost, but "industry" is somewhat of a negative and dirty word here (*on Earth*). They work on the behalf of the second dimension in several different fish tanks, and if a note were to come from Earth, which it has, then they look into how the species and how the system operates when it comes to excavating and using minerals and natural elements, such as the sun and the wind and the water, and also heat that comes from the sun. So they use certain elements—and first of all they have to know what elements are available in that specific reality—and then they do tests on how to improve and upgrade. That's what they bring back to the second dimension councils, the notes on what they perceive. So they can, in their little laboriturium, which I have not come into yet, they can do modifications and they can do tests and then they bring back the notes, –which are the ones Gergen is picking up here.

D. I guess the second would do that because they are so closely tied to the natural aspects of Earth?

B. Indeed. So that's what they do, but they don't work only for Earth. If there is another reality that are imbalanced when it comes to need of supply, when it comes to energy resources, they look at that. First of all, they have to read the core, so they communicate and they read the core of the planet, and then step-by-step, layer-by-layer, all the way up to the surface, they read the vibrational keys and how the planet is holding the experiences. They also said that sometimes a planet can be too full and it has too much resources and it WANTS to be excavated; it wants to be released because it might feel like it has food coma. So they look into that also. They said your planet, your world, is guarding a little bit because it feels like if it lets everything up to the surface for the humanoids, then the beings will take all the resources and they don't really know how to recycle it into the system again so it regenerates new. They just take out and do not put back, so it's one way—up, up, and nothing goes down. Nothing rotates (*circulates*). So on Earth, that is the case. But they say that there are certain worlds that are so full of minerals and resources and energy within the planet that they actually want to remove some. And that's when they send either incarnations or they send different visitors to just excavate or to drill, for instance. So that's why certain humanoids have a memory of visiting places where they drilled or worked in mines and so forth. It could have that one and only purpose: To release the pressure on the planet.

D. Huh. It's like milking a cow.

B. Milking a cow, that's it. And there are those who are milkers, if you like, visitors who go around with that assignment. If one planet needs to be milked, and that cow doesn't feel well, the whole system will go, "Mooo, mooo." And you want them to have a happy moo, so it's the same thing, it's a balance in everything. If there are certain planets in systems that are too full, that needs to be drained, or milked like you say, then they send in visitors. And visitors can come either like me here, falling asleep and waking up manifested in some way, not necessarily going as an incarnation—which is not very common—they normally just send in visitors who are equipped to drill, to milk.

D. I remember Gergen said the Tiddle–Taffles work with color a lot.

B. Indeed, because different vibrations in the colors gives away the well–being of, let's say, the planet. So in many ways they read colors, they don't read words, in that sense. So when they are given information it comes as a color map.

D. Fascinating.

B. So, you know. Ah. So that will probably be it now. (*He paused, looking reflective.*)

D. What are you thinking?

B. My friend here, he says there's gonna be a party.

D. Are you going to go back to his planet now?

B. I AM here on the Tiddle–Taffles planet. Haven't you followed anything? I've been dancing, I've been looking at things, like the huts!

D. (*Laughing*) I thought you had left already and were just telling me about it.

B. I am at the moment revisiting where I was.

D. So are you going to stay there for a while?

B. There's a party in my honor, so I'm not gonna go anywhere. But I said that I'm not ready to retire, I'm not ready to emigrate here. But I'll be happy to come back, and there are absolutely insights here.

D. That sounds like a wonderful place for you to visit.

B. Ah. I've got new friends.

D. Tell them we all say hello from Earth.

B. They're gonna come and talk more, they say. But Gergen said that they would talk through me today.

D. Thank you for sharing all of that.

B. I'm gonna go now. But exciting, exciting indeed.

D. I'm happy you successfully traveled there.

B. I can't say that it was a success from my part, because the Merlins just made me fall asleep and then I woke up in this colorful outfit.

D. At least you can trust them now.

B. It was because Gergen said he would come as well. I wasn't really, –it's hard when you want to trust someone, but you don't feel like you can communicate so they could answer my questions about certain things.

D. You need Ole as a translator.

B. Ole was a translator. Gergen came with because he had business to attend to. He had to leave new notes and also bring back certain results. So I'm gonna go now, but next time we talk more.

D. Alright, my friend. Thank you so much for coming and sharing with us.

B. It was really exciting for me to go and meet them, because they are doing so many interesting things. They do, like, the groundwork, the level one work, for EVERYTHING. You know how I talked about how Gergen and Ia work with DNA and light and everything, they know what to do based on what the

Tiddle–Taffles have found out and the results they provide as they do tests. So it's not just energy like we talk about, like oil, gas, electricity, it has to do with resources, minerals and the maintenance of light. They are specialists in different things. Some are working with the seas, but there are also those who work with DNA and the transmission of waves, energy waves and light waves, through different modifications of DNA. But it's basically the same because they do the groundwork for life in whatever shape or form that might exist in a reality.

D. You'll have to explain sometime a little more about how DNA and light are related.

B. Ah. Probably ask Gergen to do that. We'll see. But they are very skilled and they say they like being here because they know everyone, and everyone are friends, and they share. They don't have hobbies in that sense, their work is their hobby, but now and then they apparently like singing.

D. They like visitors too.

B. Ah, ah, it seems like they do.

D. It gives them an excuse to throw a feast.

B. Ah. Even though it seems like the meals are kinda the same. They don't seem to mind, and who am I to judge? I don't necessarily eat, so this was a new experience by itself, just to feel that.

D. In some way that is human–like, without the karma.

B. Ah. I did feel a little bit sleepy afterwards. That was also another kind of experience. Well, I'm gonna go now, but we'll be back to talk more.

D. Alright, my friend. Thank you for coming and sharing. I really enjoyed the stories today.

B. Ah, okay. Bye bye.

The Spiritual and the Manifested Blueprints (Feb 9, 2020)

Ophelia began the February 9th session, and while leaving, she told Bob he could briefly deliver a note. He proceeded to give a captivating talk that contained more than one note and was not brief (for which we are grateful). He began by elaborating on the two blueprints that are present in each soul. The main blueprint is the energetic core, the consciousness and purpose given to each spirit by the Creator. It is this core blueprint which creates forms in either the spiritual realities or out in the fish tanks, where elemental matter exists. The spiritual blueprint is divisible, making it possible for a spirit to be in multiple places at once. A human body also has a blueprint, and when a soul incarnates on Earth, they assemble pieces of their spiritual blueprint and send it out to join with a body. The blueprint for the human body is modified by the incoming soul and its Coat of Karma. Therefore, during the time of incarnation, the soul would be attached to and operating within two (or more) separate forms, one at home in spirit world, and the other on Earth.

Bob then moves on to another note about parallel realities in our fish tank. When an astrophysicist says "Universe", based on their understanding, it implicitly excludes the parallel realities. What the spirits call fish tank five is our Universe plus the parallel realities. The spirits describe the parallel planes as being physical realities with connecting highways, and should not be confused with the spiritual dimensions. Alien visitors to Earth travel and perhaps even reside within them. In order for an object, such as a UFO, to move back and forth from the visible Earth plane into the parallel reality, some bizarre physics is involved. An odd feature within one of the parallel planes is that everything is miniaturized by several orders of magnitude. If we were to observe a UFO leaving our Universe into this parallel reality, it first begins to glow. The glowing would increase as the object shrinks, appearing like a bright ball of light until it vanishes from our sight. The elements glow because they are changing state from the vibrational frequency of our Universe into another, higher frequency. The parallel planes are phase shifted outside the bandwidth of human perception, and are therefore undetectable by any of our instruments.

B. Ah. Briefly, briefly. I'll just come in and say something about that, since I was dissolved and I was moved. Clearly, I heard here that they somewhat divided my being, my two blueprints. What is said here is that there are actually two blueprints, one that is based on the form, the materia or the object itself, but there is also the spiritual blueprint. And understanding that you have both, then that indeed makes it possible to solve and to understand the endless possibilities that lies before you in how to move things, –such as myself! So what we did with me was that we in some way—I mean, I'm not physical like an object such as a rock, but I still have two blueprints;

one that is indicating my form and one that is my spiritual blueprint—so in order for me to move to Tiddle, I left the form blueprint behind and I merged into my spiritual blueprint, and that was the thing that moved. When we use the washer, Seth said, then the form goes with me. That's different.
D. That does actually make sense to me.
B. It's a way to split up. But if you want to go with both form and spirit through barriers, Ophelia says, then you have to understand and handle two different vibrations and they rotate differently. Once you understand that you are built by two blueprints, then that creates the object to potentially move. So when you sleep, for instance, you leave the form and you in some way merge with your spiritual blueprint. So you have the ability, she says, to not only go up to the dream field, which is in the fourth reality, but she says that you can also travel in that time when you sleep, if you are highly developed. She says, "It's not like everyone does that, it's way later in coming into human form that the soul tends to do this. But it is to gather information from the parallel universes, –and that is not in dreams, it is a transportation that takes place. You do that!
D. Do I?
B. Ah. And you don't just go up and float in the fourth. I can see when you do that, I can see when you dream if you only go to the fourth reality and have a rest, just sort of look around. A lot of times you look around at what other people dream, that's what you do. So you gather information because there's a lot of things to be told by dreams, so you gather information and you're more passive when you go to the fourth reality in your sleep. But sometimes you continue your journey and you go out of my sight, so I don't know where you go, but you say that you will come back. I sort of accompany you in the fourth reality. While the form is still sleeping, sometimes the soul has a different agenda, and that is when you rotate to meet parallel realities—which are not in the fourth reality—to gather information. And some souls do so, and that is how certain advanced technologies, for instance, occurs. They say they got it in their sleep. No. The form thinks it slept and it gathered it in the sleep, but it wasn't received in the fourth reality, in the fourth dimension, –it was that the soul took off, and it took off to gather information in the nearby parallel

universe, which is not the fourth reality. It's a physical, manifested reality, but a soul can visit there in sleep time. I don't go. I see you sometimes, –when you say, "I'm going to go and collect information," –then I know that you go, and it looks like you are going into a fog.

D. So you have never traveled there?

B. I don't go with you there. When you sleep, I go with you and I'm with you when you're in the fourth reality, or if you say, "Let's go home," then we go home and we go to the lab. But sometimes you say, "I'm going to gather information from the neighbors," and when you say that, then I know you go to those who are in the parallel universe. Then you come back and you have ideas. You did that a lot when you were that scientist person, the one in Italy, and that is how you understood all these advanced technologies, for that time. It wasn't that you slept and went to the fourth reality, you actually went to neighboring parallel existences and they told you, and then you brought it back.

D. If you ever travel through the washer, would you be able to access that reality?

B. If I travel through the washer, I will access not only going to different fish tanks and universes and planets and so forth, I could potentially also, after a while, access a parallel universe to a physical universe—and I'm intrigued by that! I'm thinking that there's all sorts of knowledge that exists in the fog and with the neighbors. Since I've been kind of cautious about neighbors, I said, "Do I have a parallel universe around my living planet?" And you said, "No." Then I said, "I might wanna have one of those," and you said, "But you don't like neighbors." And I said, "Well, if I can interview the neighbors who are gonna occupy my parallel universe on my living planet, then I might be fine. Where do you go and gather neighbors? Where do you go and pick?" Then you laughed, and Ophelia laughed, so what took place was that Isaac came. Isaac always comes when I'm concerned about neighbors and when I'm concerned about evolution. So he said, "I heard that you wanted a parallel universe to your living planet?" And I said, "I'm thinking about it, because I might wanna have neighbors who look after, not only spiritual friends, but those who are actually present, and could potentially be of assistance, and also be a little bit like a firewall, a guard for others. I would like the birds that are at the border to Etena—I like those." And Isaac said, "Well, the border of birds that you experienced when you went to Etena, they were actually placed there by a joined work from the councils on the seventh dimension versus those who were occupying Etena, and because of the fact that they are highly connected to the vibration of birds, that's how they manifested birds." And I said, "But I'm highly connected with fairies, so I might have a whole bunch—they will look like insects and no one will come in, if that is the case."

D. Around Etena, were the birds around the planet like an atmosphere?

B. Well, that too. But there was a bigger border of birds when we entered the fourth fish tank. And they were several. And I was like, "Oh, I wonder how I'm gonna navigate through here?" But it was no problem. There was also some, but less birds, around Etena. Similar like now, you have the water mammals occupying the seas, making sure and reporting about the sea, they have big birds—they look almost like seagulls, the big white ones—and they sort of occupy and observe the atmosphere. It's different though, you don't have birds that clean up and fly around and clean up and observe your atmosphere. Maybe you should. Because of the fact that they are highly connected to the seventh dimension, that's why they have birds. And then I said, "So I can only use the form that is of my knowledge, like fairies or sparkles or something like that?" And you said, "We can't put fairies in the parallel universe around your planet." So I said, "I want to go and see what sort of neighbors I can choose from."

D. Well, if we talk about Earth and the parallel reality around Earth—

B. They have Little Greys in there.

D. I almost pictured it was a band they could travel on?

B. Indeed. Travel horizontal alongside it, and travel up and down through (*the fog or portals between Earth and the parallel reality*). They are present, it's just that your eyes can't see them. From the spiritual realm, I see when there are those Little Greys coming in, for instance. They just drop down from that big cloud.

D. I remember we talked about the highways that connect all the different fish tanks, like a web. Is the web also like a parallel reality?

B. Well, we give you little by little, Ophelia says. And it expands. So you have to think of, that there are layer upon layer, and even in the spiritual realities, there are levels and layers, similar as in the fish tanks and similar in the whole disk. And it moves, it's like an ocean that moves. So when certain levels merge, that is when interaction takes place and that is when sometimes you can see things. It's like a big wobbling going like this (*as he rocks side-to-side*).

D. I was just trying to picture the relationship between the web that entities can travel on, fish tank to fish tank, and the parallel realities?

B. They travel on the one that moves, and you have the fish tank like this, they can tap into that. (*He was holding his arms up in front, hands near the opposite elbow, moving each up and down like waves. When the hand touched the elbow, he was indicating the realities merged. In Wave 2, they described how there are parallel wheels, stacked on top of each other, like layers in a cake. The lowest one is the main wheel. It remains in a fixed position, and it holds the patterns and intentions of the Creator, which are segregated into 12 different fish tanks. The wheel above also has 12 fish tanks, but it rotates, such that each of the fish tanks on the upper wheel eventually pass over the patterns held by the lower wheel. The static fish tanks project patterns upwards into the wheel above, creating form using the available elements in whichever fish tank happens to be above the main wheel, similar to how images are projected onto the ceiling of a planetarium. The lower wheel has no manifested form. The moving wheel is where all the drama of creation occurs. There are also parallel realities that are part of the upper wheel, and it is in these parallel realities that visitors travel.*)

D. Then around the planet are parallel realties that are in some way connected to the planet? Or are they different vibrational fields that extend through the whole solar system or galaxy?

B. I can only see fish tank disks going here, and then there is a disk going like this (*indicating one above the other, like stacked plates*) and when they merge, they can tap into that.

D. But then beneath that, around the planet, there are parallel realities that are connected to the planet?

B. Uhh. I can only see like fish tank disk (*a level in the Wheel*) going here, and then there is a disk that goes like this (*one disk above the other*) and when they merge, interactions between realities takes place. But that is not the spiritual, we're still talking about the manifested one.

D. I follow that.

B. (*He looked quizzical*) Well, maybe you can tell me more then. I think we should take a class about this. Now when I see that there is a big parallel disk that hovers above the physical fish tanks, and sometimes they are wide apart and sometimes they interact. When they interact that's when visitors can come.

D. Both of them are outside the spiritual dimensions?

B. Indeed. But the spirits can travel on that energetic disk, if you like, the one that hovers above the physical disk or the physical universes. So the spiritual realities can travel on both, like outwards.

D. It's a pretty complicated subject.

B. Ah. So I might need to take a class on this. If you're gonna ask me more questions, I might need to take a class first. Huhuhuh. Ah! I tell Ophelia and she says I'm tricky again. I told her, "If he's gonna keep asking these tricky questions then I might need to take some sort of class first." And she said, "Well, maybe we will let Jeshua answer, or Ari answer." Then I said, "It's highly desirable if I'm aware too, because there tend to be questions when I'm sitting here so it's better if I'm up to speed and I'm up to date with the topics, so I don't just talk about birds and bees."

D. You must have been around when they were building the pyramids and other structures? Did you see?

B. I did! I did! I saw things. I saw activities, I saw beings coming in.

D. Did you see the process?

B. I saw from a distance, I could see that. And I could see, looking in rewind when I access other, not only your films, but sometimes when I look at this one's film.

D. I remember one time I asked if you knew how they moved the rocks and—

B. I did, I do!

D. And Ophelia cut you off. Here came the finger.

B. Ah. And maybe that's why they don't want to put me into more training. But I'm gonna go now and we're gonna talk more about this.

D. What kind of classes are you taking now?

B. I'm not taking, I'm conducting classes. We are talking about human activity with Tom and the ones from the sixth, about what to expect from your person and how one can encourage your friend when the friend comes back from the mission, if the mission wasn't a success; and that one should not put that on oneself to think that, "I have to solve this, my complete blueprint and mission, in one trip." There is one blueprint here, but you can also have—even if you don't go to other fish tanks—other blueprints and missions on the spiritual reality where you belong. It can be certain projects, or that you are a mentor or a helper or that kinda thing. Like Ia, for instance, she's a helping hand for me, she keeps reminding me of maintaining my light capsule. So even though we have different missions, she has still a purpose for me, and I'm pretty sure that there is a purpose that I have for her, even if it is just to be a disturbance in the choir.

D. (*Laughing*) You make her laugh. You make us all laugh.

B. I wanted to sing in the choir, but I had to co-sing. It ended up though that we did a duet.

D. You and Ia?

B. Ah. We did a duet. So it's to inspire couple unity. And that is also sometimes when people feel lost here on Earth, –if they are very tight with a soul companion at home in the spirit realm, that can be crucially disappointing when one tries to find a friend–, because one is programmed to know what a friend is, and if you are put in an environment where the people are not acting as the friends that you consider a friend to be, and the signals that you are trying to read or the signals that you yourself try to give to others, if there is a disconnect between signals then a friendship cannot start to blossom. Like from the second dimension, we are very much coupled up and we are very much group activity. I have never seen your couple (*on the sixth*), you don't seem to have a couple. You have your brothers, you say, but you don't have an Ia, like that. And you don't sing, you're not in a choir. Ia and I, we were doing a duet, and it was to inspire everyone participating to bond with their companion, because even though you are a companion, you have different purposes and different paths to go. And sometimes for those who are here as a human, your counterpart in the spirit realm, the one you would consider your closest friend might have a completely different path. But you still have projects and you still assist each other, both when you travel and when you are at home.

D. I have a couple questions. On the fifth dimension, are they like male and female type patterns, or emotional and mental, or is it more ambiguous?

B. They are more coupled up. A little bit fifty–fifty there. And for them it's very important with their counterpart. They are coupled up very similar like we are on the second. On the sixth it's more solo, flying solo, but you have friends. Whereas on the seventh, they are more in big groups. I don't know if Ophelia has a twin, –not that I have seen.

D. She's right beside you, what does she say?

B. She says that they are one big unity, not just one.

D. Does the group size increase as they advance?

B. No, –the opposite, she says. It gets smaller.

D. Another question I had: Do the souls coming to Earth see their entire blueprint before they start out, or is it sort of a surprise as they move along?

B. You mean if they see the whole journey on every incarnation on Earth before they start coming?

D. Well, if they understand and know what their objective is, what they are expected to achieve over the cycles of incarnations?

B. They can see it like a long–term project, they get glimpses. However, if a soul is about to come down to Earth, it will see the outline of that general travel there, but there will be surprises and dots and colors that will be added along the way. So all challenges and all struggles and all treats are not shown, but the general outline is.

D. So they can see the general pattern in the Coat?

B. Indeed, indeed. And they are discussing the Coat and the general intent of the Coat, you know, pros and cons and so forth, and what to look into. But again, it is the general outline; as the soul advances and progresses it can analyze and look into the Coat by itself and get information without having someone showing them how to do things.

D. So when you go and do things, you must have a general idea where it is headed?

B. I have a general idea. But when I travel, Ophelia blocks, sometimes, my view. And that's what she means about me having treats under the tree. Ah. So I'm gonna be short now because this one needs to save energy.

D. Good. I look forward to hearing about that. Thursday, I guess?

B. Ah. Thursday, I'm available. Huhuh. I'm gonna go now.

D. Alright. Thank you for coming, and thank you Ophelia.

B. Ah. Okay. Bye bye.

Sneaking into the Pyramid of Knowledge (April 15, 2020)

Setalay began the session by giving a rather ominous warning about the current direction humanity and technology are headed. A spiritually enlightened society would not tolerate many of the modern scientific pursuits. DNA manipulation, nuclear weapons, microwave pollution, chemical toxins and innumerable other technologies would not exist. We are well on our way to reproducing errors made by previous advanced societies, including some that were alien to the planet. Earlier visitors to Earth also tinkered with DNA and produced biological agents that were incompatible with natural life forms, with disastrous results. When humans or visitors become too destructive, the spiritual dimensions intervene and restore balance, even if it requires millions of years.

When Bob is on Etena, he observes, with great interest, what everyone else is doing. After Lasaray and others went into a pyramid where lectures and meetings are held, he became very curious to find out what type of knowledge was being hidden from him. So he resolved to disguise himself and follow along behind a group walking into the pyramid. He flashed a picture of the scene to Christine, who remembered it after coming out of trance. Bob found a white robe, like the others were wearing, and put it on. Because he is a bit smaller, it hung loosely on him. To keep it from dragging on the ground, he grabbed a handful of the bottom half of the robe and held it up against his midsection as he walked, in a most dignified manner, behind the group of four he was shadowing. The ones going into the temple carried tablets, so he plucked a rhubarb leaf and balanced it gently in the palm of the other hand, hoping no one would notice the difference. It was a very endearing image of my Little Friend trying to blend in and be part of whatever was going on inside the pyramid. However, his actions did not go unnoticed, and Setalay intervened as he crossed the threshold. Instead of sending him away, she invited him inside to see a room near the entrance. The exchange between them is amusing, but it also exemplifies the compassion and lack of deception that exists in the spirit world.

S. This is Setalay.

D. Hello, Setalay.

S. How are you?

D. I am well.

S. We are indeed following the progress, or I should say the development, on our sister planet, Earth. As of this time, here on Etena, your friends are eagerly seeking and observing the progress in your species. We feel the pain, we feel the fear radiating as an increased heartbeat in your fish tank, as we ourselves are not affected from this karma that is encased around your system at this time. Know that it is karma that is being forced to be release out of its chains. There are incidents in your history relating to biological misuse. As man increasingly reaches higher in its consciousness, in its development of understanding the connection of elements and minerals, physics takes on a path that one might not fully comprehend. There are remains stored here of certain events in your past, stored in libraries here, containers encasing misused biological components. The karma relates to understanding the amount, or to balance the understanding one have over assets that one possess. To blend biological components, creating chemical outcomes, has been a saddened part in your history. There are episodes in your past on this planet that relates to chemical explosions, where minds came together using the technology existing at that time in order to create an upper hand in the biological pyramid. Biological upper hand is something that is greater to possess, even greater than possessing oil. The ones who have the equations, the formulas to master different components, chemicals or biological functions, has the upper hand in how a species and world develops. This is a repeat going back to the last episode, which occurred about 10,000

BC. When that episode took place, there was an effect that made the lungs inside the species, mammals at this place, to burn. It was a burning sensation in the breathing. This is not the same, but it is a replica, a memory, of an ancient disaster where misuse of biological and chemical components did not match. At that time, no one was safe. Animals suffered, no one could breathe.

D. In what geographic region did this take place?

S. There was a huge part in northern Africa. The Americas were less affected. There was a part around the Mediterranean, the eastern part—Turkey, Greece, southern Italy—where there was an outbreak. This is when the...hmm, I would not call it a hospital, but a healing zone was created. It was created to assist that region that suffered due to misuse of chemical components. There was also earlier, in the region that is central Russia, an episode that occurred about 50,000 BC. So you can see, it runs in cycles. The effect was less damaging when it occurred 50,000 BC, as it occurred during a time and in an area that was freezing. At this time, certain places were freezing, 10,000 BC, but not in the region where this exploded. The response from the spirit realm and the Creator is to increase ice, increase cold, decrease temperatures. Once temperatures run wild, run too high, then it is more likely, even though in this case you read it to contradict, but it is more likely for mutations of disasters such as biological imbalances. Once they are frozen, in some way they are encased. There are remains in the region in Russia where these cells, these virus cells, are encased in ice. You do not seek to make your ice melt, not only for those animals who depend on ice, but it also stores some leftovers and remains of encased diseases, or disasters that the Creator put a lid on.

D. Was this activity done by humanoids, or was it done by visitors?

S. Visitors. Visitors who tried to implement bases in order for their advancement, to blend in with the less developed species, meaning mankind.

D. Speaking of disasters, the great floods that are mentioned all the time in ancient literature, did that actually occur? Was there a great flood that went over a lot of the Earth, or was that just a story?

S. It is not one big flood. There are incidents, episodes of tsunamis, but there is not just one big flood. But there are occurrences when flooding takes place. It is an effect of imbalances between the elements in your host, meaning your planet. Once there are imbalances in nature, in the roots of your mountains, deep down the fork responds. The response you hear or see is either floods, meaning tsunamis, but there is not just one big flood that developed across your planet. It's merely little ones. But for those encountering it, I'm pretty sure they were big enough to be considered one big flood.

D. (*Laughing*) Well, thank you for that.

S. You are welcome. And I would also want to say that both Siah and Tess are happily rejoicing their reunion and their activities have once more continued. They are highly active.

D. Siah must be very happy.

S. Siah is happy indeed. Highly active, they both are. They can barely wake up enough to start their day, so to speak, and explore in nature and their surroundings. One can equally say that they do not have time for their morning coffee before their day begins, even though they don't drink coffee.

D. Thank you for taking care of them.

S. Oh, you are much welcome. It is a great responsibility of course, and it takes a lot of effort. That's why we share the so-called burden, even though there is no burden. More to come. But I wanted to stop in and just give you the comfort of our companionship and our care of the phase that you are at this time enduring (*the 2020 worldwide lock-downs of society*). It is similar as being on a big ocean of waves and storms, and you have your little boat and you do not know fully how to navigate this boat, as you do not fully see shore at this time. So in many ways, the flood that you referred to before, it is a mental flood in many ways, locked in a cell memory in the species that reincarnate here. The flood of turmoil. The actual floods were similar as tsunamis, and they come and they go.

D. That's so nice to hear. Thank you for that information.

S. You are much welcome.

D. How do you see this playing out?

S. You are in the middle of this repeat. This is not the only episode in that chapter. Just know that for now, man feel like they have lost their oars for their boats, and they are drifting on this unsettling ocean without the ability to reach shore. Always know that your species will be protected, even though there will be those who exit this reality.

D. I understand. Thank you, Setalay.

S. Oh, you are much welcome. So I'll see you at another time.

D. Alright, my friend. I really appreciate you coming today.

S. So there. Bye bye.

B. (*Bob immediately came in.*) Ahh! Ahh!

D. Is this Jeshua? (*I was teasing, as it was obviously Bob.*)

B. Haha. I'm blocking Jeshua.

D. How are you my friend?

B. Oh, wide awake, wide awake. I have been, I feel a little bit that I have neglected my part in taking care of Tess. I did see that Setalay was tending to both Siah and Tess. I like her, she's like Ophelia, she's very much like Ophelia, but on Etena. And she knows when I'm drifting off into territory that I'm not necessarily invited, –I have no business there, to be frank.

D. Oh? What are you up to?

B. Well, it is the fact that I am curious about the storage unit of knowledge. As I can see that Tess and Siah are out and about all the time, then it's like, "Ohh, how should I spend my day?" and I kinda drift. I'm like, "Ohh, where is everyone going over there?" If I were to give you a picture on how they appear, it's like they're dressed in white and they have big tablets, but it's not like an iPad, it's not a tablet like that. But it's a tablet that they hold and they have like a pencil kind of thing. And they walk around normally in groups. So what I did—it's not like there is a laundry room—but I did disguise myself in a white gown. You might think that I looked like a ghost because it's a little bit too big, but I rolled it up and I'm trying to blend in. I'm walking sort of in the back, and I don't have a tablet, so that was suspicious. But I found myself like a big leaf, like a rhubarb leaf, one of those, so I took that and I went like this (*he held an arm out to support his leaf, and gripped his chin in a thoughtful manner with his other hand*). And I walked silently behind a group, just trying to follow them, not making myself too obvious. And they didn't seem to mind so I thought that I was safe, that I was heading inside. BUT right at the threshold of me getting in, huhuhuh, there was a little hand on my shoulder. And I was like, "Ohh! There you are, Setalay!" And then she said, "Yes. And there you are, Little Friend. Where is Lasaray?" And I said, "I'm pretty sure he's inside," and she said, "Did he invite you, really?" –And I don't know HOW to lie. It's a human invention, to lie–, so I said, "No." And then she said, "Well, considering that you actually owned up to your little foolishness here and your little trick, I'm going to go with you and invite you to one of the secret chambers, without Lasaray." And I said, "Is this a secret chamber that even Lasaray doesn't know about, so that I can potentially tell him?" And she said, "No, he knows." Huhuh. Ohh, but sometimes I want to surprise you with something new that you don't know, that is not just like, "Oh, you know about the pine tree. Here is a palm tree." You know?"

D. You're the one that recreated Tess. I couldn't do that.

B. No, you could not. But I didn't recreate Tess, I mean, I tended to her. BUT, anyway, I went into this sacred chamber and inside, you should know, were like glass containers similar like the ones you have in your lab, similar like we used when we created my solar system. And I said, "What is this?" and she said, "These are secret and sacred minerals that comes from a different fish tank."

D. Interesting!

B. Interesting. And she said, "We're going to look at these and we're going to look at the different results that can come, what sort of growth can come, if a soil is not just Earth based soil, but is actually—" this specific soil, she say, belonged to a system in fish tank seven.

D. Haven't heard much about that one.

B. This is brand new. She's very patient, –she's like Ophelia–, and it's just she and I. So we went through and she showed me on somewhat of a screen, but not as big as the one you have. When I asked if we can zoom in, she said, "No, this is not where we zoom in." But I'm pretty sure they can if they want to, but she did not want to, probably. So this was good enough. But I was looking at a planet, a system, that was located in fish tank seven. The individuals on this specific reality, they were kinda furry. The seasons were different, she says, than Earth. Here there are four seasons. She say there were four seasons but they were longer, so a year was not like a year here. She showed me the topography and the environment, and also the individuals that existed there. So we went through and I said, "Why is this stored here?" and she said, "This reality does not exist anymore. This reality is one that is going to be reintroduced in the sleeping fish tank three, because they did so well. Fish tank seven," she says, "is about to go through a hibernation phase." Not a full sleep, not like a full bear sleep, but she say that they did their lessons so well, so this specific reality is gonna be reintroduced and they are looking into, with other councils, I'm pretty sure, but she say there is a high interest of councils coming observing this specific storage unit where we were in. Because they are looking into this as a model, like a phenomena to reawaken. Similar like we woke up Tess. So we're looking at certain memories that existed there. And she said, "This specific reality was not very developed mentally, they were not technologically advanced. This was like a greenhouse planet. There are different systems, like galaxies and so forth, that operates like a greenhouse hub." And she said, "This specific entity that we are observing was that galaxy in that region that operated as a hub for growth."

D. So when they move from one fish tank to another, isn't it a completely different structure?

B. The conditions are different, indeed. But she said that this specific solar family, galaxy, operated as a—it's like going to a big greenhouse—so this galaxy, their purpose was not technological advancement, but they were to host conditions for a productive soil, predominantly, and where certain flowers would be located. So in some way it was a remote storage unit in fish tank seven. And she said, "Once that was put into hibernation, when it had completed its purpose by being there," she said, "this is a good model to reintroduce and potentially these councils are looking into using some of the soil." She say that this specific soil was highly nutritious for earthworms, for growth, for plants, –the roots seemed to have liked this soil pretty much. And they are looking into using this model in a new planet waking up in fish tank three.

D. So you got a sneak-peek about what is going to happen in fish tank three?

B. Ah, indeed, indeed. So I'm looking here at little glass containers of different things that one can use if one wants to create a very lush planet where flora and fauna are just left alone. The atmosphere council, like I want to call them, she say they are highly interested in analyzing this specific galaxy in fish tank seven. So they are looking into the connection between atmosphere and soil because they are just relaunching fish tank three soon. I don't know when, but she said it is high action in fish tank three, because it's not starting like fish tank six with a big, big sun, she says it's not like that. (*In an unpublished session, it was revealed that fish tank six is in the early stages of forming. It has an enormous ball of energy in the center of the universe, which will eventually fragment to form the different sheets of galaxies.*)

D. You said it's in a dream state at the moment, fish tank three, that is.

B. Indeed, and they are just placing different scenarios and different conditions at this time. She said, "It's a prototype to help other fish tanks later on, because fish tank three is completely in hibernation." It's a big snooze. So she say, "We harvest here a lot of the different results after certain systems have completed their purpose. And then councils and other entities can come and have a look. And what they do now is that they are trying to, using a lot of those systems that are highly durable, that can endure conditions much more." Because it is a fact that fish tank five is not very...it seems like it is very tender. It doesn't seem like it is as sheltered and it's more effected by conditions that occurred. But then, she say that it is a part of their purpose, it is to explore the levels of karma and how one can be trapped and how it can reoccur.

D. It seems like over time, if we can talk about time, there is a gradual evolutionary improvement that occurs from fish tank to fish tank, isn't there?

B Ah, indeed. But they're very different. So like fish tank seven, that we know very little about, and me, nothing, she say, "It's not like the whole system is in hibernation, we're just talking here about a system in fish tank seven that has completed its journey." Fish tank seven as a whole is alive and kicking.

D. Oh, okay. I saw you tried to open your eyes there.

B. Ah, I'm trying to see, if there is like something to see. But I kinda see—it's more like a laser.

D. Too bright?

B. Ah.

D. It takes a while to interpret all those signals coming in.

B. Ah. So, I did enter this sacred chamber with Setalay and I was very pleased about that, because now I know that there is something going on in fish tank three that is a prototype. They are the builders. If you think of like they are completely designing a new existence, a new development, a new evolution, then they are looking into what was considered like a top–notch reality, in different ways. So I'm not sure if we're gonna go there because I had questions. I said, "What sort of evolution exists in fish tank three?" And she said, "We're going to wait for that. Now we're just talking about the conditions that the planets had that we are potentially looking into restarting in a new model."

D. Doesn't the second dimension get involved with the life forms in every fish tank?

B. You would think so, wouldn't you? But I'm not involved in that, it seems, because this never came into a cloud to me. I'm pretty sure—oh, Ophelia said I lied. She said I ignored those clouds because I thought our clouds were more fun. Huhhuh. Ohh. She's always present, in some way!

D. (*Laughing*) I thought you didn't know how to lie!

B. I don't! It's just, from the perspective of me, I only saw certain clouds. But Ophelia said there were other clouds that I neglected to see. BUT, from the perspective of ME, they were never there. I never saw them. And I said, "If you want to make yourself known, you should not just hide behind another cloud." Oh, now Ophelia laughs and says, "You can play that card if you want to, but those clouds didn't seem as interesting to you." She says I have a tendency to look for the interesting clouds. And there is a lesson in this because this is what I'm trying to teach Tom. So once again, it's good to look in the mirror sometimes, because this is what I'm trying to teach Tom, to not just ignore the boring clouds. Because in a boring cloud could be something QUITE interesting and it could lead you into a more joyful cloud. Huhh.

D. You might be involved on the team working in fish tank three if you had looked at other clouds.

B. Ah. Ahh. Gergen and Ole, they have their hearing aids on to hear all this commotion in fish tank three because they are involved in kickstarting realities, of course, and I'm pretty sure that Joel, he's gonna be there because he's like a mountain expert. And if there's gonna be mountains, he's probably involved. But I'm not an expert in anything, really, when it comes to—I mean, I did the coffee bean.

D. Thank you!

B. But after that, my path went in a different direction. Like Ia became like a nanny taking care and raising everyone, and I took the path of great travels.

D. That's a good objective in itself.

B. It is indeed. And I can always change.

D. You wouldn't be in that pyramid if you weren't a great traveler.

B. Indeed. I don't think that Joel will go to this sacred chamber, for instance. But he doesn't have a need. That's what I think. But anyway, I've been around a little bit.

D. Yes, you have. You've seen all kinds of things that most have not.

B. But the thing is—the lesson in this is—it pays off if you sometimes trespass. Because if I hadn't been so inventive in taking that rhubarb leaf and follow and try to blend into that group, I would never have gotten in to the sacred chamber, I would not have known that there are councils looking into using some of the old-fashioned—the old models—in fish tank seven, to maybe potentially start existing again in another reality. I would not have known that if I hadn't trespassed! Curiosity leads my way! I'm like the Sniffer, I can detect if there is some sort of interesting topics or something secret. (*Later in the book, Bob describes his travels and friendship with a type of spirit from the second dimension that is able to locate disturbances or problems in energetic fields on Earth. He initially called his new friend, "Old Sniffer", but in later sessions he dropped the old and just calls him Sniffer.*) I do respond well to secrets, when the secret is there for me to open. I don't respond well to secrets if there is a secret hiding something FROM me. I feel like, not offenced, but I take it less good. But if there is a secret, then I'm there! If I can sense there is a mystery. Like this big storage unit—and you should know I did not get that far into this big building. My sacred chamber was actually just to the right when I got in, so it actually appeared to be like a gift store! You know, you have the gift store downstairs in the museum where they just shoot in everything else, something that everyone can have a looksee in. So maybe it wasn't much of a secret chamber, maybe I just went into the gift store.

D. (*Laughing at his observation.*) Well, at least you got in.

B. At least I got in. And once you are in, you're in the group, you're in, and then you can expand. And once I'm in, I can advance and go further in, as long as I'm in the mindset that it is okay to trespass. Because next time, Setalay is gonna come and I will advance from the gift store a little further down the hallway. The worst thing that can happen is that I'm returned to the gift store. But now when I see it like this, when I'm standing here looking in and I can see all the different corridors that go places, and different groups—you know, normally they seem to walk around in a group of four. So the mistake I did was that I joined a group of four, so the group became five. What I'm thinking here is to try to locate a group of three so that we are four with me, so I'm less detectable next time. (*Christine and I laughed about this, since his description of wearing an over-sized robe and holding a big rhubarb leaf would, in our minds, attract more attention than him trailing along behind a group of four.*)

D. You might want to find something that looks more like their tablets.

B. Ah. I'm pretty sure that I can find something here in the gift store, because as I can see now we just went into a corner here. But at least I got in! Huhuhuh. So trespassing pays off! Ahh. And then you came and you fetched me.

D. Where did we go then?

B. Out.

D. It's nice to hear that Tess and Siah are doing well.

B. Ah. You barely see them. It's like they don't need me. But I'm pretty sure the little ones are gonna follow this secluded companionship that they are engaging in. And then it's gonna start all over again, I'm probably gonna tend to one. They eat a lot!

D. Yeah, you were going to become a farmer to help them.

B. I might do that. I am grateful that I got in, even if not that far, but as a thank you, I'm gonna offer my assistance in the gardens to make sure that I can help the plowing and the seeding and the harvesting.

D. That might earn you enough credit to get further back in the storage temple.
B. Ah. I'm thinking that if I do something then they allow me to trespass. I do something else, –they shut their eyes when I trespass even further. Huhuhuh. You (*Lasaray*) said, "Oh, you wish!" But you said that we will go in and we will explore further. Anywho, I'm gonna go now, but nice to see you.
D. Well, it's nice to see you too. You almost did see me earlier. (Bob tried to open Christine's eyes, but was not able to see.)
B. Ah, ah. I'm working on it.
D. Pretty soon you'll want to walk around too.
B. Ah. If I only could. This one is kinda clumsy and there's a lot of wires that's not fully connected. So that might be a boundary I'm not ready to trespass, because the outcome might not be what I expected it to be.
D. You don't want to drop the microphone.
B. And I don't want to make him angry, because if he gets angry, he might reject me totally, and I don't want to disturb the peace in the group just by me doing something that was not in the manual for this mission. So I know when I'm not supposed to trespass.
D. There's always a grey area, I suppose.
B. Ah. And I'm looking for those. Because if it is a grey area, then I can paint it in a color from my choosing. But Ophelia says that in the manual on how this was to be conducted, there are not that many grey areas or grey zones. She says I'm pretty well informed.
D. This seems to be working pretty well, so no need to change.
B. Ah, ah. We'll see. I still have tricks and I'm still thinking about certain things. But there's so much to do. Now I am gonna go and harvest and I'm gonna help in the garden.
D. I appreciate all of your information today. It's always very entertaining, and it's always a pleasure to see you again.
B. Ah. I'm gonna go now, but I'll be back.
D. Good. Probably this weekend.
B. Okay. I'm looking forward to it. So I'm gonna go.
D. Alright, my friend. Talk soon.
B. Okay. Bye bye.

Teaching the Students

The spiritual dimensions are fundamentally concerned with creation and education, which are inseparable. Bob is a teacher and member of a council on the second, and many of his talks are about how he mentors younger spirits. Spirits start out as blank slates. They have to acquire all the knowledge and experience needed to fulfill their blueprint. Very soon after being created, every spirit is assigned a primary mentor, whom Bob refers to as their "peer". The mentor will guide them for nearly the full duration of their existence, although other teachers take active roles at times. Some mentors have many students, and some, only one. Bob and Ia are both guided by Gergen, and Gergen, in turn, is assisted by Ole. Depending on how the Creator intends spirits to develop, spirits from other dimensions are sometimes joined together as companions, similar to how Lasaray and Bob help one another. We learn and then we teach, and the cycle never ends.

In *Volume 1*, Bob described how he (eventually) became the primary instructor for twelve students. Lasaray asked Bob to go back to the second dimension and discretely interview younger spirits he thought would make complementary companions for three little Elahims. The Elahims are being prepared to incarnate on Earth, and those from the second will be their guides. Bob got excited and broadcast the opportunity to a group of students and was inundated with volunteers. He had at least eighty who were interested in being helpers. Most of them were matched with spirits from the fifth and seventh, until Bob was left with six. Those six from the second dimension were paired up with six from the sixth—including the three original Elahim—who will be incarnating. He described how he began to train them in *Volume 1*, and at this point in his story, he is responsible for preparing these twelve students to embark on their Earth adventures. Bob shows them models of human bodies, types of personalities, how the Coat of Karma is modified for each life, how guides communicate, what to be wary of as a human, and many other bits of information. The spirits who are incarnating also study with their peers on their home dimension. Everything they learn is stored within the soul and available at a subconscious level to help them navigate during an incarnation. The education will continue after every lifetime, becoming more advanced and refined as the soul progresses. Bob embraced his role as an instructor with his normal gusto, and now organizes large gatherings where he shares his wisdom with young souls from the second, fifth and seventh. Although these talks are given to his students, embedded within the stories are teachings that are obliquely directed towards those of us already incarnated.

The Walkie-Talkie is Off (April 30, 2019)

In *Volume 1*, Bob compared the transmission of ideas between a spirit guide and the incarnation as similar to a discussion through walkie-talkies. Spirit guides have to get thought bubbles into the human consciousness, and this process of remote teaching is a difficult skill for guides to master. Although the guide and the soul are always in communication, the guide's role is to influence the physical centers of the body. The soul itself is often ignored by the vehicle it occupies, so their guide assists by sending messages directly into the mind or emotional centers of the physical body. When the incarnation doesn't hear their guides, Bob says, "the walkie-talkie is off". Then the spirits need to find alternate ways to reach their person.

D. Your students are getting pretty good at remote teaching, I guess?

B. Ah. Oh, my sparkle students, they are doing really well. I'm so proud of them. Tom is doing really, really well.

D. That's not a surprise. He's had a lot of extra instructions.

B. He images (*imitates*) me sometimes, I've seen that! Haha. He's doing with his person what I did to you, because I told him certain things. He uses certain lines, like instructions, that I did.

D. Can you give me an example?

B. Like giving direct feedback, because we did talk about the fire, so he's giving direct feedback—he instantly shoots the alert signals of danger. He's very observant of that—quick on the warnings. He's a little bit disturbed because of the fact that in later plays, that we will talk about later, I shut off the receivers in the six from the sixth.

D. That's tricky.

B. Because now Tom and the other ones, the spirit guides, are somewhat gonna get a little bit of sneak-peek of a receiver that doesn't hear them! So he was like, "Why doesn't he respond? He's gonna go into all traps, he just doesn't hear me!" And I said, "You have to work without the walkie-talkie!"

D. It must be a real art form to be a spirit guide?

B. It is an art form to be a spirit guide. It's not an art form only, for the ones going in (*incarnating*) with an agenda, it's a HUGE responsibility and art form to be their spirit guide.

D. When you are communicating directly, is it mostly just putting thought bubbles in their chimney?

B. Indeed. That is like the last resort. And because of the fact that neither of these have a button inside that they can just squeeze to crank up the volume. I'm NOT telling them that you had that, because then everyone would be like, "Oh, I want a button in mine. I want one of those volume buttons in mine. He doesn't hear me, phut, phut, phut (*imitates blowing on a microphone*), come in, come in, come in." So I'm not telling that.

D. Did I listen to you pretty well, most of the time?

B. Indeed, but it was after I had adjusted the volume in you. These are adjusting the volume, but in a different way. They are being trained as regular spirit guides, in that respect. So I have actually taken a repeat class—

D. A refresher?

B. A refresher on how to be a spirit guide. And that is actually with Zachariah. A general class for us being spirit guides, who have a person down for at least a hundred times. So it was a repeat.

D. How many times have I incarnated?

B. Oh, you've been down about—not only in human—but in human bodies, about 1200 times.

D. 1200! That's a lot.

B. Ah, over a vast time-frame. But some of them were also in the furry ones. Before that you said you were down here in a mixed appearance (*manifested*). And I said, "What kind of appearance was that?" And you said, "You wouldn't have detected me, because I looked a little bit different. Sometimes I was invisible." And I said, "Oh, that's even harder for me to detect you then, even though I can see through all energetic levels on Earth. But if you're like the wind, it's hard to know if it's a storm, or is it just Lasaray?" So anyway, I go now.

D. Alright, my friend. It was really nice to talk to you.

B. Ah. Okay, I'm gonna go. Bye bye.

The Museum of Previous Costumes (May 5, 2019)

Bob covered a lot of subjects in this session. He introduced a group of spirits he calls the Tailors because they select and custom fit bodies for each soul. These Tailors belong in the eighth or ninth dimension, but have a work center on the fifth where they fine-tune the energetic patterns of chosen body to intentions of the soul. They also have a showroom where noteworthy lives are on display for students to study. Bob compared it to a wax museum of historical figures dressed in clothes worn during the incarnation. Included with each figure are little holographic movies showing the pre-life plan, which is always positive, and then the highlights of how well the incarnation followed the plan. Or, as Ophelia says, "Look at the footprints!" Bob took his students to the museum to see what certain characters did with the life they were given. By observing these films, the students get a sense of the difficulty they will face once they blend with a body. They also realize how a single life can dramatically influence an entire society, for good or ill.

At the end of the session, I asked Bob about activities that souls engage in once they return home. I had read about a medium telling a grieving mother that her deceased son was still snowboarding in the afterlife. Bob's answer is classic. He found it very amusing, but explained why spirits will sometimes reflect what a human needs in order to heal. The same occurs in the fourth, when guides will appear as religious figures to calm the recently deceased during transition.

B. (*Bob came in making odd, smacking noises.*)

D. Hello?

B. Oh, you found me! I tried to be more settled in my approach, like I'm more of a grownup. I gently entered. Good morning. (*Said quite solemnly.*)

D. Good morning. It's like you're addressing the Moon People.

B. Like the Moon People, indeed! How are you, great spirit, how are you doing today? Making progress on your moons and so forth? If you would like to share, please, let's do. I'm also considered somewhat of a great spirit, in the reality of beyond.

D. Well, that's because you are.

B. I'm traveling around indeed.

D. Where are you going now?

B. Oh, I have actually been trying to make new scenes, new dramas, and then I was like, "Ohh" (*sounding discouraged*). Because it is a great responsibility to be a teacher, it keeps you up at night, I must say. Ia told me about this. Then I was looking back and I went over your journals, our travels, and I was looking into what could be beneficial to teach them. But I also have a little bit of a manual to follow in this training program. We have worked through certain topics; the sensation of fear, the sensation of group activity, and so forth. I have a checklist that I have to somewhat follow in my training. But Ia said, "Use a puzzle," she said, "just take bits from all the experiences that you had with Lasaray, and you create a picture, a puzzle, –you take from each. It doesn't have to mirror exactly what the two of you did. You just use your favorite puzzle pieces from each incarnation."

D. You have a lot to pick from.

B. I do indeed. So I'm having like a scissor, and I'm cutting and creating different things. Because of the fact that it became a big discussion when we marched to France, and the discussion was about group activity and how group activity is different at home than it is on Earth. (*He is referring to his training exercise he did with his students. Bob dressed up as King Henry the Eighth of England and recreated the invasion of France. The story is found near the end of Volume 1.*)

D. It's more joyful at home.

B. And because of the fact that the ones from the second are more familiar with group activity than the ones from the sixth. They are more flying solo, if you like, and they are more in that phase of being by themselves and reflect. And when they merge with groups, they are more in a phase of learning. And I said, "Going to Earth is a phase of learning. You will interact with other souls; some, their walkie–talkie is not on. Others might not be from your home base, you might not recognize the inner being, you might not recognize any tones whatsoever. That will create a sensation of solitude and loneliness, and you will have to be more centered in your mission, and that is why it is important that you communicate with your spirit guide from the second, because they will direct you to the right groups in order for your mission to blossom and become a great success. They will address you to find groups. You have a tendency, as a soul being, to enjoy more solitude because you are reflective by nature. That is why it is very valuable for you to have a spirit guide from the second, who will push you to be more social." Like this one, this one takes on extreme personalities in order for the personality to be more present and guide the soul to groups. Even if this one is a little bit different than you in many ways, it still, its original pattern, is solitude. The Elahims are like that. And even the others from the sixth, even though they are not Elahims, they are very close in that pattern, in that melody. That is why I got them too, even though they are not the same as the three (*Elahims*), but you humored me and you said, "Okay, I will double the quota. You can have three more, but they are not going to be exactly the same."

D. That's a hundred percent increase.

B. Huhuh, a hundred percent increase. Quite generous, even though the other ones (*Ophelia and Zachariah*), they were giving me much more, but they have different assignments, and they ARE more group activity. (*Bob had about 80 volunteers from the second who wanted to act as a guide. Ophelia and Zachariah matched most of them with young souls from the fifth and seventh, who are more group oriented.*) So, I have one of my own that is like you, that I needed to push to be more social, sometimes. So I know exactly how to train my students, the spirit guides, and what to look for when their person might just, by itself, withdraw, and how we are supposed to make them engage in the physical reality; because why are they otherwise coming?

D. I felt like I was disconnected almost my entire life.

B. Ah. That's why you needed me. Because first of all, you were disconnected here in the end (*the last thirty lives*), but that was when your Coat was folded, and we re not gonna tell them that this is an option. It's not an option to leave, like you do, so that is not on my training manual here, like, "Oh, if it's not comfortable, simply leave and your spirit guide will do the work for you. Just work as a remote incarnation and take notes and you will have progress here, –you can just leave." No, I'm not saying that, because of the fact that you have to have a folded Coat in order for you to have that possibility and the option—because you have deserved it! They still are in the progress to deserve their treats. And I say that, "There are many treats coming your way if you simply engage with the others and try to remember and radiate your mission. And that is what you need as a presence from the second." Tom is really all set to go, he's like, "I'm ready, we're ready, my person and I are ready to go." And I said, "No, you're not ready to go, we have not been offered a vehicle yet for the two of you." And the other ones were like, "Are you ready to go? Where are you gonna go?" and I said, "No one is going. NO—ONE—IS—GOING, because we have not finished training." There is a group, and we can call them the Tailors, who tailor bodies. We have not been there yet. That means that they will go into (*a building*) similar like a museum, and they will see different physical appearances, combined with—if you touch it, if you press it, then the physical experience that took place will start to roll as a film. The Tailors are important, it's one of my treats on my training program, that we will go and see this. Like, for instance, when I myself went there, because I was curious about this. I never went to the Tailors with you, because you just said, "Oh, there I am, this is what I'm going to look like," and you kinda gave me just a picture. And I was like, "Okay, let's see," and I tried to memorize how you looked. And like, with Mr. Mustard (*I had a previous life as an ostentatious musician in France named Charles Dijon, but Bob jokingly calls him Mr. Mustard. His adventures are described in Volume 1*), you said, "It's important that I show you this in advance, because you might not detect me, because I am going to be quite different." And I said, "How are you going to be different?" and you said, "Let's give you a little preview," and you played me a little movie. And you said, "Just so you know that I'm taking on a different persona this time. This is what I'm going to be, I'm going to be singing and dancing, and all sorts of strange activity, because I'm monitoring high society—shifts in their consciousness and shifts in how they perceive advancements, and what they perceive treats to be. So I have to blend in, so this is what I will look like." So I only saw the ready costume. BUT, there is a museum where the Tailors have different costumes on display. For instance, this is where I got my personality as Henry the Eighth.

D. Was he in the museum?

B. He was in the museum. There is also, oh you showed off, you also have a suit here.

D. Which one?

B. (*He identified an ancient Greek philosopher.*) You have a suit here. Huh. This one also has a suit.

D. Which one is that?

B. It's a warrior from Roman times. A warrior character indeed. Ophelia probably humored him with that one. But, you can go in here and have a look at old suits—what was in fashion before you are gonna come. And then, you can look at this, – there is a little button and you can press it, and a preview or a little film starts to roll on what this individual did.

D. Is it like the whole life?

B. No, it's not the whole thing. It might be that you can, but it's not very long. If we say that a lifetime, a regular lifetime, is like two hours, then you have the ability to see like fifteen minutes, –the highlights. So this is coming; and I have been by myself, just in order for me to be able to train this later on, I have visited the Tailors just to somewhat see what is there.

D. Sounds like fun.

B. It is indeed. It's very active. They belong, they say they have their dots, their offspring are all over, so they sort of hover all over the spiritual realities. I tried to see if they are from the fifth, from the sixth, or where they are from.

D. The Tailors?

B. Ah. The Tailors. The Tailors seem to operate a little bit around eighth or ninth, like a little council, but they have like runners that just run down to six and run down to five and look at all the fish tanks, and then run back and tell the designers what they should design. They have those scouts, like runners, like star falls that just shoot into a fish tank and they look and then shoot back, sssttt (*imitating the sound of something shooting by*), and say, "Okay, let's use the fabric of cotton for this specific reality." And then, sssttt, shoots down and says, "Oh, and within this specific cotton design, there should be a lot of emotional flickers sewed into the costume." So when someone comes in and later will pick this costume, they will have a costume that fits for the destination. The destination, let's say Earth, only has cotton at its disposal for the physical, but the inside will mirror the lessons and the personalities that are sewed into the costume. If there is another fish tank and another one, sssttt, shoots off into the eighth fish tank, or the fourth, where Siah is, it's a completely different—well, they don't have costumes, they just go—but if they do to another place where there are bodies, they may say, "Oh, this group will only have a costume made by polyester." Huhuh, so that's what they do. So the physique is based on the material that these Tailors are using, –it's not cotton of course. And then, there are others who sew IN the experience in this costume, they sew in the Coat of Karma in the costume.

D. Is this individually done for each soul, or is this like a general pattern?

B. They have a general pattern. It looks like a factory, so you have all these costumes hanging, ready to go to Earth, let's say, BUT, when a soul comes, –and this is probably like a spirit guide who chooses–, so let's say like when this one comes, Isaac probably goes, "Oh, let's see, which costume should I show this one for this next mission?" So let's say he takes out three different costumes, all designed to go to Earth, all sort of prepared for Seth to go. BUT then, combined with a spirit guide, the Tailors sew in the Coat of Karma, which is individually experienced from the soul. He can also sew into the costume surprises. That is when you have risen to the fact that you are allowed to sew in the experiences in the costume, then you have gone a long way in your spiritual development as a spirit guide. I don't know why I was not involved in sewing things into your costume, that would have been fun. Oh, you said that you hid this from me. (*Lasaray communicates with Bob during the sessions.*) Jeshua sewed your costume at that point. It's the primary guide that actually sews in the Coat of Karma and the experiences, and if there are surprises, then the main spirit guide is involved in that. The rest of us will sort of clean up the mess. So we're gonna go and see the museum of prior costumes, and they can look at different things. They can look at like, "Okay, here we have someone looking like this, and we're gonna observe the behavior of greed. Over here, the behavior of trying to enlighten others." So we will just press the buttons. There are certain known entities that we will go back and look at.

D. How far back in time? As far back as the ones with fur?

B. Well, the furry ones, there are just a few, way back there (*in the museum*), but mainly I would say it is more recent. My students are not gonna come down for a while, so we're just gonna look at five thousand years back, tops, of costumes. Nay, Ophelia says her students are gonna look at those ten thousand years back, she says. Why can't I? (*He was looking left, talking to Ophelia*). Oh, I'm gonna be allowed to show them something that mirrors a sixth dimensional soul and the appearance from those.

D. I think the Shea were down here about 10,000 BC, in South America.

B. Ah, so they're gonna show that. Different suits, different Tailors. So you're gonna show the costumes where a similar soul like yourself has occupied a similar costume.

D. That's fascinating. So then animals, they wouldn't have the same type of Tailors?

B. No, it's more like a group. It's not on display in the same way. You can see them, how they look, but it's a different museum. This is the Tailors for incarnations. The other ones are in the regular museum; this is like Madam Tussauds.

D. Who's that? (*He was referring to the wax museum.*)

B. Huh, the museum in London. Like that, that's how it looks, like Madam Tussauds. That's what we do, we go and we look and they (*his students*) say, "Oh, how grand!" and I say, "Let's see if this was a grand person. Just because someone has a great portrait doesn't mean it's a great inside. Let's look at Henry the Eighth." So we press the button and look at the little film. And then we look at others, and they go, "Ooohhh", and sometimes it is like (*and then he claps, showing approval*), and sometimes it is like, "Uugghh" (*he made a grimace*). But they had all this fortune and all this going for him or her, but the inside did not reflect that. And I said, "No. This is why you need a spirit guide. In this case, the remote is not on (*about the unspiritual ones in the museum*), so just because someone looks grand and pompous and has their nice portrait on display, has the nicest clothes and the nicest physique, doesn't mean it is the greatest inside." So I said, "Don't be fooled. Never be fooled. You're going to be tossed into groups, and you might be attracted to certain attributes and how they portray themselves, but you have to look for the inside. Remember," –we have not gone yet, but I'm gonna say–, "remember when you pressed the button of Henry the Eighth? Look how grand and shiny, look how nice the clothes are, – was it very grand?" And in that case (*during his play when he dressed up as Henry the Eighth*), I really went into character, so they have more than just what's in the museum to compare.

D. So what is shown in the museum is their spiritual development or how they treated people?

B. Ah. And there's a little note you read, before you press a button and see the highlights, what the intent was to go down with. So the mission is on a little bit of a sign next to a suit where you can see, "Oh, this one came down to gather people."

D. Is that what Henry the Eighth was supposed to do?

B. Ah. Gather people, but he didn't, really.

D. Well, he did break with the Catholic Church, so that was something.

B. That was something, and that was applauded. He did have different things, but you can see the mission on the display, by points, the general ideas that soul had by picking that suit, and then you can look at the little film. So the Tailors are up, and I have been fortunate to have been up there and just look around and see. It's like a busy workshop, indeed. You have to be like, "Oops, sorry! I'm sorry, I'm in your way. Oops, I have to duck, sorry, oopsy-daisy." They are extremely noisy; if you are silent in your dimension, and Ophelia's, they sing, but here it's like singing and talking—they're really loud! And I said, "Have you ever been to Earth, any one of you, –those who are designing Earth suits?" And they were like, "No. No no no no no no." (*He said it a sing-song way, rising and falling with each word.*) This is how they talk, "mum mum mhum mum mhum mhum," it goes really fast. But I was instantly greeted and welcomed. And one was like, "Look here, I'm gonna sew this suit. In here I am sewing in the experience of development when it comes to scientific shifts." And I said, "Oh, okay." Then he said, "So a soul coming in choosing this specific suit will have a purpose and a mission that will be easier felt in my suit."

D. That makes a lot of sense.

B. The Tailors, I like them. This is happy! My students will go on like a school trip to see this. If it is allowed, afterwards, this one, who was extremely friendly and showed all his skills in sewing this suit, he offered to come and meet them half–way, in the Tailor museum, and just talk about his work, so to speak. It's like when parents come to school and they tell them about their work. So he's gonna come, if it's allowed, and I'm sending a request to you that I have a guest lecturer later on. I am in that phase where I'm looking for guest lecturers, and this one is great, because he's very enthusiastic and has all sorts of experience. He said that he created suits for as long as suits were needed. Oh, he's old; he's old in this profession, he said.

D. The upcoming bodies, they haven't designed those yet, have they?

B. Nay. The physical is another thing, that is where the second is also involved. These suits are energetic, oh how can I put it for you so you, clumsy, can understand? The full physical is a joined effort from all—not the Tailors—but from all spiritual realities. Should it be slim? should it be tall? should it have hair? what organs should be inside it? –and so forth. When that is established, the energetic costume, like these ones, it's connected to a physical reality, a physical vehicle, so they merge. It's like putting on clothes, first you're naked, and the naked one is the original ones from the second and all the spiritual realities, then you put on your underwear and a little sweater, which might be like this one, and then you put on— and the cotton would be considered like the underwear and t-shirt, and then whatever you sew in, let's say the experience of growth in the scientific field, that would be considered your socks; so it's like you're dressing someone up.

D. That makes a lot of sense. So could the energetic bodies that they're making go to any different type of physical form?

B. Indeed. But they're not involved in the physical form; they are involved in creating the costume.

D. So you could blend that costume with a different type of body?

B. If it fits. If you're only allowed to have a cotton costume here, then you cannot put on a polyester one. So that is how it is. So Ophelia says it's been a joyful experience and a joyful discussion today, but now session is over, she says.

D. I did have one question. I get confused about some accounts I have read, about souls leaving and they are doing activities like they were doing on Earth–

B. Leave where?

D. When someone dies and they report back that they are skiing or snowboarding or things like that, –where are they located, is that the upper level of the fourth?

B. Normally a life review...when a soul is younger in its evolution, the life review, if that is your question, takes place at the end of the fourth reality. A spirit guide can descend into the fourth reality even halfway down and have a life review. When you established the journeys for a while, and you have been here a few times, you instantly transform through the fourth back to your home base, and whatever reporting is needed is done there.

D. Okay. But like when spirits say they are golfing or doing human–like activities, that would still be in the fourth, wouldn't it?

B. In the life review? (*My poorly worded question completely confused him.*)

D. Well, no, when souls communicate back to the living, through a medium.

B. Ah, you mean a person died and they say they are golfing in the spirit realm?

D. Exactly.

B. Huh! There's no golfing on the fifth. They show themselves—they descend into the fourth reality and they show human–like activities. It's not a spiritual activity. Huhuh. However, singing or dancing or reading, they do those sort of things, but not golfing and skiing.

D. I was sure of that, but wanted to hear you say it.

B. Nay. Huh huh huh huh! (*He started laughing heartily, so he must have thought the idea was beyond silly.*) I've never seen snow, like a mountain with snow, in the second dimension. However, we have encountered, when we studied up on mountains and snow, we encountered mountains and snow, but it's not like it exists in the spiritual realities. It is also sometimes a wish from the one who is still down on Earth, you know, like, "Oh, my person really enjoyed skiing. Now when this person is dead, I hope this person is still skiing." So they create a need, and the spirit can sort of meet that need and say, "Oh, yes, I do ski."

D. That's brilliant, I appreciate that.

B. Sometimes you can just let people think that they ski. It's mainly those souls who haven't been here that long, who have a need for someone to ski like that, or to play golf. They might say (*he mimicked an English lady*), "He really enjoyed golfing, my husband, –I hope he still likes that. Is he golfing?" And then someone can say, "Yes, indeed." And a lot of psychics, they say, "Oh, yes, he golfs. He has all these medals and he has a greater handicap now when he's up on the spiritual golf course." And it's just to meet the need, really. Those who have been here (*incarnating*) for a while, they understand that their person is not golfing. Might be reading up on things. Oh, there we go. Ophelia says, "Sometimes it's nicer to just think that someone golfs or skis, than to just rip off all their perceptions. Because at least that person thinks that the other one is doing something, that the person is still alive. It's not like they just disappeared. The person left behind thinks the loved one is doing something it liked. So sometimes you can do the generous thing and not engage in that. It's a lesson for this one—don't engage in a question or conversation, simply resign. Take a breath, and move aside," Ophelia said. And she said to this one, because this one said, "I'm–I'm all sorts of quiet, I don't do anything." And Ophelia said, "You roll your eyes sometimes, and we see that." and he said, "I don't roll my eyes!" Ophelia said to just let things pass by, sometimes.

D. Don't attach any emotions to it.

B. Nay. And just don't poke that things are stupid. Oh, it's like that. Oh, Okay, Ophelia's dragging my arm. Okay, I come, I come. Bye bye.

So Many Questions about the Coat (May 26, 2019)

After Bob introduced his students to the physical suits, they started bombarding him with questions. He called in Ophelia, Jeshua and Isaac to calm and reassure the students that there was nothing to be concerned about when it came to entering or leaving the body and the Coat. Every soul has a unique pattern and reason for coming to Earth. This blueprint is imprinted into the Coat before the first incarnation, and covers all future lifetimes until the Coat is folded. The Tailors perfectly fit each new body with the Coat and the soul's mission for that lifetime. During each mission to Earth, different parts of the pattern are worked on, until the soul fulfills the entire pattern. Each incarnation has three aspects; the body, the Coat, and the soul, which Bob explains magnificently.

> B. Someone is having a snooze! OH–LA–la–la–la (*He began toning the medieval song he remembered from my previous life as Charles Dijon, trying to elevate Christine's energy.*)
> D. Hello, my friend.
> B. Hello to you.
> D. It's nice that you could join us.
> B. Oh, I'm always present, of course, always on standby, having somewhat of a claim for my spot. But it is a fact that it takes a lot of time, this training, I must say. There are endless questions that arise that I did not foresee. And sometimes it feels like we can't really move on in my training camp, due to the fact of concerns. So, we have been given the opportunity for guest lecturers, those who have been to Earth, but don't carry a Coat. Because that was a little bit of a concern, –when we came to karma class, that became a concern–, because of the fact that they understood there will be conditions that will be placed upon them and how they will have to navigate in not only a physical body, but also in a suit, a jacket, that someone would place upon them! So Tom said, "This is like a straitjacket!" Because it kinda is, and you don't want to lie, then I felt that we should invite someone who is a little bit more encouraging of the suits.
> D. The second dimension doesn't take on suits? (*Tom, a second dimension guide, must have been experimenting with the suits.*)
> B. No. But the Elahims and the other three from the sixth were the ones asking all these questions in my training camp. And the spirit guides, they were just giving different ideas on how these different suits will appear to them. But the ones from the sixth who are gonna go into the suits and go into the different vehicles, the bodies, they were a little bit concerned about the fact of not being able to operate freely, that there

were conditions placed on them that might hinder, they said, the intentions that they initially had to go. So we have guest lecturers coming in to somewhat calm the situation.

D. Who came in to speak?

B. Ophelia came, Jeshua came, Isaac always comes where there is distress in a group, upcoming to incarnations. BUT, we also had a visitor coming who is in charge of the karma suits. So there was, I wouldn't say a workshop, because it was not like everyone was engaging, but they got a preview on how the karma Coats were designed. One might think you go through a whole spectra in your karma suit, –and some do! Some goes through empathy, beliefs, lack of judgment, focusing on needs, emotions—but some suits are more mentally or emotionally inclined. And the ones from the sixth, they're gonna have more mental Coats. So they're not necessarily gonna have that many, in the beginning at least, emotional experiences. Those who come from Ophelia's place, those suits are completely different.

D. Huh. What dimension designs the suits?

B. Ohm they're up at eight, nine, that's where they have the factory, it seems.

D. The factory to make the suits? (*Normally, we capitalize Coats when it is an abbreviation for the Coat of Karma. In Bob's following responses, he begins using coats as a general word for the combination of the physical body and the Coat of Karma, so it is not capitalized.*)

B. Make the suits. The Tailors who create suits, who create different conditions to, –it's like you have the physical, and a soul can, in some way, choose a preference, you know, "Oh, I want to be tall. I want to be short. I want to be somewhat round. I want to be white. I want to be black. I want to be yellow." They can have somewhat of a preference when it comes to the physical, but then the Tailors come in and they dress that physical, meaning they implement this suit, the coat, with different conditions for this yellow person to experience certain things. "So for instance," Isaac said, "we can see from the perspective of level eight that certain regions have predominantly a specific kind of coat, –like a mental coat or an emotional coat. So we can see that."

D. Is that based on countries, or is it a smaller unit?

B. It's a little bit both, but you can see in countries there is a difference. If a soul says, "Oh, I want to go to Scandinavia," then the grander councils and those who design the suits, they can say, "Well, if your gonna go up there, you'll have to dress in an emotional coat, or you have to dress in a mental coat. If you go there, this is the coat that you will be given."

D. Are the Scandinavians more mental, or emotional?

B. Ah, they're like fifty–fifty. They operate a little bit more from their center point, but I would say that they are a somewhat more mental. But it's a blend, it's a shift.

D. The Africans are more physical, aren't they?

B. Ah. So those coats are not as much, –it's wider apart. If you see your coat and you can sew in different experiences, personalities also exist in the coat a little bit, and you sew in different—(*he gave a big sigh*) oh, so many words that seem to be missing here—but you sew in emotional, mental, the whole spectra of emotional, the whole spectra of mental. But in certain countries—and a lot of them are below the equator, or around the African continent and Middle East continent—the coats and the experiences are wider apart between the different occurrences that should be experienced within this specific life. It's not as clear as in, let's say the Scandinavian countries or that little friendly dot, Iceland, those coats there, the experiences are more sewed together so they navigate easier in that coat. So even if the little dot, Iceland, even if that coat has more experiences and events sewed into their coat, it's easier to navigate because they all are somewhat in unity. When a coat goes to, let's say, the African countries, sometimes it can be a little bit more of a distance in between, which can indicate that they feel a little bit disconnected, in some way, but they are more grounded to the Earth, so they are more connected like that. But they don't have the same ability to access the higher consciousness, necessarily, and the mental aspect. However, the emotional is more present in that region, as a gift from spirit, to somewhat manage that kind of experience.

D. I understand that.

B. It is because of the heat. If you go down to certain countries, certain coats are not fully prepared with a lot of mental capacity, because of the fact of the heat. And because there is a spot over those regions down there, an atmospheric spot, that is more open. So if they were given suits that are more mentally inclined, it would be more and more out of control. So for souls coming into those countries, they delete more mental connections, to balance and somewhat minimize the events that they do not want to take place. The mental and the heat is not a good combination, always.

D. Okay. That makes sense.

B. So, due to this show in the training camp, we had all these guest speakers coming in. The Tailors came in and they showed, "How do they even create a suit." And everyone was kind of curious to know, "Is this what I'm gonna travel in?" and they said, "Your spirit guide is going to sew in, based on your purpose, different personalities, different occurrences and feelings that you will have during your journey, –some to help you, and some to challenge you." And they were like, "Are they gonna sew in challenges into the coat? How will I navigate? Why would you send in like a minefield? Why would someone do that?" And Tom was like, "I'm sure this is all good," he tried to calm his person. And I said, "We're gonna watch a documentary here when Lasaray went, and what could happen," and then I said, "We're gonna look at Mr. Mustard."

D. Did they laugh about Mr. Mustard?

B. Yes, because they were like, "Is that Lasaray?" and I said, "Yes! Look what a strange suit he was in here. BUT, he was on a secret mission to investigate group behavior in a society that was highly connected to mental needs. And because of the fact that you are more mentally inclined, the Elahims and everyone from the sixth, then in some way, you do investigate that. You investigate the development, or lack of development, in the mental capacity. And that's what Mr. Mustard did." And they said, "Why is he dressed like that? Why is he dancing? Why is he looking like that?" And you said, "It was to blend into the surroundings. You have to be somewhat of a chameleon at times." (*Bob mimicked Lasaray, using a stiff and formal tone.*)

D. Did I come in to give a little lecture too?

B. You did indeed. Everyone was present, because of the fact that it's somewhat scary—it was similar like going into my bubble—you want to know you can get out. They understand that when the body dies then they leave, because they cannot operate anymore. The physical has laid down and gone, the capsule is gone. BUT, when we also then said, "That is when you have to exit your Coat," then all sorts of questions came up! They were like, "Where do we leave the Coat? and how long is this gonna be attached? and is it just my Coat? and how do you change the Coat?" It was similar like the feeling I had of being trapped in the bubble. (*The bubble he first traveled in to go visit his solar system.*)

D. So is that the process that souls go through when they pass through the fourth, taking off the Coat? Releasing their attachments to the Coat?

B. Taking off the Coat. Looking at the Coat. Releasing attachments to the Coat. And if you don't release attachments to the Coat, you might stick around. And again, that was the same thing, you know, stick around where? So we had to go through all that. We are indeed having a separate class coming up about how to navigate through the fourth.

D. What did Jeshua talk about?

B. Jeshua came in, because they know him, so he came in and just was encouraging. He told stories about when you traveled and how you were also a little bit concerned. So he kinda played that card, to make it a little bit more amusing. And then they said, "Can't we go without a Coat?" and I said, "I'm in favor of that!" Because they asked me, and I was like, "If it's up to me, I wouldn't mind you going completely clear into a physical and simply fix things." And then everyone (*Ophelia, Jeshua and Isaac*) came and said, "You're not allowed to say they can travel without a Coat, because that is a condition to come here, you have to dress in a Coat."

D. Did Jeshua ever incarnate?

B. Nay. Nay. Ophelia did, and they were wondering about her Coat. Then someone said, "Can't you recycle them? Can't you just use someone else's Coat?" And then the Tailors were like, "No, you're going to get your own Coat, and it's going to be completely unique. Because you want to feel accomplishment when you solve different things in your Coat. And the soul will see how the Coat changes over time."

D. So when a soul first begins to come, the Tailors make a Coat, will that Coat cover all the future lifetimes? Does it have a certain pattern?

B. Indeed, it is that. If you see it like that, we have our Coat, and in the back, the whole back is like you said, containing all intentions, all lives to come, the general mission this soul is having coming in. BUT, for each life they sew in different things, let's say in the sleeves or in the front, that are unique for that specific mission. BUT there is always a specifically designed coat, depending on the journey itself.

D. So that's based on the soul's pattern that the Creator gave it?

B. Indeed, it's connected to the soul's pattern. That is always present in the Coat. So if you are allowed to have a cotton Coat, that is the mission that you are having, then you cannot operate in a polyester Coat. So you have established in this Coat the general journey from beginning to end, and then they sew in different events, depending on the specific journey that you are trying to engage with.

D. As the soul progresses, are their lesson or accomplishments noted on the soul's jacket somewhere?

B. Indeed. And that is how the soul can see that, little by little, the events sewed into the sleeves are dissolving, and eventually they will just have a purpose Coat, which is the intention of that Coat in the beginning, and that's how you can fold it. So, we're looking into that a little bit, and the spirit guides are like, "Hmm, so I'm assisting three here? The soul, a Coat, and a person?" So there is all sorts of questions coming up here, like "Which one should I mainly focus on?" And based on each unique different mission, from these three—soul, Coat, body—one will be more lit up. It will always be that one of these are more lit up for the spirit guides, from the view of the spirit guides. So let's say that the Coat is much more visible for a spirit guide, then they know that they should address all their teachings and all their efforts to address and communicate with the Coat to trigger karma, to trigger events that will be connected to the Coat. If you have a soul that has the walkie-talkie off, then the spirit guide will see that the Coat and the soul is a little bit more dimmed, but the physical is more lit up. So they will have to try to make more physical manifestations for their person to stumble upon.

D. Huh, that makes a lot of sense.

B. So, from a spirit guide, how they prepare how we prepare when you go down, is that we get a little bit of a preview, like

I do with you. There is a difference between guiding a spirit from let's say, Zachariah's classrooms, because then Coat–body–soul will be more in a conjunction, whereas for these here that I am training, it might appear like three different entities; soul, Coat, body. Sometimes, after a while, the soul will communicate to the spirit guide, like you did, and you will say, "Now I'm shutting down my Coat and my soul a little bit, so you only address the body." So from my point of view, it was like having three lives lit up. Well, you don't have a Coat, but when you did, there were three entities lit up, and then I would see, "Okay, now he shut down the Coat, so I'm only gonna focus on communicating with the soul and the body." And then when the Coat lit up again, I could help you trigger certain things in your Coat. So I see three different entities, that's how I see it.

D. It takes a lot of skill on your part.

B. Ah. And that's what I'm training Tom and the other ones to see. It's not just a walk in the park, it's not just to make them not burn, hehehe. You have to identify, because they're gonna have a Coat, but you have to identify in this specific life, –and we don't want to confuse them, that they can have several lives at the same time, because at this time we are saying that there is one–, but when they go down, they have to see, "Okay, which one is the strongest light; the soul, the Coat, or the body?" And that's how you can see what sort of journey you can expect the person to be on, and what your efforts should be. If the soul is very lit up, then you can indeed work on soul communication, meaning that you can address your person to ignite their intuition easier.

D. You mentioned a soul splitting and having multiple bodies at once; that must be a lot more difficult for the guide?

B. It's more tricky! When you had John 32 and the professor, then I was like, "Oh, oh, I have to go over there!" and then Ophelia said, and Jeshua said, "No, we're taking care of this one, it's not gonna be around that long. You can focus on the professor up in Germany." So I was like, "But Lasaray is over there too (*in the Catholic army*)," and they said, "Lasaray's soul is very dimmed. This is simply a physical experience." So, you might not even have heard me. But I wanted to make sure you were okay, because you were in that Catholic army and that didn't seem good, it didn't seem like that would end good. And

I was like, "Ohh, he's gonna be pissed when he comes home. He's gonna be like, 'Look at what happened—I got killed instantly'." Then Ophelia said, "We will take the blame for that". "Okay," I said, "as long as I'm not to blame, because it didn't go that well in the fire. If you take the hit, I'm gonna go watch Lasaray over here being the professor in Germany. That's what I'm gonna do." Because he (*the professor*) was in more of a solitude, more like sitting and writing, journaling.

The Tailors and the Coat of Karma (June 15, 2019)

During the Paleolithic (before the end of the last Ice Age), humans were more open and had a greater awareness of the unseen dimensions, nature spirits, and the migration of the soul than do we. It was common knowledge that spirituality was a solo quest, and that engendered a more receptive attitude to new ideas. Between 10,000 and 15,000 BC, human bodies were intentionally reengineered to suppress soul input to the mind. The disconnect from the spirit caused greed, violence, exploitation, and oppression against other humans (and the Earth) to become more prevalent. This was especially true in the Levant by 1000 BC, where the Semitic tribes of Canaanites and Israelites organized their communities around child sacrifices to Moloch. The ruthless cult has survived to this day within Judaism, Islam and Roman Catholicism, which are all trees growing from the same poison root of religious–state tyranny. Recent trees in this forest of tyranny include the international banking cartel, along with the corporations, media conglomerates and communist ideals that have merged into centralized governments. During the past 2500 years, wherever repressive regimes have grown in power, dark clouds of anti–intellectualism and anti–spiritualism have descended over the land. A spirit on a mission to bring enlightenment knows before it comes down if society will oppose those teachings. But yet, the councils need souls to come in and bring change. So the Tailors accommodate the challenges by altering the way the soul interacts with the Coat and the body. For that reason, there are a large number of spirits who will incarnate to bring changes to the materialistic, mechanistic, and soulless organizations who rule the world at this time. The media constantly promotes a bleak and dreadful future, but Bob reminds us that the play we are observing is transient and illusionary. The will of the Creator will prevail, as it always does, and future occupants of Earth will live in more spiritual and peaceful groups.

B. (*Bob came in making smacking sounds.*) I'm gonna clean myself here.

D. It sounds like Siah licking honey!

B. Ah, ah...that was a tricky thing. Well, not tricky, but I didn't want to mess him up. I didn't know he was gonna be so clumsy, but since he's your pet I should have known he's a little bit like that. It's more that he can just get so excited about the bucket, and when I later saw that everyone else were using spoons, then I was like, "Oh, that's probably better." So next time I will indeed use a spoon. Okay, okay, let's see here. So, training camp continues, we are still a little involved in the karma class and we have discussions about, – because they kinda want to know what sort of suit they're getting. So we have been in the suit museum where we could look at different things. And they could see Henry the Eighth, and they were like, "Oh, there you are! That's the clothes that you were wearing," and I said, "Yes. Now let's see how he did. Let's read here on the little post–it here, to see what sort of intention did he come in with, and where on the journey is he, based on his Coat." So we looked at different things and how different lessons were established, solved or not solved. And we also went back and looked at different scientists, –there were very many, it's somewhat divided into different expertise–, so I took them, because they're going to be in a little bit more mental Coat, so I took them in (*to the museum*) to look at different scientists that have existed. You were there.

D. Which one was it?

B. (*He mentions an historical figure from the Italian Renaissance.*) ...was there, and there were others who were in astronomy, knowledgeable in that. So we looked at different things, and I said, "These are some of the greater results, here when we come to different scientists." When we look at the suit and we read on the little sign, saying what the intention was, we also can press a button and see the surrounding events, the time frame that this person was in, how different knowledge was received. Before AD, astronomy and the higher sciences that these are gonna work with, it was more embraced as a light and as something that people wished for and wanted to be a part of. After AD, it became a completely different resonance, where science did not belong in the human pocket—science belonged in higher realities. It was like human and then god—and everything in between was erased, or they wanted it to be erased. It was much harder for those who operated as scientists and forerunners when it came to understanding astronomy and scientific changes, especially if there were two grand designs, or two advanced technologies that came forward, –where did it come from? Because it was not allowed to communicate with levels between. It was like some men put themselves in a position where they wanted to possess the higher understanding. And it was just like one, in a group, who tried to be the one setting the pace for advancements in general. What are you allowed to read, what you are allowed understand, what are you allowed to receive? And they put like a big blankie over the whole civilization, meaning that those who came in (*incarnated*) with the agenda to create new cycles of advancements in, let's say in technology, it didn't go that well. That's why there is a huge gap from zero there to around 1400 to 1500 AD. Souls like the Elahims did not come that much at that time, it was like the atmosphere became more heavy. So we looked at that and they asked, "So when we're gonna come in, is it gonna be like this, just grey?" And I said, "I'm not really fully part of when you're gonna go down. You have to ask your personal peer, but I will help you and your spirit guides to navigate." Because from that nothingness, from that space of not feeling progress, some are still needed to go down and create new cycles. And I'm not involved in their greater and grander progress, I'm simply here to help them understand prior experiences that others had. And then they said, "Why would no one come here?" (*Most Elahims avoided incarnating when the Abrahamic religions were at their worst.*) and I said, "It's just because it was a cloud and man tried to encapsulate the knowledge at the human level, not connecting with all levels that were surrounding the human, which prior civilizations did and embraced when their societies seeked for the access to the greater mysteries. But after AD, then man hijacked mysteries. What we wish now is that mysteries will be reintroduced to mankind, to understand that there is indeed a greater mystery lurking just above your head or behind your back.

And it can be different depending on what soul you are and what mission you have. And these little scientists coming in, they're gonna be part of creating and kick-starting new scientific cycles and progress. So we talked about karma and they were a little bit concerned about the Coat. But now indeed they have been provided a Coat, and we are in the fitting room and we are just trying to get accustomed to having a Coat. So, you know. (*Looking thoughtful and popping his lips.*)

D. Can you see what their general Coat looks like?

B. Indeed.

D. So they can see also what they are up against?

B. Indeed. At the moment they have been provided, –we have six Coats sewed up for us here, and we are in the fitting room, kinda, and they are looking at their own Coat, but they are also looking at each other's Coat. And they're like, "Oh, so you're gonna do that!" and they want to know a little bit about how it came about. And it is based, of course, on their unique makeup and what the Creator wants them to do.

D. So the Coat sort of mirrors the pattern in their being?

B. In their being, and the blueprint and their mission. So we looked at that, and I can somewhat, based on a little manual I have been provided here as a teacher, I can see like, "Okay, you're gonna go down and do that." I can also see that of these six, not everyone is gonna go down at the same time. Elahims might come a little bit later, whereas the other three might go first. The Elahims suits looks a little bit heavier, it looks more dense, it comes in with more tools.

D. More scientific abilities?

B. At the moment it seems like it is just that they are provided more tools, and they are gonna come in when it's gonna be more BOOM, and the others lay the foundation for the boom. But they are working simultaneously, AND what they also received news of here, is that when the first three go down, not only will they have us as a spirit guide, but the three Elahims are also gonna practice, because they are so familiar with each other. They're friends, so they are gonna practice as spirit guides for the first three going down.

D. I guess that's common, because Eli works as a guide to me and Seth, doesn't he, even though Jeshua is my mentor?

B. Ah, umm–hmm. So indeed, it's like if someone goes down from the seventh, then Julia would be someone who participates. And Julia might incarnate later, and then you have Ophelia who might assist Julia, to assist the person in human body, and then you have someone from us, who are tightly close, so someone doesn't trip and burn! Huhuhuh. Taking more care of that. So they're starting to see the adventures that lie before them.

D. Are they nervous?

B. Not nervous, because they start to feel the responsibility and the honor placed upon them from the Creator and the higher councils, so they are more eager, I would say, than nervous. What we are trying, also, here now to establish, is that it is not a one–time quick fix. It's not like they can come down and fix things instantly, because here enters physical, and it's gonna be completely different because they have this Coat. Soul goes into Coat, goes into body, –have to portion themselves out into the inner worlds of the physical body to make sure that the mission itself becomes a success. And that is the tricky part. But they have help, of course, you all do, but what we have to make them understand, because I don't want there to be sadness, so I said, "Lasaray has been down twelve–hundred times, his Coat was folded around eleven-seventy lives. So the last thirty lives, coatless." So I have to give them somewhat of a frame, so they understand that it's not like coming down to do a quick fix and then go somewhere else. They wanted to know about somewhere else, and I said, "I don't know if you're gonna go somewhere else," I kinda do know that they're gonna go around the circle here, to different fish tanks, but I'm not gonna tell, I'm not allowed to.

D. Are the other Elahims, their teachers, with them also?

B. Indeed. It's a whole group effort every time a soul goes down.

D. I meant in the Tailor room?

B. In the Tailor room–, well, Zachariah is here. Zachariah seems to know all these people, he has a lot of friends, I would say. Isaac popped by, but this is about understanding your Coat and your general purpose. At this point we have not sewed in the different experiences in the Coat; we have established the purpose Coat and are trying to just be comfortable in that Coat.

D. Can they slide into it to get a feel for how it is?

B. Indeed. And that's what we do here in the fitting room. So, we did that and the spirit guides are very interested, –I never got to go to the Tailors, I missed all this, there was no preparations, there was no Tailors, there was nothing like a Coat to see. I was informed that there was a Coat, but I did not see the whole background of becoming a Coat and stuff like that. I got you when you were already established, you were like a grownup. You were maybe considered like we were just around thirty.

D. We're about the same age, you and I?

B. Ah, we were grown. But these are sixteen to twenty–year olds that are gonna go now. But they have different teachings. I don't know if there was a haste for you to come in, like, "He's gonna go down, he needs someone—oh, okay, let's activate Bob." I don't know if that was the case why I did not get full training about you.

D. You were uniquely qualified.

B. Ah. I learn differently. So the spirit guides are here, and they have to be very well familiar with their person's Coat, because they're gonna observe the Coat. So it's important that the spirit guide closely connected to the soul has a little bit of a preview of the Coat. The main spirit, their main peer, is part of creating the Coat, so they already know. But here with Tom and everyone, –and Tom, he's like a me a little bit, he said, "I want to do this," because he has already seen a preview of some suffering on the seabed, and he wants his person to do well, fix it really fast. And then we have Little Seth, and Little Seth is gonna come down and work a lot with what now is considered communication, but through satellites. He's gonna be an engineer and will bring an understanding of the disks that will exist around satellites, and how to mirror them in order for signals to be pure and clean.

D. Not like microwaves that are damaging to the atmosphere?

B. Indeed. There has to be a cleanup in your atmosphere around Earth when it comes to the satellites, because they are angled and directed in all sorts of directions. It's like putting them up like, plupp, plupp, plupp, and they are not functioning correctly. Let's say you have a hundred up there, but they are all mirrored, some are mirrored and facing each other so they read each other's signals, instead of reading other signals that are correct. So he's gonna come in as a scientist, I can see what the intention is with him, and it is to eliminate un-pure signals, exchanging them for disks that operate and are mirrored and facing realities and operating correctly, that is not harming the inside. When there are too many, let's say we have these hundred, and he is programmed to come in with the understanding that you could have the same or better result only having three or five, but positioned correctly. At this point it's a jungle up there and it's not operating correctly for the environment. So he's gonna come in with new ideas on how to increase signals, but at the same time reducing the amount, so it is more pinpointed and not scattered and harmful for the inside. All of these, not only the Elahims in the sixth, but everyone coming in, their general mission—because everyone comes in with a collective mission, in some way—and the collective mission for all of them coming from Zachariah's school, coming from Ophelia's, is the protection of the inside, the planet itself. And then we have some that is gonna come in, and I don't think they're gonna be from the sixth, they're gonna be from Ophelia (*souls from the seventh*), but they're gonna come in and somewhat become doctors that will change how the healing process in the physical as well as the mental transforms over time. To heal the mental with light and different tools, than just put a pill in it. It's what I see over there when I get a preview here with Ophelia, they're gonna come in and a lot of them are gonna work in the medical. The general idea of the next group coming in is to protect species and the host. And Little Seth is completely ready; he was a little bit angry when he started to see what's going on and what he is coming down to do. He wanted to come in like a storm and do a quick fix, –similar like Big Seth! Come in and do a quick fix! But he's gonna have things sewed into his Coat that is gonna slow him down a little bit. And his spirit person here is, he is to help him be in the right pace.

D. This is going to happen fairly soon then, from a human perspective?

B. Ah, Ophelia says this is in a hundred-year cycle, or so.

D. Is Ophelia going to take out all the satellites with a solar flare or something?

B. Maybe they try to do it through Little Seth first. But he's gonna have a lot of lives where he will be placed in like big, –I would say space programs. He's gonna be very social, but we have to work on his personality a little bit. His Coat is filled with tools to make greatness, but we have to somewhat, like with this one, we have to make sure that the personality, the physical, maybe slows the Coat down a little bit so it's a balance, so we don't leave a red spot—eventually we leave a green one. (*He has used colors to categorize the type of footprint a life leaves behind. Red indicates karmic problems, whereas green shows a positive life.*) But he is, like all of these six, here to create new understandings. Since I know this one, I can see that there is a tendency here for a repeat, so we have to understand the physical. It's not like by chance, so his peer, he's gonna make sure that he gets a physical that is well adapted to this tremendous Coat filled with tools, like with this one. And that might create frustration in the soul, because the soul will understand and feel limited, and feel like, "Why do you put up roadblocks for me, if you want me to come down and do something?" So it's a whole balance of soul, Coat, physical, and the end result is to be able to blend in and to create new ways of doing things and understand things.

D. You have a really important job then, within this group.

B. Ah. And you know, Tom, there's a reason Tom is not with Little Seth because Tom is like trying to whisper in the ear here, I see. And I said, "What are you talking about over here, Tom? You can't put ideas in Little Seth, you have to welcome the process and honor the greater beyond and what the Creator has intended with your person; you might not know what the greater idea is." And I'm still learning, because there were several times with you where I didn't want us to leave as quickly. You had a tendency, throughout, that when you felt content, the soul felt content, it just left. But the Coat might not have been completely fulfilled, so your Coat might have been folded earlier if you had stuck around a little bit longer. I also had discussions with you when you were home, and you told me about what you were gonna do, what probably Jeshua asked of you to do, and then I say, "Can I have an input? Can I also say something here what I would like to do?" And you said, "Sure, you can have an input." And then I had, but I don't know if everything was heard or acknowledged. But I did my best to make sure that we came down...a huge task in my lap was to make you more social, to make you somewhat—because you were just captured in the mission, just very focused on the mission—but I also wanted you to not be perceived as somewhat of a loner and somewhat of a, you know, odd character in the group. So I tried to make you more social.

D. Don't be such a crab.

B. Don't be such a crab! Don't just sit there and write in your journals! And you were like, "But this is the mission. It is to create changes." And I said, "Yes, but try to engage with those around you. Be curious about them, because you are studying human behavior in some way." Anyway, I'm gonna go now.

D. That was a really good talk.

B. That's what we've been doing. We're gonna study the transitions here in the fourth, like how to leave the Coat, how to enter the Coat, where is the Coat gonna be, looking into the closet kind of thing.

The Cells of Enslavement (June 15, 2019)

We talked in the previous section about how humans were relatively peaceful during the Paleolithic. There were, however, aliens who came to Earth that caused problems for the humans. The Council of Nine identified a group they call the Cell, who are modern humans influenced by the past. Their discussion is part of *Wave 3*, but we have included a brief excerpt here about the origins of the Cell. Alien visitors came to Earth about 150,000 years ago, intent upon controlling the planet. Their technology and their actions were very disruptive, because of their total disregard for the life forms here. Subsequently, the councils banned the visitors from Earth. However, the memories of what they did and the thought–forms they created are stored in the fourth dimension surrounding Earth. When souls come down to take on a new incarnation, they must navigate through the energetic debris that exists within the fourth. There is always a risk the soul may encounter and be attracted to certain memories that will influence their incarnation. This is what happened to a group of souls who lived approximately 2500 years ago. They tapped into and reignited this pattern of desire for domination and control left behind by the visitors. They may have been warlords, emperors, moneylenders, or religious leaders in the Middle East and southern Europe. Each of them contributed, in some measure, to violence and oppression on a large scale. Because of their actions, they were joined together in a soul-specific karmic debt. The Creator and the Councils set up a system to resolve this group karma, which became part of their individual Coat of Karma. They cannot return home to the spiritual dimensions, but must continue to incarnate as a group until they independently, but simultaneously, overcome the patterns of dominance. The Jewish and Muslim conflict in the Middle East is part of the Cell's karma. Interestingly, certain members of the Cell incarnate on opposite sides of the religious war after each life. One life as a hardline Jew, the next as a dogmatic Muslim. What better way to learn the Golden Rule? The souls affiliated with the Cell incarnate into positions where they can influence changes on a large scale, such as in the commercial, political, military or financial arenas. The Cell controls the IMF and the World Bank, who use fiat money and debt to enslave all nations under their despotic privilege. Other parts of the Cell reign over the large media conglomerates that, through relentless deception and propaganda, create false realities for people to believe. The Cell has infiltrated and corrupted all of the pillars of society; laws, politics, commerce, religion, family and individual rights, education and culture. The Cell and their lackeys are the ones who perpetuate turmoil and start wars between nations—all done to expand their personal fortunes and power. The Council of Nine said that some of the offspring are involved in promoting dangerous technologies, such as 5G, 6G, and 7G.

> CN. The Cell came around the time 150,000 years ago. It started with a colony, civilized entities that came from another star system. The ones you see today are the offspring. It is in some way a bloodline. They were not incarnated. Incarnation hadn't started in that way. Fifty-fifty existed, soul pioneers, souls that came as a blend, but not fully incarnated in the program that you are addressing and caught in at the moment. The Cell that came 150,000 years ago, that's when the Cell started to become. They set camp, came from a nearby star system, (*they were originally from*) fish tank three. Fish tank three is now in hibernation. They came when the window was open for more to observe a new project. They were interested in tapping into a third reality, becoming something else. They were interested in understanding the minerals and energy

sources that were placed on this Earth. They came highly advanced in understanding energy resources, but they didn't leave. They claimed energy, they claimed to be the ones kick-starting that aspect of this world. That claim, which connects to power, energy is power, remained in the consciousness, in the bloodline (*the fourth dimension*) for others to come. They travel differently than you. They are still here in some way, and you might ask how is this even allowed or possible? We will come to that. Understand though, that there are different ways to tap into a physical reality and bypass matter. They came with the knowledge of power, energy, how to use different resources that existed here. Uranium in mountains, receivers in many ways, they are the forerunners of what you see now of those who try to establish 5G. They did the same using uranium, using mountains as receivers and transmission centers. Those who are promoting 5G—not necessarily everyone that works with it—but the council, the elite, those who sit in the positions of power of making changes within power and energy, they are offspring from this Cell. When this occurred, eruptions took place. Several came to clean the planet, and they (*the visitors*) were indeed banned. But it was still a mark in your karma, in your atmosphere, a memory was still there and souls tapping in have the ability to mirror an old memory or pattern. Even if those who were here at that time are banned and gone, there are those who have the ability to transform and use old occurrences, tapping into a physical body. It all occurs in the fourth reality. Most souls can't attach these memories as they travel in, but there are those who are bypassing certain laws, and they find these different occurrences. Like your Little Friend says, finding a note, putting it in the pocket as they travel through the fourth. You should know, though, that most have not the ability to find these more destructive notes hanging around in your energetic atmosphere, the fourth reality. Most souls, as they incarnate, as they travel from, let's say the fifth dimension, through the fourth, they are accompanied by light beings. Meaning, if I can make a picture for you, if you see the debris in the fourth reality, things that still exist as a memory, spirit guides do not wish their soul companion heading for Earth to be confused by the debris that hangs around as an energetic memory. There are helpers, light beings, assisting souls through the fourth, focusing on their Coat, having blindfolds for the debris, if you like. So if ninety-nine percent are assisted like that, then there is a small amount of souls who still find the debris on their way through. Those are the ones who create the Cell that you see now, trying to manipulate energy and power.

The remainder of the Council of Nine's talk can be found in Wave 3, in a June 30, 2019 session. We felt it would be helpful to Bob's talk if some background on the Cell was provided. Bob draws a comparison of their behavior to spiders who trap and poison people's minds with toxic fear and deceit. The West was built upon the philosophy and principles established by Socrates, where individual sovereignty is acknowledged as an irrevocable gift from the Creator, and where human interaction is conducted according to reason and virtue. For most of recorded history, governments have abandoned these ideals due to the corrupting influence of the lost souls who control the Cell.

D. I had a question before you leave. The cloud that came in around zero, was that put there by the spirits, or was that a result of religion?

B. It was caused by actions from this plane. All clouds that come in and are placed upon or removed from your consciousness, at this particular cycle for the last, –we're talking several cycles back–, but it is the end result of actions taking place on this plane. And based on certain actions around the year zero, especially in, it started around fifty to a hundred BC and then it continued to like two, three hundred AD, so we have like a five hundred year span where actions were so tremendously non-spiritual and not connected to source and soul, that the cloud came in and it was placed there.

D. Is it getting better now?

B. In some way it's getting better, because more are moving into proclaiming their own power and proclaiming their own light. However, there are different dilemmas at this point, and that is placed upon humanity from a small group, a Cell, similar thing. But it's not religion in the same way, it's more a claim of territory and a claim of possessing—holding the strings to the whole society functioning correctly, according to this Cell. So the Cell tries to hold the strings to how an entire society should operate, and that Cell is not the Creator. I said that, "Why don't we just do a reboot in that Cell? And then the other ones can be left alone." It's like as soon as humanity and consciousness are regaining strength, it seems that something happens within this Cell, like a spider controlling the web, and then the little bugs, the rest of society feel like they have no control, trapped, and they feel like they can't move, like they are immobile, because the Cell and the spider send out poison in the web making everything around connected to that web to feel paralyzed. So they make the society and the will within your consciousness, the will to progress as a species, as a human, it makes them paralyzed from the web, –because you're all connected in this earthly web, the whole society, the whole group. But the spider, I wanted to do a reboot of the spider because it's not that many dots. There's like one dot here (*New York*), there is another spider like around London, and then there's a spider in Germany (*they have mentioned Frankfurt before, as a hub of nefarious men*), there's also a spider over in Japan. So there are different spiders that send out poison in the web, but they are less in numbers. If you understand that you have the medicine to not be paralyzed in this web, then the spiders, being less in number and not very powerful as is, –they are powerful because of the fact that the little bugs, they don't raise up, they don't try to self-heal, they just feel like they are paralyzed. And a lot of it has to do with the medical establishment, who put pills in the bug and pills in the web from the spider, making sure that the creature, the bug, remains paralyzed. So that's why there is a lot coming in from the seventh, Ophelia says, that's going to be providing a balance within the medical establishment to understand. And that's also what (*he names a friend in Sweden*), her part is to show first-hand about self-healing, because the bugs need to understand that the spider is feeding them pills, making them paralyzed in the web, meaning that they feel like they are glued to the web—in many ways just only waiting to move on—and that's not why you came here. You didn't come here just to move on (*waiting to die*). Similar like with you, I sometimes said, "You left too early." And you were like, "Well, I don't really enjoy the journey, I just wanted to come down and do my thing and then leave." And that's why you also have this one, because this one will make you want to stick around. But you didn't have that before, well, when you were in Scotland you had each other, so you wanted to stick around then. But you needed the companionship and a reason to stick around. So that's why this one was selected.

D. That is a very intriguing lesson.

B. So, maybe just reboot the spider. I'm gonna say that would be something for—

D. That might involve a chat with the Evolution Group.

B. Ah, I'm putting that in my velvet bag, I'm absolutely putting that. I was gonna say otherwise, who can I put this on, whose Coat can I sew this in? But I'm not supposed to meddle with the suits, –so I'm not. But if Little Seth saw this, it would be like coming in like a wind and blowing all the spiders away. That's what he wants to do, so I'm probably not gonna tell him. I'm sure there's gonna be discussions with him when he first comes in contact with this and he comes back and talks with his peer, he's gonna know, eventually, about this. But he's very eager to go. He says, "Check on the hammer, check on the saw, check on that, check on all my tools." So he's like when you see those like a SWAT team, that's how he operates.

D. That will be wonderful when he gets a chance to do good.

B. We'll see how wonderful this will be, but that's why he needs crash cushions, like this one. I'm sure he would like to just incarnate directly into the spider family here and make a rumble in the whole net. The whole web around the globe is connected by these spiders and if he saw this, he might want to come in and do a rumble in one of the spider's nests.

D. Become the heir to their fortune and power.

B. Ah, and take over one of the spider's positions. But it's also the fact that you have to regain strength and regain power in a way that is beneficial, that is not just a rumble. That's what this one was taught: do an imprint on your surroundings that is not just a rumble, that is just a little ripple. A little ripple continues indefinitely, but a rumble can scare others, and it might not have the desired end result, Ophelia says, if you just come in like a storm, come in like a thunder god, like Thor with his hammer. It's the same thing here, have enormous potential in the Coat, BUT how to package this tremendous toolbox and personality, soul personality, into a human personality so it doesn't become like a huge rumble. So that's not what we want. Sometimes the biggest challenge is to operate in disguise. And that's a problem with this one, doesn't like to work in disguise. You don't mind, so there's a difference. This one has to sometimes work in disguise, silently and for the higher good, whereas you have been told to engage. So, it's different. Anyway, it's time to go.

D. Well, it's really nice talking to you.

B. If we're gonna come down more times, then I'm putting in a request to come in in one of the spider's nests with you, and maybe bring more (*soul*) percentage from you. Maybe pump up the volume to the max of what you can have, like twenty-five percent—that is max. That's what Ophelia said and Jeshua said; max, twenty-five percent.

D. If I get born into one of those spider families with the big yachts and mansions and I lay around eating caviar all day, you'll have to poke me.

B. I'll have to make sure you hear me, and that is somewhat of a balance—how to put one in a human surrounding that is lacking spiritual awareness, coming in with an agenda of change but not hearing the spirit guide necessarily, fully. You know, balance, balance. But since you don't have a Coat, I might try what they did with John 32, to just somewhat steer you remotely. I said, "If you're not gonna come, can I borrow like two percent and tap it into a body and then I can—" (*he looked suddenly to the left*), OHH, Ophelia, she heard that.

D. A whole new way of incarnating.

B. I said if you're not gonna incarnate, if I can only borrow like two percent of you and just put it into a body, and then I can just remotely make changes. Oh, Ophelia says, "That's like bypassing evolution again." Well, THEY did it with John 32, so why can't I do it? (*He was having a side conversation with Ophelia.*) She said it's not my role, really. And I said, "Maybe it will be." But it's silent about the topic, so I don't know. But my idea is, since you said this is gonna be the last hurrah for a while, then until you come back and do similar like an incarnation again, if I can only borrow and then remotely control. Because I have, –following you on all these journeys, simultaneously based on the things I observed–, I said, "Huh, this is how we could have done it differently," and then I created a new kinda life. So I have several lives lined up that I can use and missions that I can use, if I can only borrow two percent. So I have put out the request, and it's silence about the topic for the meantime. BUT my feeling is that maybe just have it land in everyone's consciousness. It's like here (*on Earth*), if you put out a great idea, it has to somewhat land. And it's the same thing here (*in the spirit realm*), here comes me with a great new way of solving things, and maybe everyone has to think about it for a while. That's what I think. But I have several agendas lined up. And this is probably not gonna be approved, but if I can have two percent there, two percent there, two percent there, do them all at one time. Let's see, if you give me twenty percent, then I can have ten and be like a puppet master. (*He held his hands out, spreading the fingers and showing how he would make all the bodies do his bidding.*)

D. You might have to bring in Ole and Gergen to help.

B. Indeed, and I don't need to take all the credit by myself for all this greatness, –but maybe Tom wants to be an assistant, and maybe Zachariah. It has not been approved, but I'm thinking that they're thinking about it.

D. That would be one way to make positive changes in a hurry.

B. And then you don't have to come, necessarily, all in, because you can just be elsewhere in your haste, and I can tend to haste here. Because I said, "There's haste here too. If I can only borrow two percent, since clearly, I cannot come in. And I have to start from scratch in that karma program, and that's not what my intention is." I have a person who is trained to come here.

D. Perfect solution.

B. Perfect solution for everyone. Leaving that note, I've said it out loud, so now they heard it. Might just have to somewhat absorb itself and land in everyone. And then they'll say, "Maybe that's a good idea."

D. Give Bob a shot with his plan.

B. We'll give him a shot and see. What's the worst thing that could happen? The worst thing that can happen is that something good comes out of it. So, nothing bad can happen— oh, Ophelia says that having someone with two percent is tricky, because they will not always hear you. But I was gonna remotely operate.

D. You'll need to install a volume button in me.

B. Ah, we'll see here. It's an idea. Anyway, so I'll go then.

D. Alright. We've got your book (*Volume 1*) out there now, and it was well received.

B. Ah, ah, happy about that. Make people happy, make people sing, make people not take things so seriously all the time—see the amusement and teaching and learning. Oh, okay, I'll go. Bye bye.

The Runway Show of Bodies and Personalities (June 23, 2019)

One attributes of life in the spiritual dimensions is the flexibility given to teachers. There are common lectures that students attend, but as they advance, instruction becomes more personalized. Bob is always thinking of unique ways to prepare his students, and wanted to give them a preview of the types of bodies and personalities they would encounter on Earth. He created an elaborate show and called upon his many friends to take part as actors on the stage. He then invited several hundred students, his council, and other teachers to see the play. Zachariah spoke before Bob, and mentioned going to Bob's educational party for souls who were about to begin incarnating on Earth.

B. Ah! Here I am!

D. Hello once again.

B. Always present. I have been selected to host a party.

D. That's what Zachariah said.

B. Ah. It's a huge festivity, and even though not everyone are going (*to Earth*), everyone is invited. So even those from the sixth come here and salute and congratulate those from the fifth, heading for their destination. And it's a very merry occasion indeed.

D. So you're the grand master of the party?

B. I am the initiator and the party planner of this event. I have different things, like we have role-plays, we have films, I also had the Tailors come in to somewhat show how the Coats become. In this department of Coats, there are also those who manufacture the physical. I have asked you and Ophelia and Zachariah and everyone that I know, "Who are involved in creating the physicals?" and there has been somewhat of a silence on the topic. But I have not caved in to silence this time. I have continued to be inquisitive, to be persistent, going outside of my comfort zone (*he laughed when he said that*). Huh huh huh.

D. That's a big zone!

B. Ah. You said that I was just being me. But anyway, so I have asked repeatedly, and so I thought it would be like a very nice ending for the fifth souls to somewhat see what sort of vehicles are available when they come, and what sort of personalities, SO, I created a runway show with physical and personalities! I have like a runway and everyone is sitting around and I am kinda the one behind the curtain, checking off the list, like, "Okay, here comes you, you're gonna be grumpy, off you go." They have like a little sign on them. Well, first we actually had different physical that is just physical that has no personalities. So first they came in like, "Here is someone a little bit round. Here is someone like a version of an Asian individual. Here is someone with Caucasian qualities. Here is female. Here is male." So we had all these different physical attributes first, and it was a great success. They were like, "Oh! I wanna have THAT one!" Because they kinda knew a little bit, they had like flyers where they could read up a little bit, you know like, "Where is this specific individual normally launched? Where do you find an Asian?" Then they can see on, –it's like an energetic little tablet that they have–, that they can see where normally this individual is launched. So they can see, "Ah, so this one will be around Burma. Hmm, do I have a drive and need to go there? Do I have a tingle in me that resonates that this is the location where I'm supposed to go? And if it is, umm–hmm, I'm gonna be dressed like that!" So they look at that, individually sitting there, and there are all these different physical attributes coming on the runway. And I have music to accommodate this because I want to make a full effect of what is happening. So it is a very merry show. I mirror a little bit the physical attributes, and I'm gonna do the same later with the personality attributes. I somewhat give a flavor or a tease to that specific body entering the runway. So I had different melodies, just to make an effect. So we had here someone coming up like someone who is a little bit round. They can look at different physical attributes that they might have, because the thing is, you normally come back a lot of times in somewhat of a preference form. So you can look at that. And then enters personalities, and that is different. I have a little game. When they come in, they come in and they don't show the sign, but they come in and they display different personalities, different behaviors.

The ones from the fifth and everyone sitting out there, they have on their little energetic tablet all these different personalities and aspects, and they can press, –because this specific physical coming in like an actor showing different displays of behaviors–, and then they can choose like, "Hmm, number one, that must be grumpy."

D. Do they have to guess?

B. It's a game! It's all about being a game, it's no right or wrong here, it's just to make it a little fun. So on my runway, first came out grumpy, went out there a little bit grumpy. They have all these different categories to choose from and they can choose that, and later on in the end of my runway show, the grand finale, it will be somewhat revealed. It's no right or wrong, it's not a test.

D. That sounds like it was fun.

B. So I kinda check them before they go out, because they're not grumpy by themselves, so I said, "You're gonna be grumpy." And they say, "Oh, what is that? Remind me." And then I have the keywords for that, so I say, "Go out now and be grumpy, off you go on the runway." And next comes and I say, "You're gonna be motherly; empathic and caring." That's more close to a soul personality, so there were no follow-up questions on that one so, "Off you go, and display in all the ways you can, with the physical here, that personality." But the physicals here (*in the personality display*) are more blank. When the first physicals came out showing different physical attributes, they were more a variety. When we're looking into personalities, they come in more like white physicals because I want them to focus on the personalities here, and behaviors and so forth. They all look kinda the same, white.

D. Are the personalities something the Tailors put on the blank canvas?

B. Indeed. So we have like a blank canvas, like you said, as a physical, and they have to somewhat display in other ways, different characteristics of human behaviors and personalities. And then a soul can say, "Oh, that looks friendly. This one here, what is that? Oh very caring. What words can I have on my tablet that will match with that? And then I press my button," and the show continues with different melodies. You have someone who is narrow-minded. (*Right after this session, he told Christine he also displayed personalities on the runway that were shallow, passionate, high-maintenance, and friendly*.) It's all about making them aware that if they feel like that—because they will remember deep, deep, deep, deep, deep, deep inside their soul memory and being, they will remember Mr. Grumpy, they will remember the one who is narrow-minded—so first of all, if they detect that within themselves, they can go like, "Ohh, I remember that show on the runway, I'm gonna change that." And if they encounter someone, they will recognize that personality. This is on a subconscious level, of course, but it's all about creating a sensation of memory. It's an extension of my theater classes. So we have the show and all these different personalities come out. You have someone who is very bold. And you're all here too, because this takes place on the fifth, so everyone is here. This one is there, and you're there looking at this show. Ophelia of course shows up. She wants to make sure it goes wells, so she's actually behind the scenes with me, whereas you are in the audience looking at the end result. Ophelia is there to add a little touch before I send them off on the runway. It's a very merry and happy occasion, and even though not everyone is going (*to Earth*), like the ones from the sixth, they still appreciate this. Everyone is invited.

D. That was quite a task then, to put on the show.

B. Ah. It's a huge thing to be a party planner and to create this runway show.

D. What did Ia say about it?

B. Ia laughed a little bit. She applauded it and she said, "This is a really good party, Bob." And I said, "I came up with this all by myself. I had to pull some strings. I had to be persistent and ask for not only the Coat of Karma to come in," which is the personalities, "but I also wanted to have the physicals, what sort of vehicle are available to me."

D. Did you see any new models, things you hadn't seen before?

B. Some are a little bit more red-headed coming in. They're a little bit more pale and with red hair. That's sort of a new model that came in. They're more sensitive to the sun, and that's because there are holes in the atmosphere that causes different problems on the skin. You might think instead that you will design something that is more endurable and also like a shield, like a turtle skin, but instead they're making upcoming models, a couple of them here, a little bit more sensitive to the sun. So they're gonna be more avoiding it. Ophelia, she's there assisting.

D. Well, congratulations. It sounds like quite an impressive graduation ceremony.

B. Ah, it was fun, all these different personalities. And at the end when everyone was standing there together on the runway, – both the physical and the personalities–, then the personalities had little signs and they flipped the sign, showing like, "I'm grumpy", or "I'm motherly", or "I'm shy".

D. Did you have a contest to see who got the most correct?

B. Indeed. It's not, like I said, it's not like we say, "You came last," it's not like that, but the ones who got the most right will have a little bit of an extra treat. But it's just for fun, it has nothing to do with their teaching—and I told Ophelia that, because she was concerned that I was gonna be, similar like with the (*musical*) chairs, that it would be like, "No, you're not ready to go." So I said it's not like that, it's just gonna be for fun, to see who does the best. It's not like I'm gonna grade all of them, it's just that the ones who do well will get a treat. And I wanted the treat to be somewhat like a nice treat, a unique treat. So the one who won, I said, "You will now be able, for your first assignment, to freely pick a physical and a personality." They're kinda programmed already what they're supposed to do, so it's not like I'm interfering. They're still in some way programmed to like one physical or somewhat be drawn to a specific personality. It was just to somewhat make them excited. Because later on you still choose, but it's just a little game.

D. So there are some that are ready to come down?

B. Ah, from the fifth, ready to go with spirit guides from the second.

D. So you had some from the second that were already trained up?

B. Indeed. They're gonna go to northern climate areas, that's what they're gonna do. So, that was that. It takes a lot of time and preparation to create and put on this grand show. But I'm well suited for it. It's very well established in my personality to create a party, so it wasn't that tricky. I just needed to collect some favors! And so I did.

D. How many souls were there in total?

B. We were like two, three hundred.

D. I was going to guess a thousand or more.

B. Nah. Well, souls and spirit guides, maybe three hundred. And then there were guests like this one and you. So with that combined, maybe five hundred.

D. What about your council?

B. They were there too, they would be considered guests. The council was like, "What's gonna happen here? What's this big stage for? What are we going to observe here?" And I said, "We're gonna observe the selection of physical and personality coming into body as a human individual. So just relax, sit back and see the show."

D. You have a human that you follow, but did all of your Council members follow a human? (*His Council on the second.*)

B. Some of them have followed a human, indeed.

D. So they are familiar?

B. They are familiar with following a human. But it was a lot of preparations, and like I said, I had to collect some favors. So that's what I did.

D. That sounds like you created a fun show.

B. It was a huge gathering, so like I said, we were probably in total about five-hundred. So, I'm not gonna be too long in the tooth here today, Ophelia says, but I wanted to tell about my show.

D. We're going to talk about your book today. What would you like us to say?

B. Ah, I'm gonna be there. Tell them to embrace the magic, I want you to convey magic and the ability to communicate and connect with someone like me! Or fairies, and to just create a short moment of wonderment, introducing the importance of the environment and how the environment is communicating to you in different ways. And to also embrace your pet, because someone could be inside the pet. To talk about spiritual helpers that are really close by, that are just around the corner, so to speak, or perhaps just in the basket next to you on the floor. Ah, umm. So I want there to be just a very easy going and relaxed talk, not too advanced, not too complex. Go into yourself with a sensation of laughter and amusement and provide that for them. Laugh a lot. It's all

about being excited, and that's what I want to launch. Talk about how a little sparkle becomes, because it exists everywhere.
D. Didn't want to get too involved in the solar system and things like that.
B. You can briefly mention just like it is an activity that sometimes can go on. But the main focus here is to make it a very amusing and light-hearted conversation.
D. Alright, that's what we'll shoot for then.
B. Okay, okay, Ophelia says it's time to go.
D. It's nice to hear about your graduation party, so thank you for sharing that.
B. Ah. It was a nice ceremony. So, okay, I'll go and see you soon.
D. Alright my friend, thank you for coming.
B. Okay. Bye bye.

Mixing and Matching Personalities to the Body (June 30, 2019)

Bob's runway show stirred up his students and he got a lot of questions about bodies types and personalities. In the course of explaining how some bodies are not suitable for certain missions, he gives us a little bit of information about advancements in understanding the Earth that are planned for future generations. The ability to read the subtle energy changes that cause earthquakes, tsunamis, changes in weather and other physical processes will be a gift given to certain incarnations. The humans of the future will look back on the 21st century as a time of unbridled mayhem in the sciences, a time when objectivity was lost.

B. (*He came in looking rather despondent but didn't say anything.*)
D. Why the sad look?
B. I was on time! I was here on time, ready to talk, but there was like a door. And I was like, "Why did someone put up a door?"
D. Did you hear who was talking, before?
B. No. There was a door. (*Both the Council of Nine and Gergen had talked before Bob was given his turn. They must have not wanted Bob to hear, so they put up an energetic door to obstruct the conversation.*)
D. I could tell you who was talking.

B. I could see Gergen come OUT from the door, and just sort of passed the torch forward, put a little crystal in my hand. But he didn't say anything, he just left through the door, so I don't know where he came from.

D. He came from right here.

B. So I don't know why it was necessary to put up a door, I know Gergen, there's no need to put me outside and to lock the door. That's kinda rude.

D. Well, he must have had his reasons. What's been going on?

B. Ah, I'm proceeding with my programs. (*He became happy again.*) I'm looking into the final touch of certain things. Even though I'm not responsible for making the souls from the fifth go, I'm not responsible for their training and so forth, and their Coat and their suits. But because of the runway show, there was a lot of questions coming out. Ophelia said, "This is the end result of being too outspoken. But you wanted the show, so now you have to answer the questions."

D. What sort of questions are you getting?

B. It was questions how to mix and match. Someone wanted to come in and be very passionate, and then I said, "Okay, you saw passion on the runway show, you saw that. So what sort of physical did you have in mind?" And he said, "I've been given three options." So we kinda looked into that, so it was a little bit of a preview on a tablet thing they have. So I said, "Well, sometimes certain personalities are better expressed through different physical attributes—have to mix and match a little bit, so the whole intent doesn't disappear just because the physical cannot channel it." Like with this one, for instance, he couldn't really fully channel the soul. The inside was very much in some way the same, but it was overshadowed by low self-esteem in that specific Coat that was available when this one came into the life of Alicia. (*Christine had a recent life in Virginia as a woman named Alicia.*) So the mix and match in that respect didn't make the soul heard. So we're looking into that, how to best be able to channel the intent that one have. First of all, "What is your intent? What are you gonna go down and do?" I asked. And then one said that they're gonna be like geologists, –there's a lot of geologists coming down, understanding the curves (*energy waves*) in the ground, understanding to read the planet. It's very important that there are expertise coming in to understand how to read the planet. And it's not just reading, "Oh, here comes a tsunami!" It's understanding WHY does it come, a tsunami? What is causing the end result? What is the tsunami representing? What have we been missing through these different occurrences leading up to a tsunami? You have to understand the whole chain. At this particular time, there are a lot who are like, "Uh, okay, I can read the tsunami, it's gonna strike here in two days." But WHY, and what caused it? Some are natural effects, but some are a product or an end result of other things. These geologists come in with more tools in the toolbox, let's just say that.

D. So they'll be able to read what's happening with the Earth?

B. And WHY. WHY are these end results? For instance, you might want to know why are there so many clouds and thunder traveling through Colorado at this particular time?

D. Yes, please tell me! (*In 2019, summer was slow in coming, and storms came in almost every day for months on end, which was very unusual.*)

B. It's because there are things going on on the west coast, and not everything has to do with environment, even though it's a big part of different occurrences that you see in your environment, of course. BUT, certain actions—everything is connected—so at this particular time it's a wave moving across. It originates from certain actions on the west coast, but it is meant to awaken and send an alarm on the east coast.

D. What's causing—

B. Vulnerability in your ecosystem, understanding that you are not always on top as a country and as a species. To understand that Mother Nature, like you call it, might have a need for assistance.

D. Yes, it's been producing a lot of rain in the Midwest, in the farming areas, so the crop yields are way down.

B. And that will make you vulnerable. There is a wave of understanding and consciousness coming in, and the end result is what current geologists see and understand, and biologists too. Maybe a little bit can be detected in the atmosphere and so forth. BUT—what is the behind cause of it all?

D. Is it coming from the spirit world, or is it something man is doing?

B. Well, man is doing something, and the spirit world is responding with the phenomena that you see, to make you understand that you are vulnerable. It's a signal to the east coast. It's to make you understand that you cannot always put yourself on a pedestal, you cannot always be on top. You have to go through cycles where you lift others to the top, where you yourself are not put on a throne. So you have to understand, –and it's a way to make you understand that you are connected to your host, that you cannot just do everything you like. And it's the same thing with the heat in Europe. It's to understand that it's an end result of actions that goes on, that Mother Nature responds to, puts down the foot, and to make an awareness that you are vulnerable, that you have to allow your host to take the lead for a while. You don't have to run around like ants all the time. Sometimes remain in the ant haystack kind of thing, and not just move around all the time. Everything that goes on is an end result, an answer to an action that has been taking place. Those that are coming down here from the fifth, they are trained in understanding—it's a new model of geologist—to try to find the source behind what occurs. Now it's like, "Oh, here comes the rain and thunder, up with the umbrella!" No one thinks of WHY has it changed so much.

D. Is it more of an atmospheric response, or is it coming more from the Earth?

B. Well, the Creator respond by sending...uhh, this is gonna be tricky for you, but the Creator sends, –the planet sends out from its core, the first dimension, where the center point is, it can send out an alarm or a signal to other systems and to the spiritual dimensions, and in the end to the Creator. The Creator can, of course, also look into the source, just tune in on the first dimension and read the whole situation. It's constantly being given information from the center point, not only from humans, your center point that you send to your spirit guides, –you don't know that you do, but you do–, and we read that. It pops out like little clouds in the fourth dimension, and all spirits say, "Oh, okay, now my person is trying to say something, it feels something," or different things can happen and we read that. The Creator and the councils read the same coming from the center point of the planet. So the planet sends out like an S.O.S. and the councils read it, communicate with the Creator, who responds with different things. In this case, they want to do the reboot differently (*than previous reboots*), moving in more consciousness in souls coming in. They're gonna be predominantly born in the northern hemisphere. Canada, some will actually be in northern America here, US, there's gonna be a group around Chicago, also Norway, understanding different things. But when they have grown up, physically being adults, they're gonna migrate and do good in different ways. So I'm here and I'm helping them to understand, "Okay, you want that personality, but is it really suited for the mission you are going on? Do you really need that?"

D. What kind of bodies do most of them want? Like a Roman soldier?

B. Nay, not the geologists. Seth Junior, he has been drawing what sort of suits that he wants to dress in. Ah, some don't exist anymore. He made himself a little bit too tall. And I said, "That size doesn't come. It's more like one size fits all, and you have to do with smaller modifications, you can't come in like Zeus." Nay. This one wanted to come in like Thor, it's the same thing. Did not go well. So anyway, the ones coming in here from the fifth, they are, when it comes to gender, it's predominantly male bodies they're gonna come in to. Some will be females, of course, but most of them will be males.

D. What kind of personality do they like?

B. They have to have—they're programmed already for the mission—but they have to have somewhat of a passion, and they have to be outgoing in a way, because whatever they learn and whatever they find, they have to put that out there. They're not gonna be so much in the room of decisions, most of them, they're gonna be operating in organizations, so there's no need to dress them up too fancy. I mean, if they want to, they can be fancy of course, but it doesn't serve the mission. So I said, "Put more effort into your personality than into the physical, more thought should go in, in this case, to make sure that the personality and the intent shine through." But sometimes there's a preference. One wanted to be like a little round one here in the museum that had suspenders. But I said, "I think that's more for gardeners. You can have that but if you're gonna be a geologist and go into the fine room of decisions, you might want to put on a nicer human suit, just to make a stronger impression." It's all about the portrait. I'm saying, "Build your Coat of Karma, build that, and then make sure the suit mirrors your intent."

D. You're a good teacher.

B. They were kinda curious about that, they were curious about all these different personalities that I displayed on my runway show.

D. This one said you mentioned other personalities you showed.

B. Ah. High maintenance was one. So I don't think they're gonna pick that one. Not the geologists, that would be a conflict in that incarnation. If you put in high maintenance and someone is programmed to understand the greater mysteries within geology and your host, then why pick high maintenance? There are those, actually, who are a little bit hesitant to come, and they can absolutely choose more of that personality, just to come down in some way to experience before they go into high action. Just come in and be someone's wife. There are those who are a little bit reluctant to go and they're gonna be coming in as a partner to one of the other ones that they know, on a soul level they know them. So it's soul group, in that sense. But they themselves might not have activated, for the first couple of lives, a true mission. So they might indeed, just to understand human behavior, pick high maintenance.

Role Playing to Mirror Earth Life (July 4, 2019)

After the success of his runway show, Bob decided to augment his lectures with some additional role playing. He put together another large play and invited some of the advanced teachers to perform. His aim was to show the little ones how family structures, personalities and society can interact and affect the incarnation. Bob is very observant and the play he put on contains many insights about life as a human. As he often does, Bob gives very beautiful and uplifting ideas about how we should try to find joy in life.

B. I'm here with Zachariah. I have been sending some final thoughts to the souls that are coming (*to Earth*) from the fifth; coming with the sparkles that are gonna continue the journey with their person from the fifth (*the sparkles and the young souls from the fifth will work together during all future incarnations*). So I have been providing somewhat of a first-hand insight of what can happen at different locations and in different experiences, depending on what mission they are on. Huh, so I've done that. I made a full display on, I–I–I did want to bring in, make a play, by those who have been to Earth, like Ophelia, Zachariah, you, Seth, to make like a theater expression or to show what can happen in a life. I wanted to dress each up, and first Zachariah was like, "Why don't we just show them a film? That's how it's always been done." And I said, "Why not make it a little bit more exciting, a little bit more of a show?" And I asked everyone, including Zachariah, if they were willing to dress up in character

D. Did he go along with you?

B. Eventually he did. Ophelia came in and just said, "Why don't we humor this activity. It's all for the good of the little ones." So we did that and I dressed everyone in different costumes.

D. So was it like one big play, or did each of them have a little part?

B. It's one big play where each has a part, a role. Some were family, –like Ophelia, I made her the mother. And Zachariah, he wasn't sure he wanted to participate in a play, so I thought, "Why don't you just become the teacher?" That's gonna come up, that's for little people. And then I did want to mirror the different stages that one enter, I wanted to mirror childhood, teenage, going into study, so depending on what phase I was trying to show them what will happen, and I wanted it to be a vivid display, not just a screen. So I thought, "Hmm, what can I do to mirror children?" and then I actually used some spirit guides from the second to mirror childhood.

D. What did you have them do?

B. First, the importance of, –they're gonna pick parents, first of all, from a group of souls that are a little bit older in their development, but still comes from the fifth. So they're gonna pick different constellations when it comes to family. Most will not be having someone like Ophelia as a mother, but in the beginning there is no need to scare the little ones off. So before they come into the greater teachings on how to persevere and grow self–esteem in an environment that lacks that sort of energy and foundation of love and support, –I did not show that, there is no need. This is all good, there is no lessons necessarily here, in that sense. The only lesson is that you come together similar like you come together in the spiritual reality. So I'm showing them "child", someone is here like a three to five-year old, and Ophelia teaches this child, who is actually played by Ia. So Ole is gonna come in and be a grandparent later. I asked him if he wanted to play and he said, "I can come, I can do something like that, I can be like the grandparent." So I have different characters. In this big play, Ia plays the child and showing how it is to be in some way physically limited, but on the inside more connected and more strong than when you are like an adult, because you are more in-tune and in direct contact with your home because you just left. Just because a child is limited by expressing oneself verbally and maybe not have the mobility yet to move around like later on in life, inside it's actually a stronger light in the children up to the age of about six. If man knew that—it's a strong light directly sent as a gift from the Creator in this little encased body, that might not be able to express fully this light that is carried within. The mother here, Ophelia, recognizes the light and allows this child to express this light in different ways than verbally, because the human words might be lacking. However, the spiritual language is more activated. It somewhat dims along the way, but in the beginning it's more activated. So if one tries to communicate with their child from their center point instead of through their mouth and verbally, they will find a source of direct contact—not just that they love the child—but they will have an insight that this is a direct offspring coming from a source of growth and love.

D. Ah, that's a really good teaching. (*Bob talks without interruption during the next few pages. To make it easier to read, we inserted breaks where there were no questions. The speaker designations have "B." for Bob and are continuous.*)

B. Ia mirrors that, blubbing her words, can't express, but makes her light capsule expand, making a full effect how the inside is more of a light. So the little ones say, "Oh, look how shiny!" and they know about Ia because Ia has been around and everyone likes her, everyone wants to have her coming (*with them as they travel*). And then Ophelia mirrors that, she is silent, but she is tuning in on this child, represented by Ia, and they can see communication going on and how, in certain times, when the adult might be a little bit dimmed due to circumstances that might have happened in one's day and in one's life during work and so forth, then if they knew how to communicate directly to a child, then they will see and receive that light directly. So they are looking here on how, first of all, how to expand their light capsule as a child coming in, how to radiate this light in the family that might lack the natural ability of their own light at the moment due to different circumstances. So Ophelia suddenly plays a little bit like she is saddened, and then they show what you can do as a child to radiate comfort and love to your parents if they might, let's say, they might have a bad year in their farms, and not having enough food to go around, so they might be feeling stressed. So here they come in, and Ia shows, "How do you expand your light capsule, how do you radiate the strongest comfort without words?" Because you lack that in some way, you don't have the vocabulary yet.

B. As soon as the vocabulary starts to come in more strongly, the light starts to somewhat, –it's not going away–, but it dims a little bit because one has to change the way you communicate. Instead of knowing that you have several ways TO communicate. As you grow up as a person, you will start to feel like the only way to get your opinion across is to say it out loud. And the louder the better, some feel, instead of radiating like they did as a child, like they were programmed (*as a soul*). All souls coming in are programmed to radiate love and compassion and their wisdom with no words.

B. So we have that scene coming up here, and then Ophelia plays that suddenly she starts to be a little physically sick, like not feeling that well, and a grandparent comes in, Ole, there he comes, and he shows the importance of the linear compassion in a family, how assisting each other is important. So Ophelia is laying down, mirroring that she is tired. Ole, who is older, he shows how to lead the way for this little family unit, and to somewhat mirror that just because one gets older, they don't lose their importance. In some way, the society on Earth today can mean that they neglect the older, they do not invite them into family constellations and to family meetings, like we are showing here. It is important that all units, all family members still feel and are connected and invited to share. It's important, like Ophelia is mirroring here, to not suffer by yourself, it's a way for humans to understand that it's important to share your story, that it's not whining just because you share that you might need help a little bit. And then he comes in, Ole comes in, and he reads stories to Ia, to the little one here. So we're showing how it can happen, because it's easier in many ways to be a child and to be a grandparent; the struggle lies in between, when you're sort of torn; you want maybe to be a teenager, you want to be young, but you feel pushed to the elderly corner, you somewhat feel like you are limited. All these different ages are to show that there are no limitations—there is never a stop—there is only a stop in your mind. You CAN continue to progress and increase the light.

B. So I have that, and then Ole steps aside, because Ole, being an elderly here, he doesn't suffer in the same way of the need to work, to provide, –he can move into an elderly infant, if you like. He can start to enjoy the late season. And in between, you also have the ability as an adult to enjoy all seasons. But you put yourself above it, or below it, I would say, so that you don't recognize that you all have the same ability as a child and as an elderly to be just you.

B. So Ia here shows that, coming in as a child, it is important to radiate the light. Then you become a teenager, –all sorts of different things can happen here–, and you have to start to mold into somewhat of an individual that will fit in to the surrounding, the setting, and the society and so forth. And then Julia comes in and mirrors a little bit of a teenager. Eventually this teenager has to take the step into the adulthood, and here enters Zachariah, because we're moving into learning. I have you also as a professor, so you and Zachariah mirrors two different professors. And even though you are kind of similar, it's some way to show that you are growing up and that you are starting to become something. And they know Zachariah, so they know about the sort of activity that goes on in a classroom. The problem in a classroom, a lot of times, is that you are forced to sit still, and the soul doesn't necessarily enjoy sitting still. So those children who are sometimes a little bit overactive, they are more in resonance with the mobility within, and struggles with the physical being somewhat slower, needing to be still. So what sort of teachers can you come in contact with? Zachariah shows like the way he trained them on the fifth.

You come in, and I told you, "Now you show them how you trained me, –not being stiff–, but that you took me to different places when I was a little bit discouraged. So you mirror a different activity where teachings are more about moving around and touching things." I told you, "You don't show yourself like you are taught (*on the sixth*), show yourself how you taught me!" So there are different ways. And this is just so the souls coming in from the fifth can see what to expect. They really enjoyed being in training with Zachariah and you, they felt very safe. A lot of souls feel very comfortable when they are in a school environment, because everything is taken care of for them. The only thing they have to do is be sponges and become a star (*an inquisitive soul*) and start to investigate.

B. When school is over, whoopsie–daisy, here comes demands that you have to start to provide for yourself, or perhaps for another individual. Some souls here said, "Oh, it looks a bit scary to becoming someone in charge of everything and providing and everything. Maybe I just remain in the school setting," because they like that.

B. This show is about progression through all stages and to not be paralyzed just because one enters a new stage in their life where the demands start to jump on you. Because even though you have demands, that you have to work and you have to pay bills and you have to take care of maybe children and so forth, you also, in that age, have the most means to do good and to progress. Nothing comes with just one side of the coin.

B. So I showed this show and everyone was happy. And to the spirit guides—because I'm the next guest lecturer here—so I said to them, "Pause the scene." There is an infant child here. "What would you do here with your soul being in this specific stage in their life?" And they were like, "Oh, it's almost like taking care of the soul itself. I only watch so it doesn't take harm, so it doesn't trip. I will sing to it when the child sleeps." Because they are trained, a spirit guide is trained to sing and to provide comfort for their person when they sleep. It's a way for the soul to easier go in and out. If they have a spirit guide that hums next to their person, to somewhat show them that there is a safe place to leave and that there is a safe place to return, because their spirit friend is guarding the physical. As a child, you are leaving more frequently, and it's a big role for the spirit guide to create that safe exit and entrance for the soul, to show the way to come back to the physical and to just be encouraged and to go out and explore being a soul when the physical is asleep.

D. Does the spirit guide go with them as they leave?

B. They stay behind. So like when you left I didn't necessarily leave WITH you, fully. You met me in the vault, you met me in the lab, and so forth, but I always remained with a huge amount of my soul energy next to the physical. And in that space, I hummed. I sang for you like (*he began singing*) and you learned how to recognize that, so when you wanted to return, you tuned in and tried to find the melody of (*he sang again for a while*). And because you had a tendency—and I knew that about you, that you might not always want to necessarily return—so I made my melody, I planted my melody in you to be somewhat encouraging so that you would LIKE to return. That's why I made it like (*he resumed singing his pleasant melody*). So that's programmed in you, and it means "Soul come back, physical here", –and there I sat. Other souls have different melodies, and they establish that. I'm not creating songs for everyone, but the end result of this class is that afterwards, they will go and connect with their person and they will decide what song that will be best suited for the soul leaving and coming, the fifth soul, to remember within as a signal to return. (*He then sang again.*)

D. That does sound familiar.

B. So I send that out, and sometimes you were like hovering around and I was like, "You come back now, it's almost 7 o'clock, it's time to wake up down here!" And eventually you did come back. So that was a nice show, we did that. After that, I bowed and I thanked for the applause. They really enjoyed my runway show because there were different characters to choose from and they were kind of interested because none of these characteristics, except "friend", exist in the spirit realm. A lot of the other ones are somewhat manufactured, so they have to study up on them, because they will be familiar with that. But it's important for them to know that these souls from the fifth are coming down in huge soul groups, big connections. So in my play, I showed someone in all ages so it will mirror in some way the physical family.

D. It must be easier to travel like that, in big groups.
B. Ah, it is easier. So at this point I'm not having the ones from the sixth here, because I can imagine that there will be questions why they should go solo when everyone else goes in their group. But there are different conditions, indeed. As I left this grand lecture that I hosted, everyone was happy. There were siblings too, and aunts and cousins and so forth, but they didn't have like all major parts, they were more like side–effects (*supporting actors*).
D. Did you show how when they are adults, they should work on their spiritual connection?
B. Indeed, and how to remember how they increased the light, and how they worked the light and the magic that existed as they were a child. In many ways, that disappears because of the earthly demands and circumstances that will affect mainly the adults. And adults would be considered, it starts around twenty–eight. Up to twenty–five everything can be kinda playground, in many ways, but from about twenty–eight, up till around fifty–seven, fifty–eight, it's a huge part of the human life that one feels maybe they don't fit in; maybe they picked the wrong path; maybe they picked the wrong partner; maybe they wanted to do something else. If those feelings and thoughts occur, it's a sign that you are sniffing around on your life purpose, and you might indeed be off–route. If you feel all these things: wrong partner; wrong line of work; wrong location, then return to the sensation of being a child around the age of five–six, when all roads seemed to be open and amazing to explore. You have to remember the sensation within that you are here to explore, to not become paralyzed by a situation or a person or an event that is there to test you, whether you seek the path that you initially planned for yourself.
D. People have a really hard time knowing if they are on the right path or not.
B. Indeed. And what they do, they go, "Oh, I think I'm depressed. I'll take a pill. That's probably why I'm not content with my partner. That's probably why I'm not content with my work, I'm just depressed, –I'll take a pill!" And instead of pausing and moving into the sensation of, "What did I, as a child dream life to be?" And not everyone can go like, "Oh, what is my soul purpose," because they do not necessarily think that

they have a soul, but, "When I was a child what did I dream of? What was my greatest joy? What did I aim for? What did I picture life to be? How did I picture people in my life? Where did I feel most happy?" If I felt like, "Oh, I remember when I was on a beach and on a boat with my family. All these summers by the sea, by the lake or by the water, and oh, I find myself in the desert in Arizona!" Maybe something is a little bit off route here, maybe I am programmed to be at my full display in a surrounding that has the open sea or the element water. It can be as easy as that. Or, what people did they like? "Oh, I really liked my kindergarten teacher, –why did I like her? What did she display? Oh, she didn't say much, she just sat and looked at me and listened to what I said, she was just present. Hmm, maybe I don't have people in my life that are present. So, how can I make a change and a shift. Is it something with ME that I need to change, in order to make people around me to be present?" It doesn't necessarily have to be the other ones that there is something wrong with, it could be YOU, not showing people that you want them to be present in your life. You have to make a little bit of a—I say soul search—but to a human, a lot of humans, I would say to do a little bit of child search. What did you like? So they say, "I like to play sports, I like to be part of a team. Uh–oh, here I sit all by myself on a mountain top. Maybe I am programmed to be with others, so maybe that is why I feel a little bit off-route." That doesn't mean to take a pill. That means to change your perception, make an effort to become, to return to that sensation. Again, here we're talking about (*younger*) souls coming in, and their family foundations in the beginning are gonna be all protective —like most family units are— they are loving foundations. Later on in their progress, –and we haven't got to that class yet, there's no need to put in that-, but they will have to face more challenges as a child, and it will be more difficult as an adult to say, "Return to your childhood memory and find happiness there," if there was no happiness there. So when that test comes about, there will be different teachings and a different preparation for those lives, and you have to instead create the life that you initially were supposed to have as a child. If life was dimmed when you were a child, it doesn't mean it has to be dimmed till you die. How do you do, as an adult, to bypass sensitive memories where people, soul friends dressed up in uncomfortable parts to teach you to look around events and occurrences; maybe you are trained to help others. That's way off, later on, so we're not showing that. But in general, most family foundations are loving and caring. BUT, if the adult put themselves in a mindset that it's better to take a pill then it affects the chain. The child cannot be seen, the light in the child cannot be seen. The adults, like Ole, might feel rejected and would not enter at all to help this person, Ophelia, when she was feeling tired in bed. So it's a chain effect here.

D. That's a really good play.

B. Ah. So I said, "It's better to just show in a play, instead of showing them a movie, because then they also get to know everyone." But the ones from the sixth are not here, they're going solo. So there is no need to say, "Oh, everyone comes in a big family group, even if they dress up in uncomfortable parts sometimes."

D. Are the Elahims lives more difficult? (*Again, note the speaker is Bob for the next two pages.*)

B. In some way more difficult, but you also have more tools in your toolbox. It's not difficult in that sense, you are more programmed on your mission, I would say. And some, like you, don't want to change character just because you come here, so you pick suits and Coat of Karma, when you had one, you picked personalities that was very much like yourself. But you came down more reflective, more still, more silent.

B. This one did differently. He came in with the same agenda, like you, to collect information. You more collected information and were programmed to find different knots in consciousness. Then report back where the knots were, so that the spiritual realities could engage and see where things had gone wrong. Whereas this one came down and encouraged consciousness. So in some way, this one came down and poked people, you know, like, "Display your consciousness. Display where you are at." And then you monitored and reported back.

B. So, in some way, you had the same agenda, but this one was doing different things to make the consciousness, to make the awareness, to make general social structures coming forward in the current civilization and cycle; and then you monitored what came forward. So this one sometimes came in and did a lot of poking on people, things that were like, "OHH!" and started commotions in groups. And then you looked into the response. A lot of times the knots had to do with, "How do you solve problems?" So this one caused problems, for you to see how a group being forced into problems by this one; or forced into a new thought pattern; forced into a new way of acting or thinking or reacting.

B. So this one did certain things—it's almost like when you see sheep, like a big group of sheep and you have the dog circling them around, doing things—it's like that with this one. So if you see the general public and this one came in like the dog, run around and collected the sheeps, but poked one here and there. Poked, –not bite but poked–, just to see what will be the general response in this group of sheeps. (*Bob's plural for sheep.*) And then you analyzed the end result of what took place—how do humans solve problems?

B. This one provided problems. Meaning, let's say one life was about finding a way to heal yourself that was your true right by birth, –you find solitude in nature. Sometimes you don't even have to put something in the physical, you don't have to nibble on a root, you don't have to put in a pill, the biggest healing resource that you have is to just go and sit in stillness in nature and let nature do its job. And nature meaning someone like me (*snorts and laughs*), or sparkles. Mainly, I would say, that when a humanoid puts themselves in nature, just sit there asking for help to be healed, fairies and similar like those, and sparkles, will come.

B. There's a little group of sparkles that have not started to merge yet, connected with someone like Ia, they are in nature and if they see someone sitting there sending out a prayer to nature to help heal them in some way, –and it can be a physical need, or it can be an emotional need, or mental–, but if the humanoid sits there, then believe me, all little sparkles, those who have not been training yet to merge, but they come and somewhat surround that person and they provide healing.

B. When there is a mental problem or healing needed, they're different. So if the person sits in nature by itself, asking for help, asking for healing energy to radiate through some part of that person within, the mental, which tends to be a little bit overactive in humanoids, then there is a group that comes in and just sort of flies around, circles around the head, and just calms thoughts.

B. If someone needs emotional healing, there's a lot of fairies that comes, similar like fairies, and they just sort of tickle the heart and the center point in the chest area, and they tickle the person.

B. If there is a physical need that needs to be addressed, then there are all sorts of—there's also entities that belong in the soil that have a heavier energy frequency from the second dimension, working with density—but if you sit down on a rock or sit down on the ground, try to find a place with moss, because that's like going to the hospital in nature! So if you find a place with a lot of moss, then if you sit there and ask for help, different entities from the second dimension will help you.

B. The Creator has also the ability to directly, –similar like it's assisting and reading the core of the planet, it has the ability in some cases, not all–, to go directly into the person and do some tricks. But you have to sit still, it's not like, "Okay, I go hiking in nature and I'm healed." You have to sit still in nature and you have to ask.

B. This one, in one life, showed that this is the way to heal yourself, and then those who were like doctors to become, they felt threatened because they had all new gears and new things they wanted to try on humanity, and this one said, "You don't need them, you can go directly and fix everything, or a lot of it, in nature. Just ask for healing." So this one poked and created commotion in the sheep group, "Oh, where to go, what to do!" And this one said, "Do you really think that those who are playing doctors over there can fix all your emotional and mental distress? Where do you think you will have the greatest result? In nature, or from someone who might, as you, suffer as a human from the same distress, trying, instead of fixing themselves, trying to dissect you like a frog?" And when this one said that, it became somewhat of a commotion, one could say. So he stirred the pot, and then you read the pot.

D. So we must have had a number of lives that were in the same proximity to one another?

B. Indeed. You do like to be in Europe. In central Europe a lot of this took place in the time from around 1400 to 1700, you did a lot of poking then, and reading. So even if you were not down together, this one poked and you could still read the effect of where humanity was heading. And you were looking for the knots, you were looking for how one made choices when one is poked. So.

D. That's a really good teaching. I wonder sometimes if I should put this in Wave 3, or keep it and put it in your book, *Volume 2?*

B. Ah, I don't want to be selfish here, but I think this will probably be in my book, this specific discussion. It's more personal and it might fit there, but it's also a little bit of what Ophelia says here, it has to do with group activity. So, we will see, she says.

D. I think it's a really good piece of advice for people, so maybe I will put it in both books.

B. It can be, because it's important that it spreads out and that people become aware, and to find the resources for healing. The biggest one is to just go out and find silence in nature and ask. You might not believe in fairies or believe in us, but the end result, just you asking is a sign for us that you DO believe, –and then we show you.

D. A lot of people do believe in the Creator.

B. Ah. It doesn't matter if they think a fairy came, or if Bob came, or the Creator came, –it doesn't really matter. Just try to find a spot in nature that feels very alive. Not dry, because a dry spot might be in hibernation. It doesn't mean that if you sit in the desert you can't be healed, but it's not as intense and not so many sparkles present there. But some can also find, just by putting their feet in water, like a lake for instance, just put them in. Like those who have problems with joints, those who are stiff, if they put their feet in water, –a lot of elderly people start to feel they're suffering in the feet, the feet are the first of, "Oh, heading south!" Nay, nay, Ophelia says, "Don't say that." (*Then he listens for a moment to her.*) Moving to the end cycle, one can say. Those who suffer from problems with joints, having lack of mobility in hands and feet, for instance, those do best not to just go into nature and find moss, but to go and be in water. Water is the best element and the best part of nature that will help stiffness in joints, especially feet and hands. And those who suffer from Parkinson disease, those who have shaking could also use water therapy.

D. Is that sometimes caused by mineral deficiency, like magnesium and potassium?

B. Ah, indeed. And sometimes an imbalance with iron, as well.

D. Speaking of iron, how is this one's iron? (*Bob mentions the Tallocks in his following response. The Tallocks are a group of spirits from the sixth dimension, who manifest on a planet in the eighth fish tank called Vlac. Vlac is an advanced scientific center used by the Elahim, Tallocks, and others, primarily working with elements and energy. The Tallocks have been directly involved in the Earth project for hundreds of millions of years. They are the ones who monitor the boxes placed around the planet, and work closely with the Little Greys. They also had some involvement with ancient Egypt, traveling here within a parallel reality. At one point they described how they modified the vibration of elements to assist in the movement of huge blocks of stone. They have communicated several times, and we have presented their observations in the upcoming Wave 3 of The Spiritual Design series.*)
B. It's better. This one should avoid wheat, mostly. I'm saying that, it's not like it's my suggestion, I was told by Seth and everyone that the Tallocks wanted, the new friends that you have, Tallocks, –I met them briefly, you know, so I have somewhat of an inside foot, I would say. Maybe this is a place we will go and explore. I don't know where they come from, but they come from somewhere else, and I might want to go there. I'm waiting for an invitation, because you have to be invited. It doesn't help just because I have a peanut suit that I can go anywhere if I'm not invited. So I told YOU to tell THEM that I am open for visits.
D. They're from fish tank eight, and the planet is called Vlac.
B. Oh? I don't know if I have to go through six, seven, to reach eight, or if it's like a shortcut I can make. Because otherwise I might need to, I–I–I don't know if I have to pass through all fish tanks to reach eight.
D. I would think we do it the same way when we go to Siah's world?
B. Yeah, but that's next door.
D. But we start out from the lab, so that's in the spiritual dimension.
B. I might...maybe we find like a magical room or cave in the vault or in the lab where I can just pick a fish tank. Maybe that's what it is! It's like a magic room that I can just beam myself to different locations, –or they can come get me. Maybe

that. Maybe I wait on beaming here, or maybe they come and fetch me.

D. Maybe we will travel together. A lot of people go there; Ophelia and Seth go there all the time.

B. Ah, so there's no reason that I should not go.

D. I don't think so.

B. I'm waiting for the invitation to the party.

D. What does Ophelia say?

B. Nothing.

D. She's thinking about it.

B. She's thinking about it, that's what she does. She says that not all treats come at the same time. There's always another Christmas, she say. It's like you don't get all treats at one Christmas, you have to have something to look forward to at the next Christmas, the next tree. So she said there are more trees along my path, more Christmases to come. Ah. The problem is that even though she says another Christmas will come, another tree, I AM, as a person, as a being, I am in constant holiday spirit. I think that we should have more holidays in general. And in general, even for you people—more holidays! Doesn't have to be, "Oh, waiting for Christmas, waiting for Christmas." Spread them out! It's to rip the people off. (*I think he means that people are too focused on work, so they don't feel relaxed*.) Like we go back to the fact of adults, an adult could need the break, the pause, the holiday sensation to just be in the mindset of holiday spirit. And not put themselves in the mindset of, "Oh, sweaty–sweaty, I have to cook for all these people," That's not what I mean. But put oneself again as a child and ask, "What holiday did I like the most, and why?" And then you put yourself in the mindset, – and a lot of people like Christmas because there is magic all around–, but you can have the Christmas spirit all year–round. It's a mindset.

D. I like your philosophy.

B. Anyway, time's up, Ophelia said. I have been providing things that I wanted to say.

D. Yes, I'm glad we had a separate session.

B. Ah, separate session. I don't like to be cut off.

D. Yes, I sometimes feel bad that you might feel like you're not important, but you're very important. (*When he doesn't get to speak during a session.*)

B. I feel important.

D. You are very important to this project. We always want to give you more than enough time to speak and say what you need to say.

B. Ah. And I appreciate that because I do have things to say. Okay, I will go now, but I'll be back next time and if there is a door, I'm gonna push it in!

D. What did Gergen say about that door?

B. He said it was for my benefit, to not confuse me.

D. He didn't say anything that you shouldn't hear—

B. It felt like that. But I'm not grumpy. I know that everything serves a purpose. Ophelia, you know, when she gets quiet, it's similar like a door. I think that just because I have found my way around, even if it's a fog, I can listen in a little bit, and I think that was the intention. A different barrier came up so that I would be a little bit confused about it and not trespass. Anyway, so I go now, but I'll be back.

D. Alright, my friend, thank you for coming today. Always a pleasure.

B. If you hear the tune when you're out flying, when you're sleeping, it means "time to come back. Six–thirty, it's time to go to work!"

D. You do wake me up right on the dot. (*I haven't used an alarm clock since I was a teenager, I just wake up when I want. Now I know why.*)

B. Ah, if you're out flying too far away, I just increase my volume.

D. Well, it works, because I wake up.

B. (*He sang his tune again.*) Happy tunes, so you will be encouraged to come back.

D. Okay, thank you again.

B. Okay, I go now. Bye bye.

A Field Trip to Study Earth (July 7, 2019)

In this talk, Bob covers three topics that are quite revealing about the unknown history of Earth and the people on it. First, he takes his students on a field trip to the Himalayan mountains. In *Volume*

1, Bob tells how one of his friends, the geologist Joel, observed visitors putting boxes where the Himalayan mountains later formed. On this excursion, he described how the boxes altered fields of energy to cause movement of the Earth's crust. This field of energy is unknown to humans, but Bob repeatedly refers to it as curves, not waves, as I originally thought he meant. But he is exacting with his choice of words, so to him it must appear as a curved field, like a standing or static wave at a particular location. He describes the curves as a language the spirits can decipher. The boxes modify or change the language of the curves at that location, and as these invisible curves are altered, it causes a reflective response in the movement of tectonic plates. All natural processes are under the control of the Creator and councils, including the forming of mountains and other crustal features.

Bob also tells about activities in the Mesopotamian area many thousands of years ago, when portals were established that connected the third dimension with parallel dimensions. When Bob is talking about Egypt and the Elahim and the visitors, he is covering a period of at least 20,000 years before known history. This civilization was built by the Elahim, who were on Earth in both manifested form (Anunnaki) and incarnated form (humanoid). After this civilization collapsed, fragments of knowledge were passed forward through the Swiderians (who probably built Göbekli Tepe) to the Vinča, Sumerian, and then Egyptian. This was a time when Neanderthals, giant red-haired humans, Cro-Magnons and other species of hominins co-existed with manifested and alien travelers. Ari, an Elahim from the tenth dimension, gave a very good history lesson in *Wave 2*, in the section titled *Anunnaki and Ancient History*, which we will not attempt to summarize here. When the civilization collapsed, around 22,000 BC, there was a group of incarnated Elahims who documented some of the technology on scrolls. The scrolls were taken from Tibet and hidden in caves in Mesopotamia, which were then sealed. Later, around 12,000 BC, extraterrestrial visitors came back to the Mediterranean region and used similar technology, trying to help mankind. Unfortunately, the humans viewed it as a path to power for themselves. This covetous behavior prompted the visitors to take their equipment and decamp. The humans, circa 8000 BC, did not have all the keys necessary to fully connect with the fourth dimension where knowledge is stored. By 1000 BC, only myths and legends remained.

Most of the megalithic structures in the ancient world were built between 12,000 and 7,000 BC. The oldest were constructed with a helping hand and under the guidance of visitors, especially the Tallocks from Vlac, a planet in fish tank eight. After the visitors left, humans continued to build stone structures that mimicked the older version. However, lacking knowledge of the underlying science and purpose, the more recent buildings were only crude memorials to a bygone era. When the aliens left, they took the technology with them or moved it into another dimension. For example, huge, parabolic disks made of gold were used in pre-dynastic Egypt to harness sunlight for energy and modulating matter. Even though these tools still exist at different physical locations, they remain undetectable by us, as they are in a vibration that is outside the frequency of Earth-based matter. It may be helpful to mentally picture a graph. Along the horizontal x–axis are the dimensions, with the first dimension from zero to 1, the second from 1 to 2, and so forth, until the Center Pole is reached at 13. The third dimension is between 3 and 4. The parallel realities are represented on the vertical y–axis. Like stacked plates, these are layers of different frequencies above, but still part of, the third dimension. This is a way to visualize the difference between dimensions and parallel realities. Visitors have the technology to create portals between the parallel planes and also the fourth dimension. Incarnation, NDE's, OBE's, dreaming, mental mediumship and communication with spirit guides all occur along the horizontal x-axis related to the dimensions. Humans have no awareness of the parallel realities, and this is by design.

The third topic discussed has to do with mummification, which is a rather odd practice found in Egypt and other places around the planet. Bob reveals the metaphysical motives of mummification, which are truly fascinating. The oldest Egyptian mummification shrouds found, to date, are from burials in Mostagedda from around 4300 BC. Jana Jones (et al., 2014) researched the composition of the balm used to preserve the bodies and determined it was a mixture of oil and fat, resin, aromatics, and small amounts of sugar and bitumen. The process was well refined, meaning the origins are deeper in history. Bob tells us that non-human entities were preserving bodies many thousands of years earlier. The pre–dynastic Egyptians were only mimicking something they didn't understand. Just as the mummification process was a ritual from more ancient times, certain aspects of

Egyptian belief were also distorted remnants of lost knowledge. For example, the ba and ka were identified by the Egyptians as the two main components of the spirit. Upon death, both would leave the body and then separate. Based on the qualities ascribed to them, the ka is their idea of the soul and the ba is similar to the Coat of Karma. Egyptologists say the ka is the spiritual essence of a person, and when it leaves, the body dies. It is depicted as a bird with a human head. The ba is said to hold the personality, which the Coat does, and is symbolized by upright arms. Another part of the spirit, the sekhem, is described as the life energy of the soul which never leaves the spirit world, or the power of powers. That is very similar to the higher self. The binary nature of the soul was/is an ill-defined belief among different cultures throughout the world. The general concept was passed down through the millennia, but the original spiritual understanding was obscured by time.

- B. De de la la la la (*He continued singing like that for a long time, then Ia came in and sang as well. She began yodeling like she was in the Swiss Alps, which was quite amusing.*) I'm using Ia's voice. Oh, she came in and also wanted to have a sing. I can sing too, and I don't need help necessarily, but I thought it would be nice to share.
- D. You sing all the time!
- B. Ah, I do indeed. I'm more boisterous in my being. She is more like a songbird, like a hummingbird. So if we compare us to birds, she's like a hummingbird, and I might be a parrot! Huh huh huh. Anyway, I have been taking the little ones on an expedition.
- D. Oh? This one said you showed her a picture of the Alps. (*Bob often flashes images to Christine, which he later explains in the session.*)
- B. We are hiking. I am showing them there are treats and mysteries waiting for them to stumble upon.
- D. On the Earth?
- B. On the Earth, indeed.
- D. What did you show them?
- B. Well, we have been walking in the mountains, we have been walking in what is now Nepal and Tibet, we have been there. I have stopped on certain locations, because I have a map

provided for me and they tune in on receivers in the mountains that are placed there.

D. Are these the ones your friend—

B. Joel. Joel found them and I thought that I would do them a big favor. So in this expedition, we also had students from the fifth, because they're geologists. But I did not want to leave out the Elahims and my students from the sixth, so everyone is going from the fifth and sixth.

D. A nice little crowd then.

B. Indeed. So here I am. I am directing them to understand and listen to the mountains, because mountains talk. Because they talk, if there is a disturbance, they charge language. Like Joel, he's used to understanding, "Okay, this mountain speaks English." But when the receivers comes in, it disturbs, and suddenly it becomes with like a French accent in the English. It's still English but it's a change, it's a shift. So we are reading the energies in the mountains where it is clean English, and also where there is an accent, to somewhat understand that. Because they're gonna work with the different curves within the mountains, so they have to understand the language of the mountains. The mountains are the spine of the planet. So we are on an expedition and there are treats. I asked if we could unravel treats, or look into the boxes, –that I knew someone had put in there, because you admitted. So I said, "Maybe just to have a grand finale of that expedition, we can open up a box or something like that?" And you said, "No. No. They are where they are." But you came in and you actually talked a little bit about why these different transmitters and receivers are placed in different locations in the mountains. They (*the students*) have to learn how to navigate around those signals, because those signals are supposed to be, clearly, left alone. So we went on an expedition there. After that we said goodbye to our friends from the fifth, and me and my students from the sixth and the Elahims, we went to Egypt. We are still on an expedition, but now I said, "Let's do exactly what you will do as a human when you come here." Before, a human went on a camel. Now, I wanted to make a little bit more of a current vehicle that they will encounter, so first we took a little bit of a chopper and we flew to different sites. But I also wanted them to get in contact with their inheritance in Sumeria, so we had two grand expeditions going on in Sumeria and in Egypt. In Sumeria I said, "Here, no chopper. Here we go by foot and some will use a camel." But we were looking for clues that their ancestors, other Elahims, had placed there before, so that they would be able to stumble upon them. Some of them will read, not curves in mountains, but they will read about how to make energy circulate in a fashion that the ancients knew. Just because something is old doesn't mean that it is out of date, it doesn't mean that you have progressed in all areas. People say, "Oh, we are so much more advanced now." No, that is not the case. What we are trying to discover here is what made these grand civilizations so grand. And a lot of these findings that we are stumbling upon on these expeditions are findings that you and this one left behind.

D. Can you tell me more about that?

B. When we are in the Sumerian region, there are caves, and in these caves, –which are kinda hard to find but I know where they are–, I have been allowed to take them there as a preview. We are not, –how can I put this, if I'm allowed to? (*He was looking towards Ophelia.*) Ophelia says it's fine. We are on Earth but we are not in physical. We would be considered, by someone like yourself if you find us, we would be considered ghosts. But we are there on the location to look into—we're not watching a movie and we're not doing this on the fifth in classrooms—I have taken them on a real expedition, but we are not manifested, none of us. So we are first-hand looking into these caves in the Sumerian region, and there are scrolls hidden that you put there when you came from the East, hid them in caves. They came originally from further East. It had to do with visitors and the technology that they possessed. It's written down in symbols—at that time when it was moved, there were initiated people in that region that knew how to read these symbols, because they tapped into the fourth reality where these symbols were available for all who had the clearance to enter, to be understood. It had to do with opening portals for visitors to come, –and then Tom said, "Visitors like us?" and I said, "No, we're simply here in disguise. It's similar like when you start to train on merging with trees, like the sparkles and so forth, we are there, but we are not merging, we're sniffing around in energetic form." So Tom said, "What visitors are we expecting?" And the Elahims, they knew, because they have programmed within them a feeling of home when they enter this area, because there is a remnant of the Elahim power and energy in that area. But because it was misused, the knowledge was hidden in caves.

D. Has it been discovered? Does anyone know where they are?

B. No. It's to come. They are here to remember where the caves are, so that they can open up new findings. And they are to understand what sort of visitors came, and how did they come; how to establish a portal, –first, how to open it–, and also how to close it. At the moment, several of the portals are closed because no one knows how to open them. Those who come in now are less in numbers, the visitors, they can't use the old gateways that existed before. There's also teaching belonging with those visitors that came, and these visitors came in physical form. I am not teaching this class about the visitors, necessarily, because that is their peers up on the sixth who will make that known to them. I am here to make sure the spirit guides from the second understand what sort of journey to expect. They will be directly operating as explorers, a lot of them. And the spirit guides like Tom, they're all happy here, they see that they're gonna go on expeditions, they're not gonna just sit in a house in Kansas, they're not gonna just be in a farm there! Nothing wrong with that, maybe, but these are programmed, like all Elahims from the sixth, are normally programmed to move around a little bit, so this is happy (*for the guides*). The scrolls also talk about how to make certain adjustments to maintain energy. The teachings that came with the visitors had to do with opening and shutting down energy zones.

D. Is this part of the Earth's energetic field?

B. It's part of the Earth energy field to open up the gateways so that outer energetic frequencies can merge. And the teachings in this region had to do with visitors that came, putting up these different portals, they established communication centers. Some for communicating, –they were creating a fourth reality on the third, so everything that was accessed by higher priests and so forth, shamans, that were accessing information in the fourth, the project was to move that whole knowledge bank down to the third. In order for that to take place, they had to put up different disks and create centers, like portals, to somewhat try to make all the knowledge that was available in the fourth, available also directly on the third. So some had to do with energy, power to operate different machineries that existed. But some had to do with the experiment, –and you were involved here as well as this one, and this was in Egypt–, they wanted to create the fourth reality, the collective memory and knowledge bank that exists there, they tried to mirror that, to bring it down to the third level.

D. So would that be a situation like where you could enter into a zone and have all this information available to your conscious mind?

B. Indeed. So they created different pyramid forms, they created different structures that would mirror or that will be holding the energies of, not just teachings from the visitors, but to withdraw energy from antique understandings from the fourth reality into this cone. So...(looks towards Ophelia) am I allowed to say this? "Gently. Careful where I put feet. Carefully," Ophelia says. The ancients, what they tried to do in Egypt was later, it was after the visitors came to the Sumerian region. But they had learned some of this understanding that had originated from the east and was placed in caves in the Sumerian regions, in the desert area. But it had to do with recreating a fourth reality awareness to the third reality. It was accomplished in Egypt, but not fully, and when that happened, the visitors meant it to be accessed for all, and granted certain understandings along the way for that to be accomplished. However, man became greedy with that higher connection, and they started to put themselves on a pedestal, like a high priest, like a royal, because they were guarding what the visitors intended mankind to know. They wanted to somewhat dissolve the barriers between the third and the fourth. And that was part of the scrolls that exist in the caves—how to do so. And there, individuals took advantage of this teaching that came from the visitors, and this was done in Egypt and this is where it started, like I said, where people put themselves on a pedestal, proclaiming to be the only gateway for the flock to reach that divine understanding. But the intention was to dissolve the barrier between third and fourth.

D. What was the general time–frame here?

B. When it came to religion, when I see the time–line, when it started to come into Egypt, it was around 7000 years BC, that's when it started. Visitors came earlier, trying to help mankind. They had tools in their toolbox that a human doesn't have, and they gave clearance for different teachings on how to bypass matter, how to bypass even death, how to be able to control the life cycles, and it almost became like a scientific project. But it backfired because of the fact that when those who were of human form were in charge of this project, on that end, when they realized the true connection that they had—and obelisks was part of that, to gain the power—then the visitors withdrew and closed that portal. And then fourth became fourth, third became third. But it's established in the memory down there (*in Egypt*), and those coming from the sixth. We are here on an expedition where I'm telling them the stories, –and you are here too, because you planted this. So we're kinda here, we have beamed ourselves here in energetic form, because I wanted them to sniff around on the area, not just see it in my classrooms.

D. Was there a civilization before the Egyptian, that perhaps predated the Sumerian?

B. Indeed. So that was before, so when this came to Egypt, that's when it started, it was intended to become, but it also closed. Before that, when it came to the caves, that was probably 25,000 years ago when it came to the caves. But there were times around 12,000 BC when the visitors really started to come in to the Sumerian region.

D. Were the visitors from any specific dimension?

B. Visitors came from other fish tanks. Maybe Tallocks? "Yes", Ophelia says.

D. So our friends, the Tallocks, were here trying to help?

B. They were here in physical form, working with those humanoids that existed at the time, those who were in the Sumerian region. You were also here in physical form a little bit, manifested like Anunnaki manifested, and you were here together to create a base for this knowledge to come in. So it was a project. There was interference that took place that had nothing to do with humans, but consciousness was closed, and it woke up again later in Egypt. So I don't know what happened, but it closed in the Sumerian region, and Anunnaki did not come.

D. I remember they said around 15,000 BC the Anunnaki quit coming.

B. Ah. Not come.

D. But didn't the Shea come?

B. Ah. They came. Not there, they didn't go there. (*Shea, from the seventh, manifested in South America.*) It was like putting a lid on your home base that you put there, and none come; Tallock did not come, and Anunnaki did not come. It was probably somewhat of decision from someone else. But you just left, and the thing is, it felt like you left in a hurry, because the scrolls are there almost like you didn't finish a sentence and you just left. So it seemed like there was a hurry. Everything just withdrew and just put sand on it and closed the cave, like an instant close-up. It was closed there for a long time, but then it was reopened (*the knowledge was reintroduced*) in some way, –but not from the cave. The cave was not to be touched. So now it was moved and something came alive and it was starting to blossom a little bit in the Egypt region, but they didn't have all the solutions. But visitors came and tried to introduce it in a different way, so that's what happened there.

D. I know there is a lot of giant quartz stones that have been carved, what were those used for?

B. Those are just concentrated, –if you dissolve it, it becomes into like a powder, and it has the ability to, ah, I'm not saying blowing up, but it opens up and it deletes. If you vaporize it, it has a very high concentration of, –Ophelia says I'm not supposed to use like "blown up", but it neutralized certain things, and it just vaporized. Combined with gold in powder form, it became almost like it deleted certain structures and buildings, to begin new. So quartz, you like that, because it's not just something that is in a rock, you know that it has special abilities, combined with other material.

D. In what way was it used?

B. It took away certain mountains and it created space for villages, so it was used to vaporize mountains and so forth, – not green (*trees and foliage*), but mainly mountains, but it was to unlock, or open up, it was like moving the mountain, but it vaporized.

D. So that was used in combination with the disks?

B. Indeed. There were mountains on certain areas, where, for this project, they wanted to put up disks. And the quartz, combined with gold and some other (*he couldn't find the word, but he started to say, "metha–"*), it became like it vaporized and it made it flat, so the disks could be positioned there. But you can't just do that unless you know what's underneath. So we are on an expedition here.
D. Did you look at anything else besides the caves?
B. Well, we did go to Egypt too, and we studied the mummifications and the rituals that took place, and why those rituals took place. These regions have a strong ring to the Elahims. Some of them will actually be excavating here.
D. What was the purpose of the mummification?
B. It was similar to remain them (*keep them*) in that cone (*his word for a pyramid*), it was like recreating or holding that energy within. In some way, it was said to make them go to the other side, but they were creating a capsule of knowledge that the specific high priest or someone claimed to possess. It was similar to make it not known for someone else to understand the knowledge of what that person knew.
D. So they were trying to lock it away?
B. Lock it away. And some did not have magic powers at all, but they thought they did, so they demanded to be mummified. They said, "I don't want anyone to come in contact with the knowledge that I have, so I want to be mummified when I die." And they say, "Okay, okay." It's like having a portrait—so their followers thought they had special knowledge. Some of them knew things and had that connection, but not all.
D. When they mummified them, were they trying to release the knowledge the priest had accumulated over his life?
B. Well, it was to encase it.
D. Within that body?
B. Yes, indeed.
D. And then hide the body away?
B. Well, they felt like the soul divided, but the knowledge that the person had was somewhat locked and remained within the physical. So even if the soul left with a vast majority of that knowledge, some was still available and connected to the person who possessed it; and that is what they tried to encase, like a mummy. And it was also to create different

keys, –and all this was staged before dying–, so the one dying later on could say, "I want it to only be released if someone come across my mummy who has the ability to read this and this and this." So in some way they believed that certain teachings and wisdoms still belonged with the human, even if the majority left into the spirit realm. But in order for it to not be gone, they wanted to mummify it and connect it to the person.

D. So they would leave the mummies out and accessible, and if someone came along that wanted the knowledge that priest had, they could somehow tap into it?

B. The mummy itself was also placed, normally with guards, –it was not like a museum where anyone could come and look at the mummy–, it was guarded. Many things was to just make a show out of it, and then people thought, "Oh, it must be something completely fascinating and something that I am not able to reach." So it was like creating a portrait. But some of the knowledge, because the person that was gonna die and leave, prayed for some of its knowledge and wisdom and understanding of higher levels to still be locked and remain, connected to the physical. It was also believed that the soul would be able to reenter that life, in some way, into the mummy, if it left a particle, let's say it like that, of its consciousness. So it would be able to reincarnate directly into that and just be the same person again.

D. It probably didn't work that well. (*Laughing.*)

B. It's a thought. So, here we are, and Tom, he is all over the place, he likes this. Oh, he takes notes, and he's like, "Oh, I'm gonna open up this coffin, and I'm gonna do this, –and what sort of knowledge will we find here?" His person is not Seth Junior. His person—they will actually be here a couple of times, even though Tom prefers water—but a couple of times they will pick lives where they are on expeditions; whether it's here in the Egyptian region, or if it's in the waters. We will also have an expedition coming up later on where we understand the mysteries and the need of the seas, because some of the Elahims will go there too. So I have been placed and asked to be a tour guide, and we are moving around silently, but directly, on different locations.

D. That's fascinating. I wish I was on tour with you.

B. Well, we have been on tour, it was just that you were physical and I was me. But now there is no physical here, we just sort of silently, like the wind, snooze around and look at things. Ophelia observes, of course, to make sure of what I say, look into what I'm saying.
D. Was there anything else you discovered on your travels?
B. Well, when we were with the geologists, we did also go to a jungle area in that region, like up around India. I wanted them to come in contact with certain plants that would be beneficial for different healing methods. We will talk about that, but that was an expedition by itself, and that's also where some from the seventh also came (*on his expedition* because they're gonna come in and they're gonna be doctors. I am grateful that I have been given the opportunity to go on different expeditions, and I put in different suggestions on how to unfold certain things, and then Ophelia and you, and you are very nearby, so you sometimes put a muzzle on me.
D. Ophelia did, or I did?
B. Both did. You said, "Shh," and Ophelia said, "Oh look, everyone, over here!" Because I'm not fully engaged in exactly the details of each life, but I want them to get a preview because I'm planting the awareness of this visit within them.
D. So when they come there, they will think it looks familiar?
B. This is familiar, this is like déjà vu, –and déjà vu is that. It could be similar that you were on an expedition with a spirit guide before you came, so not all (*déjà vu's*) are from what you have done in a past life. Most of them are, but a lot of déjà vu's are a memory of when you silently might have been moving around and looking at different areas. So, anyway, that will be it, Ophelia says. We have started to sniff into territory, she says, that will be somewhat explosive if I'm not careful with my tongue. So I will look into more of the directions that I, as a teacher, should follow. We have a new expedition coming up, also, where we're gonna go into the South American region. I'm not leaving the sixth, but selected souls from five, six, and seven will be joining me on my future expeditions, based on their mission, so it doesn't have to be only five, or only six, –and that is out of my control. So their peers will choose which one should go on which expedition, to not confuse the little ones.

D. Is there anything down in Antarctica that you are going to go look at?

B. Oh, I am, we're going there, but that's the sixth, that's only the sixth going there. But I have put in a request that I also want to go to the North Pole. What I have planned for that expedition—and it has not been granted yet; Ophelia says, "We're thinking about it," and you say that as well—is that I want there to be a little group from the sixth on the North, and another little group on the South Pole, and I want them to communicate through the fork, so that they learn how to navigate and read the energetic stabilizer going through. So I'm putting out a communication expedition between the Poles, that is what my intention is here. I'm thinking ahead that it might be something that might come up as an incarnation, –and I do know that the fork needs to be attended to. So I'm thinking that I will divide the group into two camps and they will know how to communicate through the fork and how to read different signals between. So in general, what my expeditions are, is to locate and...(*there was a long pause*). Ophelia took that away from me. We will wait about that, she says. Oh, anyway. She just erased it in the middle of a sentence!

D. That's a pretty handy trick.

B. I'm not sure, I might see if I have the same ability to erase things between Tom, let's say, and his person. It seems like a tool for the next level of spirit guides, since I'm there (*at that level*), to just be able to delete thought bubbles. Like Ophelia made mine disappear. Anyway, it's probably a sign that time is up and I told too much. So, we are on several expeditions, and it was only one time that we went into a chopper because I thought that could be funny to just sort of tag along. We just placed ourselves in one, since we're energetic here, we just placed ourselves. But mainly we are just here to sort of sniff around and walk around.

D. I bet they enjoyed that.

B. Ah, and so do I. There are certain things that we never went to, but I get reports from others and I do see things. Like here for instance, at the Poles, we never had an incarnation going to the Poles. You said that you did not necessarily care that much for the physical to be cold, so we never went there. But these ones have no understanding of temperature as of yet, so I thought, "Why not place in their memory some sort of fondness of ice?" The main agenda here is, again, to understand and read the fork, because it connects South Pole to North Pole.

D. Through the Earth, or around on the surface?

B. Through. And this is interesting, we never had an incarnation like that, where we—oh, "That's not true," you say. (*Lasaray, my soul energy, and Seth, Christine's soul, are always present and communicating during these sessions*). You said that you work with the fork all the time, but you didn't have to go to the Poles for that. Oh, there's gonna be questions about that. You work with the fork all the time, you say. That's how you tune in on the Earth and can feel how the host feels, it is to feel the fork. Just circle around and center yourself at the fork, and then you can feel just exactly what is going on. Oh, you say that you don't have to move at all. You said, "If I tune in and become the fork within, then I can just travel within my mind and in my being and I can just see how the sea feels, or the lake over there, or how the country Australia feels." You can tune in on different geographic zones or elements and the Earth will just tell you. And that's what I want them to understand here, so we're ABSOLUTLY having an expedition to understand the fork, because the fork will tell them secrets and its needs on different locations.

D. So, someone can do that when they're incarnated?

B. You did. You said that sometimes it's harder in a human body, but in the beginning when you were here, especially when you were here as an Anunnaki, you said it was just a shift of consciousness to be one with the fork, to be one with the core. That's what you say is the teaching from the sixth, from the Elahims, is that you become one with the core, or in this case the fork, and you just read exactly by moving around in your mind, and you can understand big things, like a continent, or you can go down to a single piece of land. So the fork and understanding it—this is interesting—so I'm putting a note here that that is something I'm going to pursue. Ah. So anyway, Ophelia says I'm talking and talking, but she lets me. It's because questions come of my own. So now I want to go on an expedition with you! There are certain things that I also want to know that might not be suited for the little ones at this point. I'm sure we can arrange a little trip. Ophelia says she will join. Group outing. I do like that, I do like to go with you and Ophelia and Isaac and Zachariah, just like the family group because it's all about my questions. Everyone is very accommodating, and I feel heard, normally. It feels like, in many ways, I'm not flock anymore, –well I am flock with you.

D. You're not part of the flock on the second?

B. Well, when there's a party, I am, and when we have second dimension activity. But sometimes I also feel like I need to just be my own satellite. It's a balance to wanting to be my own satellite and going on my own expeditions, and then taking the little ones on expeditions. Passing the torch forward, so to speak.

D. Do you like to go by yourself, or do you like to be accompanied?

B. I don't need to be by myself, all alone. I do like company, because I do like to elaborate on what I come across. Anyway, so I'll go now, but more expeditions to come. I'm gonna take them also to the South American region, and we're gonna go on a water expedition, because we're gonna understand how to communicate with the mammals. Ophelia says there is gonna come in more Master Mind in mammals, who will be directly communicating with humanoids who have their walkie–talkie on for that. All sorts of things have happened here, so expeditions continue and I'm wide awake and I'm gonna go. Ophelia says we have been running over here.

D. Well, that's some really good information, so thank you, and thank Ophelia.

B. Ah. More to come. Oh, okay, okay, I go. Bye bye.

Sending Souls to Earth (July 13, 2019)

Ia's July 13, 2019 talk was mostly about Etena (see *Ia brings Siah to our Session*), but Bob's introduction is included here. Some of the souls Bob was instructing have already begun the process of incarnating. When we think about spirit guides following us, sometimes we imaging them walking along or sitting beside us. Some guides do that. Bob, for instance, is always with me, usually within a couple of meters of my physical body. Most of the guides from the second dimension stick close to their person. Guides from other dimensions usually watch their companion on Earth while remaining on their home dimension. They maintain a constant energetic link to the incarnation, and those guides are just as close to their companion as Bob is to me. What we perceive as third dimensional space does not separate spiritual connections. Jeshua and Ophelia, my other guides, are only a thought away and always available.

We know that there are about 8 billion humanoids on the planet, having doubled since 1974. It is reasonable to question where all these 8 billion souls came from, because populations in the past were much smaller. Recently, I asked Ophelia about the ability of the spirit world to provide all those souls. She actually gave a surprised laugh and said, "Oh, there is more on the line waiting to come, there are more souls wanting to come than there are bodies to have." Many of the humans now on Earth are occupied by souls that are neophytes to this plane. There are untold billions of souls on the fifth dimension who want to take part in the Earth school. We will never know where the random actors in this grand play come from, but each are here to learn. That right, however, can be suspended after a poor performance during life.

   Ia. So we will see here. Bob, of course, has been highly active the last couple of, well...days? He's been a little bit, I would say, not nervous, but it is because of the fact that the little ones from the fifth are going, and it's departure time. It's similar like he is taking them to the airport, making sure they have everything checked in. So he runs around a little bit, making sure they have all their notes with them, programmed in the sparkles, trying to refresh their memories, so to speak, on what the journey is, ahead. He is eager, he said, to follow this, even though he also has the students from the sixth to take care of. But he is very active at the moment, and I have encouraged him to sit in silence, to center himself and to draw in the light in his light capsule, but he has not been listening, I cannot say that. He says there is haste—I don't know what that means, because there is an order in everything here. I think that he creates the haste, but there is like final thoughts, he says, that he needs to make sure that the sparkles, the guides, are aware of. So he gives them a lot of information as they are ready to leave. Zachariah is observing this and trying to calm Bob a little bit, saying that everything is under control, that it has been done over and over again, numerous times, and everything seems to go fine. Bob, on the other side, countered that and said, "Well do you think it is going really fine?" So he wants to make sure that there is information provided so that things have a different outcome, he says. And Zachariah, he sort of shakes his head a little bit, having a greater picture of the whole process. Whereas Bob only aims for a shift and upgrade and a new era to come in— as he said, it cannot be done quick enough.

D. Hence the haste.

Ia. Indeed. So there we go. (*As Ia stepped aside, Bob immediately came in.*)

B. There is no need to take ALL sunshine. I mean, it's not like I don't have a voice. It's not like I can't speak for myself. Huhuhuh. Oh, I wouldn't say that I have been running around, I have been a little bit nervous about this first group going and the sparkles going with them, even though I am not in the full charge of the sparkles attending to the souls from the fifth. But it's also that I wanted to make sure that they are well prepared.

D. You're kind of responsible for a lot of their training.

B. I am. And eventually they will come back and there's gonna be meetings about this. I have to somewhat, you know, it's like giving that last piece of information, that last push and boost, to make them be in the mindset of, "Oh, okay, adventures coming up. What am I supposed to do?" And so forth.

D. So have they picked the bodies and locations and everything like that?

B. Indeed, the souls from the fifth. My runway show was a huge help, but I did ask Zachariah if I could be included in the process of selection, but he said that is not my job. And I said, "Well, I'm sort of involved, shouldn't I be involved in the whole process?" And he said, "There's no need," and I said, "I kinda think there is a need." And he said, "Well, you don't want the other spirit guides to feel like that they don't have a purpose and a mission and an input, do you?" And I said, "No. But I don't want to be excluded!" Then he said, "You will be included, as you will monitor these events first-hand, from a viewpoint here with me," he said, "in the fifth reality." There are rooms in all different realities, or like a space, where you can be and you can monitor your person more closely. A lot of times there is activity in the spirit realm, and in order for you to be in full connection with the person and the spirit guide, –in my case, I'm monitoring the spirit guide from the second–, but I also have a little bit of a preview what's happening with the soul from the fifth. But since I'm not in charge of being the spirit guide to the one on the fifth, I can assist the spirit guide from the second, so they can directly progress and work with their person.

D. Do you also have to know what the spirit guide from the fifth wants for his person?

B. Indeed, indeed.

D. So you work with them?

B. Indeed, I will work in this space, it's a silent space where a spirit guide for a soul, the one that is assigned as a primary guide, as well as me, being the mentor for the spirit guides from the second, where we can meet and somewhat try to guide this couple.

D. And then there's probably another room beyond that where—

B. Where Gergen monitors me! I think that Gergen always has, – I might have one of those chips in me, because it always seems that he knows exactly what I'm up to. And so does Ophelia! But Ophelia, she kinda reads my chimney in some way. But if I'm going around trying to sniff up information, or look into different locations and so forth, it's always like Gergen shows up, and sometimes Ophelia. So he must sometimes communicate TO Ophelia, that's what I think. Now when I sit here with the spirit guide, I know that there is a whole family mission here, and I can see my sparkle, exactly what he's up to and where he's going. So then I know that someone like Gergen, he knows and can see ME.

D. You can monitor the younger guides that you are helping?

B. Ah. So someone can pop in on me, and I don't know how long that will be. When I understood this, then I did want to know how long that will go on, –and Gergen said, "Don't see it as a surveillance camera, it's not the same thing. It's a way to be assisted, it's a way to always be connected. Otherwise, you would be completely left alone and you would feel like you are not cared for, like you don't belong. This is a way to always be connected to your family."

D. Someone might even pop in on Ole from time-to-time.

B. Who knows? Ole also has someone, even though I haven't met that person. So, they're going now, and there is some going to

Germany. There's some going there to work in an environmental organization that is about to be established, it has to do with waters. It has to do with maintaining and preserving the cleanness of waters. So there is a huge effort that needs to take place, a shift, Zachariah says, about how you preserve and take care of the waters, so it's clean. There will be different departments that will be established over time. The problem is that man only reacts after something has happened, instead of preparing before something happens. But some of them are coming down here and they're gonna go to Germany and they're gonna be in somewhat of a government position, almost, but it's not government in the same way, it's more of an organ within the government that has to do with cleanness of water. And they do research, constant research, to maintain the quality of the waters, the drinking water that is.

D. People are often unaware of what they are putting in their body and what it does to them.

B. Umm. So there is a group here, and two or three are gonna go to Germany. The other two—there are five going—the other two are gonna go to the US. One is gonna be on one side of the border in Canada, and the other is gonna be in the US, but they're gonna be like, –it's sort of the northern US, around Boston one will be–, and the other one will be on the other side. The one in Canada, he will do research on ice, on the North Pole and ice, the melting process and the effect. So all of them, in some way work, with waters. So that's the mission here that they're gonna go on. They are forerunners for something that's gonna happen later when the ones from the sixth and Tom come. So they come down here to do research and planning for the other ones to come later.

D. So when they leave the spirit realm, are they going to come in soon, as far as we are aware in linear time?

B. They're already here. They are dropped into the linear time.

D. Did they come in sometime in the past?

B. No, kinda recently. They were born in 2005 to 2009. There's a lot of souls born around 2005 to 9, especially 2009, that's gonna be very influential in different ways. There are in your timeline, like you call it, there are certain times when there is more of an awareness of souls coming in, in certain times. There were some coming in '99, there was also around...

D. '62? (*The year I was born.*)
B. HA HA HA, or '72, huh. Well, there was actually, in that shift around '60 to '70, there was a lot coming in. If I look at the timeline, I can see if it is a buzz, if it is activity, meaning, that there is a lot of souls coming in, providing and bringing somewhat of a change. I am not however, fully capable of seeing WHAT sort of change, normally, or always, that will occur.
D. There were a lot of souls that came to Earth after WWII up through when I was born, that was the baby-boom.
B. It might be a physical baby boom, but it's not a spiritual consciousness baby boom. It's not—oh, Ophelia says, "I don't know if you should say this. Watch your tongue, Bob, watch your tongue." It might not necessarily be just because there was an increase in physical, –but it's like the lemonade was more watered in that time. And it was to somewhat understand your story and your history in order to prepare for someone else to come. However, there are souls born in '65 to '69, and some, like I said, in the '70's, they were a prototype of change to receive spiritual energies. But there was a huge amount (*of people*) who did not fully understand how to receive energies. I'm not saying that '62 and '72 were peaks, even though you came. (*Christine was born in 1972.*)
D. Well, they had a couple of good souls come in.
B. But–but, you don't necessarily—here, when I talk about these big cycles, I talk about groups. I'm not talking about individual souls. I'm talking about a general collective downpour of souls.
D. Downpour! (*I was laughing, and Bob got confused that it wasn't a good word.*)
B. Is that not...they rained down, they came down?
D. That's funny. No, it's a good word.
B. And sometimes when it rains, the environment, the receiving end cannot fully take all that rain. And sometimes it's just a drizzle. It depends on how you read this rain. Sometimes you can see it's just raining, like in the '50's, it was just raining, meaning it didn't have all the colors, to give you a picture, in the raindrops. But I can see here, indeed, around 2005 and 2009, the rain is more controlled, it's not pouring, but it's more colorful, it's more concentrated. So I can see on the

timeline, and I see souls coming in like downpour, or a drizzle, and so forth. When the two of you came, in '62 and '72, it's more of a drizzle, especially when this one came, it's more of a regular rain. It's interesting to see this. If I look back, let's see if I look back, to give you more (*he is leaning backwards and forewards as he looks to the left. Whatever he was viewing must have been quite expansive, because he was trying to see around Ophelia*), Ophelia moves aside a little bit so I can see. I do see that there was, the rain coming in around 1911 or 12 to 1923, there were also a lot of souls coming in to kick–start transportation and how to work with resources, like coal and so forth. So there was a lot of effort coming in to make transportation and a shift of your society at that time.

D. So in some way, the spirit world must have been involved in developing hydrocarbons?

B. They are involved in everything! Ophelia says, "What I see as rains coming in and different colors of the rain, is how the spirit realm meets the events that take place and what the spirit realm wants the next phase to be." So she said if I really analyzed the rain here, then I would see that there are different colors, –and I do see that, but I cannot decipher what all the colors are. This is a class that I will take with Zachariah and Isaac, to analyze the rain. What I can just say, when I see the rain here in the '50's, there is no colors, there is just a downpour. But when I see the color coming in in 2005 and 2009, they have a variety of colors.

D. Can you see where the rain is landing, geographically?

B. Ah. I can see here in 2005 to 2009, huge effort is ongoing in Scandinavia, Canada, and even Russia. A lot are coming into Russia, to somewhat assist. But like here in the downpour in the '50's, there was a huge amount coming here (*USA*). Australia also had some.

D. What's the rain look like in Africa, the Middle East, and Asia?

B. Africa lacks rain in some way, even though there's a lot of bodies there. It's not a downpour, but it's a constant rain, whereas the other places, I can see like rain, but then it becomes sunshine. When I look at Africa, there's constant rain. I can't decipher this. Zachariah said that this is how you monitor civilizations and group development and evolution. This is how higher councils operate. They can make it like a quick downpour, and then sun, or constant rain, meaning constant souls coming in. But I can't see the raindrops on Africa, –they're kinda small, there's no colors, there's no intention–, I see here. Oh, Ophelia says I need to be careful with my tongue here again. But there are actually coming in some here in the Russian area. So I see things, and now I feel like this is clearly something I need to know... oh, Zachariah says, "No, you don't need to know this."

D. If you're going to join the higher councils, you will.

B. Indeed! If I'm gonna join–, he said, "You might not join the rain council." Huhuh. But I might come in as an apprentice, because this is interesting to just see the general design behind the intention. This has nothing to do with sending in spirit guides, like when I said, "Oh, waters are in need. This egg (*bundle of new spirits*) is gonna go and help the waters," this is the general idea of selecting where souls are gonna go, and what kind of souls, and what intentions are going in different locations.

D. This is like the great design?

B. Indeed. The greater and grander design of soul incarnation. But I can't decipher the raindrops, and that confuses me. But I have seen it, and now I need to take this class, I feel.

D. Well, you have a general idea?

B. I have a general idea. I can see that there is a constant rain and drizzle going down, but I cannot see that there are colors going down in the African region. I can't see what the intention is. I see that they are coming in, but they are different. With the other ones I can see, like, there is a centimeter raindrop, meaning a soul, then looking here at the African region, they are like a tiny grain of sand. So I can't decipher, it just seems like there is a constant incoming.

D. Are they actually souls, or is it part of the Master Mind?

B. Indeed, it might be. Questions, questions come up here when I see this. So, we're not gonna say that to the public, Ophelia said. But just know, just know, she says, that you can follow these rains, –and you can see it as different rains–, and once you start to decipher and analyze the differences, then you will be able to understand what souls are present, what is the general design. In the '50's, they were somewhat preparing, meaning that souls came in but they did not necessarily come in with a huge change.

D. I guess it's like when it rains and then there are flowers that spring up, or weeds?

B. Indeed. Or just a drought here in the '50's, similar if it were to rain on a desert, it would not be able to absorb it. So the receiving end, –let's say a desert, or if it is something that is flourishing–, that is the general state of development in that area. So it could be, since I see that it is just a downpour of people coming in, but the environment, the receiving end, doesn't absorb it. It might be that at that time the general evolution here on this plane needed to be somewhat recharged and to heal, or to just prepare to become. When I see those now coming in here, it is like you say, more green, so the receiving end for those who come in have more of a welcoming environment, when they, as raindrops, fall down here. Ophelia says that's why I'm not fully involved with the rain, because I might add extra raindrops, and they might not fit. But now I have seen the rain, meaning the amount and intention of souls coming in. Sometimes the rain is just the amount of bodies, when there is not as much percentage of the soul awareness from the collective soul bank; and then other times there are less raindrops but more of a concentrated soul awareness from the soul bank. That's what I see here when I see rain.

D. That's a good thing to know, and quite fascinating.

B. We will, if Ophelia steps aside a little bit again, we will be able to look even further back and give you more of an understanding of how the rain fell down over your known history.

D. It must have been pretty colorful at certain times, such as when there was no warfare?

B. There was a little bit, it's a little bit of a silence around 500 AD to like 700, there was silence there. I can't really see, but it's sort of a silence there, a bigger silence than there was in the '50's. That rain, if it was a downpour in the '50's, but not from the soul bank, there was not that many coming at all over there (*on the timeline at AD 500 to 700*).

D. A little hibernation.

B. Well, I'll go now. Okay, Okay, I'll go.

D. Thank you for taking care of Siah.

B. Ah. I'm sitting here and I'm reading, I show him, I send him mental pictures of our journeys, different things that you do.
D. I bet he really likes that.
B. He likes to be a part, he likes to be acknowledged.
D. As do many of us.
B. So this will be developed further, but now I'm off. I have said my piece about the importance for me to—
D. Well, if the souls are already here, they must be ten to fourteen years old, so I guess you've been helping the guides to manage their people?
B. I'm like a general manager, indeed. So I take care of and I help, combined with the spirit helper for the other ones. So that's sort of what's happening here at the moment. Ophelia says that that will be it; we're having a short session today, saving energy.
D. I guess we might go for a little ride today.
B. Ah, that's good. She says, "Be out, be out, gaining energy, gaining sunshine." (*He began singing*) Sunshine, my only sunshine...Okay, so I'll go now. Bye bye.

Bob finds Remains of Atlantis (July 20, 2019)

When it comes to ancient civilizations, this session is fascinating for several reasons. The Shea, who are manifested entities from the seventh dimension, established a large city in the Atlantic, west of Africa. Ophelia, through Bob, pointed out that there were several locations where the Shea had cities, but all were part of the same Atlantis culture. One healing center was on an island in the Mediterranean northeast of Crete. The area is seismically active and commonly experiences earthquakes and volcanoes. He explains that a large area of sea floor northeast of Crete suddenly sank down and caused the island to collapse. Sea level at that time was about 120 meters lower due to glaciation, so if any archaeological evidence could be found, it would be quite deep. The southern edge of the Eurasian tectonic plate includes the Aegean plate, which extends south of Crete and forms the Pliny trench to the east. The topography in the target area has a lot of submarine mountains which could be candidates for the location of this lost city. Since portions of city walls can still be found, perhaps the site may yet be discovered. As always, when the spirits give specific dates, every effort is made to corroborate the information. It gives a tremendous amount of credence to everything they say when their casual observations match with scientifically verified research. Bob mentioned volcanic eruptions on a number of islands in the southern Aegean Sea around 15,000 BC. At exactly that time, an explosive eruption occurred on the island of Nisyros, Greece, followed by 100 years of effusive eruptions that blanketed the entire island with pumice. Nisyros is the eastern edge of the Kos-Yali-Nisyros volcanic field. The eruptions at 15,000 BC produced the geologic rock of the Nisyros Upper Pumice. Based on Bob's remarks, it seems the island of Atlantis broke apart and collapsed into a trench or graben when there was movement along a fault line. The earthquakes from the fault probably triggered the eruptions on Nisyros and at other submarine volcanoes along the Aegean Volcanic Arc.

B. So, I've been on more excursions!

D. Oh you have?

B. I have indeed.

D. By yourself?

B. No. I was complaining so much that you eventually took me, and everyone else took me. (*He means a group of us went.*)

D. Where did we go?

B. We went into the sea, because you know that I have not so much experience from the sea, because of the fact that I did not want to blend with the fish. BUT, I do appreciate excursions to explore. So this is like, how can I explain this? It's not in a physical shape and form that we went, but similar like when I go to Siah in my peanut suit, we did the same thing when we went to explore here. So we went, and I wanted to look around and I wanted to see, because there were mammals that exist in the sea that were communicating, you said, and just because I don't want to blend with them, I can still come there. You said, "You like to talk to Siah, don't you?" and I said, "Yes I do." And you said, "This is similar." So we went together and we explored, and you showed me there were things that existed before water covered it up

D. Oh? What did we see?

B. There was like a big wall that surrounded a civilization, a city. It was a wall that circled. This was actually in the Mediterranean. There is another one, a bigger one, that is west of Africa. But we're looking here at one that is just a little bit–, it's sort of north of Crete, a smaller one.

D. As far as Santorini?

B. Nay. Closer to Crete, more east. Northeast, there's a smaller settlement, you say.

D. What time period was that occupied?

B. It was about 15,000 BC, and there was like a civilization there, BUT because of the fact that there was an eruption of SEVERAL volcanoes in the region, it created a—it collapsed, similar like Santorini, and water covered. But it was bigger, there were several volcanoes in the region, in the Mediterranean region, that went off at the same time. It wasn't just like the island Santorini collapsed, it sort of made the whole area sink.

D. Was it above water and then it just sunk?

B. Ah, it sunk.

D. Did it get covered up with ash?

B. Uh? Covered up with water and stuff (*sediment and mud*).

D. If someone went down in a submarine, could they—

B. There are remains, there can be found remains. There's a wall that surrounded this, it can be found. It's sort of closer to Turkey, in that direction. So it can be found. It was a very large civilization that lived there. It...(*he seemed to be listening to Ophelia and didn't speak for a bit.*)

D. It wasn't what people called Atlantis, was it?

B. It's the same civilization, but the other one was west of the African continent.

D. So that was where the main Atlantis hub was?

B. Indeed, and this was a smaller one.

D. About what time did it go down?

B. Around that time.

D. 15,000 BC?

B. 15,000 BC. That's when it went down. But it can be found. It's trickier to find the main one over there in the Atlantic. That was like the Mother Ship, you say, and that one is, –when the little one suffered the extinction and waters (*drowning*), the bigger ones could not assist. What is talked about as Atlantis disappearing is the one in the Mediterranean. However, the big one was over in the Atlantic, and that was a decision to depart. Different.

D. How long did they stick around after that?

B. Not long.

D. So they also left about the same time?

B. Ah, around the same time, roughly.

D. What was Ophelia saying to you earlier, when I interrupted?

B. She said that there were several, and that is why there is so many different legends about Atlantis, because there were several bases similar that were connected in spirit and connected in the fourth reality, all these centers, and mainly occupied by the Shea. So a lot of souls from the seventh dimension have a strong connection, but also a fear, a cell memory of fear, when it comes to waters. So they have a fondness of the sea, but there is also a sensation of being slaved (*entombed*) underwater, in some way. So it's a dual sensation, mainly a sensation of love though, but also a memory of disappearing.

D. So the main inhabitants were Shea?

B. Indeed. In these regions they were. You were not there, –well, you said you visited, you had lectures, you say. (*Bob appeared to be listening and repeating what he heard, so my higher self, Lasaray, must have been talking to him.*) Huh! You had lectures on how to excavate and use different minerals and biological components in a way that would create energetic tools to assist doctors. These were highly skilled Shea in these centers, this place. This one in the Mediterranean was like a big hospital, they could do surgery with light and sound and different, –it's like a laser almost–, and you taught about physics, biological components, chemicals. You were like a chemical engineer, visiting, teaching, but they were the ones executing. It was like a big center in that region. Ohh, it was because of the fact that there was a lot of suffering in that region, so the center over there in the Atlantic created like a field hospital, it seems, with all these highly advanced doctors. We were never there.

D. Was I manifested?

B. Ah. I'm seeing this, but I don't remember that we stayed there. And you say, "I didn't stay, I didn't incarnate, I just came in and visited and taught and left."

D. I get around! (*Laughing*)
B. Visit, taught, and left, you say. That's what you prefer, you say, –visit, teach, leave. That's what you prefer, and that's what you're able to do when your Coat is folded. But here you did not go through the pickle of incarnation, you just came in like a guest lecturer.
D. I remember that Edgar Cayce said that one of the pyramids in Egypt was used for healing with light and sound.
B. Well, they had structures that looked like pyramids—very similar, I must say, to how Etena looks when I see this little city that was established here. But it was a field hospital in some way, –doctors without borders!
D. They had a wall, so they had a border!
B. Yes, but there were several coming in because there was disturbances in the region, there was a lot of humans...
D. To keep them at bay?
B. Yeah, and to work on, here.
D. Were they trying to improve them, or heal them in some way?
B. It's a sort of a surgery that I see here, and they're using light beams, like a laser, and it's combined with some sort of sound, and as you combine them you remove organs and you heal tissues.
D. Was it to just fix the physical, or was there another objective?
B. This here is physical, but you say it was an all–around hospital in that sense. They healed all sorts of different dilemmas.
D. Make people smarter?
B. Ha, I don't know if they could upgrade, that's beyond what can be done because these are incarnated. Maybe a lot of, –you say around this time, those who came here, they came in with like seventy–five percent of their soul being, so even though they were incarnated, they were very much operating from soul capacity.
D. So this was before they changed the human so it couldn't take as much soul energy?
B. No. This is different. But it's not a one–size–fits–all; certain beings were allowed to operate with a higher intellect, more soul capacity and so forth. It's also based on where you come from. There was a lot from the seventh here and also some

from the eighth. You came in as a guest lecturer but did not remain. This one did not really go here.

D. If you were to guess, how big around was that walled city? Was it like a kilometer, ten kilometers?

B. I would say the circle would be, in diameter, maybe twenty kilometers?

D. It should be easy to find–

B. But–but–but, the whole wall is not there anymore. Parts of it remain.

D. How high was the wall?

B. Not very high. It was to endure certain elements, –it did not. (*I'm guessing he means protection from waves.*) The wall was just like three to five meters tall, not very tall. Several gates, entrances.

D. How deep underwater do you think it might be?

B. Around, there is some that can be found around 2,000 meters deep, but there is some that sunk that cannot be found that went into a canyon, it (*makes a slurping sound*) it swallowed. There are certain places like that, that were swallowed.

D. I can see why some would be afraid now, if that is part of their soul memory.

B. Ah, you don't want to be swallowed like that. But I'm not gonna show this (*to the little ones he is training*) because it's not very common that this happens, but if they think the house they live in can just sink into a canyon and be swallowed, then who wants to come for that experience? So we've been on excursions, and I have put in several requests of different excursions that I would like to participate in. I have a fondness to go and see the poles, and to somewhat detect the activity, especially the North Pole, –it's very much connected to the sixth, whereas the South Pole is very much connected to the seventh. The connection in–between would be considered the Creator and councils and others going through.

D. And you're talking about the axis, not the magnetic pole?

B. I'm talking about where the ice is, because there is occurrences there, and I feel like I want to go on an expedition there.

D. What sort of occurrences?

B. There is like receivers put there, visitors put stuff in the ice. And there are different storages as well, under ice, of certain findings that has been locked in ice.
D. Like records?
B. Records, indeed. Mainly up there in the North, BUT, there's something on the South Pole as well, but you say it's different there. You have mainly been operating and having a contact with the base on the North.
D. I know the governments, for some reason, are very interested in the South Pole.
B. I know indeed they are, and you're happy about that, that they're not so interested in the North.
D. What are they finding in the south?
B. It's activity, it's like gateways as well for visitors. But the main hub, the main central is actually on the North. But you can read the activity through the ball, through the planet.
D. That's interesting. So what other excursions did you want to go on?
B. I–I–I feel like I want to go on this one, (*to the North Pole*). You said, "There's no need to do that, you're not going to teach the little ones this anyway." And I said, "Well, what if the Elahims are gonna come down and they're gonna be great explorers to the north. I might need to be able to train them a little bit." And you say, "If they're going there, their peer will train them." And I said, "But my guides are also gonna go, like Tom. So I feel a need to know that."
D. You did say some of them were going to settle in Norway and then go north.
B. Go north, they're gonna go north. But after some established phenomena has taken place before, from other incarnations. So they're not here right now, they're not gonna come right now. But I have also an interest in going on an excursion in the South American regions. There is several interesting findings, if one has only their eyes open. And this expedition I actually took with the little ones. And I'm showing them deep, deep, deep, deep inside the jungles are records, as well as hidden gems, hidden plants that are beneficial for medical treatment and so forth, so I'm showing them around.
D. I remember you said you hid a plant there.

B. I have hidden a plant there, yes indeed, and I'm showing them where it is and how it looks. Those from the seventh are here also, some of them, like I said before, these expeditions ahead is not a general expedition, it is based on expertise and mission. So when we go and look for the plant, I have some here from the seventh who are gonna be doctors. But also some from the fifth because the fifth are gonna, –doctors are not necessarily gonna go into the jungles by themselves, they need someone from the fifth.

D. Is the place you took them to, could it be detected by humans?

B. Indeed.

D. Is it just hidden in the foliage?

B. Indeed. It's hidden.

D. Is it in a temple or a pyramid?

B. It's hidden in nature.

D. Well, I mean the first place where you said there were records?

B. Ah, the records, they are hidden in caves in the jungle, jungle caves.

D. That would be a little bit harder to spot.

B. Indeed it is, and I know that. So we're looking around about different things. I'm gonna be not too long here, Ophelia says, but expeditions continue. And those from the fifth will find, eventually, different plants and herbs in the region, in the South American jungle to later introduce to some from the seventh who will become doctors. It has to do with healing the, –it has the ability to heal the circulation and the blood. Because a lot of diseases could be avoided if the blood did not affect all the organs and shuffle it around. So this specific plant, an idea is to help bring light to recreate white cells, and to recreate, rejuvenize the blood—make it clean, it's a cleaning system.

D. When do you think that will be introduced? After the next human? After the pharmaceuticals collapse?

B. Ah, it's not supposed to be put together with a lot of other things, it's supposed to be very concentrated.

D. What do you think about the ayahuasca that people drink?

B. Do not like.

D. It's not good, is it?

B. No it's not. It is just to somewhat bypass neurological impulses. It creates disharmony in the web it's not pure, it's not sent as a spiritual connection. It causes damages, neurological damages, afterwards, in nerves and so forth. It makes the inner more hyperactive after, and it's hard to clean.
D. I've always suspected it wasn't a good idea.
B. No, it's no good. So, okay, I'm gonna go now.
D. Thank you for protecting us yesterday (*when we were out on the motorcycle*).
B. Ah, always with, always looking into things. Ophelia says, "Time is up," so I'm not gonna be dragged away this time, I'm gonna walk away voluntarily.
D. (*Laughing*). Alright, my friend. We'll talk soon.
B. Talk soon. Bye bye.

Transitioning through the Fourth after Death (July 29, 2019)

This next talk by Bob is the most educational descriptions I have ever heard about the transition of the soul after death. Before the soul reaches home in the spiritual dimensions, it must navigate through the fourth dimension. Bob's students have not yet had their first journey to Earth. But they have learned enough to have considerable apprehension about both living and dying in a human body. Bob wanted them to be as prepared as possible, so he explained the process of dying and returning home. While I am not a leading expert on the subject, I had an NDE at an early age and have sifted through most of the books written on the subject during the past 150 years. When Bob describes coming in contact with nothingness, it really resonated with me. I experienced that sensation during my NDE. In that state, I felt connected to the Creator in a void where nothing exists beyond thought. The emptiness seemed (to me) to be the impetus for why the Creator creates. I then found myself moving above the timeline of lives on Earth, trying to find and rejoin my body. The lives appeared as dots along a continuum, and if I focused on a dot, I could look into the entire life. I actually merged with one and experienced being there for decades, and even relived the death. When I finally found the current life and merged with my body, lying on the ground where it fell, it felt as though years had passed. What I mistook for time was only the realness of the memory that I stepped into. We have emerged as companions and co-creators in this exceedingly complex reality we share, even though we are generally unaware of the larger purpose from which it originated. The uncertainty of death is part of the human condition, but when that uncertainty creates fear, it drains the enthusiasm and joy from life. We hope you appreciate this truly remarkable teaching from our Little Friend about the process of returning home to spirit, and the care provided by our spiritual companions to assist us on this journey.

B. Ah, and I'm always last.

D. But you're given the opportunity to speak nearly every time.

B. Ah, but who knows if someone is gonna drag my arm, so to speak. I have been with the little ones, and we have preparations that we've gone through. We have actually also taken the class on how to navigate through the fourth. That did not become like a one-hour class, I can tell you that! There were questions, especially if there was a possibility to not find one's path home. And I can relate to this, because it's similar to when I went to visit Siah in my peanut suit. Who knows if I will come out on the other side? Souls who have never been and done the journey yet, when they see the documentary, so to speak, on "There you die," –we show kinda a nice death, that they died in their sleep with family surrounding them or something like that. There's no need to put in trauma as of yet. And most souls in the beginning as they come down, they don't have traumatic deaths in the beginning, there's no need to go in like that. So they see themselves putting on snooze, the jacket just falls down. And then we show how to transition and what one will encounter. The first part that you will encounter is, –it can be just like a mish-mash of signals, mainly related to the physical life you just have left. So in some way it's a repeat or a rewind of several incidents that have somewhat been asleep in your memory within. And the memory can be the emotional, the mental, or even the physical has memories. If one has hurt oneself, then that is a physical memory, and one can encounter that, how it really fully felt to fall off the bike, so to speak. You somewhat transition and you leave certain layers behind. So first you go through all the physical things that happened to you, and then you move into the ideas and thoughts and the way you communicated; how was your ability to communicate? How was your ability to receive? Did you try to convey to others your ideas in a positive or in a negative way? So you look at that, and when that is somewhat gone through—the human life review takes place almost immediately as the soul starts its journey back home—then it moves into the feelings; how it fully felt to be a human, how it fully felt to be loved, how it felt if someone did not love you, what sort of residual energy is within your memory, how can you grow from that next time? So you are investigating your Coat as you leave, these different levels. When you have investigated your Coat, –and this is in the first centimeter or so (*he is using 10 cm as the reference distance through the fourth, so 1 cm is about ten percent of the way through the fourth*), before we transition further, some do that by themselves and some, if they need help, there is always, normally not spirit guides, but spirit friends who are not in body, they can come and help a little bit in the beginning. So it's like friends helping friends. But if it is needed, then absolutely a spirit guide can come and assist if they feel like the process takes too long, that the soul leaving gets stuck in understanding actions from the mental, let's say, if they see that that light is not shut down, then indeed interventions from the spirit guide can take place, to assist.

D. So the soul in some way processes its life, evaluates it?

B. Indeed. Evaluates actions, evaluates events, evaluates the Coat. This is the first time it has the ability to fully get in touch with the Coat it had, then can compare the Coat that it came in with, and compare it to how it was mirrored in the life, – and how did these two align? So you do that a little bit, and you are encouraged to do this by yourself. But if you get stuck, if you feel like this is tricky for you, if you feel, –because sometimes if a death is very abrupt, then a soul can be in the midst of understanding whether "am I the Coat, or am I the physical?" It can be confused in between, and then is when assistance can come. So as you transition, the first thing you come in contact with is the Coat, and the Coat contains physical, mental, and emotional activities that was placed in the Coat before departure. This is the first time that you can actually, like I said, investigate the Coat, combined with— because you have a really close look here on the life—so you sit and somewhat investigate the two. And it's not like you have to fully, one–hundred percent understand it, but you have to release and...

D. Detach yourself?

B. Well, you left the body, now you are leaving the Coat, and as you do, then you start to transition and transform, and from that point you are in the very beginning of the fourth reality, where you have to navigate and find your way home. And this is where they (*his students*) felt a little bit distressed; they didn't know how to find their way home because it was not clear, –it's not like there was a bus stop saying, "Fifth Dimension, Library, coming in ten minutes," so you can just stand there and wait with the other ones. So they were concerned about the transportation device that was not very visible in this documentary. And I said, "Similar like you enter a life, similar is when you exit. But when you enter, you have friends, spirit guides, that join you up to the point where you put on the Coat. So in some way you can say that the border where the Coat begins and ends, that is where you have to be by yourself in many ways, unless there is a special need. But when you have left the Coat and you are transitioning back home, then it is normally connected to parts from your spiritual home that are familiar. So the fourth is mirrored in the first part from the Earth point of view, based on your thoughts and actions as a human. The next part, as you transition further, is mirrored by your spiritual home." So if someone from the fifth transitions, there is a lot of colors, normally, and there is music. Sometimes there can be music also if a soul from the seventh transitions. Souls from the sixth rarely hear music unless there is like a special need, again, but they normally transition by themselves; whereas those from the fifth can transition in a cluster. So there can be several leaving from the fifth, but a soul will only see, normally, the ones that are from the same reality, –to not confuse–, as they transition through the fourth reality. After you have been here a couple of times, then you will, as you transition after the Coat is left, put in the closet until next time, then you will indeed be aware of souls that you are actively aware of not belonging where you belong, but they are friends. You will just see them passing with you, but they're not going to the same place.

D. How many centimeters in, –you said one time to call the fourth about ten centimeters–, do you lose your Coat about three or four?

B. Indeed. The last part is more of a blend with the spiritual realms.
D. So the transition zone closer to Earth contains more human energies, and then as you rise up through the fourth it becomes lighter and more spiritual?
B. Lighter, and depending on where you're headed, different colors.
D. I've been curious, because of all the ideas about souls getting stuck, or souls going to—
B. If they get stuck, they are still in the Coat, in the first thirty or forty percent. You can never get stuck once you've left that. So if someone is either stuck or is not necessarily, –let's say for instance, –oh, Ophelia says to watch my tongue a little bit here, but it has to be said, and she said "gently"–, let's say that someone ends a life beforehand (*he means suicide*); it came down to teach and let's say that one had a disease and it was not fully able to operate. A soul can be overwhelmed, – ahh, the soul is never overwhelmed–, I would say the container is overwhelmed and it's coloring the soul, it is dimming the soul so the soul cannot be heard. But you pick a life and you pick experiences in the Coat, sometimes for yourself but sometimes also to teach others. Let's say you become disabled and the teaching is actually for your family to become caretakers because they have never understood the importance and the beauty of taking care of someone like you do in the spiritual realm. So then a soul can pick a life where you are a close companion, a loved one, and you become disabled. The lesson is actually for the family to nurture someone, to learn how to nurture in a human environment. It's not hard to nurture in the spiritual realm, but it's hard to nurture sometimes in the human reality if your soul is too dimmed, if you follow your mental capacity too heavily, then you lose the ability and the direct link to compassion. BUT, if a soul, let's say ends a life beforehand, before the whole lesson of allowing the family to nurture this person, –which was the general idea of this mission–, then that soul can, when it investigates the Coat, it will be able to see the whole scenario, the whole planning, but at that point it could be too late. At that specific time, a soul can be asked to directly return down and continue a new life.

D. So they will take that part of their soul energy and go into another body, before returning home to merge with the higher self?

B. In a new one, in a new one. Not the same family though, but come in in a similar situation. Otherwise, that specific part in the Coat will never be folded.

D. So when souls, when they are real religious on Earth and they go to a place that matches their concept of heaven, are they still in their Coat, or is that in the spiritual part of the fourth?

B. It's still in the Coat. If they talk about certain things, –the reality is that most souls, when they are in a people container, have not the ability to fully grasp the spiritual realities. They still operate in the first, let's say, four or five centimeters. It is a wishful thinking, –and that is good, Ophelia says, that they think of heaven in some way. But to fully experience it, you have to also meet the sides of you that might not have been fully developed as a spiritual being. So you have to meet first your Coat, but as you continue your journey, you will come in contact with what you believe is the heaven, so to speak. It might be something completely different (*for each soul*). If someone says, "Oh, I'm gonna go to a gate and there is gonna be this person with a key and he's gonna give me the key and I'm gonna go in," indeed, as they leave the Coat, they might see that, but they will also understand that that is a human perception. There is no one standing with a key, anywhere.

D. So they would still be loosely attached to their Coat?

B. Indeed. It's still a little bit like that. Sometimes a soul leaving the body and the Coat will come in direct contact with nothingness. As they do—this nothingness is nothing bad, it is actually to come in contact with the Creator, because the Creator is neither or, it simply is—but if you expect to see gardens and people with keys and you come into a sensation of nothingness, it might be confusing. Because you still have, in the fourth reality, somewhat of a connection to the human form. That's why the transition takes a little time, sometimes. But the nothingness, the vacuum, as you embrace it, you will become aware that you are neither good or bad, light or dark, you simply are in the presence of spirit. And nothingness is the cradle of the Creator.

D. Is that projected within the fourth reality then?

B. It is indeed. As you leave the Coat, when you come to the last fifty percent of the fourth reality, you come to a blend of the spiritual dimension that you belong to, as well as the presence of the Creator. And if you feel the nothingness, then you are in the cradle of the Creator.

D. When people say that God spoke to them and they hear a voice, what is it exactly they are experiencing?

B. Oh, they experience the, –a lot of times it's a spirit guide that communicates to them, and it doesn't matter how they interpret it. If it's someone like Joel (*His friend, on the second, who monitors the Himalayan mountains*) who is saying something but the person is so in a box that they can only talk to Jesus, then Joel will not be sad or angry, because at least the person is hearing something. What they hear is the connection, normally as raindrops coming through the fourth reality. It's different when you are still in body, or when you have left the body. When you are still in body, then you don't sniff up and look at the Coat, necessarily. You can if you do certain things like regression work and so forth, then you can indeed investigate the Coat. But normally, if you do like meditation and so forth, you simply communicate directly to some spiritual being in the first part, the closer part of the fourth reality to the spirit realm. But if you want to investigate your Coat as a human, that is encouraged! It's always encouraged, because it's gonna be easier when you eventually leave if you have somewhat of an idea. Because like I said, you are very much like a mix, human–soul for a while, and as you are that mix, if you have done a little bit of work beforehand when you were a complete person, like up and going, then it's easier to investigate the Coat when you are not running around anymore. So we looked at that and it was a whole lecture about that. I showed them how helpers come in and assist on different levels, if needed. So a soul can indeed, either by themselves, you know, send a little honk–honk horn to a spirit helper and either a guide or a friend joins somewhere. A spirit guide, based on their own expertise, will be able to see if they need to meet their person on any levels as they transition. A spirit guide is very alert when it's time to go, –and I learned that first hand–, you have to be aware when it's time to go.

D. Did you always accompany me to a certain point when I died?

B. Well normally, like here the last few times (*lives*), Jeshua has, in the beginning (*when coming into an incarnation*), Jeshua walked with you through the fourth reality, just having a last briefing kind of thing. I normally met you when you put on your Coat, ahh, and then just did a high-five, here we go again kind of thing, and helped you dress. And then I left you again, so you could just sort of become. I normally met you early, in the beginning when you had a Coat, or early before being born. When you passed, I also—because you're different—so we sort of talked a little bit as you just left.

D. I said, "Where did you go, Bob?" (*I was teasing him about one of my first lifetimes, when I accidentally burnt up in a fire after he wandered off to look at a plant, as described in Volume 1.*)

B. Ahh, that was one thing. You were already in the fourth reality in your Coat, and I was still down on Earth, so that was quick retreat back up there to sort of assist. But, normally, as a soul is about to die, NORMALLY, –if they don't have someone like you who just leaves because you feel like you are done and not giving a heads up to anyone else–, then normally a spirit guide is fully aware when it's time for their person to leave. So they are, leading up to a departure, a spirit guide is very present, normally trying to in some way help the person look at the Coat if they haven't. It can be like providing thought bubbles, making the person reflect on childhood, making them reflect on relationships, making them reflect on choices they did. So normally a spirit guide is fully aware when their person is about to leave, so the last week, day, month, they try to encourage reflection, they make them aware of the Coat's existence, in different ways, for their person. It's a way to help them as they transition.

D. Since that would be considered like a life review for the soul at an incarnated level, there's another life review that occurs later once they are back in the spiritual realm?

B. As they come home, yes indeed. Then they look at the Coat from a soul perspective. In many ways, when they transition through the Coat, they look at it from a blend of spirit and human, because they are a little bit fifty-fifty at that point.

D. So they are still a little bit emotionally attached?

B. Indeed, indeed. And as long as you are emotionally attached to it, you can't leave the Coat. But a spirit guide normally promotes the Coat for their person when it's time to go. I mean, they do it gradually throughout life in different ways, but extra effort is put in as the soul is about to leave. They want to give that extra help because they know their person is gonna have to travel through the Coat of Karma with one eye as a spiritual eye, the other eye is a human eye, that's how you can see it. In many ways, as long as they are transitioning, one eye is spiritual and the other eye is human. But it's more obvious as they transition through the Coat area. You can see it in the eyes of a soul returning where they are in the fourth reality, how much of the human energy is still present. A soul has eyes in some way, even if they look different, but a spirit guide and a spirit helper can see where their person is. Even if someone is on Earth in a human body, a spirit guide has the ability to look into the eyes of their person and see if it is mainly human or if it's soul.

D. How do our eyes look at home, like when you look at me as Lasaray?

B. The eyes are spiritual eyes when you're at home, so there is no remains of human.

D. Are they like points of light in the spirit world?

B. Indeed. The eyes, yours are a little bit smaller; some are bigger, rounder. Yours is more oval shaped.

D. You have big eyes, don't you?

B. I do indeed. You said that, that I looked like a lighthouse, that's what you say.

D. *(Laughing)* That's all your brilliance.

B. All my brilliance, shining right through! Huhuh. And I have never been in the pickle of blending my eyes to a human or something else. I did blend a little bit when I went to Siah's, and then I have to be in a different way, –so that is my transition. I like that place because there is no Coat, I don't have to dress in something else that is not mine. I have my Coat, I don't need another one that someone has made FOR me, that I did not order, maybe.

D. One size does not fit all.

B. One size does not fit all. Okay, Ophelia says we're gonna make it a little bit short now. But I'm gonna be with you, to make sure you don't trip, so just be careful with your toes in those sandals. I was sending an alarm to this one to tell you, and he did, I think. So just be careful with your toes. Sometimes you don't lift your feet that much. Feet are meant to go up and down, up and down. When you glide, that's more what you do at home, so sometimes just think of that, might wanna lift them. Anyway, I'm gonna go now.

D. One quick question before you go. Once they leave the Coat, is it pretty much smooth sailing through the rest of the fourth?

B. Indeed. Then they feel the familiarity of their spiritual home. A soul from the fifth, they normally hear a lot of singing, they normally experience a lot of colors, they can experience different animals, –like unicorns and butterflies are very common.

D. Do they see gardens, too?

B. They start to see gardens, they see flowers, and all these things. A soul from the seventh normally also hears music and there's a lot of light, no gardens.

D. There is no other reason a soul would stop in the fourth once it drops the Coat?

B. It continues home indeed—in various speed, I might add. Like when you two go, you tend to just have a quick sniff on the Coat and then you just shoot off. I have to be on alert, because it can go kinda quickly. You don't have a need to fibble around in that area. But a lot of souls enjoy the transition, so that's what I also want to teach them; first you have to look at certain things, but then it's an enjoyment to travel through the remaining part of the fourth reality. And some have no rush because they KNOW that they are heading home. But this is a very comforting travel.

D. They don't join their higher self until they are fully back in their home dimension?

B. No. That's when they merge back.

D. That's really good. Thank you for that. That's something that people are really interested in. So that was very educational.

B. Okay, so we'll go now. Ophelia says we are saving energy.

D. Alright, my friend. Thank you.

B. Ah. Talk soon. I'll join you, of course, to make sure you don't trip, and to make sure you eat well and so forth, and that you sleep well. It's important.

D. Thank you so much. You're a good friend.

B. Ahh, Okay, see you. Bye bye.

Picking Guides (Sept 25, 2019)

This brief talk illustrates one of the steps in preparing for a life and mission on Earth. They need to find partners to incarnate with during their journey, and the little Elahims were going around soliciting traveling companions. We are including this because it is really endearing to hear about Little Seth (a.k.a. Seth Junior) going to Ophelia, the biggest star of them all, and asking if she would join him during his first incarnation. The reality is that the mentor is the one who will do most of the planning. The soul will take on more of that responsibility after a few hundred lives.

D. Well, we've been looking forward to talking with you again, it's been a while.

B. Ah. So, I've been busy! It's not been a vacation for me! I have been piling up different cases, in order for different, –I've been going over certain lifetimes, certain scenarios, with the three little Elahims and the other three (*from the second*), giving somewhat of an input. It's been like parenting meetings without the little ones. (*He has also been meeting with the peers of those souls who are going to begin incarnating.*) We have gone through different scenarios that could happen, and I have been giving my input as a spirit helper, from my own experience, what one can encounter and what pickles they can get into, –like fire and so forth. I've been giving somewhat of an outline on different things that can happen from a spirit guide's view, and some concerns a spirit guide might have. Being now in the position of looking in rewind I can see—I have several events, several episodes—that could have been handled differently, if I wasn't just freestyling.

D. You mean with Lasaray?

B. Lasaray and me. So I thought that maybe I should give a little bit of a heads–up on certain things. So we've been going through a little bit on looking into what sort of lives will they go down in, so I can prepare my spirit guides correctly. And I've been giving my input from different journeys with you. You were also there, of course, giving your input on how did you hear me? was I available? was I loud enough in my guidance? You also had like a review of me, a little bit!

D. I bet you've been a good guide.

B. Ah. But in the beginning, –no one rides a bike without assistance in the beginning!

D. So you're going to be helping the guides for the little Elahims?

B. Ah, a little bit. We're talking about what sort of activities they should engage in; and co-workers, which souls they should go down with, you know, who should they be. I brought my catalogue of available spirit guides, if there is a need for more, and so forth.

D. Have any of the little Elahims been paired up with spirits from like the seventh?

B. The fifth. They're gonna go with a lot from the fifth. And then some here wants, –because we've been on an excursion here, we've been around (*to various groups of spirits*) and we met Zachariah, we met Ophelia, we met Josephine and Julia. A lot of them want Julia to join, they feel really happy with her. I also like Julia—and Julia sings—so they like her. Like Little Seth, he had his own notebook and he was going around with his spirit guide, asking questions if someone wanted to go. He asked Ophelia if she was busy! Huhuh. And Ophelia laughed, –Seth Junior didn't understand that she laughed, but I saw that she laughed because I can read her. But he didn't feel like she was making fun of him or anything, so he didn't take offense. She just said that she had engagements elsewhere, but she would be happy to see his journaling when he came back. So he was happy with that—but I saw that she kinda laughed. So he went around and he talked with Josephine, Julia, and there are others here too.

D. So I guess a soul can ask someone to be in their life plan?

B. Indeed. Goes with the peer (*their main mentor from their home dimension*). Little Seth had his peer, and I was there in this case with his spirit guide from my place. And we moved around, we want them to feel encouraged that there is an option for them. It's not a given, because it wasn't a given that I was gonna create a life (*for Lasaray*), but here their peer is guiding this whole excursion. But we want them to feel like they have a hand in it, that they can make questions and look into different souls to travel with. But I did not foresee that Little Seth would just run off to Ophelia, the biggest star of them all, and just ask her to come! It's like picking the biggest treat under the tree!

D. He clearly knows the good ones!

O. Ophelia said she doesn't have a Coat, and that he's gonna go with those with Coats so they can help each other dress correctly in their Coat, that's what she said. Eventually they will go with no Coats, but she said, "If I did have a Coat, I would be happy to come with you. But I'm not able to because I don't have a Coat." So she put it like that, so that's nice. But I saw she laughed inside.

The Preacher–Man and the Recipe Book (Sept 29, 2019)

The way the spirits present ideas can be disarmingly entertaining. Within the stories are often very serious observations, as here, when Bob displays himself to his students as a religious cleric from the Middle Ages, also known as the Dark Ages (in Europe). While the main target of Bob's satire is religion, it applies to any field of study where intolerance prevails, including the sciences. Spirituality can only flourish when people are free to have their opinions heard. The Dark Ages were a time when knowledge, science and reason were submerged by tidal waves of religious fanaticism, famine, and war. Beginning in the 4th century, the emperor Constantine allowed his mercenaries to plunder innumerable Greek and Roman temples, burning books and pagan priests who protested. Constantine, although a worshiper of Baal, the Sun god, organized the Katholikos (καθολικός) Church by blending Pagan and Christian practices into a universal religion. By the 7th century the bellicistic Islamists had joined in the carnage. They despise not only the Pagans, Jews, and Christians, but they abhor the classical Greek philosophies of inquiry into the nature of truth. Collections of ancient writings, including those in the great Library of Alexandria and the Temple of Serapis, were contemptuously burnt to ash by the benighted Umar. In the following centuries, logic and reason, the greatest enemies of tyrannical cults, were weeded out of societies through blasphemy, heresy, and apostasy laws. The spirits have warned that the Western civilizations risks descending into another Dark Age. Lockdowns, health passports, laws that prohibit criticizing religions, mandatory injections of pharmaceutical nano–toxins, and social credit systems are similar tools for elimination of dissent and establishing tyranny. People are attacked for having logical opinions the Cell does not want shared. Even though we are in the early phase of electronic book burning, the human spirit will, in the long run, win the ideological war. The Cell will not prevail in sacrificing humanity to Moloch.

Repressive regimes, both religious and ideological, arise from adherence to a particular set of beliefs, and those beliefs are typically gathered into a book of "truths". Bob portrays them as cookbooks full of recipes, which must be followed exactly in order for the subservient member to find enlightenment. The library of recipe books would include such classics as the Bible, Koran, Hadith, Talmud, and Torah, as well as modern articles of faith, such as the Communist Manifesto; Relativity: The Special and General Theory; On the Origin of the Species; and innumerable other misleading theoretical tomes. I'm not saying the entire contents of any particular recipe book are inaccurate, since they each possess some valid observations, but they all contain errors that are accepted as gospel by their followers. According to Ophelia, the greatest of spiritual errors are ones that compel people to focus on separation, and all the aforementioned books are culpable in that regard. Bob tells us that we must listen to and follow our inner guidance and not fall into the trap of carelessly believing what we are told, especially if the ideas are culturally popular.

D. Welcome, my friend.

B. Ah. I've been doing a lot of journaling, because it's important to somewhat stop and document your progress, to look back and see how far, –this is what Zachariah said to me, that it's important that I do this–, so I am indeed looking in rewind, seeing the steps I've been taking so that I can fully put my attention and my effort and my longing into a new step, a new development. We have indeed continued different classes on what could happen on Earth. I have portrayed myself as a preacher–man.

D. Oh, that's the image you flashed this one the other day? (*Bob had shown himself standing in a 17th century priest outfit, holding an open book with both hands.*)

B. Ah. I have put on my finest preacher outfit and I have also in my possession a little bit of scripture that I proclaim is the truth. I have gathered my students in an auditorium—it would be considered like a church here—and I have placed myself on a little stage in front. I'm reading out of this and I'm also wanting to see what sort of activity ignites in the mental realm (*of the students*) as I read out of this book considered containing truth.

D. What sort of things are you reading to them?

B. I am reading about how to proclaim your light, how to find your inner light, and how I am extremely important to them to find this light, and this book in general is extremely important to find that light. And without this book, and without knowing it exactly word–by–word, they will never find that light. I'm putting forward that this is like a recipe book, you're not going to be able to cook unless you know the recipe. And this is the same thing, you're not gonna be able to find your light unless you have this book, you have to have the recipe that I am here to give you. For a small amount of fee, I will indeed give you the recipe. This week we're talking about how to access the light within and how to access and to be safe after the life has been shut down, how that light, your light, will guide you to your destination. It's not according to me here (*as the preacher*), it's not just a given that you will find your way home—unless you know the recipe. (*Bob is warning the little ones that once they incarnate, they will encounter religious teachers who pretend to have special insight about life and death, as outlined in their particular recipe book, and without their guidance the soul will become lost and unable to find its way home. He then contrasts that type of religious ignorance to the inner wisdom possessed by the soul.*)
D. Maybe the recipe doesn't lead anywhere, it's a dead–end?
B. It is indeed, and I'm trying to tell them that there will be those who proclaim to have the recipe for all sorts of things. There will be a recipe, for me here (*as he plays the part of the preacher–man*), talking about finding your way home, finding your connection to your soul particle. In many ways, I'm using all sorts of fancy ingredients and strange spices so that they will be confused. I see that they sit there and try to write down all the ingredients in my recipe of how to find their way to their soul particle. I'm trying to make them understand that me standing here with a recipe book is not how you cook. You can have the greatest soup just cooked with water and compassion, and it will be the greatest dish. So you don't have to have all these different spices, all these different ingredients, in order for you to cook that soup. But I'm very charismatic here, and I'm really putting in a lot of dramatics; I change my voice so I'm somewhat high and low, going in all these different directions, I even sing a little, putting a melody

in my words so I, in some way, put a spell on how I deliver the importance of my recipe. And I say, "You might encounter this, especially if you are placed in a life where you lack companionship; you might be drawn to institutions like this where you will find some friends." Because in spirit, we seek companionship. Even I, when I was put in that phase of self-study, I felt lost. Because in my being, in my core, I crave and want companionship. And that doesn't change just because you are incarnated. You still crave to belong with others. The problem is that here you are in a mish-mash of others. First of all, you do not necessarily travel with those that are from your tribe. Secondly, you are likely to be with those who have a heavier Coat than yourself. And then if you come into a stagnated society, you might feel drawn to find something where you can join with others, and that is how you might end up in my building here.

D. How do they respond to your teaching?

B. Well, first of all, I put my recipe book aside and I said, "So, how many of you have put down, exactly word-by-word, all my ingredients that I told you that you need to create this soup, to create this connection to your light?" And there were some here that had been taking notes, they thought that they had been really good students. Because that is the thing, they wanted to do good and they thought they were supposed to write down and listen carefully and follow my instructions. But I said, "When you are on Earth, you have all your instructions inside. You have the recipe inside. Your soup might not be the same as your neighbors' soup. There is not a universal recipe for each to find their light. So here I stand with a big cookbook on how to manage life, how you are expected to behave, how you are expected be passive and follow this specific recipe book." Then I said, "You cannot just listen to the directives that comes from the people around you, you have to be centered and look for that tickle. You can't just think that you are a good student if you just copy and write down everything I say to you. You don't know if what I'm saying to you as a human is the same advice that I would give to you in spirit. And you have to see, –that is the tingle–, is this the same message that I would consider to be of value, like if it came from my spirit helpers?" And that is the tingle in your center point, in your belly area. (*He is saying that if you hear something that is spiritually accurate, it will immediately be detected in your body, usually in the center point.*) But some can even feel the tingle in the scalp, so don't just focus on the belly, it can come in many different ways. Some will have a sensation of how their ears get warm.

D. I feel the tingle on my scalp if I hear something that is spiritually true or accurate.

B. Indeed. So, if you don't feel that tingle, then the message is coming from a manufactured idea that has no core or roots in a spiritual teaching. You have to be aware of that. It's the same down to the littlest things, you know. If it is politics, or if it is me standing here with my recipe book, it's the same thing—you have to be aware of if it's a manufactured, created idea that has no relevance, and it doesn't lead you to a sensation of development. The true preacher-man will close the book and ask its audience, "How do you perceive the light? How does it make you feel if you close your eyes and I say, 'You are light?' How does it make you feel that you have the awareness that you are light, regardless of where you are or who you are with?" And then (*the preacher-man should*) uniquely go through each and every one and just assist them. So I told them, "I'm gonna shut my book, my cookbook here, and I want you to shut your eyes and I want you to just feel the presence of light. And if you can't, just visualize that you have a little growing light in the center of your chest, and how it rotates and how it is you, –how it becomes you. And how you, from that sensation, extend that sensation to like a bridge to a home that you as a human might not know what it looks like. But from this sensation, create this bridge out, up into the Universe, and see where it leads you. This will never be broken, this will never be altered or taken away from you. You can always find your way through this connection that is yours. And some will feel like a color, some will feel the connection like a sensation." So I said, "If you feel like this bridge is a connection that, let's say, provides a feeling like you want to giggle, you feel happy, and you want to maybe snort, even." Then I said, "That is what you should establish within you—that is your spice, that is your ingredient—that the connection to home is a laughter, it's a giggle, it's something fun." Another one might feel the sensation of sound, let's say. So when I say, "How do you individually experience this bridge?" And then I go through and I listen (*to each of his students*). And I said, "That is your ingredients." I want them to be aware of that. There will be people who mislead. As a spirit, we want to grow and learn, and that doesn't change when we come here, so we might be tricked by those who appear to us as one of the teachers at home. We are always very eager students, so we have to make sure that what we consider a teacher also has our best interest in mind. So, my class here is to make them understand that there is no recipe that is specifically and uniquely the same.

D. No universal recipe.

B. No it's not. It's not McDonald's. And I want them to find how they connect within.

D. I've been wondering about the connection between the part of the soul that is in the body, and the part that is remaining. Is there a continuous bridge between the two, or are they separated during the incarnation?

B. It's a bridge, and this is the bridge that I was trying to make them understand. Some will appear, or some will perceive, this bridge as a tone. Some will perceive this bridge as a sensation, and it's important that you try to just sit in your power and try to find that bridge. And you can visualize this bridge taking form, and then from that, ask your inner being to give you a sign or a feeling that relates to YOUR bridge. And some will hear a tune, a melody, and once that is established, you can always return to that sensation and you can somewhat travel on that bridge back and forth a little bit.

D. What is mine?

B. Yours is a sound. Both of you are sound. It's like those sounds that are theta waves, very monotone. It's not like (*then he began singing Yellow Submarine*). And it's not like that song they played when people went onto that field trip, which was not a field trip at all. I mean, it was a field trip, but it didn't have a great intention.

D. Which one was this?

B. In France. (*He intoned the French national anthem, which was played to motivate French soldiers marching off to war with England. He observed some of the battles between England and France, and has used those wars as examples of how people are misled by rulers.*) And when I heard that I said, "Oh, this is a happy field trip! Look how they are dressed up in their finest. Off they go on this field trip. And then on the other side there was…

D. Not so happy?

B. Well, not so happy there. But it sounded happy before they met. And that is my whole idea. If you put a happy tune or an encouraging being like myself, here with my book, then all sorts of things can encourage individuals to move in the wrong direction. You can see how happy they were on this field trip with this jolly tune cheering them on; they became happy, they felt inspired. And it's the same thing with my cookbook. Here I stand and I put great effort into persuading them, in how I raise and fall in my tone and how I sing and how I move. So the recipe takes form into something that everyone wants and everyone seeks. I'm not saying that everything is bad, but some are not working for your higher good. So you have to be aware of, even if it comes as a great inspiration or with a song, or like me with my cookbook, it could actually be leading you AWAY from that source of happiness and achievement. So these here, going on a field trip, they were cheered on and told this field trip is a great achievement, of sorts. But it didn't become such a great achievement for everyone as they marched over this field, because on the other side there was another group, and they had a different song. So it wasn't a joined field trip with the same song, because on the other side there was this ahh nah nah (*he then sang the melody for the beginning of "God Save the King"*), and when these two came together and merged, each thinking, "This is a great field trip, and we are encouraged by someone behind, with a portrait." And they are moving together, these two songs, and it did not end up like a happy gathering. So I'm saying, just because you are cheered on by different things, whether it's me here with my book and my recipes saying, "This is good, this creates the best soup."

D. Unfortunately, with most religions there is something good in them that is uplifting, but then it often leads in the wrong direction.

B. And that is what you have to look for, "Is this a recipe that is just going to confuse me? Does it put a spell on me, does it limit me so that I cannot reach the light?" So if I tell them, "You have to have this curry, this salt, this pepper, this vegetable, and you have to cook it for twenty minutes here, and then you move the pot over there," you know, it becomes completely confusing for someone who has never cooked. BUT, if I say, "All you have to do is fill your pot with water, put in your favorite vegetable, and the soup will be exactly perfect." Then they know that they can manage.

D. I like that analogy.

B. You have to encourage people on their level. You can't just say things to confuse them, because that will make them feel like they are in the maze. But if you say, "Put water in the pot, put in your favorite vegetables, and your soup is ready to go. You don't need all these ingredients to create this soup." So, I'm not gonna be long in the tooth here, Ophelia says.

D. We wanted to ask if you had any little bits of wisdom that you would like to pass on, that we can put on our website?

B. Ah. As we are moving into the fall season, people tend to be more reflective, and I think that that is important. Because now is a time to somewhat harvest and look in rewind on what you have collected over this year, this last cycle, –to appreciate the little steps that you have taken. It is a time to also look at every challenge that you had or still have, and to look at how you solved them. Are they still present in your life? Are they still affecting you? If so, how can you potentially do things differently? How could you potentially release stress or anxiety or other things that you encountered, let's say, over the year? But it's important to look back and count your blessings, count the things that you became happy about. It could be the simplest thing, for example, maybe you had time to walk in nature and when you did so, you felt the greatest relief and the greatest calm and presence around you. So, as you are moving into the season of fall, look back month-by-month on this year and see what you learned, see how you grew, see the treats that came your way; not only focusing on your challenges. If you had a year with a lot of challenges, then see from this perspective how you grew and how that challenge might assist you to transform and create a new level of progress.

D. That's a beautiful teaching. Thank you so much for that.

B. Ah, ah, you know. I'm gonna go now, I'm gonna march away. Bye bye.

The Traveling Magician (Oct 17, 2019)

It is a true blessing to talk directly with our spirit guides. One of those benefits is hearing about past lives from a first-hand observer with a perfect memory. Bob doesn't sugarcoat or embellish the stories of our adventures through the centuries, and we often laugh about the characters my soul has occupied. In this next talk, he mentions one of my lives in England as an itinerant entertainer, who once visited Plymouth in the southwest part of Britain. He incorporated that life into one of his classes, when he was teaching about secret skills each incarnation is given. Apparently, I traveled around with a monkey and a little bear that performed different tricks. When Bob was preparing this class for the students, he used a singing, dancing worm instead. While it may not be readily apparent why Bob told this story, there is a purpose in nearly everything the spirits tell us. He wants to remind us of the unique importance of each creature on the planet, no matter how small or seemingly insignificant. His second "trick" was to cure someone's sore throat with a single leaf of a plant. He is emphasizing the healing and medicinal value of plants. Not all health issue need pharmaceutical solutions. The main lesson in the story is that every person comes in with a special gift, but he expanded the idea to show that it is not only humans who carry magic inside. The Creator gives all living plants and animals unique gifts. There are many things we cannot logically understand, but the door to the world of magic can be opened from the center point.

I always end the lead-in to the trance session by saying, "And now, if there is anyone who wishes to speak, you may do so," which was Bob's cue to begin.

- B. Huhuhuh! Ah! Anyone, –it would be me! I pushed myself, I did not send out a public invitation today. It was not a general calling into the corridors of the second or anywhere. I placed this meeting in my secret chamber, in my secret calendar and journal, where only I and Ophelia have access.
- D. Welcome. Sorry you didn't get much time to speak last time.
- B. Welcome to me. You are welcome as well, I must say, not just me. But I have been progressing my education to somewhat mirror what could happen (*on Earth*). And this time I am encouraging the souls coming down, like Little Seth, to find their secret skill. Little Seth, he likes this one (*life of a*

magician) that I am portraying now, he wanted this (*as a life selection*). I say, "If you want to, you can absolutely have this. Lasaray had this life one time." I am a magician. I have my mule that I used one other time. (*He rode a mule when he portrayed King Henry the Eighth during one of his classes. See Volume 1*). I have my mule, and I have a carriage. I am moving village to village to show my special gifts. I encourage them (the students who are incarnating) that a special gift is something to strive for. Each time you come down, you have in your possession a secret skill, each and every one of you. You might not be a magician like I am, and very popular in that sense, but EACH soul has a secret skill unique to that specific individual and that specific life. So you have your skill that is yours by birth that is, you know, the way you tick; and then you also have a skill set that is given to you as a gift from your spirit helpers, in your Coat. The trick is to try to find them, even if your life is not as exciting as me, being this magician on wheels. I am in the English countryside—I am headed for Plymouth—and I have been sending out posters in advance because I'm making my rounds. So I make sure that a trumpet sort of thing is heard.

D. Precedes you.

B. Indeed. So I follow the trumpet, you know. I sent out a minion of my show to say, "Headed for next town, Plymouth," and blows the whistle. And I come after. It's a better way, because I'm already introduced. I kinda like that—drumroll—and there I am. And Little Seth, he said, "I want to be a magician, because a magician, he has a toolbox with all sorts of tricks." And I said, "Well, we'll see about that." Then he said, "I wanna see the toolbox, I want to see exactly what's in the toolbox." And I said, "Well, in this specific toolbox that I have here, I have a little jar with a worm. This worm has the ability to sing." When I showed it to the students, it sort of moved like this, (*he then wiggles Christine's body in the chair*) and as it did, it actually created a melody, a song. So it's a musical animal. People become intrigued with this because they think of it only as a worm, but the worm is actually trained to do tricks. So it looks like I have a tame earthworm, but I have trained it for this scene here. And then you (*Lasaray*) came and said, "I did not have a tame worm!" And I said, "No, but this is not your show, this is MINE, and I can have a trained earthworm if I want to." And you said, "I had a monkey and little bear." And I said, "I have a worm. It's the same thing, Because no one expects the worm to have intelligence, and that is what I'm trying to show them here, that every teeny-tiny creature comes with an awareness and intelligence, you just have to look." Ophelia says I'm not supposed to say this, but even YOU people have intelligence. There is intelligence in there, even though you might in many ways appear like the worm here, that you don't expect there to be an intelligence inside.

D. (*Laughing.*) Do you mean humans?

B. Indeed. The trick here is to understand that just because you don't expect there to be intelligence—like they don't expect there to be intelligence in my worm—there are occasions when it's not fully visible that there is an intelligence going on in your species. And Ophelia says, "It's not necessary to compare humans to a worm." But I said, "There is no difference." But I also have in my possession my secret flower. And you take petals from the secret flower and you put it in a tea, and it actually clears throats. It's similar like rose petals, but it's my secret flower. And this secret flower, –and I'm only giving it to one person at a time in every town I'm visiting, but I have several in the back here that I grow (*he had turned almost all the way around and was looking behind him where the wagon would be*), but I say I only have one and we can only use one petal. I put it in a tea and I ask someone who has a throat problem to come and drink my tea, and then I do like a drumroll, and the earthworm is dancing at the same time, and then I give them this tea. It has the effect similar like mint but it has a burning sensation first that briefly feels like...

D. A shot of whiskey?

B. Indeed. There are different things in my toolbox here, in my magician box in my coffin (*his wagon*). Little Seth, he said that he wanted to be a magician because he wanted to make the rounds, he said, to places where they lack magic. He wants to provide magic to people. I said, "I'm all in favor of that." But the whole idea is, for me here, is to show that you have the ability to move around and create magic for others. The whole idea is to extend and to reach out to people who don't believe in magic and to tell them that, first of all, they have to bypass the idea that magic doesn't exist. When you fully embrace the fact that there are things going on that has, from a human standpoint, no explanation, then you surrender to the fact that you might not have the intelligence to fully understand everything that happens to you or around you. As soon as you start to surrender to the fact that it's okay to not fully understand everything, the doors to magic opens. But you have to surrender in a way that you don't try to figure everything out. It's a human invention, maybe for everyone, that you want to understand. But that brings somewhat of a limitation to you. If you surrender, then there are no limitations to magic, there are no limitations to what you can access and what you can experience. You have to somewhat be okay with the fact that there are limits to your brain, what the brain can comprehend. But there are no limitations in your center point, and as you experience your reality through your center point, –that is what children do, they don't analyze everything, they are IN an experience, they feel happy, they feel sad, they feel enticed–, and all those instant feelings, instant responses, they come from the center point. It never comes from the helmet (*mental*) at all! We have observed there is a lack of that feeling of excitement that magic brings, in general, in your species. There are ideas (*in the spirit realm*) on how to bring in personalities, like lives, that will unfold in that field and to bring, similar like a magician, –not necessarily have earthworms that dances and sings–, but to bring that little sparkle of excitement into people's realities. That is something that is highly overlooked. And some actually have that skillset within them, it's a skillset, it's a treat, and it's something that is given to you. But it's not necessarily seen as a gift because you're supposed to go to college and you have to do this and this and this, or you're supposed to be a doctor and you have to do all these rounds, or you have to have a master's (*degree*) in this and this and this. Well, this is a master's from the Creator, a master from within, and for those who are placed here as magicians, it can channel in many different ways. So in many ways you (*through our books*) also act like a magicians, because you open people's eyes and you make them see realities that they might have encountered briefly in dreams, but they don't know whether it is true or not. The thing with a magician is that it doesn't matter if it's true or not, it matters how it makes you feel. If someone tells you a story, like a child, it doesn't matter if it's a fairy tale or if it's made up or if it's based on real life events—how boring is that! But the ones who are not just stated as "based on real life events", those are the ones that remains as a sparkle within a human being for eternity.

D. That's a really good teaching.

B. Ah. So I'm dressed up here and I have the same mule, and we're having this display.

D. Which students are you teaching now?

B. The three little Elahims and the other three, I'm mainly with them now. However, I have been invited to be a guest lecturer for the souls from the fifth. I'm more or less stationed with the Elahims from the sixth, but I also feel, –I would say that I feel a need to help them–, but I'm also curious. So anyway, I wanted to tell you about the importance of finding the magician within you because the magician is the one that holds your secret skill, and everyone has a magician within them; you just have to find it. Because that means it is a gift in some way, but it could be—

D. Maybe you could give an example of what kind of gifts people come with?

B. To give an example, it could be just that they are the one that brings humor into an environment, which is a HUGE gift, it's a huge magician gift to be the one that brings laughter into a work place or a family unit and so forth. Another gift could, for instance, be the ability to sing, or play the piano or an instrument. That has somewhat not been looked at as a gift for a long time. I would say about the last hundred years or so, that skill set of being very equipped with an instrument has not been considered as a valuable skill, –which it is! It's a way to make people pause, it's a way to meditate and move into your light capsule, which you as person don't know that you have. So those who feel drawn to an instrument should actually exercise that. Because not only will it awaken your own soul, it has the ability through you, even if you don't play in public but if you are playing even by yourself, it rubs off on your person and those who are in tune will hear you play, even if you don't have the instrument with you. And that is a beautiful gift. If you are good in, let's say, playing the piano, and you practice that a lot, when you come to the workplace, you are in that vibration of the music that you create with your piano. That radiates through your being even if you don't have a piano there. That's why we want there to be more people playing instruments.

D. That makes a lot of sense. If you were to come in, what would your gift be?

B. My gift would be that I am highly inquisitive and I have a nose for finding the things that are hidden and to bring that to the surface for others to see. But Ophelia says, "Not everything is supposed to be visible for everyone." I have also in my possession, as a skill, to bring excitement, even if there is no excitement.

D. And humor!

B. And humor. But some (*souls*), they go places where there's no excitement, and I make them see the arena and the life they have picked with some excitement and a teeny-tiny twinkle of humor. There are no gloomy souls, but they might feel gloomy on the third reality. Anyway, I'm gonna go now before I say too much.

Coloring the Mind (Oct 20, 2019)

This session came just a few days after the traveling magician, and it follows the theme of using your gifts to help others. The soul always has a desire to share, but sometimes the human is unmotivated. Bob then goes through a very detailed explanation of how colors are associated with different types of knowledge. Bob told us, in a separate talk, that if our life is uninspiring, if we see it as dull and drab, we have the ability to change it by radiating our own colors. He summed it up by saying, if you can't SEE colors, BE colors, which is a beautiful yet simple reminder of the power of thought to change the way life is experienced. We can alter the filter through which we see the world.

Zachariah began this session, which we have included in *Wave 3*. Bob calls him the Ambassador of Knowledge. Zachariah teaches students from all dimensions and has a permanent office in the Library on the fifth. He is also a member of the Council of Nine and other councils. He is a teacher for spirits who are tasked with advancements in resource management, biological systems and atmospheric understandings. As Zachariah was ending his talk, he mentions Bob had been circling around his classrooms on the fifth, looking for an opportunity to give a seminar on colors to his students.

Z. We have someone here who wishes to show you a drawing. He has been moving around frequently in the fifth, in my classrooms, and he has asked permission to host a workshop. I asked for details about this workshop, since I know that he can be tricky, and I said, "This workshop, it has to be plain. They are not going to work with the higher science, such as the six from the sixth. They (*the ones from the fifth*) are going to come and help the biological and environmental chain to improve. So you cannot have a workshop of understanding the higher science or the teleportations that the other ones are going to come in and work on in a later cycle." This workshop that he wanted to hold in my classroom had to do with creative art. So he has dressed up, as I can see, in an apron and a little hat. The hat is black—it's a little big, but it fits well. It has paint on it as does the apron, and he is full of (*covered in*) paint.

After Zachariah finished talking, Bob came in and explained how he instructed Zachariah's students to add colors to their life and to their minds during an incarnation.

B. DEET DA DA DEEEEEEET! (*He made sounds like a trumpet, heralding his arrival.*) Class in session! Huhuh!

D. Are you a master in the painting arts?

B. I have dressed up for this and I have invited all for a grand workshop. Because this specific teaching that I am here to provide actually involves everyone—including the human! It's not just on one side or in one dimension, so this can benefit everyone. I AM dressed as a great painter. I have my apron (*as he looks down*) with paint on it, just for the effect that I want to show them, that to be creative you have to allow yourself to somewhat move into the space of madness. And madness is something that humans try to avoid because madness indicates all sorts of problems. BUT to be highly creative is actually, –the higher form of creativity is found in the border or the land of beyond–, when it moves into madness. So if you have a little bit of courage to move into a sensation where you might find yourself just completely letting go of what is acceptable, what is appropriate and what is considered normal, when you move into that phase of creative madness, this is what it can look like, you know, me here with all the paint. So if I was simply drawing with one pencil then indeed I will create a nice postcard, maybe, BUT if I want to create this big, beautiful, colorful canvas that is on display in those ancient buildings, like the Sistine Chapel down in Rome, that person for instance, he moved into the madness of creation. Being creative with all the possibilities that comes when you surrender and you just fall into, you dive into, the possibilities of creation. To be creative is to surrender into vibrations and flows and inspirations, because madness, goes a little bit hand-in-hand with inspiration. And because of the fact that man is like this (*he raises his hands like he is shielding himself*), "Oh, don't want to be mad, don't want to appear like a madman," then you might not even access your inspiration, that spark. So it doesn't mean that you have to go into being like a cuckoo, but inspiration is found if you allow yourself to not be normal, to stand out and find your own puddle, because each creative inspiration and puddle is unique. But here it's like people feel like, "Oh, I'm not sure if I can swim in that one—I don't even know if I can swim—do I remember how to swim? I haven't been swimming for a while." So they avoid this puddle of huge inspiration because it's unfamiliar to them. In order to be fully blossoming as a soul, as a spirit and as a soul in a human, –and then in the far end to that, to blossom as a person–, you have to allow yourself to be different, to be that creative cuckoo, like me here. Here I stand, and to the students I said, "You can still paint, you can still do greatness, but you might only create a postcard. I'm creating a canvas that's gonna be in the Sistine Chapel. That's what I'm gonna do. So if you want to do greatness, which everyone is entitled and has the possibility to do, then you have to allow yourself to be inspired." And how can you be inspired? Each of you has the little, –it's like a chip inside of you–, that is programmed with that specific spark of inspiration. What we see is that a lot of humans are lacking inspiration. Meaning, they are numb to EVERYTHING. I'm not saying that everyone has to be a painter, but at least you would think you would have somewhat of an inspiration for your journey, –because YOU picked this journey! Why come here and just be gloomy? You picked it, and in order for you to bypass hurdles and problems, you have to move into the fact of inspiration, because in inspiration and the border, –madness is the only word you have, so we will use that–, and that combined has the ability for you to rise above the conditions that you might feel are placed upon you.

D. A lot of people struggle just to get by.
B. It's a sadness. And it's a sadness to see that others who might be more fortunate either spiritually or financially, –which is something you people find a big medal in–, do not reach out to those who might struggle to find that spark, to find that creative inspiration within them. You don't have to, like I said before, you don't have to hold hands and sing kumbaya. But you can, just by giving a smile, just by acknowledging another person is a way for that person to start to ignite within. Look people in the eyes when you meet them, acknowledge them. You might not know their journey, of course, and you don't know what they came to learn and what they came to perhaps teach others, BUT the fact that you are ignoring your neighbors, especially in the big cities, because you are so, – you know those horses that have that thing on the sides?
D. Blinders, so they don't see to the side?
B. Indeed. And not only does it make you not see others, they don't see your eyes either. But you run like that hamster in the wheel because you are in your own lane, so to speak, you are not open to see other individuals because there might be those who can give YOU the smile. Maybe you are the one that needs a smile, maybe you are the one that needs the inspiration and to be creative. Invite others, if you find, like me here, I have found my skill, you see here (*as he looks down at his apron again*). I'm painting, I'm clearly very special in this field because I have my big canvas and it has a lot of colors. I created like a rainforest, that's my contribution in this workshop. But if I have this ability, then I should invite and encourage others who might share my ability. They might just come with one pencil the first time we meet. But the next time, I will say, "Let's do something different." So you encourage those you see who have the potential that you could help them with. You, for instance, in an earlier life, you had the potential to inspire others with your painting. In this life you can inspire others with your words, the written words, and your presence. Your presence is noticed, both of you, differently. People feel the presence of your energy, and that is what we wanted you to do. You share your calm, you share your inspiration, and you invite others to be a part of that journey, but you're not here to make other people become painters. So first you have to find your own spark, your own

inspiration, and then merge with others and see others. If you see that someone is somewhat dimmed, then you can give them a smile. Maybe they have lost their inspiration and their spark.

D. So what do you specifically tell them, the Zachariah's students?

B. I'm telling them, "Once you come to Earth, you will be placed in a bottle that might not be fully as inspirational as your spirit. You will have to find that inspiration and spark in somewhat of a locked environment. And how can you do that? One way, if you don't want to physically paint, is to color the mind." What we see is that the minds here at this time are black and white. The heart is better, the heart has colors in the humanoid, but the mind is black and white, sometimes even grey. What we say to them, "You come in now as a brand-new wave of soul capacity, and you will color the brain." They're gonna color the brain, meaning that people will recognize the colors in nature, the colors in animals, the colors of the ocean. As long as your mind is black and white and grey, you don't see and you don't appreciate your host and the environment. You have to be colored. That's one of their missions, is to color the brains, their own brain of course but also others. You two are not necessarily here to color the brain to become aware of nature, you are here to color the brain to come alive to the spiritual. It's like adding different colors to the brain. The ones from the fifth, they're gonna add a lot of green, orange, red. The ones from the seventh, they're gonna also add a little bit of orange, but they are predominantly gonna put in yellow in the brain. You are gonna put in blue and purple in the brain. Also, from the fifth, they're gonna put in brown in the brain.

D. And what do those colors represent?

B. Different ways of increasing your consciousness. Like the fifth, who are here to increase the consciousness of the environmental connections to you as a species, they are given more of those colors as they come into a body. First of all they're gonna be predominantly focusing on coloring the mental, because the mental is the thing that has been in a veil at this point, and the mental is the one that is grey and black and white. So the future souls, the waves coming in, have an agenda to color the brain in different ways. The ones from the sixth, they're gonna come in with a lot of dark blue and light blue; it has to do with communication, travels, science, understanding cosmic laws, teleportations, and so forth. The purple, the spiritual aspect, will sort of circle around all the other colors. It's like the eighth is also involved, and other ones, and they represent purple a little bit, even though I see purple in the ones coming in from the sixth. This is a way for you to understand that souls coming in from three or four different dimensions, they have in their backpack more colors that they will shine through in the brain. As they shine through, these from the fifth, with the green, red, brown, and there is a little bit of orange as well, when they come in with that, as people, they will be more open and they will see nature and they will see flowers and the colors in nature. If you don't see the colors in nature, if you don't see the vibrations that the colors represent in an animal, you can have no empathy for it. So that's why, because your brain, a lot of the brains are black and white, so there is a lack of understanding to even have an empathy for water that is blue, or for green that is nature, because you are locked in a different reality and a different experience within your brain. The brain is dying.

D. Is it just a result of modern civilization being disconnected from nature?

B. A little bit, indeed, indeed. And if we go back, like when I took the color classes that was provided to me, and Isaac was with (*me*) here, I looked down on Earth and I could see, in general, if I looked at the brain and I looked at the heart area and I looked at the center point, I could see the division of colors and how much man were in tune with certain things. I could also look at you (*during incarnations*) and see what colors are represented, and what sort of life that would indicate. Is he even reachable? If I put in inputs on, let's say, green, because if there is no green in you then it would be hard for you to identify what the green represents.

D. Is that patterned determined before you come down? Do you decide not to be able to access certain information?

B. Indeed. So each color represents a different learning. But it also, here on Earth, it represents a connection to different things. So if you don't have in your brain, –and here we talk about the brain–, if you were to just think from the heart, the heart has more colors and you would indeed appreciate, let's say, nature. But as long as you are in your head, so to speak, then you don't connect; you don't connect with others, you don't connect with your purpose, you don't connect with your host.

D. Is that pattern established within the body itself, or is that just a result of the— (*Bob cuts in to answer the question.*)

B. At this time, the black and white and grey brain is a result of a pattern in your evolution. The soul itself comes in now in future cycles and will have more colors in the region that will merge with the brain. So the soul itself is all colorful, but the body that you're traveling in and because of certain conditions—a lot of it had to do with the magnetic field, the magnetic field makes the computer (*brain*) go bzzzt, bzzzt, like that— and then it becomes grey, black and white. So now souls coming in, let's say these from the fifth, they come in with a lot of green, red, brown, and a little orange, and when they dock with the body, they're gonna open up that spectra and just color as they merge with the brain. And you (*the sixth*) will do the same with blue. So depending on what body and what location you have selected to incarnate will determine what sort of soul will come in. Because, as I say, there is gonna come in a higher volume of colors that, when they connect with the body, it will transcend into the brain and dock. That's what I'm teaching; I want them to be familiar with colors; I want them to move to become a little bit like, – it's kinda nice to be a fool, ya know?

D. I've always thought so!

B. I don't think there is something wrong with that, because then you actually ARE more in the vibrations of colors, not that colors are foolish, but you ride on them and you fly on them and you become them. Colors, they are not stagnation, so I want them to just know that they will come into a bottle that might feel like a straitjacket, like a restriction. But as long as they are in the mindset that "I have all these colors to (*at*) my disposal, then when I come into this somewhat dense bottle, I'm just gonna open up the cork and I'm gonna shoot up all the colors into the mental." And as they do, they're also gonna try to merge with others who resonate with those colors. Basically, to put this in short, what I want to say is that we want to color the world.

D. Is this mostly souls from—

B. It's not my idea, if that was the question. (*I laughed at his remark.*) It comes from a higher source, but I'm executing (*expressing*) it in my way.

D. Is this in Zachariah's class?

B. Well, I am on the fifth and I am in the big classrooms, but there are actually those here from both seventh and sixth, – everyone is taking my color workshop.

D. It sounds like a big class then.

B. I have them in groups, first there are the fifth around that big table (*as he nods to one side*) and they have all their specific colors to work on. And I want to see also about teamwork, because that is also something that man has forgotten—teamwork. Everyone is like with those blindfolds, like those on the horse (*he means blinders*), so they only trot in their lane, like the cabbage. (*He is alluding to a talk Eli gave about humans walking in a karmic ditch that was so deep that only their heads showed above ground, like a cabbage. I have become less surprised they remember every word spoken during our sessions, even though years may have passed.*) What we also want to see, and that is also something that helps with colors, is that you become more rhythmical and you WANT to engage with others. So we are also looking at teamwork. So here we have the group at that table, which is the fifth, and there are the ones from the seventh, they are...they sing. You can see the difference around the tables. Here we have mine from the sixth (*nodding to the other side*), and they have been given their unique colors that they will be programmed within their being as they merge with a humanoid, with a human body. SO, what I asked is, "Can you create a picture together," each painting where they stand, "and not try to override someone else's ideas? Just trust that the end result of the whole painting will be more beautiful than if you tell how the picture is gonna be." So here I want to see the teamwork, each painting. There's a lot of laughter here in the fifth. Some of them are trying to move around, you know, like "I'm done with my corner!" and try to rotate. But that's not the thing—we want to see that they can wait for the other ones to be done. Huh, it's similar like in council work, wait for someone to be done. I'm teaching that here. And then we have the ones from the seventh, they sing. They are more patient, I must say, and they have a lot of yellow and orange to work on. And here are mine on the sixth (*as he looks in their direction*), they are also quite still, working with different kinds of blue. They're kinda silent. But the other ones over there, there's a lot of activity over there on the fifth, on that table.

D. Is that a bigger group?

B. It's a bigger group. To give you a portion, we have 27 to 30 around that table (*the fifth*), and then there is 11 to 13 here from the seventh, and here we have my six (*from the sixth*). After this is done, we want them to move around and look at the different results, and then we're gonna continue the class, which I will tell you about another time, because Ophelia says now we're gonna go. But the end result is to understand that the soul comes in with more colors in their backpack because they are expected to shoot it off and merge it and let it radiate into the brain.

D. That's very interesting. That's a good class you taught.

B. Ah. Anyway, I'm gonna go now.

D. Alright, my friend. It's a really good story, so thank you for sharing that. It's going to go in your next volume, of course. *Volume 2*.

B. Ah. So, Okay, I'll go now, but I'll be back. Always around. Okay, gotta go. Bye bye.

D. Bye bye (*I then started to lead Christine back, but after a moment, Bob came back in and began speaking again.*)

B. Oh. One more thing. Black is also part of the coloring, but it's nothing bad with black. They have that to somewhat create lines, if that is what they want to do. I wanted to say that. There's a lot of white also here in the table with the seventh. But there is actually a little bit of black used here in the table of the sixth, and it represents the complete realization of being connected to the center pole, –it's the higher mind. Whereas the white represents higher feelings. Wanted to say that, and yes indeed I will step aside now.

D. Slide to the side onto the bench.

B. Slide to the side. Because Ophelia said I forgot to say that, and I said I really needed to pop back in and say that, so Ophelia granted it, even though we were supposed to head down the hill here. But I wanted to say that.

D. Thank you, that's important, so I appreciate it.
B. Okay. Bye bye.

Bob brings his Students to a Session (Nov. 13. 2019)

Gergen began this session, and part of his talk is found in the chapter on Teachings from Etena and Tiddle. Gergen mentions Bob created his own ladder of learning, which is evidence of free will. Spiritual literature often promotes free will as something intrinsic to each soul, where individual destiny is self-determined. Religious theology embraces predestination, although their profundity is limited to a single human lifetime, given that they reject reincarnation. After years of listening to our spirits and councils describing the soul in relation to the Creator, I view the concept in a different light. Unless a soul is defective, it will ultimately fulfill a pre-determined agenda, but the paths to reach that goal are wide. Along the way, it can pursue other interests that are approved by the mentor or councils, as Gergen tells us here. When it comes to individual lives on Earth, it may be that a soul drifts off-route by exercising free will. But in the long term, a soul cannot avoid following the pattern given to it by the Creator.

Bob wanted to show his students how he blends with Christine and is able to speak through her. They were watching while I was conducting Christine up the mountain. They saw the energetic form and were aware when the human self stepped aside and Seth took over, as well when Seth stepped aside and let Bob take the reins. Then Bob had to explain that this is not something commonly done, especially during the early incarnations.

G. He has also been asking, –how can one say? He's been creating new platforms where he would like to set his feet—platforms that have not been granted by myself, Ophelia, or other members on different levels and councils. HOWEVER, he has started to create a new ladder for himself. Because of the fact that he is in some way—yes, Bob, you will soon be able to talk, I know you got your notes and you will soon be granted, but you did step away, so this is what happens when someone leaves. What I would like to say is that, because of the fact that he has been granted visits on Etena, as well as different meetings with species within the sixth dimension, foremost, he feels that he, in some way, would be able to take further steps. Those steps had not been granted or created, so he took it upon himself to create this ladder. And he has, in great detail, made his wishes known. So at this point, we will grant one of the wishes, and that is for his students to see what he is doing as he is communicating in this sacred circle. HOWEVER, the wish was granted with an exception, and that was either to have the students with muffled ears, or behind a shield—a shield of fog or a shield of glass. He himself finds himself normally behind a shield of fog where he can't really see. So he felt like the importance was for them to see, so it's gonna be a shield of see-through crystal glass. Yes Bob, indeed you have been waiting, so I will step aside.

D. So when is that going to happen?

G. Oh, right now. It's all set up, that's what he was doing; he was creating and he was putting out chairs, so they are sitting behind the glass. Bob is putting them in some sort of order here. I don't know why because they cannot hear, and they will see perfectly well, all of them, regardless of chair, regardless of position, they will see perfectly fine. So yes, it's all set up. So, here we go. I will say farewell, since it is his stage, as he says.

D. Well it is always nice to hear you.

G. It is kind of hard to squeeze oneself in. One does not want to step on someone's toes, especially if those toes are sensitive.

D. The disadvantages of being an elder.

G. Indeed, indeed. And I told him, "This will be the same for you. One day it will be the same, that you will have to step aside and let the little ones have their moment in the sun," so to speak. It is all by design, it all moves forward. Anyway, okay, I will leave at this point.

D. Thank you for coming.

G. You are welcome. Bye bye.

B. (*Bob immediately comes in.*) Ah. Hello, hello, hello.

D. Hello, Bob.

B. I did not go that far! I just went around the glass to make sure that they were comfortable, sitting well, because we have an audience.

D. Yes, this one said you had popped in a thought bubble, asking for a session.

B. AH, AH! I showed a preview so that this one would be like, "Oh, okay, let's do it today," because this one wanted to actually postpone (*the session*) 'til tomorrow. So I made sure I popped it into the chimney so that this one would say, "Okay, let's do it today." There's no need to wait around. So I popped this image into the chimney what was gonna happen and this one told you. I put a lot color on it—the trick is, that if you want to have something to develop or happen, then you encase the thought bubble, not just as an image or information, you put a color that resonates with the being, that the being likes. In this case, I KNOW that this one is highly receptive if the thought bubbles come in the indigo blue, red, or yellow. Those three colors I know are easier received and evaluated and looked upon. So I sent it in in a reddish color this morning.

D. A little tricky.

B. It's a trick! It's not just mine, all spirit guides know this! Like if I really wanted to make myself known with you, I send everything in green.

D. Ah, yes, I like green.

B. I know you do. If I want to make sure that one of my ideas…(*He then turned and, looking left towards the students, began to wave, slowly and deliberately. They must have been asking if he could hear them and requested he acknowledge them from inside of Christine's body. As Bob continues his narrative below, when he talks about the meadow and climbing, this is in reference to the lead-in we do before each session. I guide Christine to see herself crossing a meadow on a path that leads into a forest at the base of a mountain, where she begins to climb upwards towards the top. It is during this mental walk that the consciousness of Christine steps aside and her soul, Seth, takes control. The spirits see the transformation and recognize when Seth has emerged.*)

D. What do they see? What is it they see when they're observing this? How does it appear to them?

B. Excuse me. (*He said to me, before turning back and listening to what was being sent to him. He then leaned way over to the left for a moment, quietly communicating with the little ones, before turning back to answer me.*) First, they see Seth—and Little Seth, he was like, "UH–OH, UH–OH! I know! I know! I know! Because they saw the incarnation, and then they see the transformation, first from incarnation to Seth, because that's always what happens. First this one sits, appearing like the incarnation in the chair, but about the time when he starts climbing up the mountain, at the latest, sometimes even when he starts walking on the field, transformation takes place and Seth appears. It can happen gradually—let me explain because this is what they saw. I asked Seth to not just instantly move into Seth because I wanted them to see the magic, I wanted them to see ALL the magic; from incarnation to Seth to ME, because I'm now what they see, they don't see Seth anymore at all. But they see the energy, the puddle, the form in some way, the frame of, mainly Seth. It's a little bit incarnation, but not much. It's normally down there (*gesturing towards the legs*), there is where the incarnation could be seen, there. But predominantly, it's me they see now. Sometimes when the energy shifts up and down a little bit, it could be like Seth moves forward—and he said he was gonna do that, just to make an appearance for the little ones. So it might be that they will see back and forth a little bit. But I have placed them and we have the six from the sixth and the spirit guides. Tom is really excited about this because Tom said that he wants to go into training with this. So he's been asking his person to pay great attention to this because he said, "This could be you and I." And I said beforehand, I told them, "I had to wait a looong time," and then they said, "What is time?" Because they have not been on Earth yet. It's tricky! And then I said, "Gergen, do you want to have a word? Do you want to explain the concept of time?" And he said, "No. This is all you, Bob, this is all you."

D. So what did you tell them?
B. I said it took a long preparation, several levels that I had to master, several experiences that both you and I and this one—together, independently, on Earth and at home—had to go through. So when I told them, and I drew this because it's easier, so I said, "Here, met Lasaray in the forest behind the tree." I have all the images so I don't have to draw, really, I can just lift forward from the Library all these old movies. But it's not like the old ones are black–and–white and the new ones are colored; it's not like that at all. But I can bring forward all these images—it's like some are still pictures, like not moving, and some I can just (*then he blew like he was putting out a candle*) and a scene starts, it becomes motion. So I said, "Here, this is the first time we met." So I showed them, "This is where I met him in the forest, and this is where

I showed him me and my armadillo." Then they see how we began to communicate and do things together. We skipped the fire, we jumped that one. Then, here he's still learning to be a human, still not doing anything together like this (*not trance channeling him*). So I showed them all the way through different lives. And then I said, "The training to communicate started to plan when Lasaray's Coat was folded and he didn't have to come back anymore. But this one (*Christine*) had a karma of bringing barrels (*overwhelming people*), and the request from Seth was that he wanted to try and deliver different messages in cups, like Ophelia said, so this whole program was set in motion." So I showed them, "Here you can see all the steps and all the lives with Lasaray," and when they saw that, they understood that it's not just happening around the corner, so to speak. I said, "This is the first time I've been able to communicate." Because Little Seth said that it would be highly desirable if he could communicate directly with his spirit guide, like this. And I said, "I'm not sure if that is your assignment. This was not our assignment at all for several experiences." So I call it not "time", but I call it "levels of experiences". And I said, "We can put it forward like that, or what I prefer is to put it on top of each other so it becomes a cake. That's easier to understand. Like I said, now we are sort of on the top of the cake, we're the cherry on the cake, so this life is like the cherry on the cake. (*Bob considers my present incarnation to the be cherry life for him, as a spirit guide, since he is able to directly communicate and leave behind a legacy of his thoughts in written form.*)

D. Was there any planning to do this like back during (*I mentioned a couple of my past lives, which are known in history*) lifetime?

B. Indeed. It started around (*a life lived mostly in Italy in the late time 1400's*); that's when the project was started. Because there was certain things that both of you did in lifetimes at that point that was meant to relive or manifest again, or be repeated in this cherry life. We can call it that this is the cherry life, and we are on the top of the cake. The icing or the frosting was a couple of lifetimes ago, and now we have placed the cherry. So I said, "You can see how long it takes. You have not even started to make the dough of the cake–", well indeed they started to make the dough, but they have not put in the first level of the cake, which is the first incarnation. Little Seth is quite eager, I must say, to go. He has been studying up, – and I don't know where this behavior comes from–, but I have indeed, with permission, taken him to Zachariah. And we have been sitting, me, Little Seth and his spirit guide (*peer*) and Zachariah, just to look over what sort of lifetimes could be awaiting him. What I would like to say now to everyone behind the glass is that it takes a long time before it's a cherry life. First you have to do all the groundwork to build the cake, –and you might want to put different ingredients between the layers of the cake. First level it might be quite dry—meaning it's a quite boring life, it's simply to learn how to coexist with others in Coats—because it's not the same. (*He then looks directly at them*) You guys are not gonna meet that often, but if you meet others, you're gonna meet others from the fifth, for instance, and they have to learn how to coexist, and that's several layers in this cake—just to get by, just to stay alive! HUH HUH HUH! We learned that on life two!

D. What continent do you think a lot of them are going to start coming down in?

B. Canada is a favorite. Canada is up high on the list. Australia has also been high on the list. There are beings that wants to actually go into the Russian area, to go there, because they're gonna work with communication and teleportation eventually. And I said, "The teleportation cake is not even available yet. So you can see before you do this that if your mission is to learn teleportation and communicate telepathic information and so forth, or to work with free energy, those scenarios have not yet been designed by those who design, not just the suits. So we have those who design the suits and we have been there. We have had our field trip and we have looked into different suits. BUT, we also have those who design possibilities, events, shifts, developments in different fields." And at this point, if Little Seth's purpose is to come in and kickstart somewhat of a free energy flow, you know, take on where you left off (*one of my lives was an inventor who worked with electricity and other forms of energy in the late 1800's and early 1900's*), the physical and geometric keys are not established yet for him to come in and do that. So if that is his cake, and let's say that the end result for ALL of them, the cherry, is to communicate directly to their person—this is how I told them about time. Now they understand that first of all, the cake that they are supposed to make and write and build and grow within and without, with others and independently, –the blueprint of that cake does not exist. Meaning the suit that they are gonna travel in, the bodies that they are gonna come in with into this cake, are not available. That's how I explained it, and now they understand time.

D. So when you mentioned teleportation, is that a physical movement on Earth, or between different realities?

B. It's apparently gonna be a little bit both. From the Earth level, these are gonna work on the teleportation of objects. BUT, they're also gonna be at that time different gateways opening for the upper web to merge with this web, and in order for that to happen, the ones in the lower web, the incarnations such as Little Seth and the other ones has to be in place. And at this point, their pattern is not available, so the gates and everything are closed. Meaning there is no cake to become, at this point. But I wanted to show them how I communicate...Ophelia said I wanted to brag a little bit—and that might be.

D. Well, you should be really proud of this.

B. I am very proud.

D. It's an amazing accomplishment.

B. I said, "This is something that you can strive for, if you want to. Maybe your cherry would be something completely different." And we did not know, or at least I did not know, because if I had known this earlier, like life eleven, that this would be the cherry, you can imagine how many questions, like, "When, when, when will this happen?" So I was not told until the Coat was folded. So I told them, "It might be that the giants or those who are close to the center pole, maybe the cherry is not gonna be revealed until your person's Coat is folded." Might be. So I'm letting them see. They can hear this information, because I told them and I told Ophelia and everyone that I will not talk about too many secrets. Ophelia said if I start telling secrets, then she will put in like a curtain.

D. In comes the fog.

B. In comes the fog, a curtain, she say. I think because I do want to talk about certain things, so I think I will say farewell at this point, and they can come back in a little while. So I'm gonna put the curtain up and they can have a break back there and talk with their peers a little bit. I could see the motion behind the glass wall, it became a LOT of activity back there! Hehehe, and now their peers are left with the questions! I sort of bow out and say, "Show is over. Thank you for the applause." I do like applause.

D. You should, you've done so many wonderful things.

The Spirit Guide's Oath (Nov 21, 2019)

As we go about our daily lives, we tend to forget about our spirit guides, our companions who constantly monitor us. As Bob once said about being a guide, "It's not just a walk in the park!" It can be difficult to steer a human by popping in thought bubbles or organizing synchronicities, many of which are ignored. Guides get a share of the credit if a life is well lived, so they have a personal interest in your success. However, the incarnating soul is ultimately responsible and the one who carries the karma. From the stories Bob tells, we get a look into the very personal relationship that an incarnating soul and spirit guide share through the eons of incarnation. I think the oath Bob came up with is very endearing and shows how committed a guide is to their person.

B. Huhuh. I'm back! Separate session.

D. Welcome. You had to share the stage.

B. But Ophelia had things to say, even though I said, "What we could do is that you tell me and I tell them." But she says sometimes things get lost in translation.

D. It's nice that she gets to talk too, since she lets everyone else talk.

B. Ah, that is true, that is true. So today I am back in the church. I am back in my outfit as a priest. I have gathered spirit guides from the fifth, the sixth and the seventh—it's only the spirit guides—and I have gathered them here and my teaching for them is that they will find, occasionally, that their person might be drawn into wrong beliefs. And I'm sort of portraying that a little bit here. I have a book—and then someone said, "Is that the Earth's belief book?" And I said, "This is when it becomes tricky, because of the fact that there are several proclaiming that their book is the one of truth. And you will find that, for instance, sometimes your person will go to one region and they will be hooked on one book. And next life they are there (*nodding in another direction*) and they are hooked on another book." So what I'm trying to show them here—and this is just before I invite those who are going, so this is just a little bit of a pre-talk here—but I'm telling them about different regions and what can be expected if their soul-person heads for that specific destination. The important thing to remember is that there is an outer book, and then there is an inner book. And the spirit guides are here to somewhat learn how to trigger the inner book. There are different signs and signals we are taught how to, in some way, trigger inner truths within the soul-person. And one of them is, "What sort of senses is your person likely to be receptive to?" So, for instance, smell is HIGHLY connected to happiness, and what one can engage in is to try to—because it makes the soul-person stop, and that is what we are trying to do here. If they are off-route in somewhat of a belief system that is not beneficial AT ALL for their growth, then the spirit guides need to understand what sort of inner buttons one can press, and smell is actually one. The spirit guides here, I tell them, "Find and detect some smells that your soul-person has connected to happiness in childhood. The trick is, to make your person stop and grow, is to somewhat trigger or press the buttons that trigger childhood happiness. Because of the fact that when you are grown up there is a completely different—in many ways manufactured—happiness that doesn't really relate to soul happiness. And children have soul happiness. So we're talking about that.

D. That's really good. Give them the smell of Christmas.
B. Of a cookie, of a Christmas tree, you know, –those things. A grownup, if you send a Christmas tree smell to a grown up, either it can be like sniff–sniff, feel like childhood happiness, remembering a favorite gift one year that one got, OR it can also trigger the opposite, meaning, "Ugh, I have so much to do for Christmas. I have to do all this shopping and I have to do all this cooking and I have to travel to the relatives that I don't really like," and so forth. SO, this is the work and assignment for spirit guides; they have to somewhat identify if the Christmas tree will identify that (*nodding to the left*), childhood; or (*nodding to the right and made a blowing sound across his lips*) responsibilities and having to drive ten hours to relatives you don't like.

D. That is funny, but true.
B. So I say to them, "We have gathered here in the name of spirit in this holy church, where we learned these secret keys on how to be spirit guides to the best of our ability. Raise your hands, please." And then they do. "I, say your name, I promise and swear that I will conduct, as a spirit helper and guide for my soul person, regardless of destination, vehicle, event that my person will encounter, I promise to be non–judgmental," and you there in the back, you also need to raise your hand, everyone up, everyone raise hands, "I promise to never leave my person—". I did not take this oath before the fire, because it came after the fire. But I'm not taking any chances here because it was traumatic in many ways, not just on your level, but in my being as well. So I'm putting this in my training program, that we take an oath. So, "I promise and swear that I will always follow closely, unless it is stated beforehand that the person wants to freestyle independently. If that is the case, then I will take one step back, but I will never leave. I will still be in the vicinity, but I will step out of the shadow behind my person. I promise and swear that I will always maintain the physical, emotional, and mental wellbeing in my person, making sure that my person, in many ways, feels happiness and comfort of the journey, even though it might not be from a human perspective, very uplifting." So, we have that here.
D. That's a really good oath.
B. It's a long oath. But it's really important that they understand that they can't just change if you feel like your person is not developing in the pace that you wish it did. That's what Zachariah and Isaac said to me. He (*Isaac*) said, "You have to stick with your assignment. What if I had just left when he went berserk? He's also been in the Catholic army on different occasions, so what if I had left?" He made more of a rumble before A.D. (*Seth had several lives as a Roman soldier, some during the Roman Republic, which flourished from 500 BC to 27 BC, when the Roman Empire was established.*)
D. When you put it like that, it's easy to see how much responsibility the spirit guides have.
B. And that's what I'm trying to teach them here. And then I invite the souls that are gonna go. It's somewhat of a graduation because some are actually leaving now.

D. Are they excited or a little bit nervous?

B. They are a little bit nervous. The fifth are going first. There are a few, just a handful, from the seventh. The sixth are not going yet; not mine at least. There might be others that I'm not training. But they're not gonna get a second dimension spirit helper, so I don't know where they are. But mine here from the sixth, they're not going yet, they're waiting for a better brain. Different Coat, different brain. Little Seth said, "I'm waiting until it's like a Windows 20, and it's like a Windows 10 now."

D. It would make it a little bit easier.

B. But sometimes you can actually, after you have folded your Coat, you can in some way—and this is a secret so I'm not telling them (*the ones who are incarnating*), but I'm telling the spirit guides here, because of the fact of the malfunction of the brain at this time—I told them, "Once the Coat is folded it is possible, if you get a note from the higher councils that it is okay in this specific case, that you are indeed allowed to bring in, let's say, a Windows 12 or Windows 14 into a Windows 10 body." Since I know that, that's why I said I wanted to increase your mental a little bit. But Ophelia said, "It's not like you do it for a week, you do it normally for the whole journey." You come in with a higher level of light in the top.

Final Exams for the Spirit Guides (Dec 8, 2019)

The training for becoming a spirit guide is quite intense and thorough. Even though a guide from the second only follows one spirit, each lifetime presents its own unique challenges, since the configuration of soul and body will respond differently to the same situations or emotions. Bob tries to make solving the problems fun for the students by setting up a forest of trees whose branches light up when they give correct answers. To pass the final exam, an entire ethereal forest has to be lit up like Christmas trees.

B. There's a graduation coming up here, there are certain spirit guides here with Little Seth and everyone who have different projects or assignments that they have to have evaluated. So there is this graduation coming up shortly.

D. On the second?

B. Ah, on the second indeed. Spirit guide school, different things to master when you follow a person down to Earth, –so there are certain things you learn. It's not just playing games, but I like to mix and match so that there is not just the nose in a book. Because I learn, if I'm active. But you say, "You have to learn to be active in your mind, not just active in your being. You can be as active and mobile in your mind, probably even more, than moving around and doing things for fun." And then I say the opposite! "BUT you can also learn more if you do not just sit and stare in a book." So you laughed about that and said, "Yes, it's a fifty–fifty, Bob. Let's say it like that—you do like I do and I do like you do, and then we both advance and we both grow." I think that's why we were sort of patched up (*joined together as a team by Gergen and Jeshua*), because you were a great traveler inside and I was in the making to become, I wanted to go places and travel. If I had been paired up with this one, we would probably have had eighty–five percent travels and fifteen percent would be inner travels in the head and stillness and reflection. This one says, "Oh, I reflect! I reflect as I go." Huhuhuh. But then I tried to say that to you, "I activate my inner being, my mental capacity and stillness inside, as I go." And you said, "Seth told you that, didn't he?" So you knew that, there's no way to trick you. So anyway, it's gonna be a little bit shorter today. I was just popping by, just giving you an update on certain things.

D. What has Tom been doing? You haven't mentioned him in a while.

B. Well, he's doing the assignments, he's ready for graduation and he's been reading. He says that he wants to play more, and I said, "Now we're in the phase of self-reflection and self-study. It's better to self-study here and become accustomed to the way the giants later want you to do. Since this is a preview of self-study, it's important." And I said, "When you're gonna hang with your person, he's gonna be more reflective in nature and you are more mobile in nature; so it's a good preview to know about self-study so it doesn't become such a shock. No one told me about self-study before you did. I mean I sat and I read, but I was more of a 'what I touch, I understand' kind of guy. And you said, "Now we do differently. Now what you read is the kind of guy you are." And then I say, "We mix and match with that, so I teach you that what you touch is sometimes easier to develop an understanding of, and you teach me about self-reflection." But now I can reflect—if I want to. Tom is in his phase of reflection and self-study. And he is leaving his assignment, so we can see that certain different things can happen to a humanoid as they travel, and you want to know about what you (*the guide*) should do. The test is: This happens, and then there are several options on how that manifest to the spirit guide. And then they have to choose all of the above or just one. So you have the question, and then 1(A) is "How would it be shown to the spirit guide?", and 1(B) is "What would you do to send your communication to the humanoid doing question (A)?" And question 1(C), "What could be the end result?" So you evaluate a whole chain of occurrences.

D. That's some pretty rigorous training.

B. I did not have that training. Like I said, I learned as I went.

D. This is all of your design?

B. It's of my design. Like I said, this would have been helpful, if I had some sort of manual on how you would be. So there is a first level of questions, and then you add different Coats. So it's like their person is gonna dress in this Coat, and then they look into that same specific topic again and how that will channel. Let's say, if your person travels down in a very mental Coat and the question is, let's say about anger, then you look at mental Coat and anger: (A) "How will it channel to the spirit guide?" (B) "What would you do as a spirit guide to help your individual in the mental Coat?" And (C) "What would be the end result and how could the growth occur?" Then, question (2) "Now your person travels in an emotional Coat. How would anger reflect then?" So you build a tree of occurrences and events.

D. That's very helpful to know.

B. Ah. So I created that. I'm creating a tree, and the thing is, I work with colors so it creates a web or a tree. So let's say the question is the trunk of the tree, and then you have all these branches going out and leaves and so forth. The more correct answers they make, the leaves and the branches light up in different colors. So it's a way for them to understand. And if it doesn't light up correctly, then they have to rethink and redo. So the entire idea is to have a whole forest of lit up trees.

That is the end result, that is the end result of the graduation project.

D. Wow, that's a really good program you put together.

B. Ah, so that's what I do. But now I'm gonna go.

D. Alright, my friend. Do you want a separate session?

B. Maybe I want a separate session. Maybe Thursday.

D. We'll put that in this one's mind.

B. Put that in the head, like a snowflake in the head, see if it melts. Okay, anyway, I'm gonna go now.

D. Okay, my friend. Always a pleasure.

B. Always a pleasure. I'm gonna go and watch the trees, how they light up or color. They come in like a black and white tree, the entire assignment. They look at the Coat and the travel and the assignment, and then they solve different things. Like anger; like "What do you do if your person is not doing anything wrong, but things are done wrong TO them?" That tree is a tricky one, that's a tricky question. And "How would you know this from your person? And what if the end result is that your person becomes passive and doesn't send out things in the same way, or as clear signals as you are used to? So your person might come down and not radiate signals that you are used to your person doing because it has become passive based on circumstances around them. So how do you solve it?"

D. I would assume that is a fairly common occurrence here.

B. There are several trees here and I make them into trees of color so it becomes an instant response of right or wrong, or more work or not more work.

D. It's like a video game in the spirit world.

B. It's like a video game indeed, it's more fun like that. I'm very visual. Okay, I'm gonna go now and observe this tree program, my graduation program.

D. Alright, my friend. We'll talk soon.

B. Talk soon. Bye bye

Becoming Human is NOT the Goal (Jan 5, 2020)

This is a really informative talk about the soul and how it interacts with the body. In the beginning, in the early lives, the soul is simply learning how to navigate the physical. Later, the soul works on missions assigned to it by the Creator or councils. Since no two bodies are energetically or physically identical, body selection can help or hinder the success of the lifetime. However, over many incarnations, the soul learns to manage in any of the available forms by not fully connecting to the physical, as Bob explains. Ophelia also passed information through Bob about the 5000 and 25,000-year cycles on Earth, when different configurations of bodies existed. She also advises that the 5000-year cycle we are now in is ending. As the new cycle begins, the councils will once again alter the physical vehicles to accommodate a greater soul awareness.

D. What did you want to talk about today?

B. There's been a lot of commotion in my office, because of the fact that there are several spirit guides en route to take off. Some of them I have not trained myself, because it's not the ones from the sixth, but there are several here from the fifth, helping souls from the fifth. So, it's my spirit guides from the second that is heading to Earth with an individual from the fifth.

D. Are they committed to those through all the incarnations?

B. Indeed! Indeed! You can't just give up on them just because they're clumsy, –and I told them that. We had sort of a discussion because it felt like I kept repeating. So I said, "Let's schedule a class where we will talk about this." So I did, and more came than I expected. It has come to my notion that there are more interested in becoming a spirit guide helper for Earth. So my spirit guide program has gone viral, one might say, and there are several interested in joining.

D. Well, you give a unique teaching.

B. Ah. It's important that they understand that just because their person might not fulfill, not only its own agenda, but also the intention that the spirit guide and the soul had as they prepared for the journey—if everything seems to go down the pooper—then what can you do? And I told them that, "There will be several lives that would be considered to have gone down the pooper, so what do you do? You can't just leave your friend. You have to assist them differently depending on the journey they are going on." There are some here going down now and they're gonna assist wildlife and nature and they're gonna be of assistance to work on, –I say wildlife, but it's animal life as a whole. But it's also the fact that their person is going down for the first time, many of them, so they might just go down to be a farmer, to care for animals. I told them, "Just because you and your spirit friend have the general intent and a general idea of your whole mission, don't expect that from the first time around. Because your person needs to learn and to know how to navigate in a physical vehicle, and to co-exist in a different density and a different reality than home; and it might feel just lost. Sometimes coming down to Earth the first time, you feel lost. Other times you, depending on how much of your soul energy merges with a human personality—if the decision is made that the soul merges and blends and becomes very much a human personality—they cope much better. But if they try to—(*he struggled to find words and got frustrated, then made a spitting sound*)—they might to go directly into a purpose that is designed to happened, let's say twenty lives down the line, but if they try to do that earlier, then they might feel more lonely and separated. Because it is a fact that the first couple of lives are different, it's not necessarily to come down and do a quick thing. You have to also play the game, you have to understand karma, you have to understand boundaries, you have to understand that when you experience boundaries, it is harder to make choices. As a soul progresses, as a soul develops and has been here a couple of times, they understand that the boundaries are illusions; but in the beginning, the souls tend to become the boundaries and they can become paralyzed. BUT, if they take on a life where they merge and become more a human, rather than a soul IN a human, then they cope better, but it's not necessarily influencing the mission as a whole. (*He is saying that if the soul blends and becomes more human, it usually doesn't work on the soul purpose during that life.*) So sometime if someone comes down and has had a rough path, taken on several assignments and been sort of bruised through life, they can come down and they can become a human. It means that the soul blends into the human personality and becomes a human. Otherwise, you normally come in and you are a soul IN a human. BUT, example one: If you had a bumpy path, you are bruised by several lives in the past, then you can come down and simply sort of have a bonus life. You become a human and merge into a human personality. Meaning that you experience and you learn, but you do not become bruised and you don't necessarily have a lot of progress on your soul development, but you experience—it's like taking a breath, but you still incarnate. Otherwise, example two: When you see those who simply are acting human and you see the soul is very little active, it's not a soul in a human experience, it's a human experience not aware of a soul, then that's when you see things that is considered a lack of development. Meaning grabbing, what we see when you are in conflict. Those who have a tendency for conflict, they rarely—unless they are a mole—have a soul awareness; they are becoming the vehicle, they become the human. Meaning, if we say that the vehicle itself that we are changing, at this point a soul can come in and it can become a human—meaning soul mission, soul awareness, is very dimmed. As we change the container of the human, it's less able to become a human, it will act more directly from soul. It's like making your skin thinner. Now the skin is kinda thick, meaning the soul comes in and it feels heavy in this straightjacket and it becomes the straitjacket, it becomes the human, and it acts as a human. It acts as a primitive entity that has lack of awareness from emotional, mental, or spiritual source.

D. So when the souls come in that act more from a soul awareness—

B. They don't go into conflict. They feel a need to teach others rather than holding beliefs and holding understandings and teachings. SO, you can see like a priest, they can be more of a human than a soul in a human, because they proclaim to hold the truth, to hold the path to light. And if you are acting from a soul perspective, then you simply share, you do not proclaim to possess anything. That's one example. Another example is conflicts. Those who constantly seek to overthrow others and to constantly shout out in their trumpet that they are under attack, then they are not acting from soul in human. There are those, I would say—Ophelia says here, "Don't forget the moles"—and the moles are in there and act similar as the ones that are more human. It's like the soul doesn't attach. When the soul comes in, regardless of how much soul energy, how much percentage the soul brings, it can have an easier or harder way to connect to the physical. Those who simply are (*makes a sucking sound*) sucked in to physical, those are the ones that become a human, and the soul isn't very present. But if a soul has a little bit distance—and this might contradict what you think—but if a soul has a little bit of distance and is not fully connected, then it is less human. Let's say you can connect with a thousand dots in a human body, a soul comes in and, regardless of how much percentage you bring, you can connect with a thousand dots, a soul who is connecting with let's say 995 dots, it becomes a human. It has not been here that much because it just becomes the play, it becomes the container, it becomes the vehicle that it is traveling in. BUT if a soul, after coming here a while, it understands that it can operate the vehicle as good and as productive if it's not fully connected to the body, so it connects with let's say 500 or less. Like you, for instance, you have only connected with about 17 dots, and that is why you come and leave a little bit. It gives you the perspective of a human experience—and that is when a soul has been here for a little bit—it doesn't fully connect and BECOME a human; it steers the human and it observes the human activity that it is doing itself or the surrounding humans around them, and they can navigate differently. But if a soul is just sort of sucked into and becomes the skin, so to speak, it is somewhat locked and it has less ability to operate and do changes as it was intended to.

D. That actually makes sense to me.

B. It doesn't have a soul perspective because it has merged into the human perspective. And then it simply has the human perspective, and that is quite primitive. So it has a tendency to constantly feel attacked, to constantly feel a need to be above others, to constantly have a need of like, "This is my plate, I eat this, you don't take my food." So it has a different personality at play. And that's what I said to these spirit guides, "You might see sometimes that your friend is becoming a human."

D. That would make them sad.

B. And if it's sucked into the skin, sucked in metaphorically, into the human personality and the human play and the game around them, then that's what you see when there are all these different conflicts, for instance, or those who proclaim to possess the truth and the path to the light.

D. I have a question then. Is that connection determined before the soul comes in?
B. It happens. In the beginning it happens, and that is what I'm trying to tell my spirit guides here that, "As the soul transitions through the fourth reality into the third reality, becoming a human, some of the intentions become lost. It's beyond the soul and the spirit guide, sometimes there are councils that are involved. If they want to see how a lot of riots impact a reality, they can make the fourth reality, where souls transition, different." Meaning that when a soul goes through the fourth reality and transforms into human body, the way it transitions is different. So councils can change the fourth reality; meaning that, let's say a hundred souls are going down, and if the Creator and the councils want to see how riots, for instance, or other events impact the humanoid, then they can change this path where souls travel as they enter a physical body. Meaning that as they come in, if the design itself is to make them more dimmed, more becoming a human—unless they are a mole and they don't have a Coat, they are told—but those who have Coats, they are not told, they simply are becoming part of the game that the Creator intentionally wants to see how the design unfolds.
D. So do they actually change the Coat on the way in, or is it something else that is changed?
B. Coats are similar, they are the same, but they change the conditions of how the Coat unfolds.
D. That would seem to impose a heavy karmic burden on some souls, wouldn't it?
B. Not necessarily on souls. The karmic burden that you talk about is Earth-based events. Let's say the Creator and the councils want to trigger prior karmic events, that you said is like a heavy burden, then the entrance from the spirit realm into the fourth reality and how they transition into body will change, because the fourth reality has changed. Meaning the Coats, even if they hold the same experience and karma for that specific soul, as it becomes a humanoid it operates differently. What we have seen, for instance, there is a lot of those acting as humans, meaning a tendency of conflict. So my idea—and I'm not in that council—but my idea here is to change that, because there were times when there were not conflicts at all, so it seems to have gone backwards in the

evolution. I talked to Ophelia about that and I talked to you about that, and you said there was a prior cycle that was indicating (*that caused*) a karmic debt, and that is the game that is going on at this time. Meaning that for certain souls that come in, it's harder for them, because even if they have the same Coat as other souls, the way the Coat manifests in the reality as it becomes a humanoid is different. So!

D. That's fairly complicated.

B. Ah, it's complicated. It's a grand design behind everything. Ophelia says that the councils and the Creator, based on what they want to observe, evolve, release and so forth, they change the transition in the fourth reality. But they don't change the Coats. Ophelia showed me that the fourth reality, coming from spirit realm into the Earth, it takes longer. It means that it feels heavier for the soul to dress in its Coat and come to Earth. That is why a lot of souls say that they don't really feel like coming. When there is a huge enlightenment, when there are mainly humanoids acting from soul level and not human level, then the transition is simply like falling through, gliding through.

D. That's why they say sometimes the Earth is closer to the spiritual dimensions, and sometimes further away?

B. Indeed, indeed. And at this point, the soul, as it leaves the spirit realm and moves into its Coat, it feels resistance. And it's because of the game and the play going on at Earth at this time, and some of the Coats will simply become human and some older souls will struggle because they still can feel the atmosphere that is different at this time on Earth. So even if they are with or without a Coat, older souls can feel like it is harder to navigate on Earth because of the atmosphere in general is different. As a soul comes in and, let's say, the cycle going on on Earth is very spiritually heightened, then as a soul transitions, it just falls through. It mirrors and it affects the soul's wellbeing differently, and that's the first time it can get a sense of the journey itself. As it becomes in the third reality, it simply becomes and is part of the game.

D. Is this a fairly brief cycle, like a 5000-year cycle or another cycle?

B. Ah, this is part of the 25,000-year cycle, Ophelia says. And then there are smaller cycles. But in general things go in a 25,000-year cycles, in human ways of thinking of things. But then there are smaller cycles. So at this point, the 5000-year cycle that you are in the end of at this time, it started like 3000 BC, so you are here in the end and you have the ability to move into a new cycle where souls might feel differently coming here. It might feel more engaged in the play. So you can see there are several conditions that impacts a soul coming in. And that's what I talk about with the spirit guides here, "You are in the transition. Some will experience and some will become a human being and will struggle a little bit to connect to soul. But you are in that change where we are moving into more of a healing phase." What we left behind was in some way how to balance progress and still be humble; that was a part of the last 5000-year cycle. And it's gone a little bit…

D. Sideways?

B. Sideways, you know. We'll see if this cycle becomes longer. It's not 5000 and then a new one, but you are in the end where you have the ability, you have all the knowledge, you have all the experiences from this little 5000-year cycle, along with the bigger 25,000-year cycle, and you have the ability to move into a new 5000-year cycle which will indicate healing, self-healing, and sharing. But you can see that there are resistance of those who are humanoids who feel like, and that's what that feeling is, that they feel like they are under attack, that they're gonna die. They don't understand that there is no death, there's just transition into another way of existing. And that's what they are fighting against and that is why they constantly proclaim, "Oh, this is mine!" or, "You said something stupid to me; I'm gonna punch you in the nose," and then the other one says, "No I did not; I'm gonna punch YOU in the nose." And then it just goes back and forth. As long as we see punching in the nose—it's actually a human feeling of, that it's about to wither and to cease to exist. (*The source of conflict is related to that fear.*) What they don't understand is that they will constantly exist, but they will exist in a new shape and form. But those who are very much human, they don't understand, they just see it like they will be extinct. Those who are connected to soul, they see the possibility that lies in transformation. So, that was it!

D. That was a good talk! Because souls come here over a long period of time, they get to come in when it's pretty easy and then they get the harder cycles?

B. Indeed. And they have to go through all these—it's like going through seasons, like, "Oh, summer is fun!" Then, fall is okay. But then comes the hard winter! What do you do then? It's the same thing, the seasons actually mirror soul development in many ways. That's why a soul sometimes can be a little bit confused if they are in a climate where there are no seasons, where everything is the same, because you are designed within you, your soul energy and your soul being, is designed to understand cycles. And seasons like spring, summer, fall, winter indicates those times where you can be at your peak, and you can be reflective, and you can go into hibernation, and then you blossom again—but what do you want to blossom as? And this specific teaching here with the 5000-year cycle, you are in winter. But what sort of spring do you want to be?

D. When the Council of Nine was talking about the waves that move through our fish tank, when we move into different cycles within our Universe, is this like a little cycle within the bigger cycle?

B. (*Sounding perplexed*) What do you mean?

D. (*I was laughing at the way he responded.*)

B. You're confusing. Now you're a human. Okay, Lasaray, tell me what you wanna know. Say what you want to know, Lasaray.

D. You're funny! They talk about the entire universe going up and and down in cycles, like waves on an ocean, where a galaxy will have more enlightened times, and then will descend into a canyon, where it is more separated from Source. Are we in the bottom of a canyon now?

B. Ah, ah. And you are in that winter, where you have to somewhat transform into blossoming again. So the whole system goes through cycles; the humanoid goes through cycles, the Earth goes through cycles, the incarnation program goes through cycles, goes through seasons. And at this point, Ophelia says, systems, incarnations, Earth, everything is in that phase of winter, and you have the ability now, you have to want and intuitively know, that you are heading for spring.

D. Okay. I'll take that.

B. Ah, well, you kinda have to. Huhuhuh. That was my talk today. I'm gonna take off now, but I wanted to tell you that there has been a little bit of commotion among the spirit guides in the group here. Because of the fact that I told them about what we're doing a little bit here (*channeling his communications*), and then they got way ahead of themselves and said, "Oh, that sounds great!" And I said, "It was a lot of different things, before. Some things were like him being down there digging holes, being a farmer, –but it served a purpose. It served him to understand the human game and the soul game within the human game. So everything has a purpose, and eventually it will lead to a cherry life." But some of them wanted go straight in and fix things.

D. That's understandable. How many little spirits do you have that you are working with?

B. Well, these are spirit guides that are gonna go with the fifth, and some are gonna go with souls from the seventh, but it became a group of 25. It's a lot of noise so I said, "Everyone will get their voice heard—one at a time!" And then we talked about a topic and then suddenly it became a rumble in the group and everyone had follow-up questions, so it wasn't like they had a question and I answered it and that was the end of it, –it resulted in follow-up questions. Which is very much like I am, so I can't complain too much. So that was my talk today and I'm gonna go now, Ophelia says, "Saving energy."

D. Wonderful. I really appreciate it, that was a good talk.

B. Okay. I'll be back. La la la la la la laaaaa. Du du du du! That was my farewell tune! Until next time, show to be continued.

D. (*Laughing*) Alright, my friend. I'll see you Thursday.

B. Curtain down, and scene.

D. And cut!

B. Hehehe. Okay I'll go. Ophelia says I'm just creating more words so I can be longer on stage! That's what she says.

D. We like that too.

B. Okay, okay, I'll come. I actually have things to do, so off I go. Bye bye.

What Happens on Earth, Stays on Earth (Jan 23, 2020)

Sometimes the spirits give previews of what Earth will be like in the future, and this is one of those sessions. As you may recall,

Bob is Tom's mentor. Tom was paired up with a little Elahim, who is referred to in this session as Tom's person. Tom's person has been assigned (by the Creator and the higher councils) to contribute advanced knowledge to the field of physics and develop teleportation. In ancient times, the visitors used what we call teleportation to move giant blocks of stone. My understanding, based on information given to date, is that visitors altered the frequency of the energetic structure of a stone to match a parallel reality. The object would disappear, or partially disappear, from our visible reality as elemental particles shifted into an adjacent frequency. As particles moved across the barrier, they were no longer affected by the Earth's gravity, so it became lighter and lighter or disappeared altogether. It was then moved within the parallel reality to a desired location. When energy was withdrawn, the molecular structure shifts and rematerializes in our dimension once again. Assuming the councils give this knowledge to the next cycle of humans, the future societies will be unrecognizable to us. Throughout Earth's history, there have been great civilizations that existed simultaneously with the most rudimentary hominoids. Even today, we have particle colliders in some regions, and mud huts in another. If future archaeologists dig around in parts of Africa or the Middle East and discover a 20th century village, they may errantly assume all modern humans are equally primitive. This same myopia prevails among the mainstream archaeologists of today. Great stone structures stand as evidence of lost societies that once flourished, but science turns a blind eye to the obvious.

In this talk, Bob refers to blue dots and yellow dots. He was shown a map of Earth with different colored dots at various locations. The dots represented the type of journey Lasaray made. Blue dots were manifestations, such as the Anunnaki. Then there were different colors for incarnations, depending on the purpose of the life. Yellow dots were when Lasaray came to collect information for the councils or to help another soul on their mission. Bob was only present and knew about the incarnations, so he was not very pleased to learn that Lasaray had traveled to Earth without him.

> B. Thank you! I'm always the one on the waiting end. Everyone else is sort of going (*looks to the left*)...oh, that's not true, Ophelia says. I was gonna say everyone else is going about their day and then I have to wait until they schedule me in, but that's not true, Ophelia says. She says we work around my schedule a lot, that's what she said. So she poked me and

she did this (*he raised an index finger and waved it back and forth*). Hehehehe.
D. Oh, you got the finger!
B. A little bit, but with a smile.
D. Not a stern look.
B. No, never that, never that. But what I have been occupied with, in the absence of my presence and speech (*since he didn't get to talk the previous session*), I have been indeed putting in some great and extra effort for the training of the spirit guides with Tom and the other ones going with the sixth. BUT there was an interference in the group, as the mission itself, in some way, came up as a debate. And they must have been, the little Elahims, must have been going and training somewhere and been looking into different realities and different fish tanks. And apparently, it came to my knowledge, that some of them were interested in going to Siah's world instead.
D. Oh, really? Just for training?
B. Not to go as an incarnation, because I said that's not possible. But they said they would like to go there on a field trip. And then I remembered, in the back of my mind, so to speak, that there was a lot of preparations for me to go there. There was the bubble training, which was not easy. Floating in the tanks, not easy. Having the suit shrink fitted to my being, not easy. So I said there was a little bit of preparation—it wasn't done in a day! Rome was not built in a day. Huhuh. That's what I said. BUT what I did acknowledge is that there is an eagerness to make oneself useful, and they feel like there is a lot of preparation before high action. So we are looking into different scenarios, we are observing on big screens what takes place at this time in certain locations. The sixth, these are different, the souls from the sixth, the Elahims and other ones, they are looking into more of the political scene. And they are investigating and analyzing behaviors and the way certain decisions are made, and they are analyzing the interactions between minds. Because of the fact that they are gonna go down and they're gonna interfere and blend with the communications. Some communication will be mind-to-mind, so to speak, and some will be communication where there is a transportation device involved. Tom's friend here is gonna be—I should tell you that the souls from the sixth have

gone into specialist training, each and every one of them—and Tom's person is gonna be an inventor, he's gonna be similar like when you (*Lasaray*) were (*he names an electrical inventor born in the mid 1800's*), similar like that. He's gonna invent a transportation device, and he's gonna be working a lot underground in a facility that moves objects. First of all, they're gonna try to move certain elements like protons and electrons across boundaries of physics. And after that, he's gonna create a device that is gonna be able to—and this is long term! I told him, don't expect this to happen in the first life because you also have to be involved in the karma program, so it's not just coming down and doing all these goodies with all these high-end transportation gadgets and devices and so forth. I said, "Look at Lasaray, it took a long time." It was different with you because you came down and your first couple of lives—and I had to tell them this so they are aware of the general intent and progress and cycles on Earth—I said, "Lasaray came down, he was somewhat clumsy, he did not understand fire." And I had to show this, I had to show the misdemeanor from you and the misdemeanor from me. I said, "We're gonna watch something that might be a little bit emotional and a little bit scary, but just know and see that the outcome continued, and it was no disaster. Disasters are left on Earth. Remember that, people. As you go to Earth, all disasters are left on Earth. What you do on Earth, remains on Earth." Huhuh. It's like saying, "What goes on in Vegas, stays in Vegas!" Huhuhuh. It's similar like that. So I said—and I cannot involve the blue dots (*the manifested visits to Earth*) here because that would be confusing overall, so I'm only talking about when I was present—I said, "First he came down, he was clumsy, he did not understand fire. You can see here on this screen." (*He showed them the scene of my being burnt up in a very early incarnation.*) And Tom said, "Where were you?" And I said, "Camera, swipe to the right a little bit." And the camera moved to the right a little bit, and we saw my back, deep into the underbrush. "I was not only, it appeared—as we can see on this film—it was not only that I appeared to find a flower, I actually also was communicating with the underbrush and I was actually also sitting down and having somewhat a little bit of a nap." So I said, "What we can see here, as an example, is where there is a disconnect between soul and spirit guide. BUT, there was no hard feelings. So what you can see here, if we look at Lasaray here near the fire, does he seem and appear very intelligent and capable of creating a device that will cross the laws of physics? HUH HUH HUH, he can't even sit near the fire! How would he be able to cross the laws of physics? Huhuh!" So I said, "Inside he was quite capable, but dressed in the humanoid he became paralyzed. So you have to be aware that even though your person is quite capable and fully trained and equipped to create certain outcomes and new devices and new ideas, it might not come to term, it might not come to term as they are dressed in a humanoid. So Lasaray and I had a beginning that was a little bit rough and it was a bit rocky in the start between the two of us, but you can see that everyone is happy and motion continued and progress continued as well." But then I showed the timeline and I said, "So that was there (*indicating the beginning*) and then he came down and we were having lives in the North African region, and we also had lives in the Middle East region that was QUITE DIFFERENT at that time. I said, "We had a peak when it came to understanding, a peak of scientific knowledge. Then he picked lives where he was a scientist or an astronomer, predominantly. (*Several waves of civilizations have existed in prehistory, when the humanoids were much more intelligent and spiritual than the occupants presently found in those regions.*) So we can see there, it wasn't that big of a gap from the fire person to this heightened awareness and quite skilled individual. But then, look here, there is a long empty gap where Lasaray was simply a farmer. And why would he do that, one might wonder? Because those lives are merely like the yellow dots, when you come down and help someone else come down and achieve, or rise, or address their Coat." So there was a lot of lives where he just came down to observe—and he was interested, on the behalf of Ophelia, to investigate agriculture and the ley lines and the energetic web underneath. So even though he looked like a simple farmer, SOMETIMES inside he was investigating the grid and how to be the best farmer and the best one in agriculture. (*Bob whispered that revelation with an air of great mystery.*) So I said, "It's not just to come down briefly and do a quick thing, and then go home and think, 'Oh, now I go and play with Siah and be with all sorts of high awareness and love and compassion.' That's not what we're training you for."

So to Tom's person I said, "If we take you as an example, and I'm not saying that you're going to burn," –because they were concerned–, so I said, "it's not likely that you will. But if you do, just know that the suffering and the surprise effect, one might say, remains on Earth, and then everyone is fine after that. There are certain surprise effects that one cannot navigate around, and that's why they have spirit guides." So he's gonna come down and Tom is gonna assist. He's gonna come down and he's gonna create this (*technology*) that will EVENTUALLY carry the possibility to cross space and time. That is the end result of that mission. But I said, "Similar like Lasaray came down," and we also had the blue dots that I don't talk about but I said, "he had very enlightened lives early on, and then some lives where he did not do much, –that one could perceive from the outside. But as a spirit guide, you will detect that there is indeed an undercover mission going on, even if he appears to just be a farmer. So don't be fooled by the physical appearance. When the spirits go down, the spirit guide has to accompany, it's a pair." And I said, "It becomes much more fun when you prepare for a life that you also compare notes, use what kind of clothes they will wear, and the personality," (*The spirit guides will dress and act like their person on Earth.*) Even the spirit guide can mix and match with the personality and become a human personality; meaning that they have easier access to their person if they somewhat mirror a human person. I said, "In order for you to somewhat stand out in the spirit guide crowd—because your spirits friends are gonna go down, and they're gonna have more spirit guides—and if you want to stand out, dress like a human. Mirror the life." (*Bob says he will often wear the same type of clothing as my incarnation. So when I was a farmer wearing overalls, Bob would follow me around wearing bib-pants, as he calls them.*)

D. Well the second follows a lot closer than the other guides do, don't they?

B. They do, they do. And it's different because they also have the physical wellbeing to attend to and maintain and make sure that scratches and so forth heal as best as possible. What we also do when you sleep, we actually move you around in the bed, make sure you are rolled over correctly so that you don't get—because there is a problem sometimes when the soul leaves, when it dreams, the physical is just left there like a box, and what we make sure is that even though the spirit friend is out and about, we also make sure the physical rolls a little bit. If it doesn't move, it can change and it can interfere with the process of returning, one can say. So we take care of the physical, that's what we do.

D. If someone doesn't have a guide from the second, do they not get as much attention?

B. There are different ways, but what we normally do is that we make sure that the physical rolls a little bit when our person sleeps and is off investigating other realities. And it is also to make sure that the physical, the box, is an easy access when your soul friend returns. So when you return I make sure—it's just to maintain the box.

D. Do you ever travel with me when I sleep? Do we go places?

B. Yes, I do. But you might think that I stand there—I heard you say that, that you think I stand there next to the bed and then we take off. But that's not true. I always also remain and make sure that I roll you. Since you like mathematics and percentages and so forth, I always remain with at least five percent next to the physical, making sure that it's suitable for you to return. I work on the physical being also, even though you and I take off and we explore things. But sometimes it's actually been that you say that you have places to go when you sleep and you ask me to just remain by the body, –and I do. So I maintain and I sort of look into the organs and so forth, that everything is alright. I have a little trick; I actually have my little tissue that I investigate you with. And it's easy to do that when you sleep. (*He described the tissue as something he used at the 4–H farm on the second. I can only guess it is like a little square of energetic filaments that allows for a high– resolution view of internal organs, like a spiritual x-ray.*)

D. You've been a really good friend. I appreciate all the attention you give me.

B. We have to be like the first–aid, one can say. I said that to Tom and the other ones, "Always know that in some way, you have to be the first–aid." I did not get that memo in the fire episode, but in general, that's what we do. But each of the six coming down are specialized in different fields. The one that Tom goes with, he's gonna be very much with transportation, he's gonna be a physicist. They're all like MIT Ph.Dee–Dee–Dee–Dee–Dee–D's. They're all very intelligent. But I said, "Don't be surprised if they delete some of it when they go down, it's highly likely. It's not likely that you're gonna have this bright brain in the humanoid; it might explode or implode. I don't know which is worse." I have to say that to them. But Little Seth, he's gonna come down and he's gonna do some rumbling in politics, and he's gonna be placed in a couple of lives, it seems, in the decision room. He is not—after we've been looking at these documentaries, he is not, –how can one say-, he is not thrilled or excited, he is not pleasantly surprised about what he sees.

D. About humans and the conditions here?

B. In the politician room. He feels he is not impressed, that's what he says, "I'm not impressed", that's the word he used. I said, "No. No, that is true. But also know, Ophelia said that some are moles." Then he said, "I'm not gonna be a mole; I'm gonna be quite visible and there is gonna be someone who is gonna be quite impressed about the changes that's gonna come." And again, I said, "Just rest assured and understand that when you come down, you can have all the intention and you can see quite clearly, but it's not always that easy." Like Seth Senior (*Christine's higher self*), he had similar intentions to come down and awaken the mind—not in politics, he never liked that—he felt like it was too slow. That's what this one said! I'm not doing politics, it's too slow. He never wanted to be like a lawyer. He laughs at that, he said they just go back and forth—it's not like council work at all—so he's not doing that. He came down to ignite the minds to understand the divine connection and also to pay tribute to the stars and the knowledge from the stars. He wanted people to raise their vision and have a bigger understanding of their place and understand their connection to the stars. And this one, he made the rumble in the churches, huhuh. I said to Seth Junior, "You might wanna go and talk to Seth Senior because there were rumbles, and it might be that, if you step on someone's toes in these halls of hierarchy, the life might end abruptly and it might not be as productive as you intended it to be." So we're looking at that, but his idea is to come down and he wants to change the games of policies—not only politics—but the games and the laws. He wants to come down and do some adjustments, he says, to execute an order in a way that is not so complicated. He said, "I see here a great idea comes forward to the table, but then it has to go like this," (*Bob motions to the left and then right*) "zigzag back and forth between individuals that are, first of all, not capable," he said, "I see that they are not quite skilled. And Because they're not skilled, they don't know how to evaluate and they have no idea and ability to add an enlightened comment about the idea that is put on the table." So he can see that and he said, "I can see that there is a long, endless process before it comes about." So he wants to change and make a rumble, and he wants to delete, actually. He said, "There are too many eyes, too many minds, and the minds are not equipped." Huhuh huh huh. I said, "Is that what you're gonna say, 'I'm deleting you, you're not equipped?'" So I said, "What we could do, to make it more heartfelt and not so intense, you could do the singing chair game. (*He's referring to the game of musical chairs.*) And then say it's a game, we're gonna make changes in the decision room and the halls of politics, –there are too many involved." He said, "There are too many. It takes forever for one idea to reach the end line." He says, "Delete." He just meant if we delete some of the eyes, some of the minds, then we are on a good way to make it a more progressive and efficient process.

D. Can't argue with that.

B. Nay. So that's what he's gonna do. The other ones, some are gonna work on satellite communications, and some are gonna be similar like working at NASA. But there is quite a lot of communication agendas throughout in this group.

D. Have you gotten a glimpse of what the future is going to look like?

B. Ah. A little bit here because—it's not a wipeout, I'm not saying that—but there's gonna be changes. It's gonna come to an end, –I'm talking here about Little Seth's journey. We are looking at the films of so–called progress in the decision rooms in government, and as we can see, it's too heavy. It's like when we tell you not to overeat because when your physical becomes heavy, you can't hear your spirit. It's the same here, the government is too heavy, so they can't even acknowledge a good idea because they just eat it. It just goes back and forth and then burps it up, back and forth. So when it comes to the end line, it's completely chewed up or completely modified, and the great intention from the beginning is almost lost. And he can see that, and he said, "It's like putting down like a nice big sandwich, and that sandwich, everybody's gonna take a bite of the sandwich and when the one at the end of the table who's gonna be the one making the idea go, when that amazing sandwich comes to the end, it's just like a dry piece of bread because everyone has taken a piece and chewed it. And the intention what was sent off in the beginning from idea number one, as all these people take a bite of it and nibble on it, when it comes to the end, it doesn't look like that great idea or that great sandwich, it's just like a piece of dry bread." Then that one says, "What is this? How great is this?" And the problem is that the one from the idea to the one who executes the idea, they can't really fully communicate, because if you see it as a long table, then you have all these eaters—they are eaters, that's what we call them because they don't add anything to the sandwich. They just eat and they are quite hungry, it seems. They actually just want to be fed, it's like a physical person who overeats food, it's the same tendency here. They just are there to nibble and eat, they're not there to add.

D. Useless eaters.

B. Useless eaters. And that makes it hard for those who sit down on the short side of the table, the idea end, to make themselves heard to the other ones on the other end, who is the executor of the idea. So what we want to do here is, we need to delete, Little Seth said, we need to delete the eaters.

D. I can think of a lot of ways to do that.

B. Well, we're probably gonna do something else here, he said. He has ideas on how to just delete the eaters, because the eaters are actually only there to be in the presence of power, and that's what an eater is. It's not there to cook! It's just there to eat! He said, "If they were cooks, then they would improve the sandwich as it is traveling over the table; but an eater just sees and grabs and takes out, like, 'Oh, that's a nice meatball, I'll take that.' And then the other ones become a little bit grumpy and says, 'Oh, why did you take the last meatball?'" So the eaters are just focusing on getting fed on this great idea. (*Bob's way of saying there are many bureaucrats and politicians who hijack or block good ideas out of self-interest. Most are bribed to protect the financial interests of various corporations, to whom they owe allegiance.*) It's too heavy, so we need to delete the eaters, and if we can exchange them with cooks, then that would be good. A cook would indicate someone who is analyzing the sandwich and say, "Hmm, I might add a little bit of mustard to this, or a little bit of another flavor, and see if that might work." However, too many cooks—it's not just to take away the eater and exchange them with a cook—because too many cooks is a problem by itself. And I said that to Little Seth, "Too many cooks is not gonna work. Because they are like the scientists, a little bit, they have great pride with their recipes. So if someone says, "Oh, I don't like mustard." Then there's gonna be all sorts of going back and forth with that and they are more identified, like with the puzzle pieces, with their recipes and their dish. So, in some way, it's not a good idea to take away the eaters and put in a cook. What we're looking at here, and what he is investigating is a complete remodel of government. He said, "It's too heavy, it's too clumsy." He's gonna try to mirror council work, and he has been going in training with Zachariah and Jeshua, to look into council work and the structure of councils. (*When Bob mentions puzzle pieces, he was referencing a story he told two and a half years earlier about scientists who develop a theory and then refuse to release it, even in the face of evidence that invalidates their idea. It still fascinates me they remember, with unerring precision, everything they tell us.*)

D. Kind of makes me think that monarchies, where there was just a king making decisions, wasn't so bad?

B. Ah, nah. It's actually not that bad. If they had a small group of advisors, like the knights around the round table, that sort of thing. That's how council work is, you rarely see a council that are more than 13 around the table, –and you should know that. Your council work, government, is highly overcrowded. There's no need to be that many because they just feed; they're eaters and they're feeders and the ideas just get lost. So that's what we've been doing. I've been talking to them about that. And there have been concerns about when and where to come down. And some are indeed trying to come down earlier because of the fact that it's sort of escalating into a–, I'm talking here about Little Seth, he might come down earlier than intended.

D. When you say earlier, is that like in the next one or two hundred years?

B. Ah, ah. He has placed his own idea at some council somewhere through his peer, and they are looking into that because he feels like if it doesn't come to a stop, if it doesn't come to a change, there might become more eaters.

D. Since you can see what is going to happen here, a little bit, is the Earth's population going to decrease significantly?

B. It's gonna shift, like move.

D. From where to where?

B. It's like a rotation that goes on, it's gonna be that more move— it's gonna be a little bit too hot below the equator—and it's gonna make that more wants to move up. It's not like just here (*in the U.S.*) or in Europe, it's in general that they wanna move up.

D. That's going to be a problem, because most of them harbor ideas and beliefs that predate and are irreconcilable with western societies.

B. Ah, we'll see about that. But what we are looking at is from the sixth, and a lot of the other concerns about movement of humanoids is being looked into by councils, looking into by Earth councils—Zachariah, he goes to those councils. We've never gone and you never talk about that, so you don't seem to go. But Zachariah, he has several chairs, several council chairs.

D. Is that on the fifth, the ones you are talking about?

B. On the fifth, indeed. And those councils are looking into the general movement of humanoids, and what we can see is that there is—and this is not the first time—it's a rotation, a circulation of where humanoids want to set tent. And because you are more here at this time than before, it becomes a turmoil, and that's what the Earth councils are looking into.

D. The multicultural and multiracial invasion will destroy what's left of the Western world, because we're greatly outnumbered.

B. Oh, well, but the white ones are sitting by the eating table. It's not necessarily a really good idea to mix and match because they are not souls, they're humans. If they were just different souls, not hindered by the conditions from the human activity, then it would have been a greater empathy and understanding to help those who are a little bit left behind.

But as it is channeled through somewhat of an ignorance on both sides, just different ignorance, the rotation is likely to end with conflict. We're not gonna talk more about that, but just know that earlier civilizations, you said, when you were here in a blue dot experience and you were only here to observe, it was actually the opposite. Then everyone tried to flee from the northern part of the equator and headed south. So just know there is a little bit of karma here. Those who were on the northern side invaded the southern side and at that time it was—the difference being that the intellect was less developed in those from the north, whereas it was very many on the southern side that were from the seventh and lacked ignorance, and they knew how to take care of those coming from the north. The problem being, if we flip it, it is the same ignorance in motion now from south, moving north. There are winds of interests, but those on the northern side are not similar to Ophelia. The wind, and that is what we also see here in the government with the eaters, they feed that wind of fear; it was different earlier. But just know that this circulation, this motion and movement of humanoids, has existed before. So that will be it today, we're making it a little bit short for this one. But I wanted to pop by and I wanted to tell you about certain occurrences that take place in my school. I have my school and I'm proud to say that we are moving ahead. I'm delivering treats, I'm delivering medals because I know that that some feel happy of their achievement.

D. It's nice that you remembered to do that for your students.

B. Ah. So I do that. What we are preparing at the moment, because we have had several very loud discussions here, high and low I must say, but I have been given word from the peers that they want their students to now move into self-study. They have been bombarded with information, now it has to land.

D. Is it on both sides, your students and the ones from the sixth?

B. Indeed, indeed. Because it's gonna be a division a little bit, there's gonna be less interactions between the groups here because of the fact that both sides need to contemplate. And I'm looking into Tom because I'm pretty sure he might react like I did, with complete confusion about what's going on, and maybe he will feel like he is in exile, like I did. I felt like I was in those cells in the bottom of a prison where they have the isolation cells (*solitary confinement*).

D. Where is he going to do his self-study?

B. Oh, I have a room prepared on the second. It is secluded. He's gonna feel like he is in exile, all of them will. We're moving beyond group activity, we're moving into self-exploring, self-achieving and self-becoming. As we are leaving the self-study, they will have become self-sufficient, more focused—which is what I want.

D. You're a good teacher!

B. I am indeed. So I'm doing that, but the problem is, I'm gonna focus here on the spirit guides on the second, and I'm pretty sure that they're gonna feel like they are all in exile and deserted. I felt like I was—my first response when you taught me to self-study was that I was punished. And I want to make sure that they understand it's not a punishment. It's a way to rise to greatness.

D. That's wonderful. I really appreciate everything you told us today. It's always fascinating to hear what's going on. So thank you.

B. Just know that this whole movement of people, it serves an understanding for the Creator on how to address the moving forward with either increasing or decreasing the population. So you have to look into what happens when less development or ignorance meets those who have more but are in some way drilled to be on a survival mode. It's the wind, and the wind comes from those centers, those Cells, it's a big wind machine, making like a wind in the area of London, and at this point there is a big wind machine on the East coast here in Washington and New York. Those two are in some way intertwined, but the New York one is—even though the government is placed in Washington, you should know that the Cell and the wind machine and the decisions are actually in the high-rise buildings in New York. In some way it is to remove focus from oneself, to put the decisions of government in a location a little further away. So everyone is like, "Oh, look at Washington, look at what they're doing in government." But the wind machine and the Cell up in the high-rise buildings around that green dot, the greenery park (*Central Park*), they are actually the ones that are running the whole show.

D. The interrelated tribe of international bankers, globalists and elitists.
B. So we need to somewhat—Little Seth said we should unplug the wind machines! We're gonna talk more about that, but I'm gonna go now.
D. Alright, my friend. It's always a joy and a pleasure to hear you.
B. When you go to sleep, just know that I sort of massage your body. And you should also know that a spirit guide, such as myself, we do not just sort of roll you in the bed to make sure you don't become numb and make it easier for you to return when you sleep. I do that for you, I massage your organs.
D. Huh! Thank you so much for that.
B. I do that. It's an energetic connection, it's not me putting my hands inside you, but I look with my little tissue what organs need to be a little bit more attended to, like with massage, and then I focus all my energy, I channel my focus and I massage it with my mind.
D. Is there anything I need to work on to help?
B. No. But I'm massaging at the moment your liver, I'm massaging your kidneys, and I'm doing that with my mind. I'm warming them up.
D. Thank you for that.
B. Ah. You don't want to have them cold, so I'm rubbing them with my mind, that's what we do. As a healer you use your mind and you focus on whatever you want to heal. Either like me standing next to you, working on your physical, or you can also do that by focusing on something—like Australia, an animal, a region, or a tree. You focus on it and in your mind, you rub it. That is healing, that is how you do distance healing.
D. That's really good advice. Thank you for that.
B. Ah. So I'm gonna go now. Turn off the wind machines! Then leave the eaters and soon you will see there is nothing to be concerned about and everything follows a grander plan. Ah, the wind machines.
D. Troublemakers.
B. Ah. Okay, I go.
D. Alright. Thank you and thank Ophelia.
B. Ah. Talk soon. Bye bye.

Becoming a Wheel Star (Feb 23, 2020)

Bob is enthusiastically curious about everything he encounters. He says that when your mind pulls you to follow where knowledge leads, you become like a star, radiating in all directions. Since learning about the Wheel of Creation, he has decided he wants to become a wheel star and learn more about all the fish tanks. As part of his inquiries, he makes lists of things he wants to learn about, and then gives them to Lasaray, Ophelia, Zachariah or Gergen to review. One of his favorite tools is the zooming device. He talked about it in a February 13, 2020 session, which we had to move into another book. (Volume 2 became too voluminous, one might say). On the sixth dimension there is a room that has the zooming device, as Bob calls it. From that room, which is like a planetarium, any star or planet can be zoomed-in to show it in incredible detail. Any star or planet in any fish tank can be studied. Lasaray and Seth use the zooming device to show Bob celestial objects, or what appear to be celestial objects. As Ophelia said, "Not everything is what it appears to be." We hope that as Bob becomes a wheel star, he will pass forward the information to us.

We held this session in Colorado, the day before Christine returned to Sweden for what should have been a seven-week trip. Due to travel restrictions imposed on the world, we were not together again for eight months. We held our sessions through a video link, using the internet as a middleman. While it had no impact on the quality of the communication, I much prefer sitting in the pool of energy the spirits bring through Christine. Christine also did most of her past-life regression work with U.S. clients through live video links with similar success. Since November 2020, our channeling sessions have been done with us physically together again, –in Sweden.

D. I'll miss talking to you while this one is in Sweden. But I know you're here with me.

B. I'm just one step behind or one step to the side.

D. You're a good friend.

B. Ah. I try to be. You're also a good friend, so it's a mutual friendship. I help you here, you help me there, so it's a good partnership. I'm thinking that I'm gonna see more in the showroom, and you're gonna show me certain things with the zooming device. I made a list on places I would like to see, if it's possible. I brought the list and you said, "What is this?" And I said, "These are locations that I have heard about, when

I did council work with Gergen and the other ones, that I have not been to." So I made lists of certain things that I snapped up on my travels. Sometimes I snap up things when I have been with Ophelia, I hear things and I wonder what that is all about. I made a list of certain things that I thought would be great for us to have a looksee at. You can be a tour guide at home as well—I'm gonna be the only passenger though, because I don't want there to be all sorts of commotion, – because it's my list! You looked at the list and said, "What is this?" And I said, "These are locations that I'm kind of interested in exploring in some of the fish tanks. I've heard songs and melodies and I want to investigate what they mean. So, if we can please zoom in, then I can have a listen or have a looksee." And you looked like, "Oh, we need to talk about this a little bit more. Where did you get to hear about all these locations?" And I said, "I snap up things. I'm not just a silent knob going around, I snap up things, I'm like a little receiver, I'm a little satellite. If I pass two entities, let's say on the sixth, that discuss certain things—and the more I have progressed the more I understand—and even if I don't understand the full communication, I snap up certain waves. Then I make a puzzle of it and think, "Oh, what is that?" Then when you zoomed in on certain things, and then this one zoomed in on fish tank six, I saw things and I put it in my memory bank and I put it down in my notes. And now I have a list, and it's up for review. You laugh and said, "Who told you about these places?"

D. (*Laughing*) Things I've heard.

B. Things I've heard.

D. I'm sure there are so many places to study that there is no limit to what you could see.

B. Ah, uhm. So this is good. I left the list with you so it doesn't disappear. Okay, I'm gonna go now.

D. I'll look forward to—

B. To go through my list? You look forward to reviewing it, don't you? So that we can see where we can go. Because this auditorium that you took me to with the zooming device, if that is equipped to zoom in all over, then maybe we can go there.

D. Is that near to our lab on the sixth?

B. It's a bit down, it's not next to your office, it's way off.

D. I guess others must use it too?

B. Ah. But not when I'm there. It's just you and me, and I like that. It's better because then I can point to certain things that I want to look at and we have a one–on–one discussion, and I like that. I'm not saying that if Jeshua or Ari, you know, if they were to come that I would mind. But you say that you were trained there, you took classes there when you were smaller.

D. When you look at the fish tanks and see the stars, do you see a lot of colors?

B. It's vibrations, and vibrations show themselves as colors sometimes.

D. So you can tell different functions or purposes based on the color and their melody?

B. Indeed, and the melody. I listen. Like I said, I'm concerned about fish tank one. It doesn't seem to be—it has a very strange tone in there and I'm wondering about that—it doesn't seem equipped for visitors in that sense. But one of the points on my list is to go through the wheel to look into each fish tank. I'm looking for life.

D. Is there a lot of life in fish tank two?

B. Ah. The Tiddle–Taffles...it's active, there's commotion in there. In many ways it looks similar to this one, fish tank five. It's actually quite similar. But then again, I'm limited with what I see. That's why I wanted us to zoom in. But from the perspective of me here, fish tank two and five are actually quite alike.

D. That's good, you'll be familiar then.

B. Ah. So one of my points on this list is that we should go through the wheel so that I can...I actually don't have a specific agenda, it's just curiosity. Ophelia says I'm not sent out by someone to investigate, the only agenda is curiosity, she says. Curiosity is an agenda by itself!

D. That's how you become a star.

B. Become a star. I can't become a wheel–star if I don't look into all the fish tanks in the wheel, –and that's my agenda here. That's one of my purposes, but it's designed from me, that purpose. It's not designed from the Creator that I should be a wheel–star.

D. Well, the more you learn the more we can hear about, so it helps us.
B. Ah. That's what I say. So. Okay, I'm trotting off.
D. Always a pleasure.
B. Always a pleasure, and so I go. You go through and you look at that list, and maybe you need to prepare the slides to show me. Now you know what to prepare, maybe. You hummed, you did not say yes or no or laugh. You went, "Hmmmm", like Ari does. He goes, "Hmmmm", and that's when it is not clear, it's vague, –and I don't respond well to vague! It's similar like all these passive people on Earth, vague. It's not a feeling or a word that I would pick, or that I would choose, or that I would give to someone. Why would anyone want to be vague?
D. You never go "Hmmmm" with Tom?
B. Oh, that's a thinker. I kinda do. Sometimes I need to look down the line, the ladder, to see the things that I don't appreciate. sometimes it appears indeed that I do the same. I tend to sometimes be vague with Tom. But it's because I don't want him to be overexcited about something and then just shut him down. It might be also, –and when I stumbled upon this understanding–, it also might be that we are really close to that specific request, and then I go, "Hmmmm," like it was something brand new that I never heard of. So maybe that's what you're doing here. Maybe you have already planned on my path that I should be a wheel–star.
D. That could be why you heard about it in the first place.
B. Well, someone is. Someone is a wheel–star. Mine is only fish tanks five, four, two. There is so many others to fulfill that star.
D. Eight and nine seem to be getting a lot of attention.
B. Over there, I have not been there. I've seen a little bit on six, and heard in one.
D. Well, three is asleep, in hibernation.
B. Even if someone is asleep, there might be indications of what's gonna happen when one wakes up from one's sleep. Maybe I can decipher the dream. Everything dreams, and if I can go into fish tank three and decipher the dream, because the dream indicates the new cycle that is coming. And the dream is about transforming. So every time a person dreams, every time you go to bed and go to sleep, you have the possibility

where your soul transforms your being. Meaning when you wake up, you are more soul than you are human. When you go to bed you are more human and that is why you need the sleep, it is to remember and transform into your spirit. And then when you wake up, the first five minutes you should try to detect the first initial sensation or feeling or thought that comes to you, and that is the pure intention and the pure being that is just still lingering on. So you can investigate the dreams in order for you to understand your journey as a human, but also sometimes you get caught in being a human. (*He turns toward Ophelia.*) Yes, I am gonna go, I have been on my way. (*He then turns back to me.*) But you can indeed sometimes become trapped in the human experience. So the first minute or two, up to five minutes, when you wake up you are more connected. And you might suddenly—things that bother you in life—and when you wake up you can see it from a completely different perspective. You might realize, "That is actually not that bad. That person is actually teaching me something." You might be grateful for that nosy neighbor that is trying to sneak over the fence and be a bother to you. So what does that mean? Maybe that person is lonely. So you can see that nosy neighbor in a new light, for instance. And that's what I say, just because fish tank three is asleep, I know that if I go there and I investigate the dream, I will have a feeling of where it has been and I will have a feeling of what it wants to become. If I investigate the dream, I can see the intention of the Creator much more clearly. And fish tank three is actually high up on my list.

D. It's right next to two, so it would be nice to know your neighbors.

B. It's between two and four, so I wanna go there and I wanna zoom in on the dream.

D. We should do that. I'm glad you stuck around because that was an interesting talk, so thank you.

B. Well, there's more of course, but Ophelia says, "Another time." So I am trotting off, and I will return.

D. Always happy to hear that. So thank you and Ophelia and Jeshua for coming today.

B. And you go through the list.

D. Hmm.

B. You are more going "Hmm" when we are talking about fish tank ten, eleven and nine, over there. You didn't go "Hmm" when I talked about fish tank three. So maybe that's the first place for us to go to, to investigate the dream.

D. (*Laughing*) That sounds like a good plan. I look forward to hearing about that, as a human.

B. Ah. Okay, okay. See you! Bye bye.

Everyone gets a Roller (April 5, 2020)

The whole concept of a spiritual "Roller", as Bob calls them, is yet another example of how little we know about the care and concern that is given to us throughout life. Locked in a human body, we feel isolated and alone, but that is the opposite of reality. Everyone has at least one spirit who constantly monitors and guides them. In times of physical, emotional or mental need, other healers and guides can join to lend their expertise. In addition, a special type of spirit from the second dimension, a Roller, will visit during sleep and cause the body to change positions. Bob said it is easier for a spirit to reenter if the body hasn't become stagnate. Bob calls Christine "this one" and "he" because the spirit of Seth is regarded as a male energy, since we both come from a predominately mental dimension. Isaac is Seth's mentor, and Gergen is a guide when Seth incarnates.

D. Does Gergen usually plan a lot of lives for this one?

B. Ah. He plans with Isaac for this one. When there is too much rumble, then Gergen normally comes in and he has in his possession a special potion that makes this one a little bit more accommodating for his surroundings.

D. Does he do that during the life, or before the lifetime?

B. During. You know how I say I roll you?

D. Yes.

G. Gergen sprinkles this one.

D. She seems pretty calm now.

B. Indeed. Gergen isn't as active. I mean he observes, of course, to make sure there is no rumble. But there were times when this one tried to rumble away in this life, and then during sleep Gergen came in and sprayed him. And then when this one woke up, in the little female form, huhuh, this one had all forgotten about the extravagant adventures that he had planned on before going to sleep. Did not find the idea appealing anymore and did not understand how one can change one's mind from one day to the other. Well, did not know that Gergen sparkled him. But he rolls also now, making sure this one is able to return—like I do with you—but it's also to make sure that the circulation within the body is in rhythm and in balance. It's not like I flip you, but I can move your balance and point of heaviness in either direction, and that is also to make the circulation run better in your veins and so forth if there is an unrhymical flow in your veins. It's a struggle for souls to return from sleep state into physical state, if the circulation has gone awry. You want to make sure there is a balanced flow, –that's also why we roll you.

D. Do most people have a spirit guide that follows them closely enough to roll them?

B. It's like, if you have a Roller, then it's normally someone that is either like me, following you really closely, or you can have a separate Roller. So everyone has a Roller, but it may not be a close buddy like me. I do it because I want to make sure that no one else rolls you wrongly. I don't want to find you with your nose into the cushion and your back up and everything is wrong, and who knows what happens then. So I don't leave that task to an outside Roller. But everyone has Rollers, indeed. But they are just Rollers, they don't do anything else than just roll. It's to just make sure that when souls return into body that the conditions of the physical is as ultimate as it can be. So normally it's not like Jeshua would stand there and roll you, or Isaac would stand there and roll this one, they're too busy for that. So if you don't have someone that rolls permanently, then the primary guide will just call in a Roller. It doesn't have to be the same Roller, it can shift. They occupy the second dimension indeed, and they are very equipped—like a nurse—they are very equipped in knowledge of the physical conditions combined with soul traveling. But they don't necessarily send the same Roller every time. Let's say Isaac were to say, "I need a Roller tonight because I'm busy elsewhere," then he can just go to—you know how you can call someone, like a consultant?

D. Yes.

B. And you can call that consultant firm and you say, "I need an accountant for a month?" or, "I need someone who can do the books for a week?" And they'll say, "Well, we have Todd here, free." So then they send Todd. So that would be the same procedure if you wanted to get a Roller, so it might not be the same Roller every time but they come from the second dimension indeed. I, however, do not want to call in help. I said, "I'll take on the assignment to always roll him, I don't want to find him upside down." And it's not like I don't trust the Rollers, because they're quite skilled, probably more skilled than me, it's just that if there is gonna be any progress or advancement, or, you know, any fault, then it better be me.

D. (*Laughing*) Well, I appreciate you paying such good attention to me.

B. Ah. Too many cooks, so you never know. But everyone has a Roller. Sometimes you have a Roller for life—each life one Roller. But then, other times it could be different Rollers.

D. Are they in any way affiliated with like a healing team?

B. Indeed, indeed. Because they are very intelligent and very much in the knowing when it comes to the physical body versus the astral body and the out–of–body experience. So in order for you to be a Roller, you have to understand the equation of out–of–body traveling of a soul to the fourth reality or further, as well as the connection to body. So they are in some way doctors. I am, myself, not a doctor. I am a physician with you, I help you, but I did not take the rolling program fully, so I don't go roll others. I don't roll others, and I don't let anyone roll my person.

D. Ah, that's funny.

B. I do look into this one sometimes when this one sleeps, but I don't roll him. But Gergen rolls if there's a need, otherwise just sprinkles him. Okay, I'm gonna go now, but I'll be back.

D. Oh, good, good. We'll talk on Wednesday or Thursday, my friend.

B. Ah. Okay. See you. Bye bye.

Travels with Old Sniffer (April 8, 2020)

When Ia and Bob describe their excursion to Earth with a whole host of sparkles and Sniffers, it forces us to reflect once again on our interpretation of nature. If you sit quietly somewhere in the mountains, you'll see rocks, trees, streams, animals, the sky, and perhaps hear the wind breathing through the forest and smell the richness of the earth. We tend to see each element as separate and distinct—here a tree, there a bush, above a hawk—but does that vision of the world honor the greater truth? Ia and Bob talk about families of trees, families in the seas, the children of earthworms, and caterpillars in a nursery. Beyond what we can see, there are multitudes of spiritual entities that move around and among all these creations, gently tending to them as part of a singular living planet. Because the Master Mind occupies all life forms, there is a constant interplay of communication and response between the organisms of nature and the spirits who come to assist. Just as we each have guides who monitor and help us throughout life, trees, animals, plants, and even the sea and atmosphere have their own spiritual counterparts who perform a similar function.

Bob's companion, Ia, tells us the story of how Bob invited himself on an excursion to South America with one of Ia's classes. And then Bob relates how he became friends with Old Sniffer.

D. And now, if there is anyone who wishes to speak, you may do so now. (*This is the end of my lead-in to the session.*)

Ia. Or sing! (*She then toned a beautiful melody.*) Hee hee hee. Uhh-huh! So, I am here indeed, as somewhat of a teaser, Bob said, in order to set the mood for him. I was indeed invited to just share briefly—underline the word briefly—some of the inventions that the little sparkles are preparing, treats for mankind, treats for the planet at this time. There is an enormous activity, you should know, among the little ones, who are eager to travel and to help. There is an effect that we see in the trees that needs to be addressed. It is not crucial, it is not so devastating that the trees will completely disappear, but it has to be tended to. So we have some of the little ones who have designed projects in order for the roots, the network underneath all trees, to be as healthy and connected as possible. So we have indeed sent them on this treasure hunt—something that Bob is very fond of as well, so he actually signed up for this class. And I said, "You have already taken this class. Just because one feels it is something amusing and repetitive, one cannot always expect to tag along." So I did tell him that (*she gives a big sigh*), but after some discussion, indeed, he participated in this treasure hunt. It sometimes comes to the discussion where one says something and the discussion goes back and forth, and one has to surrender to the fact that it's better to just surrender than to continue the argument of either-or. The case he presented for his joining was quite obvious. He is there to tend to their treasure hunt so they would feel excited and not stop at any boundaries that they might come across, or any roots, in this case. So indeed, he did participate. What we are indeed trying to solve is the maze underneath your feet, mankind's feet. The roots have sent out a request that they are not feeling the general pulse in the web in certain locations. Not everywhere of course, but there are certain regions, the Amazon for instance, where trees have been cut down. That has created somewhat of a disturbance and sadness among the tree family. And the request has been heard, and we are indeed taking our excursion, our treasure hunt, to that region. It is much more suitable and happy in the region of Canada and, in general, in the regions in the northern hemisphere at this time. Meaning the southern part of your planet is somewhat being neglected or feeling neglected. So indeed, we have prepared the little ones, we have given them maps and we have given them Sniffers. And a Sniffer is someone—it would be considered similar like you people have dogs that sniff out certain mushrooms, or even the police dogs you have at custom borders and so forth—so we have given the little ones Sniffers. And these Sniffers are similar like a little fairy, one might say, but they don't fly, they actually walk. The whole group was first assigned one Sniffer, but they became so excited about the Sniffer that after a while, we actually gave them each—one each—a Sniffer. What happened then was that Bob said that he did not remember being given a unique Sniffer. So that was his argument for him to go on this excursion, that he indeed needed to understand the whole assignment of having his own Sniffer. So, as I said, I rested my case and said, "Why don't you tag along." And he was very excited about having his Sniffer. So here we stand with all the little sparkles, each having a Sniffer, each ready for the big assignment, the adventure of the treasure hunt. The treasure hunt is to find a root that is lacking inspiration, that is how we show it to the little ones. It is similar how a spirit guide looks out for his person, it is to see whether the person has been dimmed in inspiration, dimmed in purpose, dimmed in the feeling of participating in the game. So the general idea to establish a treasure hunt, in this case, is for them to try to identify the roots lacking inspiration and life. Inspiration equals life. Bob, as you know, is all sorts of life, meaning that he is full of inspiration, which was the reason I said, "You might not need this specific treasure hunt," but he countered with the fact he never had his own Sniffer. So indeed, we took off and we have been—and yes, Bob, you can tell your part indeed, but I'm gonna tell them the underlying story so they understand, when you come in, what this whole agenda is about. Agreed? Yes. SO, we took off, all of us, on this big field trip, –sparkles, Sniffers, and teachers, such as myself, to make sure everything was fine. It's like a big scout gathering, one might say, and you were there. You are aware of the scouts and having these different little field trips in nature and trying to solve and find puzzles. So this is a grand puzzle where we went, and as we arrived into the Amazon jungle, Sniffers were told by teachers to assist and not take over, because the Sniffer has the upper hand over a sparkle, as you probably can understand. We told the Sniffers to, in some way, be helpful but not take over, because the little ones are the ones that are gonna go down later on and solve it, and they have to also work together with this Sniffer. So we went and researched some of the roots, and indeed we did find there is a big region in the country called Columbia that is actually in need of help. It is a central hub in many ways for the tree root network. So in order for us to be helpful for other regions such as Venezuela, we did need to look into Columbia, a little bit. Peru, we are leaving at this time, and Chile as well, because there are other activities going on with those who do not have Sniffers. We do not want groups to merge and conflict. There are different lessons going on in Chile and Peru at this time, as we are trying to move spines, and Joel is having that sort of group. (*The Andes are apparently going to undergo some significant movement in the near future, which can only result in tremendous earthquakes and volcanic activity. Joel, a close friend to Bob, is an expert on mountains in the second dimension and is leading a group of young students to study the region.*) So we do not want classes to mix and match, as it is not helpful for either one. The ones in Chile, for instance, they don't have Sniffers, so it can create all sorts of commotion if someone feels left out, you know, "Why do they have Sniffers?" and "What is a Sniffer?" and so forth. So we are focusing our attention in Columbia, as it is a hub for the general network. And indeed, we did find some roots that needed attention. What we use to create, or I should say, once we located this area in need of a reboot or to be somewhat kicked into life again, we gathered in a circle—the Sniffers were on pause—and the sparkles gathered in a circle and we created this affirmation and this initiation in order for the roots to come together and be heard and be healed. So that is what took place. Yes. (*Said as she looked to the left. Bob must have asked if she was about done.*) I have told you the story, and I'm pretty sure he will continue the story, but I'm really thankful that I was able to participate briefly—underline briefly—to create somewhat of an understanding of the work that goes on behind the curtain, so to speak.

D. Well, I'm really glad you could share with us today. It was really nice to hear from you again, Ia.

Ia. Oh, yes indeed, you are much welcome. And if I could have separate sessions, and I have not been asking for that, because the time, as humans know it, is limited. We do know that. But I do have more to say, but to the expense of whom, you might wonder, –so we share in this case. Just know that there is a group activity taking place in order for roots, the underlying networks that connects the trees, to be somewhat reconnected again, windows that needs to be merged together, so that was the agenda of that specific mission.

D. So when you find a problem, how do you resolve it?

Ia. We find a problem, in this case in Columbia, and we established the problem was that the major trees in this hub, the old ones, were not feeling the water that goes underneath; the channels underneath the roots had been cut off to the general supply. So what we did in that sense is that some sparkles, who have different expertise, went into the soil and tried to lift this flow of nutrition and water so the roots could tap into it. It is similar as you do surgery on a human body, that we do with the roots. We simply, in this case, extend it. We deleted and cut off some of the roots that were not functional and we extended the roots and we lifted the underlying canals of nutrition and water. So the trees that are considered the key trees in this network were starting to rejuvenate again.

D. Wonderful. Thank you for explaining that.

Ia. Not that tricky, it's just that you have not been taught that teaching on the sixth. So in your mind it might be highly advanced, and in many ways it is. These are not like kindergarten sparkles; these are considered like 10 to 14-year olds. So they are preparing, because around the age of what you would consider 16-year old is when we depart to fully be helpful. So this is like pre-work, in order for them to be able to, once they travel and they blend—they don't incarnate—they know exactly what to do.

D. Okay. Thank you!

Ia. You are much welcome. And so I am off. I just wanted to stop by.

D. Well I really appreciate you showing up today, Ia. It was a true pleasure to hear from you again.

Ia. (*She began humming a slow tune.*) So we can sing indeed, and it calms the trees and it calms the sparkles. Sniffers don't need to be calm, they are quite active. But in general, it's a good idea that once a work has been completed, to end with a common joined singing and a common melody. So that's what we do. Okay, I am off.

D. Alright Ia. Once again, thank you.

Ia. Bye bye.

B. Ah! Ah! Did you hear about my adventures?

D. I heard you invited yourself, along, sort of.

B. Ah. Well, if you wait for a while for an invitation, but if an invitation doesn't come, then you go and you are your own invitation. That's what you do, you just go. Because first I waited and I waited and I waited, and I showed in many different ways that I was interested. Ia, she was just passing by in the hallway, talking to all these other teachers that were gonna participate, and I popped out my head and said something encouraging about how wonderful that sounded, to somewhat show that I heard what was going on. She was passing back and forth and no indication came, so then I sat still and thought, "Maybe if I just wait for the invitation, it will come," because Ophelia said that sometimes you WAIT for the treat to come to you, you don't go TO that treat. So I waited to be invited, but when nothing came, then I took the invitation in my own hands, so to speak, and I went. Because when I went (*on a field trip when he was a young student*), I was not in the South American region, I was on a different location. I was over on the English green isle, up there. I liked it up there, so I did different things. And we had ONE Sniffer for everybody, but here I heard them talking in the hallway that everyone was gonna get a Sniffer. And Sniffers, you know, they are really cute and they're really fun—it's like a pet. And there are those who take care of the Sniffers and I've always liked them. So I said, "I think I'm gonna come because I might learn something here that I can pass on in my school." Huhuh.

D. How big are the Sniffers, in comparison to you?

B. Like maybe 25 percent of me, 20 percent of me. They're kinda round like a ball, but with feet. You cannot have your own Sniffer—I asked before, way back when I was little, if I could have my own, but it was not possible. So when I heard that this group was gonna get their own Sniffer, then I signed up and I wanted to come. And I do like excursions and I did go. I am interested in that region because I am planning a life for you and my flower is gonna be put in that specific destination. That is why I said that it might be a good idea if I explored and did some research further. Because I don't want to put it somewhere if the trees are not happy, if the tree roots are not singing. So me and my Sniffer—I got the old Sniffer. Everyone else, their Sniffer's were like really young and active. Not mine! I think it was ready for retirement. I think they just took him because there was no one left.

D. Maybe he was ready to join the Sniffer council.

B. I got him, but he wasn't as bouncy as the other Sniffers, so I came a little bit behind. But the general idea was that I wanted to participate and I wanted to go, also, and have a look–see at some of the locations that I might launch my plant for you to find later on. So it wasn't just a trick on my part, I actually had a little agenda as well. I did not have an agenda to have a Sniffer, but I had an agenda to go there. I just said, "It would look odd if everyone has Sniffers, and not me." And then Ia said, "I don't have a Sniffer," and I said, "Well, you're just gonna look after the other ones, you're gonna be like a babysitter." So I over–talked that notion.

D. It must have been a pretty big group that went?

B. Ohh, I don't remember it being that big before. This was a grand exploring group, an expedition. I would estimate it to be about 200 sparkles and 200 Sniffers, and then me and my Sniffer, my old Sniffer. I did follow behind a little bit because they were quite active. But Ia said, "If you're going to participate, you be over there, you don't disturb the expedition." And I said, "I'm not gonna disturb. Me and the old Sniffer here, we're gonna go look for where I put my plant." Huhuh. Ia knows when there is tricks, so she did this, shook her head like that. So anyway, I have indeed found a location where I'm gonna start putting the flowers for you to find later on—if you agree on this life I have set up for you. And this plant is gonna be helpful to cure grey cells, to transform them into white cells. It's a great find, but not everyone is gonna be empathic about the find. So that's why I want to make sure that it's somewhere hidden, but also it has to be in an environment where the trees, the network and the roots, are in harmony and singing. What happened was that I was not allowed to participate in the big expedition, but me and Old Sniffer, we found a location and we sat down and we prepared it and we had our own little picnic, kinda. So he sat down and I said, "What is it like to be a Sniffer? You know, here we sit, we just wait for the other ones to be ready to finish the expedition," because I had already found my location. I heard great stories, I must say, from this old Sniffer about where he had been in his days.

D. That's an advantage to having an older one then, huh?

B. Indeed! Because it turned out to be highly interesting to listen to his stories. So I found myself a new friend. And he's been around WAY before when dinosaurs came around, so he had all sorts of stories, you know, pre–ME! I said, "I came with the rain," and he said, "Ohh, yeah, hmm, that was a good year, hmm," kinda like that. And I was like, "Good year? It lasted a long time!" But he remembered this fondly, like in his early days. Hee hee huh. Ole and Gergen are kinda secretive about what happed before the big rains, before the clouds. But the Sniffer here, old Sniffer, he's wide open, he likes to share! You know how you see retired people in nursery homes, how they just talk and talk and talk. I think that old Sniffer here, he did not have that many to talk to because the younger ones are out on expeditions. So I think that I made everyone a favor of signing up for this excursion. So Old Sniffer, I think that he did not have that many to talk to, maybe. I mean, he has his equals, but they've already been there, so for them, they were just chewing the same stories over and over. I was brand new and he could somewhat shine in his endeavors and in what he saw and what he did. I myself was full of questions, of course.

D. Do the Sniffers hang out on the second, or do they always stay on Earth?

B. Ah, they're similar to the ones that go to Tiddle, the Tiddle-Taffles. In some way, they migrate and they belong on Earth or in the location where they're supposed to operate. But Old Sniffer here, he was back in the second. So he talked like Earth was a trip he took a while ago. Whereas the other ones, they are in some way emigrating down to Earth, but they still have a connection, of course, to home.

D. Well, the old Sniffer can come visit you in your office then?

B. He can indeed, and I have given him a map where to find me if he ever runs out of other Sniffers to talk to, if he wants to share—because it's important to share—then I'm always there with a big ear. But he had all these interesting talks and interesting observations about the dinosaurs, things that I never heard of because no one wants to tell me! Ole doesn't want to tell me. Gergen, he hums, and you don't know in the same way because you did different things. So I think I found myself a new channel of information in my old Sniffer here. I'm gonna tend to him, I'm gonna nourish this new friendship. And I can tell him about you, –I did indeed. He did not know about anything beyond Earth. so I told him about you, and I told him about my new solar system, and I told him about what Elahims do and stuff like that. So as long as no one sniffs us up, huhuh, all sorts of information can fly here! I'm quiet about finding the Sniffer. I don't want to tell Ophelia and I don't want to tell Gergen too much. They do tend to be one step ahead of me all the time, so I'm pretty sure they know about Old Sniffer.

D. I would assume Ophelia is standing next to you, so she knows now if she didn't before.

B. Ah. It's what happens when I blow my own horn.

D. Did he tell you any stories you can share?

B. Yes, indeed. He talked about a cycle of birth when it came to some of the big birds that flew. They were predators in some way, and they were on the top of the chain at that time. And there was an outbreak one time of big rodents, like rats and so forth, and it actually came the fact that the rodents ate all vegetation that existed in that region and it started to spread some sort of disease among them. And the disease were not just among these rodents, it actually started to effect the ecosystem. And they just kept overpopulating and were not healthy. So there were these big birds that were called in, and they were more in numbers after a while, in order for them to eliminate this problem. Because the ecosystem and the plants and so forth started to be affected about this big outburst of these rodents. And the rodents were not healthy, they had some sort of—it was something with their minds also—they had a physical problem in their blood which carried on into their offspring, and as they were highly sexually active, it spread. And he said that it was a bad memory for Earth in general and they had to do a reboot of the whole ecosystem. Because bugs, and the little black one with the shield and feet—the beetles—they started to disappear. And if the beetle disappears, it creates a chain into the whole ecosystem. So that was a sad moment and it had to be rebooted, he said.

D. Was this before the dinosaurs?

B. Before dinosaurs, yes indeed. After that it was a reboot. It was not a rain, but in order for this to go away they had to cool down, he said, that specific region, and there was sort of an ice age. That was a way to kill off this group of rodents and the virus that they had. They brought in an ice age, that's what he said. Not the Sniffer itself (*the Sniffers didn't initiate the ice age, those decision are made by councils*), but he observed the solution that came, and it was an ice age that lasted quite long. He's quite talkative. I might bring him more times because he has all sorts of things to say. And he said to tell you that this specific ice age lasted almost 35,000 human years. And this was before dinosaurs and before me, because I came way later. And when you were by the tree, that was also way later.

D. Well, the continents were still a lot closer together then, weren't they?

B. Ah. Indeed. The American continent was connected in some way to the European and African. He said that is what we do sometimes if we want to kill off a virus, we bring in ice, in this case. He said it's not the best option to bring in solar flares, solar energy, and cook the planet. He said the best thing is to freeze, and that is how you kill a virus.

D. Might have to do that again to get rid of this recent virus.

B. But he said that is just a hiccup. You don't go and freeze someone just because they have a hiccup. You don't go reboot someone just because someone has a hiccup. So he says that it's not considered a problem. He's seen much worse, he say, and this is not a problem. It barely qualifies as something that would even be talked about. But in general, I found myself a new friend and I'm gonna continue to talk to him and nourish this new friendship of mine, and I'm gonna tell him things too. He's quite interested and curious, because you can imagine if you have just been in your own bubble for about, I don't know, 500 million years or so, and here comes me and I say, "Do you know there are other fish tanks? Do you know there are other levels where they look different and they do stars and so forth?" And he said, "I've seen stars but I haven't gone." So I told him, "I'm gonna tell you about Etena, and I'm gonna tell you about the stars. Because the stars are not always what you think they are—some of the stars are just windows." And then he became really fascinated. So I say, "I share about the stars, and you share about pre–cloud time." Huhuh. So a special bond has started growing. Sharing secrets. But–but–but–but I also have my privacy, and you're not allow to just bombard into someone's privacy. So I'm gonna attend to him. So anyway, I'm gonna go. But I wanted to tell you about the Sniffers, who are a great resource to investigating the possibilities that a spirit guide, such as myself, can come across.

D. Well, that's wonderful. I'm glad to learn about them.

B. Do you have a new friend that you want to introduce me to?

D. (*Laughing*) I don't know who that would be.

B. Well, I'm thinking about Lasaray here. Maybe he has someone he wants to introduce me to, –invite to share.

D. Poor old Dave doesn't know what Lasaray is up to.

B. Nay. That is tricky. We'll see about that, but in the meantime I'm gonna go talk with my new friend. We like to wander, him and I.

D. Wander through the forest and talk?

B. Indeed. We wander through the forest, and I started to tell him about Siah and Tess, and he never saw them on Earth, so he's interested in that. And I talked a little bit about Etena, and he wondered how I got there, how I traveled there, and I said, "In my peanut suit." And he wondered if he can have a suit, and I said, "That's a whole long program to be like an astronaut in that sense."

D. You send thought bubbles to him that has pictures, don't you?

B. Indeed, and that's what I do. So we communicate and he tells me stories and I do the same, so I think that's a good solution for everyone.

D. For me too, so I get to learn.

B. Ah. So I'm gonna go now, but I wanted to share that I have a new friend.

D. That's wonderful, Bob. I'm glad you could join us today. It's always nice to have a separate session.

B. Ah. I think so too. Okay, so I'm gonna go now, but I'll be back soon.

D. Alright, my friend. Until then.

B. Until then, you go find a friend yourself as well. It's a happy feeling to find a new friend. Okay, I'll go now. He's waiting here and he might have things to say, so I don't want to miss that.

D. Okay, talk soon.

B. Ah. Bye bye.

Bake with Both Hands! (May 25, 2020)

As *Volume 2* draws to a close, it behooves us to take to heart the many lessons shared by our dear unseen companions. During most of 2020, Christine and I were living in separate countries. I was still employed in Colorado and she was working in Sweden. We talked every day and, on this date, we were discussing Bob's book. The ending of his journal was not clear to me. Christine suddenly felt Bob, who is always listening, pushing for an opportunity to speak. I grabbed the recorder and Christine allowed him to give the ending for this book, in a way that only he can. Christine saw him standing in a kitchen with a tall, white baker's hat on. He was covered in flour, vigorously working a big pile of dough. Since he easily blends with Christine, he explained what he was doing, and gave another beautiful teaching about life.

B. You don't know what life has prepared for you if you don't get messed up a little bit. If you have just one toe in life, because you are afraid to be messy, then you are not engaging. Similar like me here with my dough, I'm messy because of all the flour around me and I'm just standing in it. If you're going to do something, go all in. You won't know if you like something unless you fully commit to it. Once you explore something like that, if you don't like it, then you should go all out. (*He then showed Christine that he put one hand behind his back.*) If I only halfway engage with the dough, then how can the dough fully show what it can become, or the possibilities that it has? You explore with both hands, both eyes, both feet. People now only dip in one toe. You should ask yourself, "Are you a person who engages in life with both hands and both feet, or only has one toe in life?" You have to allow life to mess you up a little bit, –like me, I'm standing here covered in flour and I'm not sure if I like it, but I am engaging in the task. You have to engage in life, and you have to allow it to mess you up. Life might mess you up, but at the end of your life, you may discover you created a grand cake, or have created a fine new outfit for yourself. Your life may have been messy, but at the end you find the greatest result. The dough has been prepared to become something, but at the moment I don't know that it has a plan to become something. You don't give it a fair chance to become if you do not fully engage. At the moment I just feel like it's a big clegg and I'm messy and I'm dirty. But if I don't fully engage with the dough, but if I just focus and retreat based on that I feel messy, then I will miss the opportunity to see whether I like to bake, or what the dough has planned to become. Because at the moment, it's just a big clegg, tacky and sticky. But if I leave now then I can't say, "Oh, I don't like to bake!" because I have not allowed the dough to become something, –I am just standing there in the process for it to become. And it's the same thing with life, if you just stand with a toe in life and say, "Oh, I messed up, everything is messy and it's not working," then you don't really allow life to blossom and become. You have to allow life to actually dress you up rather than mess you up. Sometimes you have to be a little bit messy in order for the grand finale to become something, to be dressed up in the most fancy outfit. You cannot have a cake without engaging in baking the cake and you cannot have the best life or the best option of a life unless you put in more than just a toe, –you have to engage.

D. That's really brilliant, my friend. Is that what you wanted to say yesterday?

B. Well, there was just so little time so I was not allowed to. But now, I feel like this one is a little bit on snooze and I felt like I can come forward and I can say things. It's important that people don't just put in a toe and expect to have a full outfit, it's the same thing. If you're just standing with one hand in the dough and don't expect there to be a big, grand cake and to be the best baker person that you can become or be. But at the moment I'm deciding whether I like it or not, and the dough told me, "If I'm going to show you the grand cake that I can become, then at least you should engage with me and allow that to become." And life is the same thing, it might say that to a human, "If you expect me to become colorful and give you the great result that you seek, at least you can engage more than with just one toe."

D. That's really good advice. I'll put that in your book.

B. Ah. I wanna have that in my next book. It's gonna be in the end.

D. I was trying to figure out how best to end *Volume 2*.

B. This is how we're gonna end it. It's like a little bit of a map on how to navigate life. My ending, my book. That's what I want to say. That was it. Bye bye.

(Don't worry, Bob will be back.)

ACKNOWLEDGMENTS

From the first draft of this book to the present has been witness to the turmoil of transitions. Christine and David were living near Denver, Colorado when the world began locking down in early 2020. Christine was the first to leave, returning to her home in Sweden to work. David coasted into early retirement from the corporate world and moved out of Colorado in September. By November 2020, he was reunited with Christine in Sweden. Colorado was a magical place to live, and it was there, on a sunny mountainside, where the spirits first began dictating these books. We will always be grateful to those friends in our soul community, both in the U.S. and Sweden, who encourage us to continue the work we are doing.

Kari Pelletier, our copy editor, is owed a debt of gratitude for her collaboration and skill in correcting all the linguistic errors that are invisible to the writer. She also left Colorado in 2020 and enjoyed a year in Hawaii before settling in the blistering heat of Arizona. She impulsively agreed to edit *The Spiritual Design, Wave 3* before she left, and we hope she does.

Christine and David also extend our appreciation to Susanne Kromm. She has been participating in each of our books and has been an invaluable editor, translator and objective reader. She points out the rough edges that often creep into David's writing, and the finished books are much more agreeable for it.

Finally, and most importantly, we want to acknowledge the unwavering support of the spirits and councils in the unseen realms. They are the true authors of all our books. Their wisdom and love have changed the way we see the world, and their gifts of knowledge will forever remain as the footsteps we leave behind.

About the Authors

Christine Kromm Henrie is a spiritual channel, a certified past life and between lives soul regression therapist, psychic, and karmic astrologer. She was born and lived in Stockholm, Sweden until 2014, when she moved to the USA and married David Henrie, with whom she now shares her work.

She had an intense spiritual awakening in 2009, during a past life regression, which became the starting point for her practice with the higher realms. She began to receive messages and visions from her spirit guides about her soul assignment to develop the skills needed for them to speak through her. Accepting their advice, she studied different modalities of mediumship, psychic development and astrology in Sweden and England during the next five years. This intensive training enabled her to perfect the link and the ability to maintain this altered state for extended periods of time.

After moving to the USA, her formal training continued in soul regression and hypnotherapy, becoming a licensed regression therapist. Christine has two offices in Stockholm, Sweden, where she offers private soul regressions and progressions, assisting people to recall lessons from past lifetimes and memories from their spiritual home. Astrological consultations are also available online.

A near-death experience at age eleven and a transcendental epiphany in his early twenties led David Henrie to lifelong inquiry into the nature of the spirit. His studies focused on NDE's, reincarnation, spiritualism, and the theological beliefs within Buddhism and other pre-Christian religions. After a lengthy career as a petroleum engineer and executive in the U.S., he now lives in Sweden with his wife, where his time is dedicated to writing and research. David conducts the trance sessions and converses with the spirits Christine channels. He transcribes the recorded dialogues and assembles their teachings into the co-authored books.

Christine and David give lectures about the channeled material and the regression work, helping people to remember their soul mission and purpose. Their practice and publishing imprint is through **Access Soul Knowledge**, a Swedish company with U.S. proxy.

For further information, please visit:
www.AccessSoulKnowledge.com.

www.ingramcontent.com/pod-product-compliance
Lightning Source LLC
Chambersburg PA
CBHW030144100526
44592CB00009B/116